Educating Multilingual Learners

Educating Multilingual Learners

What Every Classroom Teacher Needs to Know

Second Edition

Carine Strebel
Joyce W. Nutta
Edwidge Crevecoeur Bryant
Florin M. Mihai
Kouider Mokthari
Donita Grissom

Harvard Education Press
Cambridge, Massachusetts

Paperback ISBN: 9798895570517

Cataloging-in-Publication Data available from the Library of Congress.

Published by Harvard Education Press,
an imprint of the Harvard Education Publishing Group

Harvard Education Press
8 Story Street
Cambridge, MA 02138

Cover design by Joel Gendron

The typefaces in this book are Adobe Garamond Pro and Univers LT Std.

Für mini Eltere—Max and Sonja Strebel

—Carine

✦

To Hugo, my emerging bilingual beloved grandson

—Joyce

✦

I dedicate this book to my dearly departed mother, Mercia Crevecoeur, who continues to symbolize the courage of all Haitian mothers and will always be an inspiration to our family. Nou renmen w, Manman! Onè - Respè!

—Edwidge

✦

For my wife, Cristina, with love

—Florin

✦

With love and gratitude, for the Mokhtari and Reichard families, for multilingual learners, and for the dedicated teachers who support them

—Kouider

✦

To my family and colleagues whose love and support have always strengthened me; and the experiences that have shaped my growth as an educator

—Donita

Contents

Even Better Than the First: What's New in the Second Edition?

It seemed like everyone was singing and dancing to "Happy" and cheering on the *Guardians of the Galaxy*. *Game of Thrones* debuted, and a company called OpenAI was founded. In education, massive open online courses (MOOCs) expanded learning opportunities globally, and teachers in the United States spent hours in professional learning to implement the Common Core State Standards (CCSS). Remember 2014? It was an eventful year that led to advancements that have endured as well as initiatives that turned out to be short-lived.

More than a decade has passed since we wrote the first edition of this book, during which many changes in educational research, theory, practice, and priorities occurred. In the **teaching English to speakers of other languages (TESOL)** field, certain changes stand out:

- New terminology for English learners, with multilingual learners (MLs) or multilingual learners of English (MLEs) becoming more common terms
- More precise second language proficiency testing data available nationally
- Merging of TESOL and bilingual education approaches to instructing MLEs and conceptualizing the process of second language acquisition
- Growth of dual language immersion programs and research on their effectiveness
- Using ML students' full linguistic repertoire to foster their developing bilingualism

In regular **preK–12 education**, growing trends included:

- Merging of teaching language arts and literacy with teaching disciplinary literacy
- Use of artificial intelligence (AI) and other technologies to support and scaffold learning
- Focus on student personal well-being and support
- Many US states using their own standards derived from the CCSS
- More new teachers entering the classroom without certification
- Increasing coplanning and coteaching in various instructional programs

Given all that has changed for multilingual learners and those who teach them, our second edition has been updated and enhanced. You will see the following differences in this book:

- We reframed and expanded how we refer to preK–12 students who are learning through a language that is new to them. Because most readers of this book are or will be teachers in the United States, our examples mainly reflect the US preK–12 context. However, by adopting the broad term *multilingual learner*, much of the book's content now clearly applies to learners of any new language in any context, anywhere. When we are speaking specifically about students classified as English learners by federal definition, we use *multilingual learners of English* (MLEs), and when we are speaking about students in dual language immersion programs for whom Spanish is a new language, we use *multilingual learners of Spanish*. This shift also emphasizes that becoming bilingual is a valuable goal for all, regardless of the pathway taken.
- We streamlined and updated our previous two protocols into a new, teacher-friendly framework that is easy and quick to use. The Teaching All Subjects, Language, and Literacy (TASLL) Framework uses common assessment data to determine the degree and type of support and scaffolding that MLs need. The new framework blends the prior protocols into a coherent process that improves classroom communication and individualizes language and literacy instruction for MLs. The framework applies to all subject matters and grade levels and is appropriate for new or seasoned teachers in states (and nations) with different standards. In the application of the framework, we suggest various new AI and other technologies that support ML students' learning and offer additional resources on our website https://www.MLSuccess.org.
- We expanded our collaborative approach to educating MLs and built it into the TASLL Framework, offering simple first steps to partner with your coworkers to meet your ML students' needs.
- We incorporated critical theoretical and practical considerations on translanguaging, illuminating why, when, and how to use the full linguistic repertoire of MLs. We also added ML student case story and classroom application details about dual language immersion and its effectiveness in developing bilingualism, biculturalism, and biliteracy.
- We expanded the stories of our four ML student cases, focusing on understanding the ecology of the learner and their family and community.

So, how will this new edition prepare you for what the next decade will bring for MLs? To paraphrase that timeless 2014 song, when teachers know how to work together to support their MLs' learning, *it feels like a classroom without a roof.* Let's make the sky the limit for *all* our students. Happy reading!

Setting the Stage for Multilingual Learner Success

Educating Multilingual Learners in Regular and Dual Language Education Classrooms

Many teachers we know feel overwhelmed and overworked. There are so many competing demands on their time, including mounting paperwork, intensifying accountability measures, rising standards, and increasing student needs. The list goes on. We know that teachers of all subjects and grade levels operate under challenging conditions. Yet, despite this, they continue working hard every day toward a single goal—to help *all* students reach their potential, not just the privileged students or those with every advantage. All students. And this increasingly means teaching students learning in a language that is new to them, referred to generally in this book as *multilingual learners* (*MLs*) and, more specifically, *multilingual learners of English* (*MLEs*).[1]

The US Department of Education identifies approximately 5.3 million MLEs in US schools.[2] Two-thirds of teachers have at least one ML in their class.[3] MLEs bring extraordinarily rich linguistic and cultural backgrounds to the American education landscape, which strengthens instruction for *all* students. However, these cultural and linguistic assets can also pose significant English language, literacy, and content learning challenges that often prevent MLEs from doing well academically. Historically, students who are not classified as English learners (the term the US federal government uses for MLEs) have consistently outperformed MLEs on tests of academic achievement.[4] Federal legislation holds public schools, state education departments, and higher education institutions accountable for the education of MLEs, requiring a close examination of their performance in comparison to their non-MLE peers (meaning native speakers of English, bilingual students who were never classified as MLEs, or students who were previously classified as MLEs and have been exited).[5]

In addition to federal accountability measures, state standards present opportunities and challenges for MLEs and their teachers. On one hand, the standards present MLEs with an opportunity to gain equal access to rigorous instruction along with higher expectations for learning. On the other hand, classroom teachers need to make the challenging standards accessible to MLEs, regardless of their English proficiency.

These opportunities and challenges will, in turn, require a change in how teachers view and implement instruction for MLEs in the regular education classroom. Educators in every state are confronting the language-centered challenges MLEs face in accessing more rigorous instruction. This book is about helping MLs meet these challenges.[6]

BRIDGING THE CLASSROOM COMMUNICATION GAP

Unlike many other books that examine achievement gaps in the aggregate, this book focuses on helping teachers meet the needs of individual MLs. In particular, we focus on analyzing and addressing the gap these students face in regular education preK–12 settings between grade-level expectations for using listening, speaking, reading, and writing skills in the language of instruction (also known as language demands) and each ML's current proficiency in these skills. Let's call this the classroom communication gap. Understanding subject- and grade-specific language demands in relation to an individual's current second language (L2, also referred to as their new, or additional, language) proficiency—in other words, understanding the classroom communication gap—is the first step for classroom teachers to make curriculum, instruction, and assessment accessible to MLs.[7] And delivering that accessibility—in other words, narrowing the classroom communication gap—is an essential part of addressing the achievement gap. Although this book mainly addresses MLEs learning in preK–12 US schools, this vision holds true for MLs learning in any L2 and in any nation's school system.

With that goal in mind, three broad areas of focus permeate every chapter of this book. The first is communication and language in the regular education classroom, predominant because it is directly under the control of classroom teachers. Of the many factors that impact ML students' achievement, teachers' actions determine most of what is said and done in the classroom. The second area of focus is the process of second-language acquisition and how MLs progress from understanding and using little or none of their new language to reaching parity with their native-speaking peers. No educator can make informed decisions about curriculum, instruction, or assessment for an ML without a basic understanding of the second-language acquisition process, how it affects ML students' ability to comprehend and demonstrate mastery of new concepts presented in their L2, and what can be done to accelerate and promote attainment of the highest levels of proficiency in listening, speaking, reading, and writing in their new language.

Examining the distance between these two areas of focus—classroom communication and MLs' developing L2 proficiency—brings us back to the classroom communication gap and allows us to consider what teachers can do about it, which is the third area of focus. Throughout this book, through the stories of four MLEs at different grade and proficiency levels and through descriptions of their lessons in different subjects, we show how the subject of instruction and the grade level impact MLs' performance. For each lesson example, we address the classroom communication gap for one of the four MLE cases by applying a framework we have developed and used successfully in preK–12. The **Teaching All Subjects, Language, and Literacy (TASLL) Framework for Multilingual Learners** offers guidance on providing precisely what an ML needs *in addition to* the general best practices teachers commonly use with all students. We developed the TASLL (pronounced *tassel*) Framework in collaboration with teachers of all subjects and grade levels who have one or more MLs at different levels of L2 proficiency in their classrooms. Unlike some other approaches to teaching MLs, which require that instruction be structured in a certain way, the TASLL Framework is a flexible approach that teachers can use with *any* type of lesson, enhancing and adapting it for the additional needs of their MLs.

Narrowing the classroom communication gap while fostering MLs' achievement of rigorous standards may seem daunting. The great news is that no classroom teacher has to go at it alone. Every educator has an essential role and responsibility in supporting MLs' academic achievement and language development. The role of each type of educator of MLs should complement the roles of others, *forming an interconnected, unified system of support.* Location and instructional delivery model notwithstanding, all MLs deserve educators who are informed, skilled, and capable of reaching them. That principle is the basis of this book. We wrote this book for current and future disciplinary subject and language and literacy teachers with one or more MLs in their classrooms. Everything we share with you is based on our conviction that general education teachers, along with all other school-based professionals, can best serve MLs when they collaborate with Second Language Development (L2D) teachers, specialists in bilingual/dual language education, or in English language development (ELD), also referred to as English as a second language (ESL) or English for speakers of other languages (ESOL).[8] Throughout the book we feature information about MLs that is essential for regular classroom teachers, and we present examples of how they can work together with various kinds of second language teachers and specialists and other professionals at their schools to support MLs' language development and academic achievement.

We, the authors, are teacher educators born in five different nations and raised speaking ten different languages (English being the one language we have in common). For the past thirty years, we have been planning and leading professional learning for practicing and preservice teachers, concentrating on what is unique about reaching different types of MLs in the regular classroom. Our aim, in our work and in this book, is to provide practical guidance focused on what teachers of disciplinary subjects and language arts/literacy can do to make curriculum, instruction, and assessment accessible for MLs at different levels of L2 proficiency, while addressing the same high standards required of all students. This book distills what we believe to be essential research, theory, and instructional practices that support this aim—to narrow the classroom communication gap—and presents them in a new way, one that is accessible to general education teachers and that is highly effective in their classrooms. We begin this discussion by introducing four MLEs and how they learn in school. Through their stories, we show how considering the ecology of each student—the fullness of their lives at school and in their homes and communities—can lead teachers to more effective instruction for their ML students.

WHO ARE MULTILINGUAL LEARNERS OF ENGLISH AND HOW DO THEY LEARN?

There are many influences on MLE students' second language acquisition. To present these influences in an individual context, throughout this book we share the stories of four MLEs—Edith, Gero, Edgar, and Tasir—who represent common characteristics and issues of MLEs that preK–12 educators need to understand and address. These student cases are based on real MLEs we have worked with, but some details and names have been changed to protect their identities. Descriptions of the schools, classrooms, teachers, and other details of the stories will seem familiar because they were drawn from schools that could be located anywhere. What may be unfamiliar is the complex array of factors that are specific to the home and school lives of these four students who spend the majority of their day in classrooms that include MLEs among a majority of non-MLEs (whether instruction is in English, Spanish, or another language).

Through the stories of Edith, Gero, Edgar, and Tasir, we portray common issues for MLEs in primary and intermediate elementary grades as well as middle and high school. Our four student cases represent typical characteristics of MLEs at different English proficiency levels, ranging from newcomers to those close to exiting or being reclassified from the MLE category. They also reflect differences in family circumstances, motivation, and engagement in school. In addition, many cultural, social, and affective factors form part of each student's portrait, offering complex considerations regarding the student's performance at school. Based on how well our four MLE students can understand and use spoken English (their oral proficiency), we categorize them as beginning, intermediate, or advanced. In subsequent chapters, further details such as their precise WIDA proficiency levels will expand on this initial categorization.

The stories take you to the scene, capturing a sliver of what we observed over the course of the academic year at actual school locations. Packed with details, the stories are subsequently explained in terms of research and theory. In other words, the stories are more than simply illustrative; they are also instructional. Through recounting these students' experiences in various lessons, we realistically depict the gaps they face in classroom communication and show how lessons can be adapted to better meet their needs, using the TASLL Framework we have developed.

GETTING TO KNOW MULTILINGUAL LEARNERS OF ENGLISH: EDITH, GERO, EDGAR, AND TASIR

Let's look more closely at the protagonists of this book, Edith, Gero, Edgar, and Tasir, and the general issues that impact their English language development and academic achievement.[9]

✦ Edith Rodriguez and Gero Jantiy at Pine Woods Elementary School, Harveston, Florida

"Why aren't you in class?" asked a grown-up voice. "Do you have a hall pass?" Edith kept walking. It was her first day at Pine Woods Elementary, and she was fifty minutes late. The fourth-grade classroom was at the end of the long hallway, and Edith was walking as quickly as she could. "Excuse me!" Edith slowed and turned toward the assistant principal (AP). "Sweetie, I'm talking to you."

"No. . . no inglés," Edith whispered. Bending down to Edith's eye level, the AP remembered one of the helpful phrases she had learned in Spanish. "¿Como te llamas?" she asked with a smile. "Edith Rodriguez," the girl answered softly, as the AP stood up and started walking with Edith toward her room.

"Ms. Oliver, this is your new student, Edith. She's an MLE," the assistant principal announced. Ms. Oliver motioned to Edith to join a small group at a table in the back. Drawing her shoulders inward and with her head low, Edith moved hesitatingly to her spot. "Class, this is our new student, Edith Rodriguez. I hope you will all make her feel welcome."

Edith's family had moved from the Hidalgo region of Mexico a month earlier, settling in one of five trailers parked at the edge of a dirt road crossing fifty acres of strawberry fields. Her parents had decided to leave Mexico to join relatives with jobs, following the harvests northward during the season. Neither Edith's mother nor her father spoke English, so knowing someone from home who worked in the fields made it possible for them to join the crew. Edith had attended school in Mexico, but her town had increasingly experienced violent crime and insurgency, which caused her parents to relocate often for safety and for work. As a result, her schooling had been haphazard, and Edith's literacy skills in Spanish had suffered, along with her knowledge of math, science, and other subjects. Despite these hardships, Edith loved school and enjoyed the attention of her teachers. She had been looking forward to finding out what school would be like in the United States.

Five years ago, Pine Woods Elementary was rezoned to include the outskirts of town and its surrounding farmland. Before then, the school had seldom enrolled an MLE, but now every grade had MLEs, all at different levels of English proficiency. For the last five years, a group of Pine Woods teachers attended a national conference during the summer, bringing back tips and techniques for reaching MLEs. Some of these teachers even chose to deepen their professional learning to better understand how to teach MLEs, participating in online classes with individual coaching. Everyone knew that the school had to shift its approach to teaching and learning, but some teachers were more eager to do that than others.

Although Pine Woods Elementary's professional learning focused on supporting the success of MLEs from a variety of backgrounds, the majority of the MLEs at Pine Woods spoke Spanish at home. Because of this enrollment trend, the school had identified two classes of each grade whose instruction would be provided half in English and half in Spanish, known as dual language instruction. Their "roll-up" plan began with kindergarten and added a grade each year, with Edith's new fourth-grade class beginning the first year of dual language instruction for that grade.

That first morning when Edith arrived, she attended a Spanish language development class (referred to as Spanish language arts).[10] She immediately felt more comfortable among the other multilingual learners of English and Spanish and their patient, encouraging teacher. Half of her school day would be spent in English-medium instruction that she could barely understand, but in the Spanish language arts class, Edith could communicate with her Spanish-speaking classmates and teacher, and she could even help the multilingual learners of Spanish. In no time, however, the bell rang, and the other students began picking up their pencils and making their way out the door. Edith wanted to stay as the new group scampered in, planting themselves in the empty chairs, but her teacher gently coaxed her to move along to her next class.

In the hallway, Edith passed a small boy with "Gero" on his nametag, who stifled sniffles and tears as he stood in line with his classmates. It was Gero's first day, too. Gero had come to Pine Woods Elementary after spending a few weeks of the new school year in another district. Gero's father, a civil engineer, had been transferred to a construction company in Harveston, so the whole family had to quickly adjust to their new neighborhood and schools. Gero's mother, a pediatrician, and his father spoke to him in French, as they insisted on doing with all of their children. However, Haitian Kreyòl, the native language of Gero's home country Haiti, was also spoken in the home, mainly by Gero's brothers and sisters and sometimes by their grandmother.

Gero was lucky to be placed with kindergarten teacher Ms. Levin, who had begun professional learning the summer before the school's zoning change but had opted to remain in the English-only classroom when offered to join the dual language instructional team. Because of Pine Woods Elementary's dual language classes, there was greater awareness of the needs of MLEs, whether their home language was Spanish or not. Nonetheless, Gero's parents chose to enroll him in a regular classroom that included MLEs among non-MLEs but that only used one language (English) for instruction. There were not enough Kreyòl or French speakers enrolled at Pine Woods for dual language instruction in either language, so Gero's parents reasoned that because he already spoke Kreyòl and French, he needed to concentrate on learning English rather than adding Spanish to his existing language base.

Ms. Levin had worked to create a welcoming environment for her MLEs, labeling classroom objects in multiple languages and providing an enticing selection of bilingual picture books in Spanish and, now, Kreyòl. "Welcome, byenveni, Gero!" Ms. Levin had greeted the doe-eyed boy at the door. At her side was a girl from Port-au-Prince who had been in the United States for two years, with English skills that had grown strong in a preschool program. Gero smiled and moved toward his class buddy. Kindergarten didn't look as scary as he had expected. Ms. Levin made sure of it. When it came time to go to lunch, Gero refused to leave Ms. Levin's side.

Within the different categories of MLEs, Edith and Gero are at the beginning level. MLEs entering school (either in preschool or kindergarten) at the beginning level of English proficiency may have been born in the United States but live in homes and communities where their exposure to and use of English may not be extensive. This is not the case for Edith and Gero, however; they are both what are known as newcomers—MLEs who have recently arrived in the United States, have emergent English language skills, and likely have little experience with American culture. As with all language learners, Edith and Gero will go through some typical, predictable stages in their acquisition of English. MLE students of all grade levels begin learning English by focusing mostly on comprehending their new language. They often show comprehension by nodding, pointing, and answering in their first language because they haven't yet acquired the wording and phrasing necessary to converse in English. Apart from language-related challenges, newcomers face issues linked to their adaptation to and integration into a new cultural environment. Schools need to recognize these difficulties and make an effort to include the family and the community in the cultural transition of MLEs because they play a critical role in the success of this process.[11]

Previous schooling experiences and first language literacy are both important factors in MLEs' performance and progress. Edith likes school, but her education has been irregular, a fact that can potentially affect her performance. Will her gaps in literacy be insurmountable? Edith's teachers will soon find out whether she has developed basic reading skills in Spanish when they gather preliminary assessment data. Unlike Edith, Gero is a bilingual French and Haitian Kreyòl speaker but is more dominant in Haitian Kreyòl.[12] He is able to use a wider set of words, sentence structures, and emotions when expressing himself in Kreyòl rather than French. He also has developed strong preliteracy skills in both home languages, thanks to time spent with his grandmother and mother, who read to him regularly. Do his teachers know that he is drawing from multiple home languages instead of just one? Do they know that his foundational literacy skills have been developed in his home languages? These are all important questions that we will look at more closely in subsequent chapters. Now that we have introduced our beginning MLEs, Edith and Gero, it's time to meet our intermediate MLE, Edgar.

✦ Edgar Ponce at Highpoint High School, Chicago, Illinois

The apartment smelled moldy. Eliminating the dampness seemed impossible given the two narrow, 1970s-era column windows, neither facing south and one of them broken. This city dwelling was far removed from the bright and airy home Edgar grew up in with his family in Puerto Rico. His "real" home wasn't big or fancy, but sea breezes blew across every sunlit room.

Edgar had become withdrawn and sullen after his father left the family one random Saturday evening fourteen months earlier. Edgar's mother said he'd be back, but that never happened. After six months, she decided to move, along with her four children, to the US mainland, to the big city where her sister lived. There was work, her sister told her, and starting anew near family gave her hope.

Every afternoon when Edgar came home to the dingy apartment, he remembered all they had left in Puerto Rico: his friends, the sunshine, and even his school. Edgar had never liked school, but after eight months away from his "real" home, his memories of ninth grade and before became more pleasant. Even though he had struggled with reading and math, his teachers understood him.

Now school had become a nightmare. Edgar's eight months of English immersion gave him budding conversation skills, but that didn't equip him for the demands of tenth-grade subjects taught in English. On a good day, Edgar would simply tune out when he couldn't understand his social studies, math, or science teacher. For too many days, Edgar would impulsively act out, talking loudly to nearby Spanish-speaking classmates and even confronting the teacher as she explained a concept that was incomprehensible to him.

But Edgar entered a different world for two hours each day at Highpoint High. There was one place where he felt at home again, where he felt understood. Ms. Myers, his English language development teacher, knew how to teach so he could comprehend. The other students, who spoke many different languages, had lived similar experiences and felt homesick and tongue-tied like Edgar. When Ms. Myers introduced newcomers, Edgar approached each one eagerly, welcoming and helping them with maturity and empathy. During class, Ms. Myers often observed him leaning in to encourage a newly arrived group member, giving clues such as "Así se dice libro en inglés, boo-k." A child-like smile would spread from his eyes downward—he knew more English than someone else, and he could help. For now, though, this side of Edgar had to be suspended until the next day. The clanging bell interrupted end-of-class group work. "Remember to take your vocabulary practice sheets home," Ms. Meyers announced as she held up the empty form. Stepping out of the classroom oasis, Edgar folded his arms, tilted his head defiantly upward to the left, and mustered his toughest stance to survive in the mainstream.

Whereas Edith and Gero are newcomers, Edgar is a US-born MLE. A great proportion of students classified as MLEs were born in this country, entering preschool or kindergarten as beginners and continuing to receive ELD support as their levels of proficiency and grade levels rise. US-born MLEs bring a different set of challenges, but they also share many common issues with newcomers, as is the case with Edgar, who moved from Puerto Rico, a US territory with a distinct culture where Spanish is the primary language. As you saw in the story, it didn't take long before Edgar got into trouble at school. But this doesn't necessarily mean that Edgar is a student with behavioral issues. Edgar's discipline problems may simply be the result of a very difficult yet common period of cultural adjustment known as the hostility or crisis phase of acculturation.[13] Edgar's displacement from his familiar environment has created feelings of frustration, irritability, and helplessness. It's likely that Edgar will need special assistance from various professionals to succeed in school. In addition to the support of his ELD and academic subject teachers, a guidance counselor who is familiar with cultural adjustment could talk with Edgar about why he may be feeling stressed, and a bilingual reading coach could offer the additional help Edgar needs to develop his academic and literacy skills in both languages.

If we compare Edgar's language performance to that of Edith and Gero, it's clear he is beyond a beginning MLE. As an intermediate MLE, Edgar is able to communicate in English. He understands conversational English fairly well but not in most academic contexts, such as his various subject classes. Like many MLEs at his level, Edgar's speech and writing at this stage have frequent errors as he tries to master the complexity of English grammar and sentence structure. This is a normal part of the process of second language acquisition. In many ways, Edgar is right where we would expect him to be. The big question facing Edgar is: Where will he go next and how can his teachers contribute to his growth?

Now let's meet Tasir, our advanced MLE.

✦ Tasir Barad at Freedom Middle School, Traverse, South Carolina

"Yes, I *am* going to school dressed like this, Dad! This is how all the girls dress," Tasir insisted as she stormed out the door. Still smarting from the confrontation, Tasir replayed the scene in her mind as she hurried to the bus stop. Why does he want me to dress, think, and act like someone thousands of miles away? How come he insists on speaking Arabic when he knows I prefer to use English? *He* moved the family here, not me, so how can he expect us to live like we never left Egypt? As the bus to Freedom Middle wound through the tidy suburbs, Tasir glanced broodingly through the dusty windows at the driveways and ranch-style homes passing by.

More than anything, Tasir wanted to fit in, to look, think, and act like the popular girls in the seventh grade. She did all right imitating the cool kids, with her style, mannerisms, and even speech mimicking the latest tween fads. It had taken time to blend in though. When she started school in the United States, back in the third grade, Tasir spoke not one word of English. Her reading skills in Arabic, her native language, were strong, but the shape and direction of the boxy letters in the English textbooks were all new to her. Four years later, she understands but rarely utters anything in the language she arrived speaking.

"I just don't see how Tasir is still categorized as an MLE. No one could tell she's not a native speaker. I have no time to make accommodations for her, and she doesn't need them anyway!"

"Ms. Parker," cautioned the ELD resource teacher, "Tasir may be able to talk about her favorite pop stars, but she can't keep up with your lectures. She tells me that just as she's starting to understand a new point, you move on to the next." Tasir had failed Ms. Parker's last test. Next to the grade of 58, the teacher had written, "You can do better than this!" Tasir reached for the paper, felt the force of her limitations rush upward from her flushed neck, and flipped the test over quickly on her desk.

Tasir hated geography, math, and earth science. Family and community sciences, where she could watch her teacher prepare meals and practice cutting vegetables, was the only class she liked. Most of Tasir's teachers thought she did poorly because of her "whatever" attitude. But even though she looked and sounded like a typical seventh grader, she read and wrote like a fourth grader. Catching up with the native speakers required learning a new alphabet at the same time she was absorbing the meaning of the most basic words and acquiring the unfamiliar structure of simple sentences and paragraphs—all this while she studied science and social studies and math in this backward language that she had only just begun to understand. She'd had barely four years to catch up with the others, but now Ms. Parker only saw a seventh grader who could do well if she just tried.

To understand Tasir's needs, Ms. Parker should become aware of how advanced MLEs become fluent in social uses of language while they are still developing proficiency in academic language. Social language is synonymous with what ML expert Jim Cummins terms basic interpersonal communication skills (BICS). This is the type of language proficiency required to converse with others about daily life and basic needs. For example, when Tasir talks with her friends about what she is planning for the weekend, she is showing her command of social English. In contrast with social language, Cummins defines proficiency in academic English, which he has termed cognitive academic language proficiency (CALP), as that needed for learning school subjects.[14] Academic language is more complex and tends to refer to more abstract notions than social language. In addition, academic language use involves more reading and writing than social language, which is mostly conversational. Even advanced MLEs like Tasir still need time and support to become proficient in academic English. Research has shown that if MLEs have no prior schooling or have no support in their native language, it may take seven to ten years for them to catch up to their peers' proficiency in academic English.[15] Therefore, Tasir's teachers should not assume that MLEs with advanced oral proficiency like her, who show a high degree of fluency and accuracy in everyday spoken English, or social language, have an equally well-developed academic language proficiency in English.

We can see that Tasir needs more support and more time, especially because her first language uses a script that is different from the English alphabet. She is fortunate that her foundational literacy skills in Arabic were strong before the family relocated to the United States. Strong literacy in the first language helps tremendously with acquiring literacy in a second language. However, because she did not continue to receive literacy instruction in Arabic, her transition to English literacy has required more time and is not complete. Tasir is still classified as an English learner, but even MLEs who have been exited from the English learner category are still in the process of catching up with their native English-speaking peers, and so they still need monitoring and support. Tasir has worked hard to catch up with her peers when it comes to fitting in culturally, but this has cost her the loss of her native culture and language and caused a clash between her home and school lives.

Individual Characteristics of Our Four Multilingual Learners of English

The stories of Edith, Gero, Edgar, and Tasir show how complex MLE-related issues are and the difficulty of a one-size-fits-all type of instructional approach. Differences in the first language, age, and social, cultural, and affective conditions of MLEs have a powerful effect on the way they learn.

FIRST OR HOME LANGUAGE

Although the majority of MLEs in the United States speak Spanish, as do Edith and Edgar, MLEs come from a multitude of home languages, and each one has particular influences on the way they learn English. Edith and Edgar can benefit from various similarities between Spanish and English, and their teachers should take advantage of every opportunity to make connections explicit. Similarly, French and Haitian Kreyòl, Gero's home languages, share many commonalities with English that can be built upon to his benefit. Unlike the other three MLEs' home languages, Arabic, Tasir's home language, does not use the same alphabet as English, nor does it have many words that are based on the same roots (typically Latin and Greek words). However, the basic concepts of print and the notion of sound/symbol correspondence that Tasir brought with her from Egypt undoubtedly helped her develop an ability to understand and use their English counterparts.

INTERACTION BETWEEN COMMUNITIES THAT SPEAK EACH LANGUAGE

As with the linguistic and cultural differences evident in the stories, some MLs have a positive attitude toward learning their new language, whereas others are more resistant if they view their L2 as trying to displace their ethnic identity or if they see no clear or immediate benefits to developing strong skills in this "foreign" language. Like first language development, second language acquisition occurs in very rich contexts where social, cultural, and affective factors are an important part of the process. Second language acquisition scholars have studied social and affective influences on student learning, examining the relationship between two linguistically different groups of people who are in contact.[16] One group consists of people who have the same first language (such as Spanish) and are learning a second language (such as English), whereas the other group is made up of native speakers of the second language. The research suggests that a number of social factors can either promote or hinder contact between the two groups, which affects whether or not the second language learners from the same native language group adapt to the culture and consequently acquire the second language. The contact between the two groups can affect MLs' attitudes toward learning their L2. The type of contact between the community of speakers of the home languages of our four MLEs and the larger community of English speakers varies greatly, and the more our MLEs' teachers know about the languages used in their homes, the better the teachers will understand how their native language impacts their learning.

MOTIVATION TO LEARN A NEW LANGUAGE

As with learning anything, motivation, like attitude, affects learners' second language acquisition process and outcomes. Two types of motivation, integrative and instrumental, have been identified as influencing individuals' second language development in particular.[17] *Integrative motivation* alludes to the learner's interest in learning the language and their attitudes toward the teacher, the school, and the second language and its speakers. *Instrumental motivation* entails the learner's perceived benefits of learning the second language. Both types of motivation have been found to influence second language acquisition, with integrative motivation seeming slightly more influential than instrumental motivation. We can see with Edith, Gero, Edgar, and Tasir that teachers and other educators at their schools have a profound influence on their interest in developing English proficiency and in maintaining and increasing proficiency in their home languages. Similarly, we will see in upcoming chapters how their teachers will clue them in to the direct benefits of developing proficiency in listening, speaking, reading, writing, and using vocabulary and grammar in English, as well as the importance of drawing upon proficiency in their home language, to progress toward reaching grade-level expectations.

PERSONAL WELL-BEING

As with any student, personal aspects significantly influence MLs' performance at school. Teachers play a critical role in sustaining student motivation, fostering self-confidence, and implementing strategies that build linguistic competence in the classroom. These efforts are essential because motivated and confident learners are more willing to take risks, engage in conversations, and practice their language skills—key behaviors that drive oral communication development. When teachers intentionally support students' personal growth, they create a positive learning environment that empowers students to overcome language barriers.[18] MLs' sense of self-efficacy in classes taught in their new language, their relationships with parents and teachers, and the degree to which the school environment encourages the use of their home languages and cultures are all examples of social and emotional issues that have been found to impact their achievement. Research has shown, for example, that at the middle school level, MLEs have significantly lower levels of self-efficacy than non-MLEs, which is believed to be associated with the slower growth in academic achievement that occurs with MLEs in grades 6 to 8.[19] For young MLE children entering school, socialization practices of parents and caregivers may conflict with those of teachers, which could lead to children's uncertainty regarding acceptable behavior at school.[20] In the early childhood grades, there is evidence that use of the home language in the classroom has a positive effect on MLs' social-emotional development.[21] Edgar's struggles with adjusting to his new environment and the cultural and social differences between his native Puerto Rico and Chicago point to various elements of the experience specific to MLs that can impact academic achievement.

AGE OF LEARNER

Age also plays an important role in language development because older MLs have to acquire highly complex academic content at the same time they learn their L2. As we have seen with our four MLEs, the age MLEs begin learning English has a major effect on their language development. This is true for both internal factors, such as cognitive development and maturation, and external factors, such as different instructional approaches.

Several studies have compared the development of older and younger learners in similar situations, finding that at the early stages of language development, adult learners are, contrary to what many assume, actually more efficient than younger learners.[22] In formal second language learning settings, older learners are successful because they have several skills younger learners do not yet possess: metalinguistic knowledge (they can compare the new language with their home language), memory strategies, and problem-solving skills. This means that they can benefit from more formal instruction about their new language that calls upon those more complex skills to learn new grammatical structures. So, Tasir and Edgar, adolescent MLEs in middle and high school, can benefit more from the formal study of English grammar, as we will see in more detail in part III. This doesn't mean, however, that older students are better at learning second languages. Younger students like Gero and Edith have many advantages, including more time to catch up, a learning environment that is generally more conducive to language acquisition, the fact that their grade-level peers are starting to acquire academic language at the same time as they do, and internal developmental factors that promote the eventual attainment of native-like pronunciation and grammar use. All of these issues play key roles in the progress of our four MLEs.

Our MLEs' stories illustrate the many differences in classifications and terms used (e.g., newcomer, native-born) to describe the students we focus on in this book: preK–12 students who are learning in a new language they are not yet fully proficient in.[23] MLs' education in their native languages and home countries may have been interrupted and ineffective, or it may have been continuous and rigorous. They may come from financially stable families or live in abject poverty. The diversity among MLs can be as vast as that of any other group of students.

Classroom Communication and Language Learning for Our Four Multilingual Learners of English

As we have seen, how one learns a second language can vary greatly, with individual factors such as native language, prior education, family background, motivation, and age affecting the process and the outcome. Along with these key issues, the school context in which MLs learn has a major impact as well. In fact, the school and classroom context is so important to MLs' success that it is the main focus of the rest of the book. Considering the quality of communication for MLs in general classrooms is a crucial first step for teachers to understand how to help them learn academic subjects and develop proficiency in their L2.

Just from our brief snapshot of the elementary, middle, and high school classrooms of our MLE cases, we see that the goal of successful communication with these students can vary greatly. Gero's teacher, Ms. Levin, is working hard to narrow the communication gap between classroom language use and Gero's current English proficiency. Being in a kindergarten environment certainly helps, but Ms. Levin supports communication with Gero with what she has learned about MLs. In contrast, Edgar's tenth-grade disciplinary subject teachers mostly teach their classes as if he weren't there, with no special attention to improving communication with Edgar. If they knew more about narrowing the classroom communication gap, they could help him master their subjects and even contribute to his language development. Teachers who know how to support MLs in this way can make all the difference for students like Gero, Edith, Edgar, and Tasir.

In the upcoming chapters, your understanding of the school context, classroom communication, language instruction, and other issues affecting ML achievement will deepen as you come to know Edith, Gero, Edgar, and Tasir. Their unfolding stories and the discussions that follow them present the experiences of these students and their teachers realistically, showing how, despite the challenging circumstances that face so many schools and classrooms, educators like you *can* reach MLs and guide them to high levels of academic achievement.

ESSENTIAL POINTS

1. Teachers must understand the gap between the specific language demands of a lesson and the MLs' proficiency level to make curriculum, instruction, and assessment accessible to these learners. This approach, in turn, will enable them to narrow the classroom communication gap and help MLs meet or exceed the required standards.
2. We present the Teaching All Subjects, Language, and Literacy (TASLL) Framework as an approach to help teachers recognize, address, and provide support to meet the specific needs of MLs. Rather than requiring a separate approach, it complements and enhances the best practices teachers already use with all students.
3. The experiences of Edith, Gero, Edgar, and Tasir, highlight the complexity of issues related to MLEs, including first language, age, and social, cultural, and personal conditions, and the challenges that can significantly affect their learning when they remain unaddressed. However, the main factor that contributes to their success is the school context, where the quality of the communication in the classroom is a key component to help them develop L2 proficiency and obtain academic success.

OVERVIEW OF UPCOMING CHAPTERS

We have divided the book into three parts and a concluding chapter. The first part, to which this introduction belongs, provides information on the theoretical and practical underlying premises. The other two parts then dive into the heart of our TASLL Framework—supporting classroom communication and targeting language and literacy development. In the conclusion, we bring the book full circle, explaining how the information from the previous chapters can be implemented in a school-based, collaborative model of instruction for multilingual learners.

Part I: Setting the Stage for Multilingual Learner Success

The introduction presented the overarching aim of this book—bridging the classroom communication gap that exists in many regular classrooms with one or more MLs. You were introduced to the four MLEs whose journey you will follow for the remainer of the chapters, and we described characteristics that affect their process of becoming bilingual and the contexts in which these students live and learn.

Chapter 1 discusses language and learning in school, explaining how classroom communication differs by the subject and grade level of instruction and how these differences affect MLs' process of acquiring a new language. To illustrate how students' levels of L2 proficiency affect their performance in school, stories of our four MLEs include dialogue from actual interview transcripts and illustrate additional important factors, such as their first language (L1) literacy and prior knowledge of the disciplinary subjects they are learning now.

Part II: Supporting Disciplinary Learning

Chapter 2 explains our approach to providing supportive classroom communication for MLs and offers an orientation to the research and theory that underlie it. After the preliminary discussion of classroom communication of disciplinary subjects and ML levels of L2 proficiency, we discuss the gap between them and how it is affected by grade level. Last, we introduce the Supportive Classroom Communication (SCC) protocol of our TASLL Framework, which is an articulated series of analyses and decisions that narrow the gap between communication in curriculum, instruction, and assessment and MLs at beginning, intermediate, and advanced levels of proficiency.

The SCC protocol of the TASLL Framework is then applied in chapters 3 through 6, which provide research-based practical guidance for teaching disciplinary subjects to MLs. Each chapter focuses on teaching a specific subject to one of our four MLEs, Gero, Edith, Tasir, or Edgar. Unlike this introduction, which presented our four MLEs in order from beginning to advanced levels of English proficiency to introduce that concept, the chapters in part II are sequenced by grade level, progressing from kindergarten (Gero) to fourth (Edith), seventh (Tasir), and tenth grades (Edgar).

Chapter 3 first presents general considerations in teaching social studies to MLs. We then apply these principles with the SCC protocol to a kindergarten social studies lesson analyzing where and deciding how Gero will be provided necessary support. In addition to this detailed description of how we used the protocol to narrow the classroom communication gap for Gero, we provide briefer adaptation examples for MLs at other levels of L2 proficiency.

The remaining chapters of part II follow the same structure, with chapter 4 focusing on Edith and science instruction, chapter 5 on Tasir and interdisciplinary, thematic instruction, and chapter 6 on Edgar and mathematics instruction. The lessons presented are standards based, and each uses a different pedagogical approach, which illustrates how various common instructional practices present particular challenges and opportunities for MLs. We also have published a handbook for using instructional practices that promote MLs' academic achievement and second language development. In *Show, Tell, Build: 20 Key Instructional Tools and Techniques for Educating English Learners,* we give step-by-step guidance for using these featured tools and techniques for MLs, with the first ten focusing on supportive classroom communication and the second ten implementing targeted language and literacy instruction for MLs, the subject of part III.[24]

Part III: Focusing on Language and Literacy

As with part II, part III begins with an orientation to the research and theory that underlie our approach to teaching MLs but focuses on teaching language and literacy. Maintaining the centrality of communication to all types of learning, in chapter 7, we isolate the primary means of communication—language—and analyze how it develops through instruction, or what is known as instructed second language acquisition. In noting the difference among teaching *through* language, teaching *about* language, and teaching *language*, we argue that teaching language/teaching about language to MLs requires a greater degree of linguistic precision than teaching disciplinary subjects to MLs.[25] We subsequently deepen our discussion of L2 proficiency, describing five levels and how to target language and literacy instruction to these more precise proficiency levels. After discussing how implementation of instructed second language acquisition (what we term "targeted language and literacy instruction" for MLs) might range from nearly complete overlap with grade-level language arts instruction to nearly complete separation from it, we move on to how this language difference can be addressed in the regular and L2D classrooms. We then show how the Targeted Language/Literacy Instruction (TLI) protocol of the TASLL Framework, a series of analyses and decisions that target language and literacy instruction to specific levels of L2 proficiency, helps guide language and literacy learning to ensure that curriculum, instruction, and assessment in regular classrooms and, where appropriate, in L2D classes (or for other learning contexts, language development classes in the majority language of instruction) meet MLs at their precise level of L2 proficiency.

The TLI protocol of the TASLL Framework is then applied in chapters 8 through 11, which provide research-based practical guidance for teaching listening, speaking, reading, and writing to MLs. Each chapter focuses on one of our four MLEs, integrating the teaching of listening and speaking with reading or writing instruction. We begin each chapter by examining grade-level expectations for language and literacy and then consider similarities and differences between the English sound system, the writing system, rhetorical organization, and grammar and our four MLEs' first language (i.e., Haitian Kreyòl and French, Spanish, and Arabic) before presenting actual reading and writing samples in the context of their stories. This all leads to a classroom application of the TLI protocol to standards-based English language/literacy lessons and activities.

Maintaining the pattern described above, chapter 8 focuses on teaching language and literacy to MLs in kindergarten, taking into account Gero's beginning level proficiency in learning to write in English. Chapter 9 focuses on teaching language and literacy to MLs in the intermediate elementary grades, looking specifically at teaching Edith morphology in the fourth-grade dual language classroom at her level of English proficiency. Chapter 10 presents teaching language and literacy to MLs at the middle school level, discussing teaching Tasir writing and public speaking in the regular classroom at her English proficiency level. Chapter 11 focuses on teaching language and literacy to MLs at the high school level, but it diverges from the pattern of chapters 8 through 10 by showing how Edgar's language instruction needs are best met in the ELD classroom rather than the general classroom.

Conclusion: Moving the Tassel

After experiencing key research, theory, and practical issues in teaching MLs through the cases of Gero, Edith, Tasir, Edgar, and their teachers, you will be prepared to take action in your own classroom and school. The conclusion summarizes how educators who have developed essential knowledge and skills in teaching MLs through learning and applying the TASLL Framework can collaborate to serve their best interests and be exemplary teachers of MLEs.[26] We describe how teachers and other school professionals can work together, spanning simple coordinated efforts to more cooperative approaches and finally to collaboration, the most integrated and connected way of working together. The chapter closes with revisiting our four MLEs, now at the end of the school year in which we have come to know them, and we suggest how teachers can get to know their own ML students as well as their families and communities.

In appendix A, we provide you with a list of terms used throughout the book, whereas appendix B consists of the TASLL Framework Protocols diagram, which we suggest you copy and keep in your planning folder for a quick reference of the two protocols and their steps. This appendix also contains an image and narrative that show the philosophical orientation and theoretical rationale of the TASLL Framework. Finally, appendix C provides lists of artificial intelligence (AI) tools that educators can use for creating classroom communication support, personalizing instruction for MLs' specific needs, and for fostering family and community engagement. Guidelines for responsible use of AI are also given.

Features Common to the Entire Book

Because an overarching theme of this book is the classroom communication gap, envisioned as the space in which every teacher works to address the specific needs of an ML, the content of every protocol application chapter is organized by a common sequence: first, a general description of the language demands of the subject or skill of focus, followed by a discussion of the challenges in studying that subject or skill for MLs at specific levels of L2 proficiency. Each chapter, then, shows an original lesson and offers practical suggestions for making it appropriate for MLs.

This book provides an overarching theoretical framework, a big picture so to speak, for the specific practices that illustrate what teachers can do to reach MLs, and we believe that big-picture books need big (and lots of) pictures. Therefore, in the theory-to-practice chapters 2 and 7, we have placed diagrams and icons that illustrate and summarize major points. We included these visuals also to walk our talk about the importance of using both verbal (language) and nonverbal (visual, in this instance) communication in teaching MLs.

Each chapter contains a summary of "Essential Points" related to the theoretical and practical discussions and ends with "Stop and Reflect Questions" and "Go and Practice Activities," which offer myriad opportunities to apply the book's content to each reader's instructional contexts. Our website, http://www.MLSuccess.org, provides suggestions and resources for further study. We believe these resources will be most useful after reading the book and developing a sense of the full landscape of teaching MLs in regular preK–12 classrooms.

This book wasn't written for a perfect world. It doesn't lay out a gold standard of practice that can only be implemented in ideal conditions with bountiful resources. It was written for you and all the other educators who are doing the best they can to help all their students reach their potential. We believe what you read here will be actionable in your classroom, and we hope it helps you to foster excellent communication and provide effective support for your ML students' success at school.

STOP AND REFLECT QUESTIONS

1. How are you currently assisting your MLs to meet the rigorous requirements of the standards in your state?
2. Think about the MLs in your class(es). Do any of your students share characteristics with Gero, Edith, Edgar, and Tasir? If so, how are they similar?

GO AND PRACTICE ACTIVITIES

1. Considering the first-day experiences of our four MLEs, during the course of a week, reflect on your communication in the classroom and how you design activities for your students to communicate with each other.
2. Make a list of what you know about your MLs that might contribute to their success at school (for example, first language literacy, personal well-being, and motivation to become bilingual) and consider how you might build on these assets.

Language and Learning in School

There's a lot of information available about teaching multilingual learners (MLs). In fact, there are entire academic degrees in that subject. In this book, we distill what our research and experience tell us is essential. To get to our core goal of accelerating and elevating MLs' academic achievement, we have divided the book into two areas of focus: (1) classroom communication and (2) language and literacy instruction for MLs. In classroom communication for MLs, we define the goal as *narrowing the classroom communication gap* between grade-level communication and MLs' current second language (L2) proficiency. That is the subject of this chapter and part II. In part III, we address language and literacy instruction for MLs, which we define as *targeted language and literacy instruction*, adjusted for each ML student's precise level of L2 proficiency. Because we believe communication is the foundation of learning all subjects and skills, we begin part I by considering its essence.

COMMUNICATION: THE CURRENCY OF EDUCATION

Most would agree that communication is paramount in teaching. Teachers communicate information about topics, concepts, and skills that students are expected to master. Likewise, communication by and among students is central to learning. Students communicate their understanding of a new concept or their questions about a skill they are developing. Communication is, in a sense, the currency of education. A great deal hinges on successful communicative interchanges between teacher and students as well as those among classmates. All teachers need to attend to the quality of communication in the classroom, reflecting on their own and their students' use of language and other means of expressing and comprehending meaning. Without communication, little is taught or learned.

Communication scholar James Carey once stated that prominent twentieth-century educator John Dewey positioned communication at the center of humanity, asserting that society exists both *through* and *in* communication.[1] Drawing on Dewey's work, Carey expanded a prevailing definition of communication from the conveyance of information from one person to another, known as a transmission model of communication, to a communal process of constructing a symbolic reality, referred to as a ritual view of communication. Carey pointed to the common root of the word *communication*, the term *community*, going as far as viewing communication as culture itself.[2] In this perspective, communication is much more than the simple transmission of a message from sender to receiver—it acts as a binding force of interpersonal connection, an exchange of meaning affected by and affecting the communicators.

Similar to Carey's culture-building model of communication is the assertion by language scholar M. A. K. Halliday that culture forms the context for making meaning through language, which he defined as a "social semiotic system" (that is, language as a sign or symbol referring to real objects, concepts, etc.).[3] Halliday's view of language, the most significant form of human communication, is similar to that of learning theorist Lev Vygotsky, who defined language as a cultural tool that serves social interaction.[4] Clearly, language can be described in multiple ways, but there is no denying its principal function of creating shared meaning.

In the preK–12 school environment, with its many different uses of language, communication both forms and is shaped by the culture of the classroom. Each individual in the class brings cultural and linguistic assets from life outside of school, creating the potential for a rich collective expression and exploration of meaning. In addition to this collective classroom culture, the socially constructed content of schooling—the knowledge and skills communicated through curriculum and instruction—exists in and through communication as well. If a child's own language and culture closely align with the larger society's language and culture as experienced at school, the gap between the child's abilities and grade-level performance expectations is small. If the gap is large, such as that between the rigorous language demands of state standards and the English proficiency of a beginning multilingual learner of English (MLE) like Edith, a substantial degree of support is necessary to meet and surpass those language demands.[5]

COMMUNICATING ABOUT ACADEMIC SUBJECTS THROUGH LANGUAGE

Attributed to Halliday, there are three aspects of language use in schooling.[6] The first is *learning through language*, such as when studying a subject like history. Information regarding the topic is presented through spoken and written language, and students develop understandings through discussion or other instances of listening, speaking, reading, or writing about the topic. Learning through language is the main mode of communication in teaching and learning. Another aspect of language use in school is *learning the language*. This is typically done in language and literacy lessons, where students develop competence in the four skills or modalities of language use—listening and speaking (oral language) and reading and writing (literacy). Lesson objectives and activities provide opportunities to practice these skills, often stressing strategies for improving outcomes. An example of learning the language is a lesson on writing a narrative that retells historical events. Halliday's last element of language use is *learning about the language*, which involves analysis of the form, structure, and rules of language, such as learning grammar, punctuation, or spelling. This type of learning would typically take place in language and literacy lessons and could easily be part of the historical narrative writing lesson just mentioned.

Halliday's distinctions of classroom language functions help illustrate the shifts that take place when teaching disciplinary subjects and when teaching language and literacy to MLs. Although both types of instruction are clearly interdependent, the overall goals of each differ in emphasis. With disciplinary subject instruction for MLs, the primary goal is to master the subject matter, and if communication of the subject matter is at an appropriate level for the ML, the student is able to also develop related L2 proficiency. Hence, disciplinary subject teachers play a critical role in MLs' language development through focusing on successful communication. MLs can use newly acquired language related to the disciplinary subject to better learn new content and skills, and therefore, a cycle of success in learning the subject and the language of the subject continues.

As MLs develop greater second language proficiency, they can comprehend more complex subject matter through language, discuss the content in more complex terms, and demonstrate mastery through higher-level language-based assessments. This process is a mutually beneficial, upwardly mobile system, leading concurrently to increased second language proficiency and subject matter knowledge. This cycle is illustrated in figure 1.1.

Conversely, with language and literacy instruction for MLs, the primary goal is to develop proficiency in L2 listening, speaking, reading, and writing, which involves learning language and learning about language. Yet by acquiring L2 skills and, more specifically, academic language skills, MLs are able to master more complex disciplinary subject content in their new language.[7] In part III, we will explore the dimensions of language and literacy instruction for MLs in more detail. As shown in figure 1.2, just as with disciplinary subject instruction, the process is mutually beneficial.

Given that all teachers need to be mindful of effective communication, teachers of MLs bear additional responsibilities. MLs are acquiring the language of instruction,

FIGURE 1.1

Purpose of Teaching Disciplinary Subjects to MLs

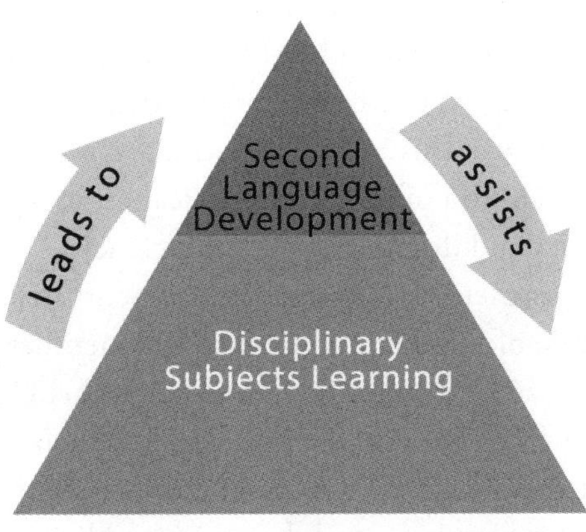

FIGURE 1.2

Purpose of Teaching Language and Literacy to MLs

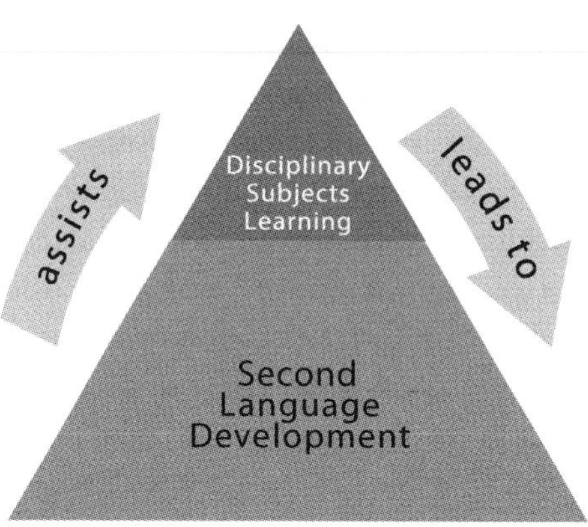

so communicating with them and helping them to communicate what they are learning take extra knowledge, skills, and effort. In essence, the primary goal of teachers of MLs is to communicate successfully with and support the successful communication of these students, whose academic achievement and L2 development depend on it. We believe that if culture can be defined as communication, so can teaching.

COMMUNICATION *FOR, BETWEEN,* AND *OF* MULTILINGUAL LEARNERS

Extending Carey's and Halliday's play on prepositions, we can consider classroom teachers' role in disciplinary subject instruction for MLs in terms of communication *for*, *between*, and *of* students. Teachers attend to their communication *for* all their students. Lessons of every type involve some sort of teacher communication that is *for*, or directed to, the learners. Similarly, teachers plan and orchestrate communication *between* students, making sure the back and forth sharing of meaning between teacher and student and between student and student goes smoothly and purposefully. Teachers also enable communication *of* their students, providing support to help them say or write what they know about the subject being learned, such as with assigned homework or in-class quizzes. No one can deny that these communication relationships are important to teachers. This is especially true for teachers of MLs. Let's take a look at Edith's class to get an idea of how communication in a general classroom can help her learn mathematics and develop her L2 proficiency.

Edith's fourth-grade teacher, Ms. Oliver, often presents new information or skills through the gradual release of instruction, or what is sometimes known as the *I do, we do, you all do, you do* approach.[8] When Ms. Oliver taught her class how to add fractions, she began by writing ¼ + ¼ = on the interactive whiteboard, naming the number and describing what she was doing with each number and symbol she wrote. She continued the same process of writing and describing, adding the top numbers and writing 2 above a line she drew, and then 4 beneath it, and so on until she had solved the problem (the *I do* part of the lesson). After she had walked the class through a couple more examples, she let them know that they would now do a few problems together. By questioning the class at each step, she had them direct her calculations on the whiteboard, coming to the correct answer by consensus (*we do*). At this point, it was time for students to work together at their tables, solving more problems first in pairs and then sharing their answers, back and forth, with the other pairs (*you all do*). Finally, she turned off the projector and gave each student a handout with four problems to solve individually (*you do*), asking them to write out each step of solving the problem as well as the answer.

Ms. Oliver's gradual release lesson involved the three communication relationships we discussed. For each stage of the lesson, she set up communication *for*, *between*, and *of* her students. Let's rename these three prepositions that represent the direction of classroom communication with their recognized terms in the field of second language acquisition—input (communication for students), interaction (communication between students and between teacher and student), and output (communication of students). In the first part of the lesson, Ms. Oliver presented and demonstrated new information, which provided *input* to the learners. Then the teacher led the give-and-take instructional process, which is a form of *interaction* between the teacher and individual students. After that, students had an opportunity for *interaction* with each other, first in pairs and then with their small groups. Finally, individual students showed what they learned through their written *output* on the handout.

Input

Second language acquisition research and theory have shown that language input, interaction, and output are necessary for anyone to develop proficiency in a new language, but just providing the three aspects of communication is not enough to ensure language learning. They must also be accessible.[9] What does this mean? Essentially, MLs like Gero, Edith, Edgar, and Tasir must be exposed to unknown language forms and structures that they can comprehend; they must engage in meaningful communication, using these new forms and structures with other speakers of the language; and they must express themselves understandably using the newly acquired forms and structures.

Comprehensible language in the preK–12 classroom means that when unknown forms and structures are directed at MLs (communication *for* MLs), they are able to comprehend them through reference to real objects or actions (and, in some instances, through background knowledge learned in the native language) or through inferring their meaning from closely related language they already know. In other words, the language MLs are exposed to becomes comprehensible through being at the level of, or a slight step beyond, the language the learner already knows and also by being closely linked to nonverbal items and experiences the learner can understand.[10] For example, if Edith hears "Write your name, Edith" when her teacher holds a pencil as she points to the top of a blank page, Edith knows to put her name on the paper. This association is described by the term that second language acquisition theorist Stephen Krashen coined, *comprehensible input*.[11] We can contrast this with hearing a radio broadcast in an unknown language—there is input (the sound of the spoken information), but it is not comprehensible because there are no visuals to support the input. In any learning environment, the more comprehensible input available for the ML, the better.

Output

The counterpart to comprehensible input is comprehensible output, which means that the learner expresses meaning in their new language (communication *of* MLs) that another speaker (native or otherwise) of the language can understand.[12] Because this is an important requirement for developing proficiency, MLs who are moving beyond the earliest stages of second language acquisition, when they mostly listen, must have opportunities to express their thoughts in their L2, through either speaking or writing. In addition, there needs to be an audience for the ML's output. The audience can be someone evaluating the output at a later point (as in a testing situation) or someone who is speaking or writing extemporaneously with the ML (communication *between* MLs and *between* MLs and others—or *interaction*).[13]

Interaction

Interaction, as the word implies, signifies an exchange between two people, in this case two communicators. The beauty of communicative interaction is that it includes both input and output, and they are connected in a meaningful way. For example, if Edgar asks his English-speaking friend, "Can I use your kay?" and the friend doesn't know what he means, Edgar might say, "for open door," or he can repeat "kay" and hold out his fist, grasping an invisible key and twisting it left and right. His friend would then say, "Oh, you mean my key!" and would hand it to him. This exchange enables Edgar to use the language for a real purpose and builds his vocabulary through his attempt at using an unfamiliar word and his friend's confirmation of the correct term and object. This attempt at communication is like a little lesson, one that uses negotiation of meaning between Edgar and a more advanced or native speaker of English as a route to language growth.[14]

In preK–12 classrooms of all subjects, teachers should do everything possible to provide the most accessible input, interaction, and output for MLs.[15] This means making instruction comprehensible, setting up and supporting interaction with MLs and between MLs and other students, and enabling MLs to express what they know and can do in the subject through multiple means that are appropriate to their level of L2 proficiency. As we saw with Ms. Oliver's gradual release lesson and with most types of lessons, instruction or presentation of new information is a major form of input (with some teacher-student interaction when the teacher calls on individuals to answer questions), pair and group activities offer opportunities for interaction, and classroom-based assessment requires varying degrees of output. When the classroom teacher is keenly aware of the importance of accessibility for all three elements, she can make adaptations that not only improve the ML's understanding of the subject being learned but also naturally increase the ML's second language development.[16]

No matter the subject or grade level of instruction, accessible input, interaction, and output are the essence of successful communication *for*, *between*, and *of* MLs. Successful communication promotes learning of the academic content and fosters L2 development. We know that accessible input, interaction, and output are necessary for second language development, but as we'll see in the next section, their feasibility differs by grade level.[17]

CLASSROOM COMMUNICATION ACROSS GRADE LEVELS

To get a more complete sense of the nature of communication in instruction at different grade levels, start with a look at your district's curriculum in the early grades—it shows concepts and topics that are concrete and can be presented by using real objects, role playing, making crafts, and engaging in hands-on activities rather than solely by offering spoken and written explanations. This is what second language acquisition expert Jim Cummins calls "context-embedded instruction."[18] A simple comparison of the physical arrangement of Gero's kindergarten and Edgar's tenth-grade classrooms illustrates this point. Gero's classroom has centers where he and other children play-act different kinds of jobs and handle toys representing the tools or equipment used. His classroom is highly visual and colorful, with labeled objects and word walls that show the alphabet, accompanied by words and pictures. There are bins and crates overflowing with sorting objects, models, flashcards with pictures and words, and sentence strip holders. Parts of walls are dedicated to vocabulary-building resources. There is abundant correspondence between objects and the printed word. By contrast, most of Edgar's high school classrooms contain fewer objects and other resources that make vocabulary and concepts more concrete. Many of the posters on the wall address good study habits and attitudes, but they don't display as many objects and images depicting topics and concepts that relate to the curriculum.

Because young learners have not fully mastered literacy in the language of instruction, much of the disciplinary subject instruction in the early grades is communicated through oral language accompanied by copious amounts of hands-on objects and experiences, pictures and visual communication, and labels and other forms of accompanying text, among other resources. The close relationship between the visual aspects and spoken or written language benefits MLs like Gero. Once children have learned to read, however, much more of the information they have to acquire is conveyed through text, and their comprehension of the content is often assessed through writing, which makes learning the concept more challenging for MLs at lower proficiency levels. Measures of text complexity generally show an increasing level of difficulty in materials spanning preK–12. For example, the following texts show an increasing amount of information and complexity, including discipline-specific vocabulary by grade levels, which Gero, Edith, Edgar, and Tasir could be expected to read and learn in their respective grades.

> *Kindergarten Water Cycle Text:* The sun evaporates water from oceans, and it turns into water vapor.
>
> *Grade 4 Water Cycle Text:* The constant recycling of water on Earth is called the water cycle. Heat from the sun causes the water particles to move faster and faster. In time, the water particles have enough energy to release into the air as water vapor. This phase of the water cycle is evaporation, the process by which a liquid changes to a gas.
>
> *Grade 7 Water Cycle Text:* The water cycle, also known as the hydrologic cycle, is the continuous movement of water between the surface of Earth and the troposphere. The water cycle happens because of three repeating processes: evaporation, condensation, and precipitation. Evaporation is the process by which liquid water changes into invisible water vapor (water in the form of a gas). Heat from the sunlight causes evaporation.
>
> *Grade 10 Water Cycle Text:* Water vapor rearranges energy from the sun through atmospheric circulation. This happens because water absorbs a large amount of energy when it transforms its state from liquid to gas. When it evaporates from liquid water, the resulting vapor contains more energy, which is referred to as latent heat. Solar radiation drives evaporation by heating water so that it changes to water vapor at a faster rate.

From these examples, we see that the language demands of these grade-level texts become more complex and the amount of language used to convey information about topics and concepts and to develop skills in disciplinary subjects increases with each grade. But what about *oral* language complexity?

We know that academic language demands include listening, speaking, reading, and writing, but most research on their increased difficulty across the grade levels focuses on text and reading. A good deal of research has been conducted on the degree of text complexity from prekindergarten to the twelfth grade, with formulas for calculating readability and grade-level passages as well as specific types of linguistic analyses, but scant attention has been paid to listening and speaking (oral language) complexity in the classroom.[19] Educators assume discussions focusing on complex texts require higher levels of language proficiency to comprehend and participate in lesson activities. Unfortunately, there is limited research on the demands of listening and speaking skills at any grade level. Absent definitive empirical research, we can look to various linguistic factors of oral language, such as the rate and complexity of speech, including word choices, phrasing, and discourse types, to understand the communication challenges in comprehending instruction.

One way to see how grade level may affect oral language demands is to consider how adults speak with young children. Research on adults' speech to babies and toddlers shows that they focus on the here and now; slow their speech; use short, simple sentences; and repeat words frequently. When adults talk to kindergarten-age children, they speak more slowly than with adults, adding pauses between each word. They naturally use repetitive sentence patterns that allow simple substitutions, such as, "Where's_____? Look at_______."[20] When adults speak with older children or other adults, they tend not to use these natural adaptations to help younger children develop first language (L1) competence. This means that MLs in general classrooms at the middle and high school levels, such as Tasir and Edgar, don't normally receive the same quality of oral language development or accessible input and interaction that Gero and Edith receive in their elementary school classrooms.

To illustrate the differences in expectations for listening, speaking, reading, and writing as well as the amount of contextualized instruction in early grades versus upper grades, in figure 1.3, we show an approximate ratio (not to scale) of context-embedded instruction (depicted as nonverbal classroom communication) to the language demands (verbal classroom communication). The graph highlights the decrease in nonverbal types of communication and increase in verbal ones as we move from prekindergarten to the twelfth grade.[21] In Gero's kindergarten class, the portion of disciplinary subject instruction communicated solely by language—for example, listening to teacher explanations and reading books—is smaller than that communicated by other means, such as hands-on experiences. However, for Edgar, in grade 10, language bears a greater proportion of classroom communication. In Gero's classroom, in addition to the higher proportion of nonverbal communication, the correspondence between nonverbal and verbal classroom communication is very close, with Ms. Levin referring pointedly to real objects and pictures to contextualize their verbal descriptions. Moreover, the integration of oral and print communication is explicit and consistent, providing a bridge between them for young children. This is less true for Edgar in tenth grade.[22]

FIGURE 1.3
Proportion of Verbal and Nonverbal Communication Across Grades

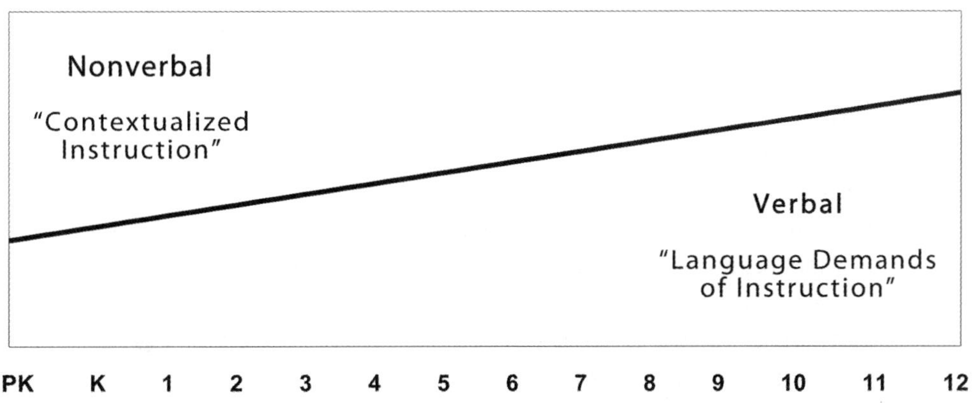

INDIVIDUAL FACTORS IN OUR MULTILINGUAL LEARNERS' OF ENGLISH ACADEMIC ACHIEVEMENT

Gero, Edith, Edgar, and Tasir represent common oral language behaviors for MLs at different levels of L2 proficiency. Although they are in different grades, their listening and speaking skills are less representational of their grade than their L2 proficiency level. In other words, a sixth-grade beginning ML has many of the same listening and speaking behaviors in their L2 as a ninth-grade beginning ML, and a ninth-grade advanced ML has many of the same listening and speaking behaviors in their L2 as a twelfth-grade advanced ML. The following stories include transcripts of Edith's, Gero's, Tasir's, and Edgar's speech, which gives a sense of what an ML at each level of English proficiency can say and understand, and how he or she says it.

✦ Edith and Gero

"How long have you been in the United States?" "Uhhh . . . ." Edith wanted to respond. She longed to please her teacher with the correct answer. She just couldn't understand the question. "Umm, one month . . . in Florida?" Ms. Oliver held up her index finger as her rising pitch signaled a question. "One . . . one month," Edith confirmed as she bobbed her head and smiled.

Even though an English language development (ELD) specialist had tested Edith and placed English proficiency scores in the file according to district guidelines, these scores were confusing to Ms. Oliver, who, as a first-year teacher, had little experience with L2 proficiency assessment data. "Why don't you just sit down with Edith and have a conversation?" suggested another teacher. "Whenever I get a newcomer, I make sure to have a lot of pictures and props when we talk."

Ms. Oliver had followed that advice, and after asking Edith about her background, she opened a magazine and pointed to a cartoon. "Who is this?" "Uh . . . eh-Stitch?" Edith offered. "Stitch, that's right, that's Stitch! Do you like Stitch?" Edith nodded with a flutter of affirmation, a wave of relief rising toward her piercing black eyes. "Uh-huh!" "Yeah, me too!" agreed Ms. Oliver. "He makes me laugh." Sitting side by side, the magazine between them, Ms. Oliver and Edith were communicating. Ms. Oliver went on. "What color is Stitch?" (Transcript follows.)

EDITH: Uhh . . .

MS. OLIVER: Is he green, is he black, is he yellow? What color?

EDITH: Eh, blue.

MS. OLIVER: Blue, very good, he's blue! And, can you point to the bed? [no response] Do you see a bed in the picture? [no response] Is there a bed there?

EDITH: Uhh . . . [asks to use a little Spanish—poquito español]

MS. OLIVER: ¿Poquito español? Okay.

EDITH: Uhh . . . ¿poquito español? [pleads for clarification in Spanish]

> **MS. OLIVER:** La cama (Spanish for bed). Can you point to it? The bed.
>
> **EDITH:** ¿La cama?
>
> **MS. OLIVER:** Uh-huh. In the picture, show me where it is in the picture.
>
> **EDITH:** ¿La cama? ¿Eso? (Translation: The bed? This?) [points to the bed]
>
> **MS. OLIVER:** Yeah, that's the bed. And what color is the bed? Is it the same color as Stitch?
>
> **EDITH:** Uhh.

Their conversation was somewhat strenuous, with both of them grasping for words that made sense to the other. Despite the strain to communicate, Edith's and Ms. Oliver's give-and-take began to form a strong basis for tailoring instruction to Edith's needs. From these interactions, Ms. Oliver gained an understanding of what a beginning MLE can say and do in their second language. She knew, though, that as a new teacher she needed to learn more.

✦ ✦ ✦ ✦

Ms. Levin was not surprised that Gero hadn't yet spoken in English. He had, however, begun to nod and point and follow simple commands. Even when his Kreyòl-speaking classmate, Merline, wasn't nearby, Gero would express himself in Kreyòl, but when an adult pressed him to speak up in English, his response was consistently, "Je ne comprends pas." With a classmate, it was always, "Mwen pa konprann."

Edith's listening comprehension and speech in English represent the beginning level of oral language proficiency. Kindergartner Gero is nearly identical to fourth-grader Edith in both listening and speaking. Common characteristics of the beginning level, which can last up to a year, often include an initial "silent period" when MLs are not yet speaking in their L2.[23] They might not talk, but they can show comprehension by pointing, performing, gesturing, and nodding. As they progress through the beginning level, MLs develop a vocabulary of five hundred to a thousand words they can understand, some of which they might not use yet. They become more capable of speaking, albeit limited to one- or two-word phrases or short answers to simple questions. For example, once beyond the silent period, MLs can answer simple questions such as yes/no (Is this a flag?), who (Who has the flag?), either/or (Is this a flag or a globe?), what (What is this?), and where (Where is the flag?). In addition, they are able to understand and say memorized frequent, formulaic language, such as "Whatcha doin'?" even though they aren't yet able to build a sentence that complex word by word, as in "What are you doing?" We saw in Edith's story that she frequently used her Spanish to clarify a question or supply an answer. It is common for beginning MLs to spontaneously use the language they know well when they are put in situations where they don't know enough of their new language to express their thoughts, even if the person they are addressing doesn't know the ML's first language.

✦ Edgar

Losing patience after her previous warnings to Edgar, the dean of students spoke sternly. "Here we are again, Edgar. Your fourth referral this month. You've got to straighten up soon, or we'll be looking at more serious measures."

"Like . . . like what?" Edgar questioned.

"We can talk about that when the time comes," the dean replied. "I mean *if* the time comes. Hopefully, that won't happen."

Edgar stared at the freshly painted wall behind the dean's desk. Grooves the width of his index finger marked each horizontal row of cinderblocks. The semigloss sheen of the gray paint highlighted underlying peeled splotches of various pastel colors from the past, their cheerful hues painted over to muffle potential distraction. Gray, and only gray, loomed everywhere.

DEAN: Edgar, are you listening to anything I'm saying? I just told you the behaviors we expect of you in every class. Ms. Myers describes a well-behaved young man in her ELD class. If you can follow the rules in her class, why are you so disruptive in history class?

EDGAR: What?

DEAN: Why do you make trouble in history class?

EDGAR: 'Cause the other class [history] is boring. I don't like it.

DEAN: Why is it boring?

EDGAR: 'Cause sometime I don't understand the work what I have to do. You know.

DEAN: Do you understand everything in ELD class?

EDGAR: Yeah, and I talk with everybody.

DEAN: So what kinds of things do you learn in ELD class?

EDGAR: We read, write, and talk, we need to talk, and the teacher, umm, they help, umm, everyone do the other for the other class. In the other class, yeah when, when someone got some problems in some class, yeah, they help with.

This was the longest the dean had spoken with Edgar in the eight months since he had been placed in tenth grade. Maybe knowing a bit more about him could help improve his behavior. Forging ahead, the dean inquired about Edgar's home life.

DEAN: Can you tell me anything interesting about your family?

EDGAR: My brother he come from this school, my sister she go to Kennedy, um, my little sister she go to King Highway, something like that. Yeah, and my little brother he don't go to school because she's four year old but he's in the chilled [sic] care.

The second-period bell interrupted the getting-to-know-you interview that the dean had been improvising in simple English. If Edgar stayed out of trouble, there might be no further reason to continue the conversation. The dean hoped this was all she ever needed to know about Edgar.

Common characteristics of MLs, like Edgar, at the intermediate level of oral L2 proficiency, which may last up to two years or more, are a vocabulary of around three thousand words and the ability to use short phrases and simple sentences to communicate. Intermediate-level MLs are able to ask and answer questions that use and require a bit more language than the simple questions that are appropriate for beginning MLs. In the interview, Edgar could understand, "Do you understand everything in ELD class?" and even elaborated beyond a *yeah* to make it known that he talks with everybody in that class. However, when trying to produce longer sentences, his language, typical of intermediate MLs, contained grammatical errors that obscure meaning. For example, when Edgar referred to his little brother, he alternated between *he* and *she* because he had not yet firmly acquired the correct form in English. Another error that is typical of MLEs at this level is not adding the *-s* to the end of verbs, as in "he come" and "she go." He also uses *don't* instead of *doesn't* in "he don't go," an error that may be due to his developing learner language or to language modeled by his native-speaker peers.

✦ Tasir

Suite 115A . . . 115B . . . 115C. 115J had to be coming up. "Have you heard her with her friends? She sounds like any seventh grader. You may think you're helping her in ELD class, but you're actually holding her back." The voices got louder as Tasir approached the end of the hall. "The problem with Tasir," Ms. Parker continued, "is she's basically lazy. She won't push herself, so we have to." Tasir paused outside the doorway. "Uh, Tasir, how long have you been there?" "Just got here," she chirped. "Come in. We've been waiting for you." Tasir's ELD teacher, Ms. Marlin, pulled a chair out from the conference table's edge. "We'd like to ask you a few questions about your classes." Tasir shrugged her right shoulder as she replied with an abrupt "Sure."

MS. MARLIN: Tell me about your favorite class.

TASIR: Um, family sciences, 'cause it's fun and it's not—it's not hard.

MS. MARLIN: What kind of things do you do in there?

TASIR: Um, we're gonna cook, but we didn't like cook yet. We, um, uh, we, we learn about like what kind of food we eat and stuff. Like what is good for me.

MS. MARLIN: Oh, so do you like to cook?

TASIR: Oh, no, not really, not really.

Tasir chattered freely as Ms. Parker and Ms. Marlin recorded her responses in their notepads. Manila folders labeled with Tasir's full legal name were stacked, unopened, at the table's edge. The school counselor and testing coordinator sat at the end of the table, listening while typing on their laptops. Avoiding looking at Ms. Parker, whose gaze was fixed on her notepad, Tasir volunteered unexpected details, sounding more and more like a seventh grader who was raised speaking English.

MS. MARLIN: What is your hardest class?

TASIR: Geography.

MS. MARLIN: Geography. And what's hard about geography?

TASIR: Um, Ms. Parker don't give us like time to do stuff, when she says do something. She just like gives us a second, and she goes okay, next person.

MS. MARLIN: So, it goes too fast, huh?

TASIR: Yeah.

MS. MARLIN: Do you have to do a lot of reading in geography?

TASIR: Uh-huh.

Ms. Parker glanced at the other educators around the table for a split second. With Tasir seated in front of her and surrounded by her coworkers, especially the sympathetic Ms. Marlin, Ms. Parker for once kept her opinions to herself. Ms. Marlin stopped her questions and reached for one of the cumulative folders. "Tasir, let's look at your progress in reading." Tasir didn't respond. Her mind had drifted to Ms. Parker's earlier outburst, to those condemning pronouncements that carried down the hallway. Tasir is a problem. Tasir is lazy. Was that the real reason for her failures at school?

MLs at the advanced level of oral proficiency, which might last two to three years, typically have a vocabulary of close to six thousand words. Advanced-level MLs like Tasir are able to construct complex statements, state their opinions, and speak at length. However, they are still in the process of learning academic language and still need language support when they experience difficulty with tasks at grade level.

Depending on the age of initial exposure and the amount of exposure to their L2 as well as other individual factors, it can take from four to seven years (or even longer) for an ML to reach grade-level academic language proficiency in their L2.[24] From the interview, we can see that Tasir has clearly mastered social language, but she is struggling with academic language. Her reading and writing in English are well below grade level (we will see samples of her work in those areas in part III), but that isn't her only difficulty. She has trouble understanding her teachers' explanations and discussions during instruction, which perplexes her teachers who don't know about the process of developing L2 proficiency.

The stories in the introduction and thus far have illustrated that a number of factors may explain individual differences among MLs in academic achievement. These factors include MLs' level of L2 proficiency and oral proficiency, in particular; their literacy in the first and second language; and the extent of their prior knowledge of the disciplinary subject.[25] We look at these factors more closely in the next section.

Second Language Proficiency Level

Learning a second language is a process that progresses from knowing and understanding nothing about the language to becoming fully proficient. The intervals, or stages, can be categorized in various ways. Traditional foreign or second language instruction often divides levels of proficiency into five or more segments until full proficiency is achieved. In part III, we will show how teaching language and literacy to MLs requires fine-tuning instruction in listening, speaking, reading, and writing to individuals' levels of L2 proficiency, and we will describe the English language proficiency standards and assessments of the US-based WIDA organization and its six stages of L2 proficiency (see part III, chapter 7 for specifics). We use this organizations framework because it is widely used in the United States, but the two protocols of the Teaching All Subjects, Language, and Literacy (TASLL) Framework can naturally be implemented with your region's or nation's equivalent standards and assessment.[26]

For narrowing the classroom communication gap, however, we believe that placing students in ranges of oral proficiency comprising three basic categories—beginning, intermediate, and advanced—is most useful.[27] With these three ranges, there are clear distinctions for what each student can understand and do in their L2. Similarly, for teachers, there are very clear, memorable distinctions for what they can do to enable successful communication for, between, and of these students. Table 1.1 describes common characteristics of MLs at each of the three categories of oral proficiency, placing Gero and Edith in the beginning, Edgar in the intermediate, and Tasir in the advanced category. This categorization of levels is an important basic tool for teachers to add classroom communication supports based on what ML students can comprehend and express at each of the three general levels and will be referred to again throughout

TABLE 1.1

Student Cases' L2 Oral Proficiency Categories (for Determining Amount and Types of Communication Support)

Beginning Gero and Edith	Intermediate Edgar	Advanced Tasir
• Points to items • Follows simple commands • Listens primarily—receptive skill development • One- to two-word responses • Memorizes simple common phrases, often as chunks	• Uses novel phrases and simple sentences • Describes items in simple terms • Frequent grammatical errors in word form (he go) • Frequent sentence structure errors (Why you don't like it?) • Pronunciation errors (in spontaneous speech and read-aloud) • Vocabulary gaps and circumlocution (describing something because its term is unknown)	• Fluent social conversation • Developing academic language use • Extended dialogue and discourse with some grammatical and rhetorical errors

part II in more detail. At this point, we provide brief descriptions of what our MLEs can understand and utter in spoken English for purposes of providing supports appropriate for their proficiency.

Prior Knowledge of Subject Matter and First Language Literacy

Gero's, Edith's, Edgar's, and Tasir's teachers face similar, yet unique, challenges. They all strive to help their MLs succeed, but this can only occur if the content is made accessible. Because curriculum, instruction, and assessment are largely afforded through language, MLs' developing second language proficiency influences their developing knowledge and skills.

MLs may already know the disciplinary content or focus in their first language, which would mean that they are learning their second language's phrasing and terms of a topic they already understand. Let's look at Edgar to see how this works. Fortunately, Edgar had learned about plate tectonics in Puerto Rico, so when his earth and space science class at Highpoint High studied continental drift and the Earth's lithosphere and asthenosphere, he could catch on to the content more readily since the concepts were not new to him. This freed up information-processing capacity for him to concentrate on the English terms used. Considering what Jim Cummins refers to as cognitive demand of instruction for MLs, we can see that the cognitive demand placed on Edgar in learning a topic he already knows is low, but he still has much to learn about the language used to teach and assess the topic. If the curriculum in Puerto Rico had not included plate tectonics prior to his arrival in Chicago, he would most likely have felt overwhelmed, trying to understand the content and its related English explanations at the same time. In this case, he would have a high cognitive demand because he would have twice the content to learn—the science concept and its related language in English.

First language literacy has a positive effect on second language literacy. Years of research have shown this to be true. MLs who are literate in their L1 have an advantage over peers with few or no literacy skills in their L1.[28] So Edith, who missed a lot of school while her family moved from town to town in Mexico, has gaps in disciplinary subject knowledge as well as literacy in her native language.[29] This will present additional challenges because in fourth grade Edith is expected to learn disciplinary subjects through reading and writing about them. Students who read widely and frequently in any language, not just their second language, are higher achievers than students who read rarely and narrowly.[30] Fortunately, important aspects of language and literacy knowledge and skills are transferable, even across languages that differ markedly in the type of letters, spelling conventions, word formation, sentence structure, and direction of print (e.g., Arabic, English, and French).[31] If MLs are competent readers in their L1, they will never need to learn to read again. They may need to learn new symbols, and they will need to learn new language, but much of what they know about reading in their L1 will help them read in their L2.[32] And, of course, there is reading involved in learning disciplinary subjects, so their L1 reading competence can ultimately help them to learn disciplinary subjects in their L2.

The L1s of MLs should be recognized and utilized as a learning support in the educational environment. This could be as simple as providing bilingual dictionaries or glossaries, like the ones provided by the State of New York.[33] Research has shown that when used as a tool to support learning, MLs' L1 has the potential of helping them understand complex concepts, reduce cognitive load, and make connections between existing and new knowledge.[34]

Despite clear individual differences, our four MLEs share several characteristics. They all go through predictable stages in their L2 acquisition, from primarily listening in the classroom to developing advanced fluency in speaking, listening, reading, and writing. Their social language develops more quickly than their academic language, which needs more time and more direct support from classroom teachers.

In addition to common characteristics of MLs that affect the process of developing proficiency in their L2, we have seen that classroom environments can vary in the degree that they narrow the gap between classroom communication and MLs' L2 proficiency levels. Classrooms with accessible input, interaction, and output narrow this communication gap and thus foster both disciplinary subject learning and language growth. When MLs are doubly tasked with learning the disciplinary content and its associated academic language, accessible curriculum, instruction, and assessment depend primarily, or perhaps even exclusively, on successful communication.

Using Multilingual Learners' Full Linguistic Repertoires

The classroom provides ample opportunities for both educators and students to systematically employ students' L1 in a manner that facilitates learning and acknowledges their multilingual backgrounds. When teachers encourage students to use their L1, they affirm home languages and cultures as assets, which benefits MLs and the entire class. One possible way of L1 use in the classroom is offered by translanguaging, which is a concept referring to the simultaneous application of two languages within a single lesson.[35] Translanguaging is used to enable MLs to bring into play their full linguistic repertoire that includes both languages.

For example, in English for speakers of other languages (ESOL)/ELD settings where English is the primary means of communication, teachers may create a multicultural environment through bilingual signs and classroom materials. Additionally, during group activities, teachers could also encourage students to discuss and brainstorm in their L1 before sharing in English, allowing them to organize their thoughts and access their content knowledge. In bilingual or dual language classrooms, translanguaging may involve alternating the language of input and output within the same lesson. This means that information was absorbed in one language (input) and then utilized in another language (output) once fully understood. However, it's essential for instructors of both language and other subjects to remember that proficiency in L1 can vary significantly. Some students learning English may not have literacy skills in their L1 or may possess limited academic vocabulary in their mother tongue. In their literature review on translanguaging, Eman Barri and Florin Mihai have concluded that extant peer-reviewed research is not yet sufficient to determine whether translanguaging is a more effective instructional method than other methods for MLs who are learning a new language or who are maintaining their first language.[36]

According to Ofelia Garcia, a leading advocate for translanguaging pedagogy, translanguaging is "an approach to bilingualism that is centered not on languages, as has been the case, but on the practices of bilinguals that are readily observable."[37] Garcia and her coauthors define two dimensions of translanguaging: (1) teacher observations of students' use of languages, and (2) teacher adaptation of pedagogy to take advantage of students' language practices. They identify three principles that guide translanguaging pedagogy. First, bilinguals use their language knowledge and skills as learning resources. Second, bilinguals learn language in interaction. Third, translanguaging is part of bilinguals' sense-making processes.[38]

To get started using translanguaging in regular and dual language classrooms, here are seven suggestions we compiled from the works of Ofelia Garcia and other scholars:

1. Encourage bilingualism for all students and guide students to effectively use multiple languages in the classroom, as appropriate for the task.
2. Display multilingual labels, word walls, and visuals.
3. Pair students purposely, such as the same first language background but different proficiency levels, as appropriate for the task.
4. Use books, videos, and instructional materials in the various languages of the children.
5. Allow students to demonstrate their knowledge and skills in whichever language they are most able to, as appropriate for the task.
6. Engage with families and communities and communicate in linguistically and culturally relevant ways.
7. Select and provide technologies that use multiple languages.

Because of some past misuses of first and second/foreign languages in the classroom, we would like to point out what we believe translanguaging for MLs is **NOT**:

- Translanguaging is *not* simply translation or concurrent interpretation; it is moving fluidly from the L1 to the L2 or vice versa in a *purposeful* way that uses the ML's full repertoire of linguistic skills in multiple languages. If interpretation of a statement that is incomprehensible to a student is needed in the moment or if translated materials are prepared or selected as supplemental L1 support, translation can be helpful. For most contexts, however, repeating everything that the teacher says in MLs' first language is not a sound instructional approach because the back-and-forth pattern of language use leads students to tune in and out depending on their comprehension of the language being used. We believe that if translation is the *only* means used in the classroom to make instruction comprehensible for MLs, then their teachers haven't done enough to create supportive classroom communication for their multilingual learners.

- Translanguaging is *not* teaching a new language (L2) in the first language of MLs. Previously used world languages instruction that, for example, taught Spanish class mainly in English led to studying a language without being able to speak it outside of classroom exercises. Using the L1 to explain a grammar point can be very helpful, but if the teacher isn't mindful of how much L1 versus L2 is being used to communicate in the classroom, students won't have an opportunity to practice their new language through supportive classroom communication so they can use it inside and outside of the classroom.
- Translanguaging is *not* teachers using both languages indiscriminately in dual language instruction by engaging in code mixing, for example, "Put your lapizes on the mesa" when giving directions to the class. Although students should be encouraged to play with language, to use their two languages in creative writing and expression, and to draw upon either language when words fail them (a very natural part of becoming bilingual), they should understand *how*, *when*, and *why* using more formal language in the L1 or L2 is expected.
- Translanguaging is *not* refusing to steer students to use a particular language in group interactions because it might discourage students from drawing on their full linguistic repertoire. Depending on the instructional context, there are times when the minority or partner language needs to be protected from being overtaken by the majority language (whose prestige and power even students in primary grades can sense), such as in a two-way dual language (English/Spanish) science class during the time that Spanish is the medium of instruction. Students can still be encouraged to draw upon their knowledge of English and Spanish when groups are given directions to describe a scientific process in Spanish, for example. We have seen many Spanish-medium classes in which all students interact entirely in English during these sorts of group activities, putting MLEs at a disadvantage in learning the topic and depriving learners of both language groups of the opportunity to develop scientific discourse ability in Spanish.

In this book's chapters about our four MLEs that show examples of lessons that have been enhanced with the two TASLL Framework protocols, you will read many examples of the use of translanguaging, such as Gero's pairing with a more English-proficient student from Haiti for group work, myriad bilingual materials in Edith's dual language classroom, Tasir's teacher's suggestion that she investigate Arabic signal words in persuasive texts, and Edgar's use of Spanish and English in his song lyrics composition.

ANALYZING THE GAP BETWEEN MULTILINGUAL LEARNERS' L2 PROFICIENCY AND GRADE-LEVEL LANGUAGE DEMANDS OF INSTRUCTION

The stories of Gero, Edith, Edgar, and Tasir illustrate the challenges in making curriculum, instruction, and assessment accessible for MLs. From their examples, we can see how grade level affects verbal and nonverbal classroom communication. But what happens when the verbal communication in whole-class instruction is too far above an ML's proficiency level and the topic or concept is new as well? This is the situation facing many secondary teachers, such as those who teach Edgar. For example, if Edgar is expected in social studies class to listen to, read about, and discuss complex aspects of the relationships among science, technology, and society, learning this new content through language that is appropriate for tenth-grade non-MLEs will likely cause him to struggle to comprehend every detail and nuance presented. However, Gero, who may not know the grade-level concepts of voting and majority rule, will more easily grasp them if his kindergarten class learns about them through voting for a class treat. So the gap between grade-level classroom communication and the ML's proficiency level is the space in which the teacher adapts curriculum, instruction, and assessment.

To get a clearer understanding of this space for adaptation, let's look at a visual representation of the approximate gap between the L2 oral proficiency of each of our four MLs and the language demands, or verbal classroom communication, of each ML's grade, presented in figure 1.4. Gero, a beginning ML in kindergarten, has a smaller gap between his English proficiency and the language demands in his class than Edith, who is also a beginning ML but is in the fourth grade. Tasir, an advanced ML in the seventh grade, has a smaller gap than the three other MLs. If Tasir had come to the United States as a toddler, attended a good-quality preschool, and consequently entered kindergarten with advanced oral proficiency, her gap could be very small, almost negligible. Enrolled in the uppermost grade of our four MLs, Edgar has a large spread between his intermediate L2 oral proficiency and the language demands of tenth grade. This classroom communication gap diagram depicts students who are literate (to varying degrees) in their native language. If they lacked basic literacy skills (or in Gero's case, preliteracy skills) in their native language, then the shaded "gap" bar would begin below the beginning line, creating an even greater classroom communication gap.

FIGURE 1.4
Classroom Communication Gaps for Our Four Multilingual Learners of English

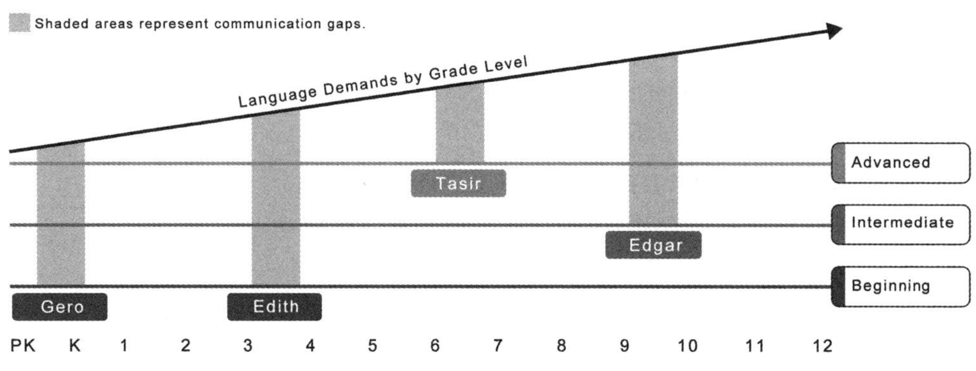

The classroom communication gap is real. Its size differs by grade level, L2 proficiency, and other individual factors, but we can't ignore small gaps because they seem inconsequential, nor should we throw up our hands at large gaps that seem too big to take on in regular classes. We owe every student the best we can give. We must do all we can to narrow every classroom communication gap.

To support teachers in narrowing the classroom communication gap, we have developed a framework offering step-by-step guidance in adapting classroom communication as well as language and literacy instruction for MLs. In this chapter, we briefly describe the key aspects of our framework. We will walk through each step in detail for supporting classroom communication in chapter 2 and developing language and literacy in chapter 7.

THE TEACHING ALL SUBJECTS, LANGUAGE, AND LITERACY (TASLL) FRAMEWORK FOR MULTILINGUAL LEARNERS

The TASLL Framework is designed primarily for MLs in contexts where they are placed in preK–12 classes composed of a substantial percentage of learners who were raised speaking the dominant language of instruction (by this we mean the majority language spoken in the country or region). In the United States, this typically would be in what we term "regular classrooms," meaning that instruction is in English and addresses grade-level standards, as well as what are called "two-way dual language classrooms," which also address grade-level standards but enroll students whose home language is the majority language of the country or region as well as MLs who haven't developed proficiency in that language yet.

The TASLL Framework is also appropriate for classes designed exclusively for MLs, such as content and language integrated learning (CLIL), and bilingual education programs, for instance one-way dual language immersion classes, or ELD and English as a Foreign language programs. However, the four case study students illustrate the framework's application for MLEs enrolled in regular classrooms and two-way dual language instruction classes for the majority or all of their time at school.[39]

Theoretical Foundations

The theoretical foundations of the TASLL Framework encompass research and theory from the fields of communication, second language acquisition, and bilingual education, drawing primarily from sociocultural, interactionist, and translanguaging perspectives. Please see appendix B for the framework's theoretical rationale in narrative and diagram forms as well as a summary diagram of the TASLL Framework's two protocols.

Four Tenets of Educating Multilingual Learners

From these broadly inclusive theoretical underpinnings, which we believe complement rather than conflict with one another, the TASLL Framework is centered on four tenets for educating MLs and encompasses two protocols that specify instructional steps that put the tenets into practice in the classroom.

Tenet 1: Develop a multilingual mindset—Include learners' home and community languages and cultures, as well as L1 literacy skills in curriculum, instruction, and assessment, and encourage MLs to draw upon both for learning.

Tenet 2: Consider the whole child—View the learner from an ecological perspective that includes the following factors that affect ML success when addressing learners' academic performance:[40]

- personal characteristics, such as age, gender, prior schooling, persistence, and attitude about/feeling of connection to school
- family and community facets, such as family economic status and whether teachers are from students' communities
- social elements, such as funding of schools/class sizes, rural versus town setting, and availability of dual language education

Tenet 3: Foster a school-wide collaboration—Form a system of support among educators in the classroom and throughout the school that complements each other's expertise and roles in enabling learners' success.

Tenet 4: Base instructional decisions on language-specific data—Collect and analyze each learner's language assessment data and samples of their language used during instruction to optimize classroom communication and to individualize their language and literacy development.

Overview of the Two Protocols of the TASLL Framework

The TASLL Framework for Multilingual Learners offers a principled, research-based process for ensuring accessibility to instruction and promoting engagement in learning. It is meant to be compatible with all types of instruction and all learning contexts that include MLs. What separates the TASLL Framework from other approaches to teaching MLs is its flexibility and adaptability of use. Designed to complement grade-level standards-based lessons and activities, the TASLL Framework serves as an overlay for addressing the needs and harnessing the assets of MLs. At the heart of the framework are two instructional protocols, shown in figure 1.5 (and summarized immediately after in a brief narrative overview), each of which will be described and depicted in detail in chapters 2 and 7.

Because all classroom instruction requires communication and MLs need **added support** to access and engage with what is being communicated, we developed the Supportive Classroom Communication (SCC) protocol. For any type of lessons and activities, the SCC protocol is the first step in ensuring that MLs can participate and learn to the fullest extent that their current proficiency in the language of instruction permits and then some. It also fosters the development of L2 academic language. You could say, metaphorically, that the SCC protocol's purpose is to brighten classroom

FIGURE 1.5
The TASLL Framework

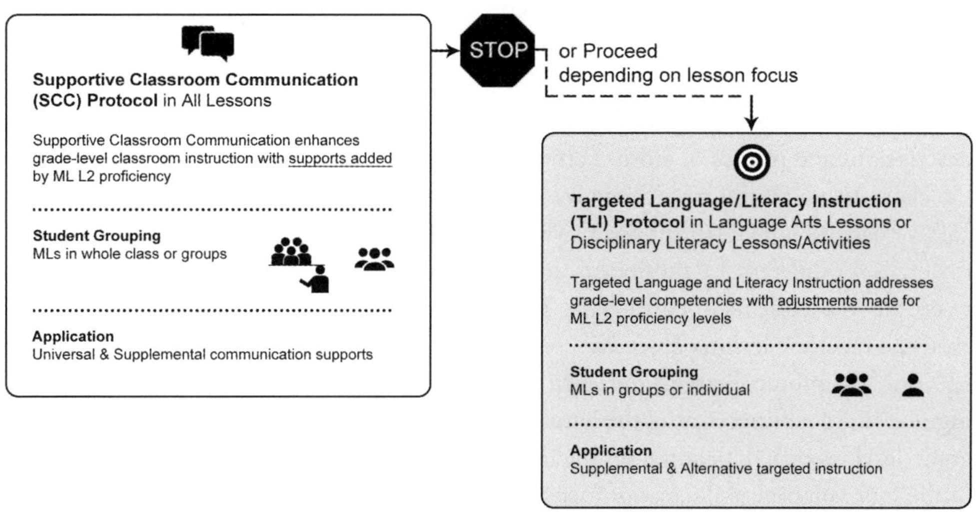

communication, to let more light into classrooms that can seem like a dim space to MLs. The key to the SCC protocol is adding verbal (language) and nonverbal (images, objects, movement) support to existing lessons and activities, according to MLs' proficiency in the language of instruction. This is typically done during whole-class or small-group instruction and involves adding supports that are either universal, meaning good for all students, non-MLs included, or supplemental, which are meant to complement and clarify the original lesson or activity for MLs only, according to their proficiency in the language of instruction. There are three steps to implementing the SCC protocol, which will be discussed in chapter 2.

For lessons and activities that focus on disciplinary subjects, the SCC protocol's added verbal and nonverbal supports alone may suffice for making classroom communication of the lesson topic accessible to MLs. However, if parts of or the entire lesson or activity focuses on language/literacy, then the second protocol, the Targeted Language/Literacy Instruction (TLI) protocol, also comes into play. This protocol is where the **differentiation** for each individual ML occurs, squarely where language and literacy are learned or learned about. It is where instruction meets individual MLs where they are.

To know whether the TLI protocol should also be followed, you can check if the lesson or activity includes an objective focusing on developing listening, speaking, reading, and/or writing skills. For example, if a hands-on, minds-on science lesson on erosion included a follow-up writing activity to build students' skills in summarizing a geological process using scientific discourse, both the SCC protocol and the TLI protocol would be appropriate. The SCC protocol would be applied for the entire lesson to provide supportive communication, and the TLI protocol would be applied solely to the writing activity part of the lesson, as would be for a lesson whose objectives are entirely focused on developing language and/or literacy skills, such as a lesson requiring students to find and explain evidence from a grade-level text to support their positions on a current event. In contrast, the TLI protocol would not be needed for a hands-on, minds-on science lesson that did not specify a language objective and that followed up the hands-on erosion experience by assigning groups of students to search online for descriptions and photos of erosion around the world and sharing what they found with the class. Although this would involve reading the online information, the SCC protocol's verbal and nonverbal supports, which would include additional online and print materials for different L2 proficiency levels (including L1 support), would be adequate to enable ML students to participate. Therefore, no reading instruction would be necessary to meet the lesson's objective.

The TLI protocol targets the spirit of the listening, speaking, reading, or writing objectives, not necessarily the letter of the objectives (i.e., actual objectives for the grade-level lesson), depending on the distance between the ML's proficiency in any of the four language skill areas of focus and their grade-level targets. Unlike the more generally applied added verbal supports in the SCC protocol, such as leveled questioning or sentence frames, the targeted language and literacy instruction of the TLI protocol goes deeper into language and literacy instruction and provides precise differentiation by L2 proficiency levels. Because the TLI protocol meets MLs where they are in listening, speaking, reading, and writing in their new language, it is used with either small groups or pairs of MLs at the same proficiency level in the skill of focus or with individuals if more explanation, practice, translanguaging, or different texts and tasks are required for the student (or if there is only one ML at a particular skill level). Depending on the distance between the lesson's language/literacy focus and the ML's proficiency level in the skill of focus, the language and literacy instruction may be closely related to the lesson for the entire class, using supplemental materials to address specific areas that the ML needs to develop. In cases where the distance is large, such as a newcomer, beginning ML in a tenth-grade writing class, the TLI protocol's differentiated instruction would be an alternative to the lesson for the whole class. Chapter 7 will explain the three steps of the TLI protocol and how they are built upon the similar three steps of the SCC protocol.

MLs are doing double the work required of non-ML students, learning the subject *and* the language at the same time. As a result, MLs need extra communication support and targeted language and literacy instruction to acquire the academic language proficiency necessary to reach grade-level benchmarks in their new language. Part III will explain significant features of the second language acquisition process that affect ML progress, showing how there is an internal order and sequence to developing L2 proficiency, which can be accelerated, but not overridden, by accessible communication and targeted language and literacy instruction. The process of becoming bilingual, bicultural, and biliterate requires students' time and effort, but knowledgeable teachers play a significant role in their success.

ESSENTIAL POINTS

1. Communication, when used intentionally and purposefully, can serve as a unifying force because it influences every aspect of classroom interactions. When teachers recognize the importance of creating shared meaning, they are more likely to prioritize the development of this skill at the highest level.
2. Effective communication creates a continuous cycle of successful language acquisition and content learning. As MLs gain new language skills through content instruction, they apply this knowledge to acquire additional content, significantly improving their language development. The same cycle occurs with language and literacy instruction, where MLs advance their proficiency in the L2 when they use their growing language skills to engage with academic content.
3. MLs may already understand certain concepts and possess literacy skills in their native language, which can support their ability to transfer this knowledge to the L2, thereby reducing cognitive load. Developing learners' knowledge and language proficiency in their native language enables them to focus on linking new vocabulary to existing concepts rather than learning both simultaneously. However, literacy acquisition can be more challenging for those with little to no literacy in their native language because they must develop reading and writing skills in a language they speak and another they are unfamiliar with.
4. The Teaching All Subjects, Language, and Literacy (TASLL) Framework demonstrates how MLs can fully engage in standards-based instruction and activities by being provided with support and instructional adjustments geared toward their current level of proficiency. The framework consists of the Supportive Classroom Communication (SCC) protocol and the Targeted Language/Literacy Instruction (TLI) protocol.

STOP AND REFLECT QUESTIONS

1. In this chapter, you read that the conversation between Ms. Oliver and Edith was a bit strenuous, but how do you think Edith felt about the interaction? How did she feel about Ms. Oliver? In a classroom context, why should Edith's feelings matter?
2. Do you agree with the notion that the basic function of language is to create shared meaning? How is shared meaning created in the classroom?

GO AND PRACTICE ACTIVITIES

1. In this chapter, you read about MLs at the beginning level who developed a five hundred– to a thousand-word receptive vocabulary yet could not use all the words. Why was that so? What evidence can you provide to support your answer? Plan to observe and interview a beginning ML in your class or school and write down what you noticed about what they understood and what they could express and whether there were any obvious differences.
2. Reach out to your school's (or district's) ELD or bilingual education specialist and ask them what approach the district takes with ML students who had interrupted schooling in their home countries prior to entering school in the United States. How does your district support newcomer students enrolled in upper elementary and higher grades who are not literate in their home language?

PART II

Supporting Disciplinary Learning

Supportive Classroom Communication for Multilingual Learners

As discussed in chapter 1, the Teaching All Subjects, Language, and Literacy (TASLL) Framework for Multilingual Learners views the education of multilingual learners (MLs) from a multifaceted standpoint, considering the personal qualities and fullness of experience of MLs in relationship to the interconnecting systems (such as the home, school, and community) in which MLs function.

Within this multifaceted outlook on educating MLs, we prioritize communication in the classroom because it is one of the elements that educators influence the most. For this reason, applying the TASLL Framework begins with the Supportive Classroom Communication (SCC) protocol. Because communication underlies all learning, the SCC protocol is the first stage in ensuring that any type of instruction is accessible to MLs, and it is often the only phase for instruction focusing exclusively on learning disciplinary subjects.

In this chapter, we describe the SCC protocol for use in disciplinary subject instruction, and in chapter 7, we describe the SCCP's use as the first of two phases in supporting accessible classroom communication and meeting MLs where they are during language and literacy development activities. In the following sections of this chapter, we explain the need for the SCC protocol and walk you through each step of its use.

WHY DO TEACHERS NEED PROTOCOLS TO REACH THEIR MULTILINGUAL LEARNERS?

Now that you've read about our four multilingual learners of English (MLEs) and the classroom communication gaps they and their teachers face, it's time to look at how you can approach the classroom communication gap in your classroom. After working with teachers of all disciplinary subjects and grade levels, we found that they weren't looking for a specific instructional format for the MLs in their regular classes. Many had tried that approach but ran into two equally detrimental problems. Teachers told us that if they had only one or maybe a handful of MLs in their classrooms, it wasn't feasible or reasonable to revise all their lessons specifically for them. There wasn't time to develop double plans for every lesson objective, and even if there were, how could they put the plan for MLs into practice when they had to teach a whole class composed primarily of students who grew up speaking the language of instruction? If they taught everyone a lesson designed especially for their MLs, then the students that grew up speaking the language of instruction would not be adequately challenged. Conversely, if they taught a lesson designed for non-MLs to everyone, then the curriculum, instruction, and assessment would not be accessible to their MLs.

To avoid these competing lesson approaches, many classroom teachers had turned to lists of teaching strategies or to universal design for learning (UDL)—using multiple ways to present and test information—to reach their MLs. That seemed like a feasible and reasonable way, especially because they were already using UDL to help their students with special needs. The problem with extending those strategies to MLs, we came to learn, was that for many teachers all these accommodations became one big blur. For them, this set of various practices was "just good teaching" for all students, and they lost sight of the unique needs of MLs. And who could blame them? At face value, teaching strategies for any students who need extra help do look strikingly similar. But something deeper is going on for MLs. The process of acquiring the language of instruction, of moving through levels of second language (L2) proficiency, leaves a gap between MLs' current understanding and use of their new language and what goes on in their L2-speaking (and listening, reading, and writing) classroom. That gap—the classroom communication gap—is what is unique about MLs, and it is the teacher's workspace for making instruction accessible for MLs. No one lesson can close the language gap for MLs; that occurs over time. But if each lesson makes curriculum, instruction, and assessment accessible for MLs, they will learn more content and develop more L2 proficiency as a result. And, as we discussed earlier, these are two mutually supportive objectives that propel MLs' eventual achievement of grade-level expectations in their new language.

So when you think about making classroom communication accessible for your MLs, picture the gap as presented in figure 1.4 (see page 42). This is the space that you will need to narrow in your disciplinary subject lessons. How do you go about doing this? To foster this process, we developed a protocol that walks teachers step by step through specific decision points for determining the appropriate support for MLs in any lesson and at any level of proficiency. Rather than asking teachers to design special lessons for the MLs in their classes, the protocol focuses on how teachers can add supports to their state standards-based lessons to make the curriculum, instruction, and assessment accessible to their MLs as well.

To narrow the gap for each ML participating in a lesson designed primarily for non-MLs, you need the right tools, materials, and people. The SCC protocol helps you develop a work habit for every lesson—to size up the classroom communication gap and identify the resources needed to narrow it. And everything you do in putting this protocol into practice serves the research-informed goal of successful communication *for*, *between*, and *of* MLs in classes composed primarily of non-MLs. Through using this simple protocol day by day, you'll help raise your MLs' second language proficiency in subtle, yet essential, ways.

NARROWING THE CLASSROOM COMMUNICATION GAP: THE SUPPORTIVE CLASSROOM COMMUNICATION PROTOCOL

This foundational protocol of the TASLL Framework, which applies to lessons and activities of all types, aims to narrow the classroom communication gap. Figure 2.1 summarizes the three-step process of the SCC protocol. Definitions of terms and acronyms in the SCC protocol summary diagram, such as SLIDE/TREAD, will be provided in the narrative section that follows (on page p56).

The protocol begins with the classroom teacher developing an understanding of the L2 proficiency of MLs enrolled in their class. Different regions and countries use various L2 proficiency tests that help teachers understand their ML students' L2

FIGURE 2.1

Supportive Classroom Communication Protocol

Referring to each ML's WIDA ACCESS* Individual Report Levels (L, S, R, & W Proficiency Level Descriptors), apply the following:

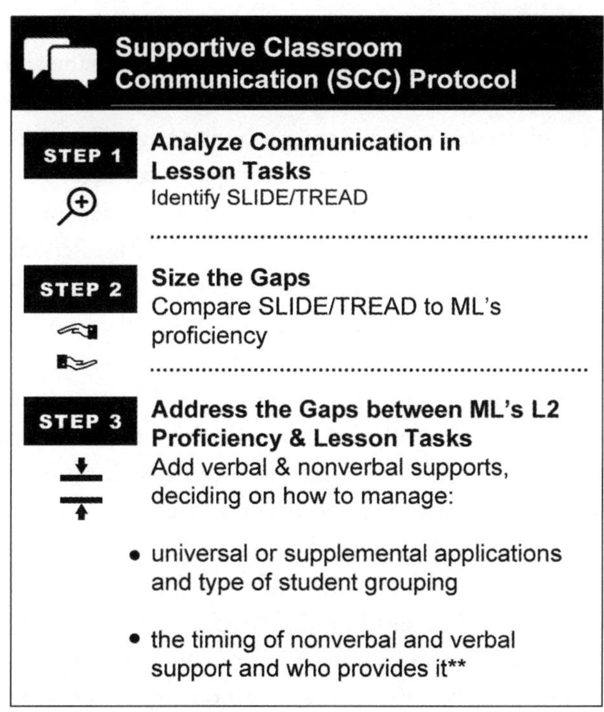

*Or other L2 assessment

**Possible variation of best fit of providers

proficiency, including the US-developed WIDA English proficiency tests that we focus on in this book. This familiarization with ML students' L2 proficiency starts with:

1. reviewing students' WIDA individual report (table 2.1), or whichever measure of L2 proficiency your school uses, which is followed by
2. ongoing informal observation of each ML's current ability to converse and write in their L2 (and also in their first language [L1], depending on the language and school/district resources).

Within a reasonably short time from when an ML student is enrolled in class, teachers using the SCC protocol can get a good sense of what their ML students can do, say, and understand with and without support.

As table 2.1 shows, this sample student is at high beginning levels in English speaking, reading, and writing (level 2 of six possible levels) and at an intermediate level (level 3) in English listening. It is common for students' listening level to be higher than speaking because MLs, as well as non-MLs, tend to comprehend more language than they can express. In general, low beginning MLs' levels of listening and speaking (oral language) tend to be similar to their reading and writing skills, but once they progress in developing more oral proficiency, their literacy levels tend to lag behind. You will see these types of variations in oral language and literacy proficiencies and how to provide support for every language domain (listening, speaking, reading, and writing) laid out in detail in upcoming chapters featuring our four MLE student cases.

Although WIDA testing reports specify four language domains, each of which have six measured proficiency, the SCC protocol synthesizes all this into three different types and degrees of needed support, categorized as beginning, intermediate, and advanced oral proficiency levels (see table 1.1 on page 37 for details). All things being equal, the SCC protocol places emphasis on oral proficiency (listening and speaking) levels, as oral proficiency tends to precede literacy skills and is essential for comprehending classroom communication and actively engaging in it.[1] In chapter 7, you will see how the Targeted Language/Literacy Instruction protocol emphasizes literacy skills in tandem with the SCC protocol's emphasis on oral proficiency.

You will only need to review your ML students' WIDA levels once to gauge the types and degree of support they will need, after which you can continue to informally monitor their language skill use in the classroom because their proficiency will continue to develop during the school year and new proficiency testing results may not be available until or after the end of the school year.

Once you categorize your ML students' oral proficiency levels into beginning, intermediate, or advanced categories of needed support, you will apply the SCC protocol. There are three steps, the first of which is to analyze communication in a lesson plan or activity description. Once the quantity and quality of verbal and nonverbal communication in the lesson are determined, the second step is to assess the gap between MLs' L2 proficiency and classroom communication or language demands of the lesson. Based on the number of MLs in class and the gaps between their L2

TABLE 2.1

Sample WIDA Individual Student Report

Domain	Proficiency Level	Students at this Level Generally can . . .
Listening	3	. . . understand oral language related to specific familiar topics in school and participate in class discussions, for example: • Connect spoken ideas to own experiences • Find, select, order information from oral descriptions • Identify the causes and effects of events or situations discussed orally • Classify pros and cons of issues in discussions
Speaking	2	. . . communicate ideas and details orally in English using several connected sentences and can participate in short conversations and discussions in school, for example: • Share about what, when, or where something happened • Compare objects, people, pictures, events • Describe steps in cycles or processes • Express opinions
Reading	2	. . . understand written language related to common topics in school and participate in class discussions, for example: • Identify main ideas in written information • Identify main actors and events in stories and simple texts with pictures or graphs • Sequence pictures, events, or steps in processes • Distinguish between claim and evidence statements
Writing	2	. . . communicate in writing in English using language related to common topics in school, for example: • Describe ideas or concepts using phrases or short sentences • Label illustrations describing what, when, or where something happened • State steps in processes or procedures • Express opinions about specific topics or situations

proficiency and the lesson's language demands, the third step is to manage different types of supports and resources to improve classroom communication for ML students.

The SCC protocol is typically used for learning that occurs with whole-class or small-group configurations, but it can also be used for individual instruction when needed and feasible, such as when there is a sizeable gap between an ML's proficiency in their new language and the language demands of the lesson. Most often, the types of support are universal, which is appropriate for all students but especially supportive for ML students, and supplemental, which provides additional assistance only for ML students that complements the class's learning materials and activities and enables MLs to engage with and in them. Alternative support, meaning learning that uses different materials and activities than those in the lesson, can be used when needed and feasible, just as with individual instruction. Now's the time to begin taking the first steps to supportive classroom communication for your ML students! The next section walks you through the details of putting the SCC protocol into practice.

STEP 1 Analyze Communication in Lesson Tasks

Before thinking about making curriculum, instruction, or assessment accessible for MLs, it's important to figure out how much of the lesson is conveyed primarily through written and spoken language (verbal communication) versus how much is conveyed primarily through hands-on experiences, manipulatives, pictures, and visual models (nonverbal forms of communication). This applies to communication for, between, and of MLs, or to state it more technically, it applies to the input, interaction, and output elements of curriculum, instruction, and assessment.

Some lessons include lots of nonverbal forms of communication, which helps make instruction (encompassing curriculum, instruction, and assessment, unless noted otherwise) accessible for MLs. Other lessons are exclusively or primarily verbal (language dependent). And of course, there are many lessons somewhere in between. When tasks are primarily verbal, MLs need extra support.

Over the years, when we asked teachers to review lesson and activity descriptions to determine where MLs would need support, we were struck that they were often blind to the language used by teachers and students. If a description indicated that the teacher should explain a concept, such as how the seasons occur, teachers often would miss that the term *explaining* most likely involves speaking. If a lesson plan required students to discuss an issue in small groups, teachers didn't always notice that this requires verbal skills in English that many MLs might not yet possess. To help teachers develop habits of practice that analyze the degree of nonverbal and verbal communication of lessons for any topic, we developed a two-part mnemonic device: SLIDE and TREAD. SLIDE and TREAD are acronyms for verbs conveying common student and teacher actions that point toward aspects of lessons or activities where information is conveyed largely through nonverbal or verbal means, respectively. Table 2.2 lists some of the most common verbs and their synonyms.[2]

TABLE 2.2

SLIDE and TREAD Verbs

Less Language-Intensive (not primarily language-conveyed) lesson aspects tend to be described by verbs like these:	**More Language-Intensive** (primarily language-conveyed) lesson aspects tend to be described by verbs like these:
• **S**how (also watch, pantomime, model, display, project [a picture/graphic]) • **L**ook (also smell, taste, feel, and other nonverbal senses) • **I**nvestigate (also measure, weigh, categorize, classify, connect) • **D**emonstrate (also draw, design, act out) • **E**xperience (also act, move, do, make, create)	• **T**ell (also present information, lecture, narrate, recount, go over, report out, share) • **R**ead (also skim, scan, review) • **E**xplain (also listen) • **A**sk/**A**nswer (also solicit, write, respond, predict) • **D**iscuss (also describe, define, brainstorm)

To review an activity or lesson description for its degree of verbal communication (language demands) and nonverbal communication (context-embedded instruction), you *scan the plan* by underlining verbs or phrases that indicate what the teacher or students are doing. Then you analyze whether those verbs signify a heavy dependence on language, marking each task that requires support for MLs (which will be added in step 3 of the SCC protocol). The point here is not to analyze grammar but rather to use the verb as a key to the type of teacher and student communication—verbal, nonverbal, or both.

Let's take a look at the following second-grade activity description to see how this works. We have underlined the verbs that indicate what the teacher or student does in the lesson (we don't underline the verbs that tell what other people or objects do).

> Tell students that each table group will design a boat using one sheet of paper and a roll of tape. Explain that they will test their boat, so it must fit inside the testing container and must hold as many pennies as possible.
>
> Each group makes its boat and displays it to the class, giving the name of the boat and explaining its design.
>
> Each group puts its boat in the testing container and places pennies into the boat until it begins to sink.
>
> Each group weighs the number of pennies its boat held before sinking.
>
> Each group discusses the strengths and weaknesses of their designs, and students write the information in their science journals.

We can see that this lesson description uses both SLIDE and TREAD verbs. The first verb is *tell*, which is how the teacher will give directions about the activity to the students. As shown in table 2.2, tell is the T in TREAD, so it is a major clue that there is verbal communication (the teacher tells the students what to do) for which an ML may need support. After *tell* is *explain*, the tricky verb that usually involves speaking (in this case, the teacher is speaking, so the students are listening). This word is a red flag for TREAD when considering the challenges of any task for MLs. The next verbs say what the students do, *make* and *display*, and these are SLIDE verbs because they involve hands-on, experiential (nonverbal) actions rather than primarily verbal ones. One underlined phrase, *giving the name*, is another way to say tell or state the name, so it is TREAD. However, the response requires only one or two words, so that is less difficult than a similar term like *give a rationale*, which involves more complex language. Next students *explain* the design of their boats, which, of course, is a TREAD word. After that, the verbs involve students' use of concrete objects, such as *putting* the boat in the container, *placing* pennies in the boat, and *weighing* the pennies, so the tasks they describe are accessible to MLs. Activities at the end of the lesson involve verbal tasks, such as *discuss* and *write*, so we know that we will have to provide support to enable MLs to participate. And you can probably guess that beginning and advanced MLs need different types of support.

So now, let's relabel figure 1.3 (see page 31) with our acronyms, showing that in general we would expect that certain topics' instruction uses less nonverbal communication (SLIDE words) and more verbal communication (TREAD terms) as we progress up the grade levels. Figure 2.2 depicts this sliding scale. To use the terms discussed earlier (and shown in figure 1.3), the language demands increase while the context-embedded instruction decreases. We believe this general principle of increasing language demands/decreasing context applies across all subjects, although the degree of SLIDE to TREAD varies somewhat by the nature of the subject, as we will see in chapters 3 through 6. This has implications for the amount of nonverbal and verbal support needed by MLs at different grade levels and L2 proficiency.

Both verbal and nonverbal communication are important, but MLs need balance between the two and special support for TREAD-heavy activities because they are language dependent.

FIGURE 2.2
Proportion of SLIDE and TREAD Used Across Grades

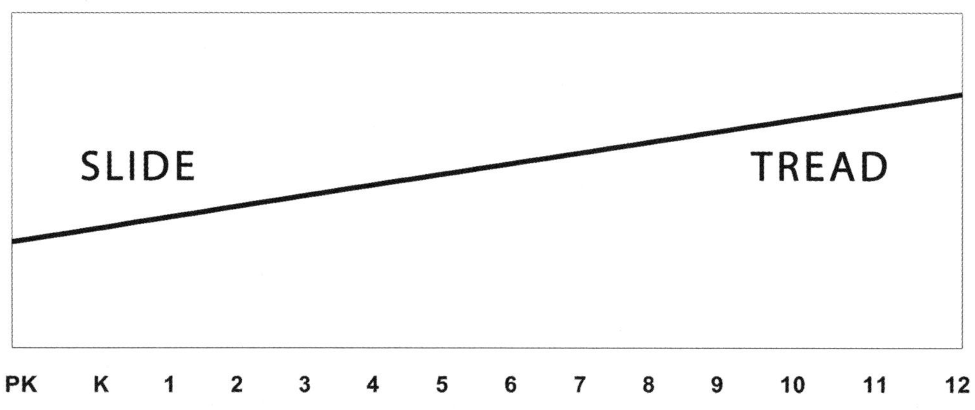

STEP 2

Size the Gaps

Equally important to analyzing communication in your lessons is knowing each ML in your classroom. In addition to the student's L2 proficiency, the ML's cultural background, native language and degree of native-language literacy, and knowledge of the academic subject matter are essential in planning instruction.

After you have analyzed the TREAD and SLIDE words for a task, determine whether your MLs at any of the three categories of classroom communication support can participate fully. For example, if a task requires small groups of students to debate an issue in social studies, is it likely that an intermediate ML could do that successfully without extra support? Of course, you must first know your MLs' general categories of oral proficiency for support (beginning, intermediate, or advanced). After examining what they can understand and do in English (refer again to table 2.1 for an overview), you then compare their skills to what the lesson's tasks demand. For application of the SCC supports, we grouped MLEs at WIDA oral proficiency (listening + speaking ÷ 2) levels of approximately 1–2 as beginning, slightly below or above 3 as intermediate, and 4–6 as advanced.

After sizing the communication gap between the task and each ML's proficiency, you can plan support to meet their individual needs while ensuring that instruction for non-MLs remains appropriately challenging. Now, you decide how to make curriculum, instruction, and assessment accessible. But what exactly does accessible for MLs mean? As we noted previously, classroom communication can take place through language (verbal communication) or other (nonverbal) means.

Nonverbal communication occurs when we perceive or use objects, images, graphics, multisensory activities, gestures, facial expressions, and movement, among other means.[3] Language-based, or verbal, communication, in contrast, involves listening, speaking, reading, writing, or any combination of the four. If we add nonverbal and verbal support to any lesson, we are attempting to support MLs' comprehension and expression of the lesson topic while developing language proficiency in the process. Step 3 of the SCC protocol thus begins with a determination of what nonverbal and verbal support teachers can add to make their lessons more accessible for MLs.

Address the Gaps Between MLs' L2 Proficiency and Lesson Tasks

STEP 3

Adding nonverbal support is the quickest way to begin making your classroom communication supportive for MLs because it benefits all students. However, nonverbal support is especially important for those MLs who are at beginning and intermediate L2 proficiency because it naturally reduces the language load by adding other ways of perceiving information. The second type of communication support you need to consider for your MLs is verbal. Because it is language-specific, verbal support is not only intended to facilitate communication with MLs rather than all students but also needs to address the MLs' L2 proficiency.

ADDING NONVERBAL SUPPORT

We define nonverbal support as either nonverbal additions to primarily verbal instruction, such as pointing to objects, gesturing, and showing pictures, or as primarily nonverbal information that includes verbal elements, such as concept maps with graphics and titles. Nonverbal support is generally helpful for all students. Any subject can incorporate nonverbal support, from manipulatives in mathematics to dramatization in social studies. If you only increased nonverbal support, this would go a long way to improve accessibility for MLs. The following suggestions for nonverbal communication support indicate its variety:

- gestures/acting out/pantomiming
- visuals—photos, pictures, video clips, animations
- pointing to real objects, demonstrating a process, and modeling tasks
- hands-on activities and experiences
- referring to picture dictionaries
- using props and dramatizations

- experiential learning
- simple graphic organizers and infographics[4] using pictures and words
- using mobile devices, tablets, and other visual communication technologies

Although nonverbal support generally benefits all students, we recommend adding it wherever possible for the explicit benefit of MLs to enhance their comprehension and their ability to demonstrate knowledge. Even though the second-grade science activity we analyzed previously includes many forms of nonverbal communication, it could be improved by having the teacher model the directions while stating them. This could be an ideal opportunity to not only make the directions accessible to MLs but also help their L2 development by associating any new words with known objects and actions. Conversely, for the existing lesson elements that are nonverbal in essence (i.e., SLIDE), such as demonstrating a process, it is equally important to state (and write key words and phrases for) what is being done or referred to so ML students connect the meaning to the new language they hear and see.

ADDING VERBAL SUPPORT

Although nonverbal support is vital, it's not enough to fully support MLs' subject matter achievement and L2 development. You'll also need to support verbal communication to enable MLs at different levels of L2 proficiency to comprehend and participate in lessons and show what they have learned to the fullest extent.

The type and amount of this verbal support vary based on the ML's L2 proficiency. That is, if you had a beginning ML, you would incorporate a different type and greater amount of verbal support than for an advanced ML. When the classroom communication gap between any ML's proficiency level and the language demands of the task is vast, using both nonverbal and verbal support throughout all parts of a lesson, activity, or assessment can help narrow the gap and improve comprehension and language growth.

We categorize verbal support into two types: support that (1) moderates the language demands of the lesson (bringing the demands down) and (2) temporarily elevates MLs' spoken and written language above what they could produce without support at their current L2 proficiency level (bringing the learner up). Figure 2.3 incorporates these two types of support, displaying their directionality and how they help to reduce the gap for the ML. Our experience working with teachers has taught us that the consistent implementation of both types of verbal support, geared to the MLs' unique needs and based on their proficiency levels, yields strong results.

It is important to be clear that the verbal supports of moderating language demands and elevating learner language are not targeting lessons to an ML's exact proficiency level for their specific language skill development but, rather, are using resources and instructional practices that require less language comprehension and/or expression to provide access to the content. Gaining access to content gives MLs the opportunity to engage with the lesson.

FIGURE 2.3
Two Directions of Verbal Support

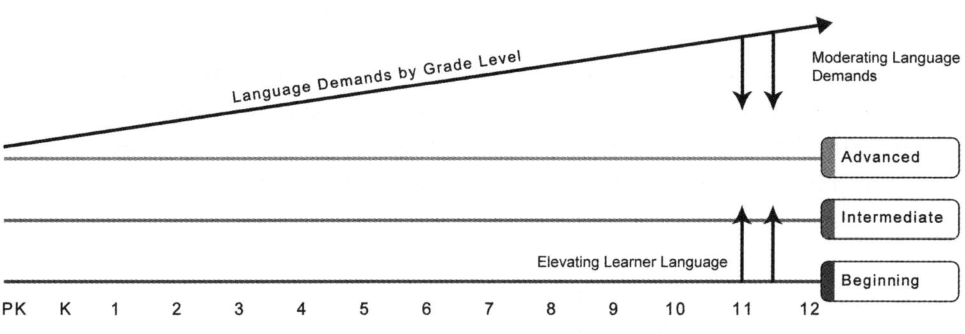

Moderating Language Demands

Moderating language demands means reducing the complexity and amount of language a lesson requires. Although this may seem like watering down the curriculum, it needn't be so. There is a relationship between topical and linguistic complexity. As the topic becomes more complicated, the language needed to understand and talk about it also becomes more complex. That's indisputable—a beginning MLE placed in an eleventh-grade American history class will probably not be able to access the content solely through grade-level reading and discussion activities in English, even when the teacher adds ample nonverbal support, such as diagrams, graphic organizers, and interactive media that show complex relationships.[5] Simplified and elaborated (through additional paraphrasing) texts are necessary when there is such a substantial gap between grade-level language use and the ML's L2 proficiency. In such cases, L1 resources can also be used to help fill in any details that are lost so that the topic is represented at grade-level complexity. Another way to moderate language demands is to use leveled questioning and tasks. These types of verbal support can provide accessible input, output, and interaction through using language that is a step above what the ML has already acquired, which will increase language development over time. We look more closely now at these two go-to tools and techniques to moderate language demands.[6]

Text Simplification and Elaboration. Text simplification and elaboration facilitate comprehension if the language structure is not too far beyond the learner's current proficiency. MLs' comprehension of vocabulary and structures in receptive language (listening and reading) is typically more varied and complex than their competence in productive language (speaking and writing). In other words, MLs are capable of understanding more than they can express accurately (i.e., without developmental grammatical errors). However, if the reading or speech they are attempting to understand uses very complex grammatical structures and lots of unfamiliar vocabulary, comprehension is more difficult.

Let's look at an original text and a simplified/elaborated text in Italian to experience the benefit firsthand. The following is an original social studies text at the fifth-grade level:

> *Si dice che Mastro Giorgio non svelasse mai a nessuno la sua maniera, ma da lui i ceramisti di Gubbio qualche cosa devono aver imparato, se ormai da cinque secoli producono terraglia di squisita fattura; e in particolare (con una tecnica scoperta mezzo secolo fa) quei vasi neri e lucidi chiamati búccheri, che ripetono le forme e i fregi degli antichissimi modelli originali etruschi.*

Did you get all that? Were you able to use your strong reading skills to learn the content? Check yourself with the following translation:

> It is said that Master Giorgio never revealed to anyone his method, but from him the ceramicists of Gubbio must have learned something, if by now for five centuries they produce earthenware of exquisite nature; and in particular (with a technique discovered a half century ago) those black, shiny vases called búccheri, which repeat the forms and friezes of the original Etruscan models from antiquity.

In contrast, let's look at a simplified/elaborated version. The sentences are shorter. There are fewer complex clauses and unusual or embedded phrasings.

> *Il ceramista famoso di Gubbio, Mastro Giorgio, non ha mostrato il suo metodo. Però, i ceramisti di Gubbio hanno imparato il suo modo di fare ceramiche. Dal 1513 i ceramisti di Gubbio fanno ceramiche squisite. Dal 1963 i ceramisti di Gubbio fanno búccheri, vasi neri e lucidi. Questi búccheri sembrano i vasi antichi etruschi.*

Here's what it looks like simplified in English:

> The famous ceramicist from Gubbio, Master Giorgio, did not demonstrate his method. But, the ceramicists of Gubbio learned his manner of making ceramics. Since 1513 the ceramicists of Gubbio have made exquisite ceramics. Since 1963 the ceramicists of Gubbio have made búccheri—black, shiny vases. These búccheri resemble ancient Etruscan vases.

We can see in this example that some information is lost in the simplification, but most of the main topics and points are maintained. The simpler language allows the MLs to access the structure and meaning of the text so that both the content and the language can be comprehended. Many commercial materials have been developed for teaching various subjects to MLs at different L2 proficiency levels, so these can be a convenient means of providing leveled texts.[7] Many commercial materials also provide elaborated texts, which unpack notions that are expressed tersely, offering added description and other details. For example, the original wording above might need this elaboration:

> . . . if by now for five centuries, in other words since 1513, ceramic artists produce what is called earthenware, or terra cotta pottery . . .

This expands embedded sentences and paraphrases unusual words or wording. When simplified or elaborated texts are not available, reducing the amount of text through outlines, graphic organizers, and infographics can help the MLs master the lesson objectives and meet the standards. These resources can be presented together with the original class texts so the MLs are exposed to grade-level text even if it is largely inaccessible and overwhelming without supplemental support.[8]

Leveled Questioning. Another very useful strategy to moderate language demands is leveled questioning. Teachers who are knowledgeable about the comprehension and expression of MLs at different levels of oral proficiency can adapt their questions about the subject matter for each student's language ability. For example, Edith, who can understand and answer simple yes/no, either/or, and one-word-answer questions, could be asked, "Does Master Giorgio make ceramics or glass?" Edgar, who can understand and answer more grammatically complex questions, could be asked, "For how many years have people made ceramics in Gubbio?" Tasir, who can understand and answer grammatically complex and abstract questions, could be asked, "If Master Giorgio didn't share his method with the ceramicists, how do you think they were able to develop specialized techniques?" Using nonverbal support together with leveled questioning will enable comprehension beyond MLs' current level of L2 proficiency. Samples of how to write leveled questions for any subject are depicted in table 2.3.

In addition to phrasing instructional questions at each student's level of L2 oral proficiency, adjusting the language of existing test questions can help make them accessible to MLs. Several language features make academic subject test questions difficult for MLs to comprehend. These include unfamiliar vocabulary, complex grammatical structures, language abstractions, and passive voice.[9] Questions and tasks need to be carefully worded to make assessments more reliable, more valid, and more accessible to MLs. Table 2.4 shows examples of these linguistically complex structures, which are typically acquired at the advanced levels of L2 proficiency, in comparison to those with less complex grammatical structures.

Elevating Learner Language

Conditions that provide MLs with accessible input, interaction, and output in the new language lead to growth in their L2 language proficiency over time. Although temporarily raising MLs' level of L2 proficiency beyond what they can do without support is intended to narrow the communication gap, these conditions can also accelerate language development because MLs are given opportunities to produce spoken and

TABLE 2.3

Leveled Questions for each L2 Proficiency Category

Beginning Proficiency	Simple yes/no questions—Is this a book? Questions that allow pointing, selecting, showing—Show me the book. Either/or questions—Is this a book or a pencil? Simple who, what, and where questions—Who has the book? What is this (point to book)? Where is the book? Questions that require only one-word answers—What is this? Questions that require simple or common two- or three-word phrase responses—Where is the book? On the table. Frequent vocabulary questions/answers (questions that use and elicit high-frequency vocabulary, such as the word *book* rather than *manuscript*) Formation of simple identification questions
Intermediate Proficiency	Restricted-tense questions • Simple present—What do you do every day? • Present progressive—What are you doing? • Simple past—What did you do yesterday? • Past progressive—What were you doing yesterday morning? • Simple future—What will you do tomorrow? • Present perfect—Have you read *Harry Potter*? Basic description (what) questions Basic explanation (how and why) questions Formation of basic questions and negative statements
Advanced Proficiency	Questions using complex tenses and moods • Past perfect—Had Harry seen Voldemort before he began following him? • Future perfect—Will he have finished his homework when he comes to class tomorrow? • Hypothetical, conditional—If Dumbledore asked you to move to Hogwarts, would you do it? Why or why not? Questions using complex passive and negative sentence structure • Passive construction—Could Harry have been hurt by Snape's magic? Why or why not? • Formation of complex negative statements—Should Harry not have gone to Hogwarts? Why or why not? Formation of complex analysis, justification, and evaluation questions and statements

written academic language, and in so doing, they will eventually be able to use academic language without support. Following are two of our go-to verbal support tools.

SENTENCE FRAMES

One strategy to support MLs to speak or write beyond their level of proficiency is to use sentence frames as conversation prompts in pair activities. To help facilitate peer assessment among classmates, Margaret Heritage offers the following conversation prompts for all students:[10]

TABLE 2.4

Complex Versus Simple Phrasing in Assessment Questions

Complex Phrasing of a Test Item	Simple Phrasing of a Test Item
Unfamiliar words *Jim expects that each orange tree will bear fifty oranges.*	Familiar words *Jim expects that each orange tree will have fifty oranges.*
Passive verbs *A game is bought for $12.95. If the sales tax on this item is 7.5 percent, what is the total amount that must be paid for the item, including tax?*	Active verbs *Sue buys a game for $12.95. Sue pays 7.5 percent sales tax on the game. What is the total cost of the game, including tax?*
Conditional clauses *If John is driving at 70 miles per hour, what is his approximate speed in kilometers per hour?*	Separate sentences *John is driving at 70 miles per hour. What is his speed in kilometers per hour?*
Long and complex phrases *Which of the following numerical expressions gives the area of the square below?*	Simple words *Which expression describes the area of the square?*
Relative clauses *The first heart transplant that was a success took place in South Africa.*	Removed or separated *(removed) The first successful heart transplant took place in South Africa.* *(separated) Heart transplants have become successful. The first one was in South Africa.*

Source: Edynn Sato et al., *Accommodations for English Language Learner Students: The Effect of Linguistic Modification of Math Test Item Sets* (NCEE 2009-4079), Institute of Education Sciences, National Center for Education Evaluation and Regional Assistance (Washington, DC: United States Government Printing Office, 2010).

I'd like to suggest . . .

Have you thought about . . .

A strength I see in your work is . . .

You could improve this by . . .

Depending on the ML's oral proficiency, the conversation prompts could be further prescribed by providing word banks, as shown in table 2.5, which gives two scenarios for a beginning ML in a high school graphic arts class.

Deciding whether to provide a word bank in addition to sentence frames for complex sentences depends on the MLs' L2 proficiency level, with more support being necessary for beginning than for intermediate or advanced students. Either way, sentence frames enable MLs to produce higher-level structures than they could utter by constructing them word by word. The dependence on sentence frames lessens as MLs hear and produce similar sentences over time.

As with other verbal supports presented in this chapter, sentence frames can be a step toward language and literacy development. For example, an ML's additions to a sentence frame requiring certain grammatical structures can be a springboard to analyzing student errors and targeting language instruction (which will be discussed in depth

TABLE 2.5

Sentence Frames

	Example 1	**Example 2**
Sentence frame	I'd like to suggest that you ______.	Have you thought about ______?
Verb word bank	lighten, raise, erase, shade	making, elongating, darkening, translating, featuring
Object word bank	the heading, the background, the template, the graph	the fonts, the template, the title, the shape
Completed sentences	"I'd like to suggest that you erase the heading." "I'd like to suggest that you shade the background."	"Have you thought about elongating the shape?" "Have you thought about translating the title?"

regarding the second TASLL protocol, the Targeted Language/Literacy Instruction (TLI) protocol, in chapter 7).

WORD BANKS AND GLOSSARIES

Word banks enable all students, but especially MLs, to use academic vocabulary as it relates to the lesson when they would otherwise have struggled to think of the words needed. Not only do these tools reduce MLs' frustration levels by enabling them to express themselves successfully, but they also save precious instructional time because students don't need to refer to a dictionary or translation device each time they want to use the new vocabulary in the L2. As the lesson topics change and new content is introduced, the teacher changes the word bank. One point to keep in mind is that MLs at beginning and intermediate L2 proficiency may need more word lists or banks than their non-ML peers, who only have to become familiar with content-specific vocabulary. For example, MLs have to acquire everyday nouns, verbs, and adjectives like *pencil, book, question, think, return, large,* and *round* at the same time that they learn the academic vocabulary and phrases.

When using text for instruction, there are different means of drawing the students' attention to important academic words, phrases, or concepts. Although many textbooks assist teachers in this task by providing glossaries in the margins, MLs likely need more than what is provided by the publisher. Instead, you could read through the text prior to assigning it to determine, possibly with the assistance of an English language development (ELD) or bilingual education specialist, which additional explanations are necessary for your MLs to comprehend the text.

In summary, when the communication gap between the ML's proficiency and the language demands of the task is vast, using nonverbal support coupled with both types of verbal support is necessary to help reduce the classroom communication gap's effect on comprehension and language growth. We have presented four "go-to" verbal support tools that you can use with your MLs every day. They can be used in combination or independently based on the size of the classroom communication gap.

There are many other tools for verbal support that can narrow the classroom communication gap, either by moderating the language demands or by temporarily elevating the ML's proficiency. We authored a practical book of tools and techniques that teachers of all grade levels and subject areas can use to reach MLs in their classrooms, entitled *Show, Tell, Build: Twenty Key Instructional Tools and Techniques for Educating English Learners*. We suggest that you begin by trying out one or two of the "go-to" tools and techniques, getting comfortable with how they work for your MLs, and then adding one or two every so often to your repertoire.

MANAGING CLASSROOM COMMUNICATION SUPPORTS

Once you have identified the most advantageous types of nonverbal and verbal support for the ML's level of proficiency, you need to examine the feasibility of their application.

Applications

We divide types of use into three categories: universal, supplemental, and alternative, as shown in figure 1.5 on page 45. For the SCC protocol, the application is primarily universal and supplemental, although alternative application is an option when there is a large classroom communication gap as well as when there are additional resources available to develop and provide the alternative support.

UNIVERSAL

As previously stated, nonverbal support can almost always be used for all students, which is why we term this application of support universal. In cases where the language demands are only slightly above an ML's L2 proficiency, such as with an advanced ML in kindergarten, the verbal support used to reach the ML would be universal as well. MLs with beginning and intermediate proficiency, however, may need verbal support that isn't appropriate for the whole class.

SUPPLEMENTAL

If the classroom communication gap for an ML is small enough to allow participation in instruction and interaction with additional support, the support may be supplemental to instruction, such as a handout with support in the ML's L1 for a complex concept or a fill-in-the-blank form with sentence frames to supplement group discussion.

ALTERNATIVE

When the gap is enormous, as with beginning MLEs who lack prior schooling in their home countries in addition to being admitted to secondary schools in the United States, support that is alternative to what the non-MLEs are engaged in may be necessary. For example, if eleventh graders in a social studies class are rehearsing debates on the US Civil War, a beginning MLE could be given an alternative task of viewing a computer-based, graphic-enhanced timeline of events of the war to develop background knowledge and vocabulary.

Closely related to the decisions about the use of communication support for each ML is determining in which setting these supports would best be implemented. This is the next consideration of step 3 of the SCC protocol.

Grouping

In most disciplinary subjects' lessons, the added communication supports can be implemented during whole-class or small-group instruction, regardless of whether the supports are universal, supplemental, or even alternative. There may be occasional circumstances where the gap between the ML's L2 proficiency level and the language demands of the tasks are so large that they cannot be sufficiently narrowed in these two settings, at which point individual instruction needs to be considered.

Regardless of whether the supports are provided during whole-class, small-group, or individual instruction, the last two considerations of step 3 of the protocol are determining when the support would have the greatest impact and who can best provide support.

Time and Support Provider (When and Who)

Would supplemental or alternative background information in the ML's first language help the most if it were provided in advance of the lesson? Or should the ML be immersed in the activity and receive support on an as-needed basis? Can misconceptions that emerged be addressed after instruction? These are just three circumstances that show the time-sensitive nature of classroom communication support. Sometimes the time of implementation is dictated more by logistics and available providers than by what would be optimal for the ML. This balance between optimal and actual practices is the reality for most MLs and their teachers.

Although you may be able to find time to implement the support strategies through creative lesson configurations, as an elementary or secondary classroom teacher, you may not always be the ideal educator to deliver them. This fact leads us to the final decision point in planning communication support that meets the needs of your MLs: Who is best suited to provide the support, given the type and time of support needed?

The person best suited and available to implement the support is to a large extent dictated by the resources at the school and the ML program model used. Can the classroom teacher work with a group of MLs before, during, or after class? Does the school have a bilingual aide who can help with interpretation or translation? If there is an ELD, second language development, or bilingual teacher, can that person support the ML while the classroom teacher works with the rest of the class? At schools with small numbers of MLs, parent or community volunteers can help provide communication gap support. These volunteers may or may not know the L1 of the ML, which would affect the type of support used. We have seen that, increasingly, instructional technology can offer individualized, targeted support, using both the home language and the

L2, or it may be the basis for pair or small-group interaction with the selected support tool (e.g., texts with glossaries or definitions that are linked to some or all of the words). Increasingly, artificial intelligence (AI) can offer instructional interactions (e.g., chatbots) and resources that support successful communication of a lesson's topic (e.g., Magibook for changing original text to an ML's proficiency level).[11]

In chapters 3 through 6, we apply the SCC protocol to lessons developed for different academic subjects and grade levels. You will get more ideas about how it works from those examples. We suggest you start by flipping through teacher resource books and searching the internet to find lesson descriptions to try out with the SCC protocol. Once you get the hang of it, it will change the way you teach. We hope your MLs will thank you for your extra effort, but even if they don't, we do. Thank you for taking the time to make your curriculum, instruction, and assessment accessible for your MLs. It will make a difference.

ESSENTIAL POINTS

1. Teachers often struggle to apply well-researched theories, approaches, and techniques to support their MLs while also addressing the needs of native speakers in their classrooms. In examining this issue, we identified a gap between understanding and effectively implementing these theories due to a crucial missing component: awareness of classroom communication. The SCC protocol emphasizes communication in the classroom, and by narrowing the gap between subject-area lessons and the L2 proficiency of their MLs, teachers make instruction more accessible.
2. The SCC protocol can be integrated into all lessons to enhance communication, which eventually will become a daily instructional habit. The easily applied three-step process to implement needed support, analyzing communication within lesson tasks, identifying gaps between the task and students' proficiency, and narrowing the gap by incorporating verbal and nonverbal support, enables teachers to assess the level and type of support needed—whether at beginning, intermediate, or advanced oral proficiency—helping teachers determine when and how to apply differentiated instruction effectively.
3. The two acronyms, SLIDE, and TREAD, help teachers assess the level of verbal and nonverbal support needed in a lesson by analyzing the language demands dictated by key verbs. SLIDE verbs represent observable actions that rely on nonverbal cues, whereas TREAD verbs depend on language to be able to carry out tasks, such as *asking* or *explaining*. This simple yet effective tool helps teachers pinpoint where to integrate verbal or nonverbal support in their lesson plans and activities, which will result in improving classroom communication.

4. Teachers can narrow the gap between classroom communication and the ML's proficiency in two directions. To moderate a lesson's language demands, we recommend text simplification or elaboration and leveled questioning. To elevate the learner's language, we suggest teachers provide sentence frames, word banks, and glossaries.

STOP AND REFLECT QUESTIONS

1. As a teacher, do you consider yourself an effective communicator? If so, describe the characteristics of an effective communicator. If not, what skills do you need to learn to communicate with your students more effectively?
2. Analyze the communication gap between the classroom language demands and the level of proficiency of an ML with few or no literacy skills in their native language who has been placed in the eleventh grade. How wide would this student's gap be? What kinds of verbal and nonverbal support would such as ML need? Would this student need to first become literate in their native language prior to doing beginning-level work? How would native language literacy development help MLs in general to acquire literacy skills in their L2?

GO AND PRACTICE ACTIVITIES

1. Over one week, analyze your communication patterns in the classroom. Reflect on the exchanges that you think occur. Then, have a colleague videotape one of your class sessions during an unannounced visit. View the video with your colleague and discuss your verbal interactions with your MLs. How often do you call on them? Do you elaborate on their answers? Do you share your opinion on a given answer to model dialogues?
2. Once you have analyzed the video recording of your session, write down any behaviors that need improvement to enhance communication between you and your MLs.

Teaching Gero About American Symbols

Academic Vocabulary in Social Studies

That smile. Tepid at first but growing expansive as he sat alongside Ms. Levin, Gero's smile reflected his sense of belonging. Before the lesson on community helpers, while his classmates worked in groups, Gero pronounced the new words with Ms. Levin in a heavy Kreyòl (Haitian Creole) accent. "Ahm—boo—láhns, oe—spee—táhl, fie—air—tróek," he half whispered. "Gero, show me the police officer." His hand glided falteringly over the tabletop to the picture book. He paused, looked right at Ms. Levin, and thumped the illustration with his fingertip. "Yes, that's the police officer. She helps keep us safe. You learned so much today, Gero! Let's review our new words quickly before I read the class a story. Class!" Ms. Levin called out, "Let's get ready for story time!"

Ms. Levin gathered her class on the rug in front of her rocking chair. Her left hand gripping the opened, oversized book and her right hand suspended like a magic wand turned inward, she smiled at the students and began to read.

COMMUNICATION IN TEACHING AND LEARNING SOCIAL STUDIES

Academic content areas have their own language, discourse, and communication demands that vary across the preK–12 curriculum. The National Council for the Social Studies defines social studies as "the study of individuals, communities, systems, and their interactions across time and place that prepares students for local, national, and global civic life."[1] As they bridge the content from disciplines including, but not limited to, history, geography, economics, ethnic studies, social sciences, government, and citizenship to the ideas of one another, social studies teachers and their students encounter various forms of academic language in their readings, discussions, and critical-thinking exercises.[2]

Social studies teachers may wonder whether abstract concepts that are part of the disciplines listed above can even be made comprehensible for multilingual learners of

English (MLEs) like Gero, Edith, and Edgar, who are at beginning and intermediate oral proficiency in English. Our response to this question is an emphatic "Yes!" Social studies, much like science and mathematics, lends itself to an inquiry-based lesson format where second language learners can be involved in meaningful interactions with their peers and the content, which assists them with language development. We focus in this chapter on discipline-specific challenges multilingual learners (MLs) face in social studies and show how teachers can provide the necessary communication support to foster their acquisition of both subject matter content and academic language.

Social Studies Texts

Of all content areas, social studies has traditionally required the most reading of informational text. Scholars note that history texts are information dense and may not make connections clear.[3] They describe history texts as having short sections with a wide variety of discourse patterns, including retelling events, describing, explaining, and debating, which makes lessons very language intensive. Let's take a look at some of these assertions and other important challenges of social studies textbooks in more detail by examining a brief selection from *TimeLinks: Third Grade*, a K–12 social studies textbook that builds geographic mastery:[4]

> Jill Staton Bullard started the Inter-Faith Food Shuttle in 1989. She saw a restaurant cashier throwing away leftover food and decided to do something about it. She serves seven counties in North Carolina and feeds more than 5,000 hungry people a day with donations.

The first apparent difficulty an MLE may face in approaching this paragraph is possible *lack of background knowledge or personal experiences*, as we noted in the introduction and will discuss in more detail in this chapter. Contrary to their native-English-speaking peers, concepts such as "throwing away leftover food" might be unfamiliar to MLEs in the United States who come from impoverished countries where hunger is common and having leftover food never occurs. This lack of background knowledge is further reflected in MLEs' lack of familiarity with vocabulary.

Another language-related challenge is *text density with fact, details, and language complexity*. In social studies passages, facts and details are often condensed and textbooks typically contain a high concentration of new vocabulary or sophisticated sentence structure. They contain complex language, an occurrence perfectly illustrated in the last two sentences in the text example. First, the language is complex because it consists of compound sentences with two clauses linked by the coordinating conjunction *and*. Furthermore, the use of the pronoun *she* forces the second language learner to figure out to whom the pronoun refers (the antecedent). Another language complexity factor in social studies texts, although not present in the sample above, is the common use of passive voice constructions. For example, instead of "I observed no significant increase in economic development," which is already loaded with academic language to decipher, textbooks will typically state, "No significant increase in economic development was observed." The passive voice, in both spoken and written language, is difficult for MLEs to comprehend because its formation is learned relatively late in the process of acquiring English.[5] As we showed in the previous chapter, teachers can make texts more accessible to MLEs at beginning and intermediate oral proficiency by simplifying or elaborating text.[6]

Social Studies Vocabulary

Social studies language contains multiple examples of polysemous words—words that have one meaning in social English and another meaning in academic English. For example, the word *party* is defined as a social gathering in social everyday English but is defined as a group of persons with common political interests in the academic language common to social studies. The word *house* has a general meaning, such as "I saw your cousin in front of your *house*," whereas it carries a specific meaning in social studies when used in the sentence "The *House* is in session." Likewise, the word *front*, as in "Meet me in *front* of the cafeteria," has a very different meaning in the sentence "Unlike previous wars, this war was waged on one *front*."

In the introduction, we discussed Jim Cummins's important distinction between the language second language learner's need for social conversation and the language they need for academic purposes.[7] Social language or basic interpersonal communication skills (BICS) are developed through informal settings such as the school playground or cafeteria. However, BICS are not enough. To perform successfully in school, MLs must also acquire the ability to use language for academic purposes. This type of language expertise is called cognitive academic language proficiency (CALP) and is developed in the classroom. In our vocabulary examples, MLs might know what a house is in a social context, but that will not help them in a social studies class where the same word has a completely different meaning.

TEACHING MULTILINGUAL LEARNERS SOCIAL STUDIES

In social studies, not only do concepts become progressively more abstract along the grade level spectrum, but also connections between the disciplines become increasingly multifaceted. This, alongside the complexity of social studies text, makes this subject very challenging for MLEs. In this section, we highlight several points teachers should consider when teaching social studies and share considerations of how to teach social studies in general classrooms with one or more MLEs.

Background Knowledge

One of the main challenges MLEs encounter in social studies classrooms, more so than in other content areas, is the lack of background knowledge needed to understand key concepts. Cultural and societal norms in the home countries of immigrant MLEs can obviously differ considerably from the values and norms represented in our schools. This is not just the case for children whose ethnic and cultural backgrounds are substantially different from what most would describe as, even among the vast diversity encountered in the United States, "typically American." Recent immigrants from Western countries may also have different understandings of concepts like values, personal rights and responsibilities, and the role of community.[8] The good news is that children who received some schooling in their home countries may be able to transfer some of their experiential knowledge to the new language of instruction. Social studies teachers who are aware of the main cultural and societal norms in the students' home countries can gauge what concepts are similar and can be transferred without much adjustment and what concepts may need to be built into the lesson plan for the MLEs. That same cultural awareness needs to be present when working with US-born MLEs. These students may have culture-specific background knowledge that may or may not be valued at school. The more familiarity teachers have with their students' cultures, the easier it is to integrate them into the curriculum.

There are several ways in which social studies teachers can build background knowledge useful in the academic context through students' previous knowledge and new experiences. For instance, when teaching about migration patterns, teachers can ask MLEs to bring items related to their own family stories regarding immigration. Gero could bring objects, photographs, or drawings of where his family came from. Students whose ancestors immigrated to the United States several generations or centuries ago could bring similar artifacts or images found online that show their own family migration history. More than one in four children in the United States has at least one immigrant parent, so it is more than likely that Gero's experience will not be singular.[9] Then, the social studies teacher could create a migration map using the collected artifacts. Gero's previous experiences with migration will help him understand the upcoming lessons about immigration and settlement patterns of American people.

In the case of migration patterns, personal experiences of many MLEs make new learning possible. However, many social studies concepts are not easily bridged. When this is the case, social studies teachers at the elementary level may consider using role play as a means of constructing the background knowledge necessary for understanding new information.[10] Following models provided by teachers (videos, dialogues, illustrations), MLEs can play the roles of colonists, the king of England, and the king's representative to dramatize the concept of taxation without representation. Making difficult concepts more concrete by acting them out can make classroom communication more accessible, stimulate interest in the topic, and engage MLEs in language practice.[11]

Developing Multilingual Learners' Academic Vocabulary Skills

A well-developed vocabulary helps MLEs build background knowledge and comprehend text and lectures in social studies classrooms. Starting with No Child Left Behind

(NCLB) and continuing with the Every Student Succeeds Act (ESSA), there has been a distinct emphasis on academic vocabulary development for MLEs. When designing effective vocabulary instruction for MLEs, one challenge lies in selecting appropriate target words. For instance, concrete nouns such as pencil, desk, or car are relatively easy to acquire. However, terms that represent relationships (e.g., adjacent, supplementary, complementary, collinear, coplanar) pose greater difficulty. Similarly, verbs that need complex argument structures to complete meaning (e.g., the sentence "Jim **told** James the story twice" requires four arguments) are highly demanding for MLEs.[12]

Based on Robert Marzano's research, the Tennessee Vocabulary Project catalogues content area–specific vocabulary in mathematics, science, language arts, and social studies and offers a valuable tool for all teachers.[13] Teachers who have a student like Gero can use this list to establish an instructional plan that includes deliberate vocabulary development activities. It is important to note that this list and others like it contain regular terms that all preK–12 students, not only MLEs, have to master. Therefore, mainstream classroom teachers who have MLEs should consider which of the words are in essence generic, or collective, terms. It is highly likely that native English-speaking students already know many of the specific words that are grouped under collective terms, so they only have to learn to use the new term, whereas multilingual English learners might have to learn individual words first. To illustrate this point, let's look at an example from the kindergarten list: basic needs (food, clothing, shelter). Beginning English proficiency learners like Gero not only have to learn the generic term *food* but also have to learn a handful of words for individual food items such as *apple*, *carrot*, *tomato,* or *beef*, *chicken*, or *fish*.[14] Intermediate MLEs have a lighter load because they already know many of these words and might only need to learn one or two food items, especially if they are not regularly consumed in their home environment.

Fortunately, in kindergarten, these words can be taught through visual cues, such as pictures or drawings. When going up in grade levels, however, the vocabulary gets more abstract, and teachers will need to find additional means to illustrate the concepts. For example, the essential social studies vocabulary that needs to be addressed in kindergarten consists of words such as *neighborhood* and *transportation*. These are generic terms that are typically covered in a picture dictionary. Moving on to first and second grade, the list contains concepts such *rights* and *responsibilities*, *rural* and *urban*, or *distribution* and *economy*. Teaching such terms to MLEs is trickier because they require the teacher to use descriptions while offering examples, even if they display images or bring in objects. Descriptions require verbal comprehension skills that beginning- and intermediate MLEs don't yet possess. Therefore, finding places in the curriculum for explicit vocabulary instruction for MLEs *before* commencing a new unit is of paramount importance. If the school has a push-in, pull-out, or content-based English language development (ELD) program, collaboration between the specialist and the classroom teacher is necessary, especially at the secondary level, to design multiple forms of practice activities to reinforce the acquisition of the vocabulary and the ability to use the new vocabulary appropriately.[15]

To promote vocabulary learning and development with students like Gero, social studies teachers can use word walls. Although this instructional strategy is widely and successfully used in teaching first language literacy in the lower grades, it is much less present in secondary grade levels. We recommend that teachers in those upper grade levels adopt and adapt the practice, including placing visual representations (i.e., drawings, photographs, or downloaded images) next to the words. Content-specific words strategically placed in the classroom allow MLEs to refer to them during verbal exchanges and/or when writing, and the teacher can quickly point to them during whole-class instruction. These words can also be used in scaffolded learning activities, such as sentence strips activities at a learning station or during group work. In addition to asking MLEs to use a dictionary to look up the meaning of new words, teachers can add to the word wall while providing written and oral explanations and examples or after drawing a concept to help convey meaning. The words remain on the wall throughout the unit, and teachers can refer back to them whenever those words occur. Frequent repetition and active learning are key to vocabulary expansion, which in turn leads to content comprehension and acquisition via language development.

Leveraging the students' first language knowledge, especially when it shares cognates with English, is a highly effective approach to expanding vocabulary that is sometimes overlooked by classroom teachers. Cognates are words that have similar origins and meanings across different languages. Because Gero speaks Haitian Kreyòl, a language with French influences, he has access to a vast bank of cognates because more than 40 percent of English words have a French origin. Many English words share cognates with Haitian Kreyòl, and many of these cognates are high-frequency social language words in Gero's first language but low-frequency academic words in English (e.g., the pair of cognates *akselere* in Haitian Kreyòl and *accelerate* in English).[16] Cognates also benefit Spanish-, Italian-, and Portuguese-speaking MLEs, as these languages are Latin based as well. Research indicates that second language (L2) literacy in Spanish and other Latin-based languages offers access to both orthographic and phonological cues for understanding cognate relationships.[17] Even students who are not literate but orally proficient in those languages can still benefit from instruction in cognate awareness. In other words, sound-based connections between cognate pairs can be valuable for all students, regardless of their literacy level.[18] Encouraging children like Gero to leverage their cognate knowledge is a powerful strategy. Making them aware of and encouraging them to harness the superpower they possess thanks to their home language enables MLEs to quickly increase spoken and written comprehension, even if they are not yet able to produce the words without prompting. Free bilingual glossaries and lists of cognates are a good place for teachers unfamiliar with their MLEs' home language to learn where to make such connections.[19]

ESSENTIAL POINTS

1. Social studies presents unique challenges for L2 learners due to dense informational texts, complex vocabulary, and abstract concepts. The academic language used in these texts, including passive voice and words with multiple meanings, can be difficult for MLs to grasp. Text simplifying or elaboration and diverse instructional strategies help MLs understand both the content and academic language.
2. MLs often lack the necessary cultural or contextual background knowledge to fully engage with social studies content. Awareness of students' home cultures is key to bridging gaps in understanding. Teachers can draw on students' prior experiences and cultural backgrounds to build relevant content knowledge through storytelling, role play, and using artifacts to help make the lesson content more accessible and meaningful.
3. Many social studies texts contain polysemous words such as house, party, rights, or economy, which can present reading comprehension challenges for MLs. Teachers should explicitly teach academic vocabulary unfamiliar in everyday contexts. Word walls, vocabulary mini-lessons, and leveraging cognates between the language used in the classroom and MLs' first language (L1) can significantly support vocabulary development and content comprehension.

CLASSROOM APPLICATION

"Class, come back together on the floor." As the groups of students moves to the front of the classroom, Ms. Levin collects the worksheets. "All right," she says as she points to the sample sentence displayed on the chart next to her rocking chair, "repeat after me: 'A heart stands for love.' Yes, that's right. Let's try it again. 'A heart . . . .'"

Speaking in a low voice in the safety of the entire group, Gero does not know that the teacher focused on listening to his speech during the second repetition. Ms. Levin, on the other hand, is encouraged by what she hears Gero say, even though he doesn't accurately pronounce the word *heart*. After all, words with the initial *h* sound are seldom found in the Haitian Kreyòl language.

After a few rounds of asking individual students what symbol she is holding up and asking the entire class what the symbol stands for, Ms. Levin is confident that her students, including Gero, know enough about the topic and language to participate in the upcoming unit on American symbols on Monday. As is her routine, Ms. Levin shakes every single student's hand at the door on the way out. When Gero leaves the classroom, Ms. Levin says, "Sweetie, I'm so proud of how you said our sentences this afternoon. You're doing great!" Is this her imagination, or did Gero just grow a half inch?

AMERICAN SYMBOLS LESSON DESCRIPTION

Ms. Levin had had great success with a unit on American symbols for a few years when she did not have any MLEs in her class. Last year, after receiving a few pointers from the ELD specialist when two MLEs joined the class, she felt that she had successfully supported them to a certain degree. After recently engaging in additional professional development and having observed Gero's promising progress both linguistically and in his demeanor during the preceding weeks, she now decides to look at the same unit lesson plan rather than starting from scratch, despite Gero being at beginning English proficiency. "Maybe a few additional alterations will do the trick," she muses.

OBJECTIVES

- The student will be able to identify and name four symbols of American democracy.
- The student will be able to identify similarities and differences between American symbols and equivalent symbols from other countries.
- The student will be able to draw American symbols and write three facts about them.
- The student will be able to verbally explain why the symbols are important to American democracy.
- The student will ask questions to get information, seek help, or clarify something that is not understood.

INTRODUCTION

Call the students to the rocking chair.[20] Display a collage of American symbols on the whiteboard and ask what they are. Tell the students that this whole week they are going to explore the meaning of these symbols just like they did with the previous symbols (heart, stop sign, etc.) but that they will also learn about the history of these symbols. Point to one of the symbols and state that it represents what the children will learn about today.[21]

LESSON STEPS

1. Conduct a read-aloud on the symbol, working on conceptual understanding of its symbolism and on vocabulary development.
2. Walk the students through each center, explaining what they will do there. Tell them that they will complete a task every fifteen minutes.
    - *Listening Station:* Each student gets a worksheet that contains a word bank on top.[22] Together they view a narrated, teacher-created presentation with facts about the symbol.[23] They copy the words into the appropriate spaces on the worksheet.
    - *Drawing Station:* Each student copies the word of the day's symbol from the board onto a worksheet, which has a large empty space for the illustration on one side and three boxes for writing on the other, and then draws and colors the symbol.[24]

- *Exploration Station:* Looking at a picture of the symbol of the day and an equivalent symbol from another country, the students compare the two as a group. The teacher completes a Venn diagram based on student input.[25]

3. Divide students into equal groups and tell them in which center they start.
4. Debriefing: After all groups have rotated through the centers, the class discusses what they learned.
5. Journaling: Students write three facts about what they learned on their worksheet from the drawing station.

EVALUATION

Evaluation includes discussion, group participation, and daily journaling/writing.

APPLICATION OF THE SUPPORTIVE CLASSROOM COMMUNICATON PROTOCOL TO THE AMERICAN SYMBOLS LESSON

As we have seen, Ms. Levin is very cognizant of Gero's current English oral language skills proficiency based on formal assessment and verbal interactions. To identify where to tweak the original lesson plan to help Gero meet the lesson objectives, Ms. Levin first reminds herself that Gero's WIDA Screener Report shows his oral proficiency at the beginning level (see table 3.1). With that in mind, she can move on to identifying classroom communication.

Analyze Communication in Lesson Tasks

STEP 1

Here we categorize the underlined verbs and verb phrases by nonverbal (SLIDE) and verbal (TREAD) elements (see table 2.2 on page 56 for sample verbs), explain them, and show the associated language skills.

ANALYZE SLIDE

At first glance, we see a number of nonverbal elements, including *display*, *point*, *draw*, and *looking at a picture*. In the introduction to the lesson itself, there are two nonverbal elements, the display of the American symbols collage and Ms. Levin pointing to one of the symbols. These SLIDE elements, however, do not help Gero make the connection to the previous symbols lesson and what he will be learning in this new unit. Ms. Levin needs to support the introduction.

Three nonverbal elements exist in the lesson tasks. They relate to the physical movement of the students (e.g., *walk* the students through the station, *create* groups, *rotate* the groups), which is consistent with kindergarten classrooms where directions are modeled rather than spoken. Although Gero can see that they will be working with images or objects and that he is supposed to move from station to station where different activities take place, he does not comprehend exactly what he is supposed to do there because the directions are given verbally. Only two SLIDE tasks can be described as instructionally related: drawing and coloring the symbol of the day (Drawing

Station) and looking at pictures of two symbols in the Exploration Station. Yet both of these stations, especially the latter, contain language demands.

ANALYZE TREAD

The oral language communication (L = listening, S = speaking) between all classroom participants and the literacy demands (R = reading, W = writing) for Gero's kindergarten class are numerous. *From their point of view*, the students will experience and use language as follows:

- Teacher: explaining the tasks associated with the four centers (L)
- Students: using a word bank (R) to fill out a worksheet (W) after listening to narrated presentation (L, R) in the Listening Station
- Students: copying the word of the day's symbol from the board to the worksheet in the Drawing Station (R, W)
- Teacher and students: comparing two symbols (L, S) and completing the Venn diagram (R) at the Exploration Station
- Teacher and students: completing a read-aloud for conceptual understanding and vocabulary development (L, S)
- Teacher and students: discussing the information learned in each rotation during debriefing (L, S)
- Students: summarizing the information learned during the four activities during journaling (W)

Clearly, the TREAD elements greatly outnumber the nonverbal SLIDE elements. With this list, Ms. Levin can also see that the verbal elements are strongly linked to instructional tasks (e.g., *tell, complete, compare, discuss, copy* vocabulary) rather than procedural ones. If Gero cannot understand these verbs and is not given opportunities to interact with the content and complete tasks at his beginning English proficiency level, he cannot meet two of the lesson objectives. Ms. Levin thus needs to identify supports for her MLEs during the read-aloud, in two out of three stations, during the debriefing session, as well as during journaling time when the students write about what they learned about the symbol of the day.

STEP 2

Size the Gaps

In chapter 2, we explained that teachers should familiarize themselves right away with their MLE students' WIDA ACCESS Reports (or, in the case of new arrivals like Gero, who do not have existing data, with the WIDA Screener Reports). This information, in addition to regular observations of the students' oral communication and language samples, provides the basis for deciding the necessary nonverbal and verbal supports. Once they are familiar with the MLE student's linguistic strengths and challenges, teachers do not need to consult this information each time they plan instruction. Gero's Screener Report is shown here to explain the decisions Ms. Levin makes to support his learning in the unit. The report consists of listening and speaking scores only because the school district has elected not to screen for MLEs' reading and writing skills in kindergarten. Table 3.1 shows Gero's oral proficiency levels and lists what he is generally able to comprehend and express.

TABLE 3.1
Gero's WIDA Proficiency Level Descriptors (Kindergarten)

Domain	Proficiency Level	Students at this Level Generally can . . .
Listening	1	. . . understand brief messages and short commands.
Speaking	1	. . . communicate using familiar words, gestures, or body language.

Although brief, the spoken language sample from this chapter's opening vignette confirms the descriptors in the table 3.1: Gero is able to repeat words Ms. Levin says to him, even if he does so hesitantly. He is likely to know what to do when Ms. Levin calls the class forward to the rocking chair, partially because he sees his peers move when she does so.

The SLIDE and TREAD analysis has shown that the students' learning of the daily symbols and their meanings is largely language dependent. For MLEs at the beginning level of English proficiency like Gero, this represents sizeable gaps between classroom communication and what he can comprehend at this point in his language acquisition journey. How big the gaps are is explained next:

- No gap: Once Ms. Levin demonstrates during the walk-through, Gero can complete the Drawing Station tasks. Similarly, he understands to which group he is assigned when Ms. Levin gently moves him to the other members, and he understands her calling, "Children, move to the next station."
- Small gap: Copying the word of the day's symbol to his drawing requires some language, but Gero does not need to produce the word on his own. In many ways, he is similar to his peers who are also developing letter formation and writing skills.
- Medium gap: Following Ms. Levin's explanation of what occurs at each station is somewhat difficult for Gero. He can see that he is supposed to listen to the narrated presentation and complete the worksheet with the use of the word bank, and he notices the students looking at two symbols with Ms. Levin writing something in two intersecting circles. However, he does not understand what is discussed.
- Large gaps: In the opening session, Gero sees the collage of American symbols and catches some words of previously learned symbols. However, he does not understand that the new symbols will be about the United States and that

students will be learning about their meaning and history. Unlike his peers, Gero does not benefit from this prior knowledge activation and stage-setting class conversation.

All remaining learning activities depend so heavily on language skills that Gero is faced with considerable challenges.

Based on the gap analysis between the lesson tasks and Gero's English proficiency, Ms. Levin is now ready to determine what specific supports will enable him to meet the grade-level objectives.

STEP 3

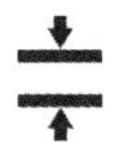

Address the Gaps Between ML's L2 and Lesson Tasks

A good start for attending to MLs' classroom communication needs is to identify lesson tasks to which movement, gestures, or images can be attached. If nonverbal support is not enough to narrow the gap sufficiently, further enhancement of classroom communication can be made through verbal supports. Both types are described below, alongside an explanation of their application.

ADDING NONVERBAL SUPPORT

The introduction to any lesson sets the stage for what the students are going to learn. It activates prior knowledge and provides background information on the topic. Making both lesson introductions and directions and routines obvious in kindergarten is especially important because all the students have to learn about movement and behavior in a classroom. When called together, they are learning that the teacher is going to say or do something important and that they must pay attention and listen. MLEs like Gero often use these floor announcement/discussion opportunities to pay particular attention to what the teacher is saying in an attempt to understand expectations. Because of the professional development sessions she recently attended, Ms. Levin always makes sure to place Gero directly in front of her so that he can watch her lips as she forms the words and hears each syllable she enunciates. Although this happens seamlessly while she addresses the entire class, his placement is considered a *supplemental* support because it is done specifically for Gero.

To assist Gero in understanding the verbal elements of most lessons, Ms. Levin also makes a habit of using gestures more deliberately when describing activities and actions. For example, when calling the students to the floor by the rocking chair, she purposely looks at him while waving her hands, palms face up, to demonstrate to him that he should move forward with the other children. In the Haitian culture, such a gesture is considered to be acceptable.[26] Applying this technique is a *supplement* for Gero.

For this particular lesson, Ms. Levin incorporates these daily habits into her modeling of the tasks at the various stations during the walk-through. For example, in the Listening Station, she not only states that the students will copy words from the word bank on the worksheet and write them in the spaces but also pretends to do so with one or two items with her hand holding an imaginary pencil after pointing to the word bank. Although this *universal* support will not help Gero identify which words need to be placed in which spaces when he gets to the Listening Station, he will remember what he is expected to do.

ADDING VERBAL SUPPORT

Although each center requires specific linguistic adaptations for Gero, one constant modification that Ms. Levin can implement is to have her other Haitian student, Merline, sit near Gero at all times. This way, Merline can quickly redirect him when he is lost or translate a word or two when he is unable to comprehend what Ms. Levin or others say. This shows the two children that their home language is an asset to learning and its use is valued in the classroom.[27]

Other verbal supports that are specific to Gero's beginning English proficiency level can be added during the whole-class activities and discussions, at the individual stations, and during journaling time.

- During introduction: Introducing the daily symbol and associated vocabulary and developing the conceptual understanding of the symbolism are language intensive, but Ms. Levin has ample opportunity to connect the oral and written words or phrasing of the target terms right away. She can point to the word, say it, invite the students to repeat after her, and then ask, "So what is this?" This simple repetition has the built-in benefit that MLEs can pronounce the words or phrases for the first time in the safety of the group.[28] After the choral repetition, Ms. Levin can write the vocabulary or phrasing on the whiteboard next to her rocking chair, point to it and say it slowly, following her finger underneath the sounds. Intentional moves like this only take a few seconds, but they help the kindergarteners who are new to reading and writing associate the written word with how it sounds. These options for narrowing the communication gap for Gero fall under the category of *universal* support because all students profit from them equally.
- During read-aloud:
  - While she reads the text, Ms. Levin can engage Gero and his classmates by changing her voice, using different intonation patterns, and using lots of gestures as she reads each page and shows the class the pictures from the text.[29] Additionally, she can instruct the students to give a thumbs up each time they hear the word as she reads the text. These verbal supports are *universal* in type because they help all students stay focused and are added for the entire class. They are especially beneficial for Gero because they connect the spoken words he hears to the target vocabulary.
  - At times, as she stops to pose questions, Ms. Levin can pretend to be thinking about the answer, with one finger on her chin and eyes turned upward, her head slightly tilted to the side. This way, Gero recognizes that she is trying to find an answer and he may even dare to offer one. She can facilitate the exchange through leveled questioning that requires him to respond with one word only

or ask him to point to the object in the picture that contains the response. Similarly, by developing the habit of placing emphasis on the word she intends for Gero to know or concentrate on, Ms. Levin can formulate a leveled question like, "Can you point to one of the *red* stripes in the American flag?" After he does so, she can then say, "Yes, this is one of the *red* stripes in the American flag," thus not only providing Gero with confirmation that he responded correctly but also giving him another opportunity to hear the sentence. Leveled questioning is a *supplemental* support because it is specifically targeted toward Gero's needs while being implemented alongside the instruction for all students.

- At Listening Station:
  - Although the class is shown what to do in each station, Ms. Levin creates a step-by-step guide with words and images for each center activity. Specifically made for and only used by Gero, this is a *supplemental* verbal support.
  - Ms. Levin needs to listen carefully to her PowerPoint presentation and decide whether the pace is appropriate or whether it would be wise to rerecord the voice-over a bit more slowly to increase Gero's chances to understand more words. She could also use a different font color to draw attention to important information on the slides. Increasing the wait time between slides so that Gero and his native English-speaking peers who have difficulty decoding are given a better chance to copy the words from the word bank into the cloze sentences on the worksheet is an acceptable modification. Any change to the narrated PowerPoint slides is seen and heard by all students and thus categorized as a *universal* support, even though the changes help Gero the most.
- At Drawing Station: Other than copying the word of the day from the whiteboard to the top of the worksheet, this station consists only of drawing and coloring, so no verbal support is necessary. If need be, Merline can show Gero where he can find the word to copy displayed.
- At Exploration Station: Many of the verbal supports identified in the read-aloud apply to this station, which Ms. Levin guides. She points to the symbol from the country used to compare, asks the students to describe it, and writes their responses on chart paper on one side of the Venn diagram. During this time, she asks probing questions for more detail, leveling them for Gero's needs when she addresses him. To further assist him, though, she gives Gero a bilingual handout with colors, shapes, and other details that he can compare to what she writes on the chart paper. After repeating the same procedure with the American symbol on the other side of the diagram, Ms. Levin tells the students to read the words with her, listening to how the students say them and helping with decoding where necessary. She can again use leveled questioning to ask which of the words Gero sees underneath both pictures, point to them, and write them into the intersection of the two circles. Finally, each student can take turns copying a leftover word from either side into the appropriate circle. With the exception of the bilingual word list and the leveled questioning specific for Gero, which are

supplemental in nature, all verbal supports suggested in the Exploration Station are *universal.*

- During debriefing: The same supports that facilitate interaction between Ms. Levin and Gero in the read-aloud and the Exploration Station and that help him learn the symbols and their meanings can be implemented here.
- During journaling: While the students write the three facts, Ms. Levin uses leveled questioning to consult with Gero about what he wants to write and encourages him to use the bilingual list to copy words into his drawing. Although she checks in with all students while they journal about the word of the day, we consider these *supplemental* supports taking place in an *individual,* one-on-one setting because they are explicitly employed for Gero's needs.

Managing Grouping, Time, and Provider

All supports that narrow the gap between Gero's current oral proficiency level and the lesson's classroom communication demands are easy for Ms. Levin to implement when she instructs the whole class or when the students work in their small groups in the stations. Assembling the list of bilingual vocabulary or making verbal adaptations to the existing presentation (e.g., rerecording at slower speed, increasing time between slides, highlighting text) could be assumed by a volunteer with instructions from Ms. Levin, if one were available.

One component that Ms. Levin might not be aware of is that although students in Haiti engage in comparing-and-contrasting activities, this is most often done through verbal interaction and not through the use of a graphic organizer. Explicitly teaching Gero how to complete the diagram prior to the unit would be beneficial, although it could occur for reinforcement after he sees it modeled for the first time. This task could be assumed by the teacher, a bilingual aide, the ELD teacher, or even a classroom volunteer who can work individually with Gero while the other children do silent reading.

After reviewing the lesson plan modifications, Mrs. Levin thinks with a smile, "I can't wait to see Gero learn alongside his peers in this unit."[30]

INSTRUCTIONAL SUPPORT FOR OTHER MULTILINGUAL LEARNERS

Based on the SLIDE and TREAD analysis as well as the nonverbal and verbal scaffolds Ms. Levin selected for Gero, table 3.2 shows suggested supports for assisting learners at intermediate or advanced oral proficiency specific to this lesson.

Lesson Summary

An overview of the SCC protocol applied to Mrs. Levin's original American Symbols lesson plan is provided in table 3.3. The nonverbal (SLIDE) elements are underlined, and the verbal components (TREAD) are depicted in **boldface**. Both fonts **combined** show that a task can contain both nonverbal and verbal elements, such as students listening to the teacher during the demonstration of an experiment. The second column

TABLE 3.2
Support for Intermediate and Advanced Multilingual Learners

Oral Proficiency	Nonverbal Support	Verbal Support
Intermediate	• Use gestures; point to items or pictures when talking.	• Read-aloud: Same as for beginning-level MLs but leveled questions, such as "What is this symbol?" or "What does this symbol stand for?" • Listening Station: Same as for beginning-level student • Exploration Station: Word bank in L2 • Debriefing: Leveled questions that require short responses • Journaling: Use of word bank provided during the Exploration Station
Advanced	• No extra nonverbal support is necessary.	• Journaling: Pair ML with a more proficient partner to proof words or phrases

points out which language skills are involved in the lesson step *from the point of view of the students* and gives a visual depiction of the size gap between the classroom communication and Gero's current beginning level of English proficiency. Finally, the third column lists the verbal and nonverbal supports.

Final Thoughts

Whenever the class completes a multiday or weekly unit, Ms. Levin's habit is to send representative work samples home. For this American Symbols unit, the small package in the folder consists of a copy of the symbols collage she showed in the introduction of the unit, the drawings and facts on the daily symbols the children produced, and a copy of the daily Venn diagrams. A few days later, Gero arrives in the classroom carrying a box in his hand and a big grin on his face. "From mother et . . . and . . . gran-manman," he said before reaching into his backpack and pulling out an envelope. In the card, written with the help of a translation app, Mrs. Jantiy expressed her gratitude for including their family's heritage during the unit on American symbols. "Gero looks forward to your class every day, and we hope you will enjoy the tablètkokoye. These coconut candies are popular sweets in Haïti."

Upon their return from physical education class, Ms. Levin tells her students that they are about to get a special treat from Gero's home country. As she starts to hand out the candy, she asks, "Gero, please tell us what these are called." She nods to encourage him to speak. No, it isn't her imagination. He grows half an inch as he says proudly, smiling at his peers, "Tablèts kokoye. Very good."

TABLE 3.3

The American Symbols Lesson at a Glance

Lesson Steps	Skills[1] and Gap Size[2]	Added Supports[3]
Call the students to the rocking chair. Display a collage of American symbols on the whiteboard and **ask** what they are. **Tell** the students that this whole week they are going to explore the meaning of these symbols just like they did with the previous symbols (heart, stop sign, etc.) but that they will also learn about the history of these symbols. Point to one of the symbols and **state** that it represents what the children will learn about today.	L, S ↕↕↕	***Nonverbal Supports:*** Intentional gestures and pointing alongside clear enunciation ***Verbal Support:*** Placing Gero nearby to better hear teacher language (supplemental)
Conduct a read-aloud on the symbol, working on conceptual understanding of its symbolism and on vocabulary development.	L, S, R ↕↕↕	***Nonverbal Supports:*** Intentional gestures and pointing alongside clear enunciation ***Verbal Supports:*** • Connecting oral and written language through (choral) repetition and tracing words with finger while pronouncing them • Using intonation patterns to draw attention to target vocabulary/phrasing • Instructing students to show thumbs-up when target vocabulary is used • Questioning leveled to Gero's proficiency level (supplemental)
Walk the students through each center, **explaining** what they will do there. **Tell** them that they will complete a task every fifteen minutes.	L ↕↕	***Nonverbal Supports:*** • Explicit demonstration of tasks, including where to consult word bank and copy vocabulary onto worksheets • Connect verbal instructions with gestures and pointing
Listening Station: Each student gets a worksheet that contains a word bank on top. Together, they **view a narrated, teacher-created presentation** with facts about the symbol. They **copy the words** into the appropriate spaces on the worksheet.	L, R, W ↕↕↕	***Nonverbal Support:*** Step-by-step guide with images (supplemental) ***Verbal Supports:*** • Rerecord voice-over with slower information delivery • Highlight important vocabulary/phrases (supplemental) • Increase wait time between slides • Provide step-by-step guide with images and words for Gero (supplemental) • Assign Gero to Merline's group for her to briefly assist with L1 as appropriate (supplemental)

Continued...

TABLE 3.3

The American Symbols Lesson at a Glance *(Continued...)*

Lesson Steps	Skills[1] and Gap Size[2]	Added Supports[3]
Drawing Station: Each student **copies the word** of the day's symbol from the board onto a worksheet that has a large empty space for the illustration on one side and three boxes for writing on the other, and then each student draws and colors the symbol.	W ↕	***Verbal Support:*** Assign Gero to Merline's group for her to briefly assist with L1 as appropriate
Exploration Station: Looking at a picture of the symbol of the day and an equivalent symbol from another country, the students **compare** the two as a group. The teacher **completes a Venn diagram** based on student input.	L, S, R ↕↕↕	***Nonverbal Supports:*** Intentional gestures and pointing alongside clear enunciation (supplemental) ***Verbal Supports:*** • Repeating and emphasizing words provided by students • Leveled questioning (supplemental) • Choral repetition of symbol descriptions after each side of diagram is completed • Provide a bilingual list of shapes and colors for Gero to compare as teacher writes on chart paper (supplemental)
Divide students into equal groups and **tell** them to go to the centers.	L Ø	***Verbal Supports:*** Assign Gero to Merline's group for her to assist with L1 as appropriate (supplemental)
After all groups have rotated through the centers, the class **discusses** what they learned.	L, S ↕↕↕	***Nonverbal Supports:*** Intentional gestures and pointing alongside clear enunciation (supplemental) ***Verbal Supports:*** • Repeating and emphasizing pertinent words in descriptions provided by students • Leveled questioning (supplemental)
Journaling: Students **write** three facts about what they learned on their worksheet from the drawing center.	W ↕↕↕	***Verbal Supports:*** • Leveled questioning to elicit from Gero what he wants to write (supplemental) • Encourage Gero to use the bilingual list to copy words (supplemental)

Key:

1 Language skills: L = listening, S = speaking, R = reading, W = writing

2 Gap sizes: No gap = Ø, ↕ = small gap, ↕↕ = medium gap, ↕↕↕ = large gap

3 Unless otherwise noted, all supports are considered universal.

STOP AND REFLECT QUESTIONS

1. Many students have stated that they were unaware of the polysemous words used in social studies. Prior to reading this chapter, were you aware of such terms? If so, when were you first made aware of them? If not, why do you think native speakers are not made aware of polysemous words? What are the underlying assumptions educators make about polysemous word use among native speakers? How are those same assumptions about knowledge of polysemous words transferred to teaching MLs?
2. When teaching social studies, have you used the following strategies specifically with your MLs: prereading, vocabulary overview, prediction guides, section reading, graphic organizers, and note taking? How effective were the strategies? Did they bring about the desired results?

GO AND PRACTICE ACTIVITIES

1. Review the textbook you are currently using and identify the polysemous words. Highlight them and create a list of the general meanings and social studies meanings and review them with your MLs. Plan time to discuss the words with your MLs because these words may initially be confusing. Have a bilingual aide assist the MLs in identifying other polysemous words throughout the remainder of the chapters and create a list with their meanings for reference.
2. Create a word wall from the social studies unit you are currently teaching. Be sure to document the effectiveness of using word walls. For example, have you noticed greater participation among your MLs as a result of using this word wall? If possible, jot down how often and in what ways MLs use the word walls. Provide specific examples.

Teaching Edith About the Earth's Rotation

Inquiry-Based Science and Language Development

In Edith's fourth-grade dual language class, science is taught in English this week. "Sit next to *me*, Edith!" Edith's classmate swats the air, motioning to the empty chair nearby. The children rush to their team tables for directions. "On each table, there is a piece of paper, a roll of tape, and a pile of pennies," Ms. Oliver explains. "Every team will design a boat, using only the paper and tape. Your team's goal is to create a boat that holds the most pennies without sinking. We will test your designs by placing the boats in a basin filled with water." Ms. Oliver flicks her number spinner. "Teammm . . . memberrr . . . *three* will lead the discussion of the design plan for each group. Let's get started!"

"Hey, Edith!" shouts the boy sitting across from her. "You're number three!"

COMMUNICATION IN TEACHING AND LEARNING SCIENCE

Science instruction can provide many opportunities for multilingual learners (MLs) to comprehend concepts and topics through observing, measuring, weighing, and using just about every sense to take in and make sense of new information, which can make science lessons less language intensive. By fourth grade, students across the globe have typically experienced instruction that shows and explains, for example, properties of objects and materials, position and motion of objects, properties and changes of properties in matter, and motions and forces, among other concepts. All of these topics lend themselves to a hands-on approach to learning, linking objects and actions with language that describes them. However, like any other academic subject, science has language demands that challenge multilingual learners (MLs) in listening, speaking, reading, and writing.

Language Features of Science Discourse and Text

Students learning academic subjects such as science in a new language face various challenges as they negotiate the language, literacy, and content needs of the disciplines. A major challenge for teachers is to structure instruction so that they can reduce the language demands for participation while maintaining the rigor of science content and process. The academic language used in science classrooms is built around expressing specific functions. Science students, MLs included, are expected to formulate hypotheses, propose alternative solutions, describe and classify phenomena, use time and spatial relations, infer, interpret data, predict, generalize, and communicate findings.[1]

Language scholars Zhihui Fang and Mary Schleppegrell note that science discourse in the English language is replete with technical vocabulary.[2] In addition, science texts, in particular, use abstract language, such as abstract nouns that are formed from verbs, as in *discover/discovery*. Another challenging aspect of the communication of science is the density of scientific texts. A great deal of information is packed into a clause, as in this example of an embedded clause:[3]

> A pattern of evolution in which distantly related organisms evolve similar traits is called convergent evolution.

The last feature of scientific texts that Fang and Schleppegrell identify is its tightly knit rhetorical nature. Referencing the "zig-zagging" pattern of thematic progression described by Eggins, they show how science follows a chain of reference from a new topic in one sentence to its further explanation and discussion in one or more following sentences, often using pronouns or other referents to link the second mention of the topic with the first.[4]

All four of these qualities of scientific texts pose challenges for MLs; the text complexity, their level of second language (L2) proficiency, and depending on their age, their first language (L1) reading ability also affect the extent of the challenge and the support needed.

Components of Science Learning

In teaching science to MLs, it is helpful to consider what defines the constructs of science learning. Science and language experts Okhee Lee and Sandra Fradd have categorized the constructs as summarized in table 4.1; characteristics of scientific inquiry are shown in table 4.2, "Science habits of mind."[5] For each of these components, we further explain ML-specific issues—issues teachers need to consider regarding the unique position in which these students may find themselves when "doing science."[6]

If MLs are experiencing any of the issues described in tables 4.1 and 4.2, it may affect their ability to fully engage in the science lesson. By addressing these linguistic differences or cultural viewpoints prior to teaching science, you enable your MLs to focus on the lesson rather than on those linguistic or cultural differences.

TABLE 4.1

Components of Science Knowledge

Component	Characteristics	ML-Specific Issues
Knowing science (science understanding)	• Building on prior knowledge • Using appropriate science vocabulary • Understanding concepts and relationships	• Terms and concepts do not always translate accurately across languages. • MLs may lack specific language or communication patterns to express precise meanings.
Doing science (science inquiry)	• Engaging in inquiry • Solving real-world problems	• MLs with little or no formal schooling or those from oral language traditions may have difficulties with scientific inquiry in school if their cultural background does not encourage asking questions or devising plans for investigation.
Talking science (science discourses)	• Participating in social and academic discourse • Using multiple representational formats • Appropriating the discourse of science	• MLs may have difficulty following discussions and sharing their points of view, especially at the lower levels of L2 proficiency. • MLs may have different interpretations of nonverbal expressions (body language) exhibited during discussions. • MLs with limited literacy experience may have problems reading complex text, interpreting data, and expressing themselves in written, graphic, or electronic formats.

TABLE 4.2

Science Habits of Mind

Component	Characteristics	ML-Specific Issues
Science values and attitudes	• Manifesting generic values and attitudes • Appropriating culturally mediated values and attitudes	• MLs from cultures that value group harmony above all may have difficulty critiquing their peers and arguing their perspectives.
Science world view	• Recognizing scientific ways of knowing	• MLs may interpret natural phenomena as the interaction among social, personal, and supranatural forces; this view might be rejected as personally useful and socially relevant but not scientific.

TEACHING MULTILINGUAL LEARNERS SCIENCE

Science lessons provide a very meaningful context for learning language and acquiring literacy. For example, when doing science inquiry, MLs use language associated with objects, visual representations and pictures, hands-on activities, and experiences with the local environment.[7] Moreover, they have the opportunity to develop their literacy through science discourse when they express their understanding in writing or by creating tables and graphs. When MLs discuss science in science class, they describe, hypothesize, explain, justify, argue, and summarize, all of which support the understanding of science concepts and the development of language skills.

Therefore, the relationship between science learning and language learning is reciprocal. The use of verbal and nonverbal communication in science classes allows MLs to develop and practice complex language forms and functions. Conversely, the use of language functions such as description, explanation, and discussion allows them to develop their understanding of science content.

Focus on Vocabulary

A well-developed vocabulary helps MLs build background knowledge and facilitates content comprehension of text and lectures in science classrooms. As for teaching and learning social studies where English is the language of instruction, the Tennessee Vocabulary Project is a resource for science teachers. It lists the essential vocabulary items Edith's science teachers will need to teach. Teaching words is an important part of teaching concepts, so the integration between the content and language domains is quite clear in vocabulary development.[8] For example, third-grade words such as *solar system* and *stratus*, fourth-grade words like *climate* and *condensation*, and fifth-grade words like *states of matter* and *symbiosis* should be identified and defined in tandem with teaching conceptual knowledge and skills.

A useful vocabulary-building strategy for science suggested by Joyce Nutta and colleagues is to address cognates explicitly.[9] Cognates are words that sound or look similar. More important, however, they mean the same thing in different languages. Science uses many terms derived from Latin, the origin of Romance languages such as Spanish, Italian, French, Romanian, and Portuguese. Consequently, Spanish and English share many cognates.[10] Cognates such as *agricultura* and *agriculture*, *analice* and *analyze*, *actividad* and *activity*, and *aire* and *air* can be compared, and prefix, root, and suffix patterns can be contrasted, as with *-dad* in Spanish and *-ity* in English. Explicit instruction in these similar words and their prefixes, suffixes, and roots can be an effective way of building vocabulary for Spanish-speaking MLEs.

An interesting fact about cognates is that some cognate words are highly frequent in Spanish but less frequent in English. As a result, Spanish-speaking MLEs like Edith possess an L1 vocabulary bank that includes many words that are common in Spanish (e.g., *sol, luna*) but are used only in scientific and academic language in English (e.g., *solar, lunar*). Such words might help Spanish-speaking MLEs understand science texts. To activate this resource, Edith's science teachers can begin by pointing out examples of cognates and then challenging her to find as many as possible in her science textbook unit. Then, cognates can constitute the basis for a student-generated glossary Edith can use when she needs help remembering the meaning of previously covered science content or when connecting new content to her existing science knowledge. Developing such metacognitive awareness will translate into all subject areas and make Edith feel more confident all-around while learning her additional language.

Promoting Language Interaction

In chapter 1, we discussed the importance of interaction for acquiring a new language. Discussions are part of science instruction, and they often follow a communication pattern of initiation/response/evaluation (IRE). The IRE communication pattern starts with the teacher asking a student a question. The student's answer is then evaluated by the teacher, who makes a brief statement such as "Good" or "No, that's not correct," after which the interaction ends. However, to integrate science with academic language development, science classrooms should include many opportunities for students to engage in classroom discussions in which they practice talking about science, challenge each other's ideas, and influence the direction of the discourse.[11]

A better approach for MLs might be the initiation/response/follow-up (IRF) communication pattern, in which either the teacher or the student asks a question or introduces a topic. After a response is given, the initiator uses the response to move the conversation forward, which can continue for as long as the participants wish to talk about the subject. In contrast to the IRE pattern, IRF may include contributions from other students in the class. For example, a science teacher who teaches in English could engage their MLEs in discussing the evaporation and condensation of water. If the first answer the teacher gets is "Condenses," it would be easy to assume that they lack the necessary language to express their ideas clearly. However, if the teacher uses the first response as a starting point and continues to ask questions such as "What is *condenses*?" and "How does it condense?" then the students' responses become more comprehensive, moving from "Condenses" and "It condenses" to "The water vapor condenses" and then "The water vapor condenses as it cools." After more discussion, one student states, "The hot water in the bottom cup evaporated to the top cup, and the water vapor cooled with the ice and condensed in little drops." These changes represent the integration of science learning with language development using the IRF pattern. Initially, students learning English may use present tense verbs only ("condenses"), without specified nouns and pronouns. As their discourse becomes more complete, it also grows in complexity to include adverbs, adjectives, dependent clauses, and tense changes.[12] By describing and explaining their observations in science activities, MLs acquire the language of science as well as science content.[13]

Despite decades of education reform that has aimed to make science accessible for all students, there still are important achievement gaps between native English speakers and MLEs.[14] Moreover, they are less likely to see science as relevant to their lives outside of school or to pursue advanced degrees in science.[15] We believe that more accessible communication in science teaching and learning can lead to greater involvement of MLEs in science-related activities.

ESSENTIAL POINTS

1. Science lessons offer valuable opportunities for MLs to develop both academic language and content knowledge through hands-on, inquiry-based activities. Integrating language development with content learning benefits students' overall progress.
2. Focusing on academic vocabulary is essential for MLs. Teachers can enhance vocabulary development by explicitly teaching discipline-specific terms, using cognates, and connecting new terms to students' first languages. This approach bridges the language gap and strengthens both language and content learning.
3. Shifting from a traditional IRE model to an IRF communication pattern promotes more engaging, interactive classroom discussions. This method encourages students to build on each other's ideas, deepen their understanding, and practice academic tasks like hypothesizing, describing, and explaining, which are critical skills in science and social studies.

CLASSROOM APPLICATION

As Ms. Oliver leans over group two's table, she overhears laughter from the left. She quickly turns toward group four and sees Edith staring at the linoleum. "So, Edith . . . what do we do *now*?" the boy asks, intoning his question with sarcasm. "Let's have Sophia lead this discussion today because I need to borrow Edith for a second," says Ms. Oliver as she hurriedly places her hand on Edith's shoulder. Edith follows Ms. Oliver to her desk, where they both do their best to communicate about the activity. Ms. Oliver had swooped in for the save, making Edith feel comfortable in the moment and keeping her from shutting down, but she knows she could have set up the lesson better. She just didn't know how yet.

During the students' lunch, Ms. Oliver searches teacher websites for just the right activity. She is a bit nervous about coplanning a lesson with an English language development (ELD) specialist that the district provides to all first-year teachers in a dual language classroom whose language of instruction is English. "I want to do all I can for Edith," Ms. Oliver tells her principal as the activity pages stack up in the printer tray, "but I can't turn my class upside down to reach one student."

"I know what you mean, Ms. Oliver," the principal calmly replies. "This is why I am excited about you being part of this professional development. You've been assigned to a *phenomenal* ELD specialist who will give you lots of insights. I want you to be the *best* teacher for *all* students, and I think you'll find that if you continue to concentrate on that goal, the professional learning will show you how to go about achieving it for your MLEs as well." "Thank you. I'll keep that in mind," answered Ms. Oliver, rushing out of the room to finalize planning for next week's science lessons before the students' return.

THE EARTH'S ROTATION LESSON DESCRIPTION

Edith and her fourth-grade classmates are learning that the earth revolves around the sun in a year and rotates on its axis in a day, or twenty-four hours. Inquiry-based lessons offer ample opportunities for English learners to interact with the topic, thus assisting with the development of conceptual understanding through hands-on exploration. They also invite verbal interaction with academic language in a low-risk environment when working in small groups. Despite the many elements that make inquiry-based lessons comprehensible for MLEs, Edith requires extra support for some tasks, including small-group interactions. The activity modified with the Supportive Classroom Communication protocol is the beginning of a lesson on the earth's rotation[16] that is built on the 5E Learning Cycle Model.[17]

OBJECTIVE

By demonstrating the earth's movement around the sun, students will explain how day and night occur as a result of rotation.

INTRODUCTION

Engage:

1. Show a picture of you and a friend and tell the class that you want to call your friend who lives in New Delhi, India.[18]
2. Ask the class what time would be the best to call her because she will be on the other side of the world.
3. Ask the class how the rotation of the earth affects day and night.

LESSON STEPS

Explore:

1. Create groups of four and give a materials bag to each group.
2. Tell students to number off in fours.
3. Explain each group member's task: Students 1 and 2 each select a sphere from the materials bag and hold it up. Student 3 makes a chart and writes the size of the sphere on the chart. Student 4 turns on the flashlight and shines it on the sphere, holding it about eight inches from the sphere.

4. The group observes the first sphere to determine approximately how much of the sphere is lighted, estimating the amount, while student 3 records the estimation on the chart. Then the group repeats the sequence with the second sphere.
5. Group members then discuss why they think that much of the sphere was lighted by the flashlight.

Explain:

1. Bring the groups back together and discuss their findings, asking:
   - What did you find?
   - Why do you think this occurred?
2. Guide discussion toward the correct answer: Light spreads only to the widest part of the object; it can't bend around the sides. So, one-half ends up being dark.
3. Ask the class what shape the earth is and show pictures of the actual sun and earth with the back side of the earth dark.
4. Using one lamp for the class and globes for each group, guide discussion toward how the earth's rotation takes twenty-four hours and causes dawn, day, dusk, and night.

Extend:

1. Allow students to scout different times around the globe.

EVALUATION

Answer the following questions in writing:

1. What is the shape of the earth? Provide an example of this shape.
2. What causes day and night? Explain completely.
3. How long is the earth's day?
4. When it is daytime in the United States, what time of day is it in India? Why?

APPLICATION OF THE SUPPORTIVE CLASSROOM COMMUNICATON PROTOCOL TO THE EARTH'S ROTATION LESSON

In this section, we show and explain Ms. Oliver's thinking and decisions on making the lesson accessible for Edith and suggest additional verbal and nonverbal supports worth considering.

Right after fine-tuning the lesson plan, Ms. Oliver reminds herself to take another glance at the English proficiency level descriptors for level 1, at which Edith was assessed, before looking at the communication requirements of the lesson.

STEP 1

Analyze Communication in Lesson Tasks

Based on the underlined verbs and verb phrases in the preceding lesson description, we categorize the nonverbal (SLIDE) and the verbal (TREAD) elements and list the associated language skill for verbal components. Table 2.2 on page 56 provides sample verbs that indicate each element type.

ANALYZE SLIDE

The group activity has many hands-on tasks, including selecting and holding up a sphere, shining a flashlight on it, and observing how much of the sphere is lighted. During the whole-class discussion, the students see pictures of the earth and the sun, including images of the dark side of the earth, and observe the earth's rotation with dawn, day, dusk, and night as they hold up their globe to the lamp. Finally, they explore different times around the globe. With all these visual elements with images, objects, and movement, Edith is able to participate in these tasks to a certain extent and develop basic conceptual knowledge.

ANALYZE TREAD

- There are a number of oral communication demands (L = listening, S = speaking) for all classroom participants, as well as literacy demands (R = reading, W = writing), in this lesson. *From the point of view of the students*, they will experience and use language as follows:Teacher: giving directions (L)
- Students: estimating the amount of light area on the sphere and recording it on a chart (L, S, R, W)
- Students: discussing why the portion of the sphere was lighted by the flashlight
- Teacher and students: discussing findings and discussing why the back side of the sphere remained dark (L, S)
- Students: answering questions on test (R, W)

Participating in both the group inquiry and the whole-class discussion requires the ability to form sentences using a cause-and-effect structure, which Edith is not yet able to understand and produce without support. The class discussion also involves answering "why" questions, so Edith needs help to comprehend the vocabulary and concepts involved. The quiz is entirely verbal and requires responses that are far more complex than she can write by herself. Ms. Oliver has to find another way for Edith to demonstrate comprehension of the process of the earth's rotation.

Size the Gaps

STEP 2

Ms. Oliver has been getting increasingly familiar with Edith's linguistic strengths and challenges based on classroom communication samples. Knowing her English proficiency levels from the ACCESS Screener Report that was sent to her shortly after Edith joined her classroom, Ms. Oliver is ready to size the gaps between the lesson's verbal and nonverbal elements and Edith's current linguistic English abilities. The report (see table 4.3) is shown here for your consideration and is used to explain the decisions that can be made to support her learning science content behind the earth's rotation.

Related to the lesson tasks, the proficiency level descriptors reveal that Edith is able to communicate with her group members and with Ms. Oliver in a few words, referring to familiar objects, and demonstrate how to do things using a few words. She is also able to interpret information from graphs, which will help her in the whole-class

TABLE 4.3

Edith's WIDA Proficiency Level Descriptors (Grades 1–12)

Domain	Level	Students at this Level Generally can . . .
Listening	1	. . . understand oral messages that include visuals and gestures and may contain a few everyday words or phrases in English, for example: • Recognize familiar words and phrases in conversations • Match information from oral descriptions to objects, figures, or illustrations • Follow one-step oral directions • Show agreement or disagreement with oral statements
Speaking	1	. . . communicate orally in English using gestures and language that may contain a few words, for example: • Ask and answer simple questions about what, when, or where something happened • Name familiar objects, people, and pictures • Show how to solve problems using words and gestures • Express personal preferences
Reading	1	. . . understand written texts that include visuals and may contain a few words or phrases in English, for example: • Interpret information from graphs, charts, or other visual information • Comprehend short text with illustrations and simple and familiar language • Identify steps in processes presented in graphs or short texts with illustrations • Identify words and phrases that express opinions and claims
Writing	1	. . . communicate in writing using visuals and symbols that may contain few words in English, for example: • Express ideas or concepts using text and illustrations • Share personal experiences through drawings and words • Label steps in processes presented in graphs or short texts • State opinions or preferences through text and illustrations • Express opinions about specific topics or situations

discussion if she is able to refer to them. Finally, she can label steps or show conceptual understanding in writing a few words.

The analysis has shown that a large chunk of building conceptual understanding gained during the hands-on part (SLIDE) is dependent on discussions (TREAD). For a beginning-level MLE, this represents a considerable gap between classroom communication and what Edith can comprehend and express at this point in time. But exactly how big are these gaps? Let's see:

- No gaps: Being assigned to a group, observing or doing the task of picking and holding up spheres or shining the flashlight onto them (during group activity), and holding the globe toward the lamp (during whole-class discussion) do not require any language, but Edith needs to be shown her assigned role.

Reading the estimations of how much of the sphere is lighted on the chart(s) during the group activity and when all groups report out consists of numbers or a few words and does not cause her difficulty, and looking at the image of the earth and sun during the whole-class discussion presents no gap.

- Small gaps: Sharing her observation of the lighted part of the sphere with her group members does not require Edith to use extended speech, and she can use gestures to show what she is trying to express.
- Medium gaps: Teachers often count off students, put them into groups, and describe the roles each member is to play. For beginning-level MLEs, however, understanding what every group member is to do, if communicated entirely by the teacher speaking, is too much information at once for Edith.

  Edith needs to learn the words *round* or *circular* because she won't naturally catch on to them when the teacher asks about the shape of the earth, and without them, she can't verbally indicate her understanding.

  During the extension part of the lesson when the students investigate different times around the globe, Edith's challenge is to explain her opinions and listen to her group members' input.
- Large gaps: The engagement part of the lesson is entirely verbal, causing Edith to disengage almost immediately when she cannot catch on to the story the teacher is telling.

Comprehending the group members' conversations of what they observed and negotiations of what to record on the chart is very difficult for Edith. She can recognize the numbers or how her peers describe the shapes, but she definitely struggles with following the argumentations, leading her to miss details. However, seeing the agreed-upon result on the chart will help her develop concept understanding.

The whole-class discussions and answering the test questions depend exclusively on listening, speaking, reading, and writing skills. They also require complex expressions (e.g., hypothetical phrasing and cause-effect phrasing) and elaboration of ideas or a hypothesis. All these verbal tasks are well beyond Edith's current oral level in English and greatly impede her ability to participate in the lesson.

Address the Gaps Between ML's L2 Proficiency and Lesson Tasks

STEP 3

Given how TREAD heavy the lesson is, Ms. Oliver knows to first pinpoint areas in the plan where adding SLIDE will narrow the gap to require less support (or eliminate the need altogether). This, in turn, impacts how she addresses Edith's remaining communication needs.

ADDING NONVERBAL SUPPORT

Building background knowledge visually is essential for Edith. In her introduction, Ms. Oliver can show on a globe where New Delhi is as she tells the story. She can then rotate the globe to show India's location in reference to Harveston, Florida, where the class is, noting that the turning of the globe represents the earth's rotation. Because each group is using a globe at the conclusion of the lesson, this *universal* support does not require any additional time or objects, and it benefits visual learners at the same time.

When assigning students to groups and explaining the group activity, Ms. Oliver counts off the students and then shows the numbers one through four with her fingers while modeling what she states is to be done at each step. Instead of just modeling the task, she could have each group follow along at their tables, giving her visual affirmation that everybody knows what to do and saving time once she signals the students the sign to start.

Whenever she addresses the entire class or checks in on Edith's group progress, Ms. Oliver should make a concerted effort to act out the earth's rotation and the way the light hits the globe, point to vocabulary shown on the board on images (listed in verbal support below), and so on to make the verbal information more visible.

ADDING VERBAL SUPPORT

In the situation of a dual language Spanish classroom, we do not consider the automatic built-in L1 peer support as an addition of verbal support to classroom communication because translanguaging often happens naturally. Being enrolled in a dual language program, Edith is used to requesting and receiving quick translation of terms or of instructions when appropriate, and so Ms. Oliver does not need to assign her to a particular group.

A prelabeled and bilingual textbook illustration of the process of the earth's rotation is an important resource for Edith to relate to the topic and to connect the terms in both languages in real time. Later transferring them into her bilingual dictionary as homework or during bell ring work the next day provides reinforcement. Alongside the illustration, Edith needs simple sentence frames to connect the content vocabulary and academic sentence structure to the hands-on activities. These frames then serve as the basis for sentence frames that help her participate during the class discussion. For example, "I think that ______ (half of, most of, a slice of, etc.) the sphere was lighted by the flashlight because ______ (light spreads to the widest part, light cannot bend around the sides, etc.)." As a beginning MLE, Edith cannot say these sentences during the discussion, but she can refer to them as she listens to the other students. The handout, sample sentences, and sentence frames are all considered *supplemental* support because they are only given to Edith.

During class discussions and when looking in on Edith's group, Ms. Oliver should summarize or repeat what students say and ask questions directed at Edith's proficiency level to check for comprehension. Aimed at and implemented only with Edith, this *supplemental* support ensures Edith's continued engagement.

During the class explanation following the exploration phase, Ms. Oliver could display a picture of the globe and the sun (nonverbal support) labeled with *sphere, rotate, rotation, spin, axis,* and similar words to help all students learn the content-specific vocabulary, in addition to writing words such as *day, night, dusk, dawn,* and *twenty-four hours,* which would allow Edith to connect the written words to what she hears during the discussion on rotation. Additionally, while checking everybody's understanding of the terms, Ms. Oliver should ask the class to say the terms aloud as she points to the axis, the sphere, and so on. This gives MLEs an additional opportunity to hear the vocabulary and pronounce the words without being singled out while also reinforcing the vocabulary with the non-MLEs. Last, by writing the different groups' hypotheses on the board, Ms. Oliver gives Edith the opportunity to compare her own group's hypothesis to that of the others. She may not understand every hypothesis, but she can recognize words that are similar to or different from the ones her own group used. These supports are available for all students to see and are, thus, *universal* in nature.

In lieu of asking Edith to respond to the quiz questions in writing, Ms. Oliver can ask her questions 1, 3, and 4 by using the globe, gestures, and other graphics to illustrate each question while stating it. While checking comprehension of the question, the teacher can paraphrase and offer prompts to clarify, such as "How long is the earth's day?" If Edith's expression shows lack of comprehension, Ms. Oliver can restate the question as "How many hours are there in a day?" or "One day has how many hours?" (said while holding up one finger during "one day" and palms up with a questioning expression during "how many"). To show her understanding of question 2, regarding the causes of day and night, Edith can make a graphic/physical explanation of the process of the earth's rotation, using clip art, simple English, and Spanish where necessary.

Because the suggested supports for Edith could be added for the whole class (universal) or provided alongside instruction (supplemental), no alternative supports would be necessary during the teaching and learning parts of the lesson. However, the test, which requires both reading and writing skills, is far beyond Edith's current reach. As a result, Ms. Oliver must go about assessing Edith's conceptual understanding through the alternative format of orally asking the questions and giving Edith the option, where necessary, to answer in her L1.

Managing Grouping, Time, and Provider

Narrowing the gap between a beginning MLE and the classroom communication in language-intensive lessons like this requires a number of nonverbal supports. Monolingual teachers like Ms. Oliver can design and implement a lot of them, but because their time is divided among a number of students, bilingual aides or classroom volunteers are some of a school's greatest resources. We will look at variations of the nonverbal and verbal supports applied in this lesson with an eye to managing them.

Time permitting, either with the assistance of a bilingual aide or a volunteer or independently, Ms. Oliver could cue up a YouTube video on an iPad for Edith to preview prior to the lesson to create context for the subsequent activity. Technology can also be utilized to firm up Edith's conceptual understanding as a follow-up to the lesson. Working with a bilingual aide, she can be directed to a YouTube video of the earth's rotation where she can express in Spanish what is occurring and why. If no bilingual aide is available, Ms. Oliver can ask a community volunteer to sit with Edith while the other students work independently on other tasks.

The more one resource can be utilized at different instructional steps, the better for MLs because they become increasingly familiar with it and the language is reinforced. It also creates less preparation for the teacher or other providers. In this lesson, the labeled illustration of the process of the earth's rotation and simple sentences are such a case. Although Ms. Oliver was able to create this support (the closing vignette will show what happened during the process), a bilingual aide or a volunteer could have prelabeled the illustration and written sentences. Because this supplemental sheet contains a lot of new content and vocabulary, Edith would best be served if Ms. Oliver or a volunteer had a few moments before the class to present these resources and encourage her to use them during the group work. Another option for making maximum use of the resource is to point to the images and ask Edith what they represent in Spanish in a follow-up meeting to reinforce the academic language.

Similarly, an ideal situation would be to go over the sentence frames with Edith prior to the lesson. That would not only allow her to better participate in the class discussion but also might help her depend less on the labeled illustration during the group activity. Because that was not possible here, Ms. Oliver, an aide, or a volunteer should go over them with Edith the next day to reinforce the academic vocabulary. The Spanish language teacher could do it prior to the next science lesson, or the literacy specialist could follow-up during her next visit to the classroom.

INSTRUCTIONAL SUPPORT FOR OTHER MULTILINGUAL LEARNERS

In table 4.4, based on the SLIDE and TREAD analysis above, we propose nonverbal and verbal supports for narrowing the communication gaps for learners at intermediate or advanced oral proficiency.

Lesson Summary

An overview of the Supportive Classroom Communication protocol applied to Ms. Oliver's original Earth's Rotation lesson plan is provided in table 4.5. The

TABLE 4.4

Support for Intermediate and Advanced Multilingual Learners

Oral Proficiency	Providing Nonverbal Support	Providing Verbal Support
Intermediate	• Make verbal content-specific vocabulary visible through gestures and by pointing to objects or illustrations.	• Provide a list of academic vocabulary that will occur during the first experiment to facilitate participation in group discussion and recording of findings. • Practice a sample sentence, such as "When it is _____ o'clock in New York, what time is it in _____?" to facilitate participation in the last exploration. • Consider reading the quiz questions to the student. Accept short answers or incomplete sentence formation in questions 2 and 4.
Advanced	• No extra nonverbal support is necessary.	• No extra verbal support is necessary, with the exception of the quiz, where allowance for grammatical errors should be made.

TABLE 4.5

The Earth's Rotation Lesson at a Glance

Lesson Steps	Skills[1] and Gap Size[2]	Added Supports[3]
Show a picture of you and a friend and **tell** the class that you want to call your friend who lives in New Delhi, India. **Ask** the class what the best time to call her would be because she will be on the other side of the world. **Ask** the class how the rotation of the earth affects day and night.	L, S ↕↕↕	***Nonverbal Supports:*** Use globe, movement, and gestures. ***Verbal Supports:*** • Leveled questioning at Edith's proficiency level (supplemental) • Repetition of vocabulary
Create groups of four and give a materials bag to each group.	L Ø	N/A
Explain each group member's task: Students 1 and 2 each select a sphere from the materials bag and hold it up. Student 3 **makes** a chart and **writes** the size of the sphere on the chart. Student 4 turns on the flashlight and shines it on the sphere, holding it about eight inches from the sphere.	L ↕↕	***Nonverbal Supports:*** Number off students and model tasks.
The group observes the first sphere to **determine** approximately how much of the sphere is lighted and **estimating** the amount, and student 3 **records** the estimation on the chart. Then the group repeats the sequence with the second sphere.	L, S, R, W ↕↕↕	***Nonverbal Support:*** None. Activity is hands-on. ***Verbal Supports:*** Labeled illustration and simple sentences (supplemental)
Group members then **discuss** why they think that much of the sphere was lighted by the flashlight.	L, S ↕↕↕	***Nonverbal Support:*** Encourage Edith to gesture along with using words from illustration (supplemental). ***Verbal Supports:*** • Labeled illustration and simple sentences (supplemental) • Repetition and leveled questioning during check-in (supplemental)
Bring the groups back together and **discuss** their findings, **asking**: • What did you find? • Why do you think this occurred?	L, S ↕↕↕	***Nonverbal Supports:*** • Gesture to indicate questions. • Point to vocabulary used in hypothesis. ***Verbal Supports:*** • Group hypotheses written on board • Choral repetition of vocabulary • Leveled questioning (supplemental)

Continued...

TABLE 4.5

The Earth's Rotation Lesson at a Glance *(Continued...)*

Lesson Steps	Skills[1] and Gap Size[2]	Added Supports[3]
Guide discussion toward the correct answer: Light spreads only to the widest part of the object; it can't bend around the sides. So, one-half ends up being dark.	L, S ↕↕↕	***Nonverbal Supports:*** • Display labeled picture of sun and earth. • Gesture during explanation. ***Verbal Supports:*** • Repetition and leveled questioning (supplemental) • Sentence frames (supplemental)
Ask the class what shape the earth is and **show** pictures of the actual sun and earth with the back side of the earth dark.	L, S ↕↕	***Nonverbal Support:*** Point to sun, earth, lighted side, and dark side. ***Verbal Supports:*** Repetition and leveled questioning (supplemental)
Using one lamp for the class and globes for each group, **guide discussion** toward how the earth's rotation takes twenty-four hours and causes dawn, day, dusk, and night.	L, S ↕↕↕	***Nonverbal Support:*** Physically rotate globe or self and point to vocabulary on displayed picture. ***Verbal Supports:*** • Labeled illustration (supplemental) • Repetition and leveled questioning (supplemental)
Evaluation **Answer** the following questions in writing: 1. What is the shape of the earth? Provide an example of this shape. 2. What causes day and night? Explain completely. 3. How long is the earth's day? 4. When it is daytime in the United States, what time of day is it in India?	L, S ↕↕↕	***Nonverbal Support:*** Physically rotate globe or self and point to vocabulary on displayed picture. ***Verbal Supports:*** • Labeled illustrations (supplemental) • Repetition and leveled questioning (supplemental)

Key:
1 Language skills: L = listening, S = speaking, R = reading, W = writing
2 Gap sizes: No gap = Ø, ↕ = small gap, ↕↕ = medium gap, ↕↕↕ = large gap
3 Unless otherwise noted, all supports are considered universal.

nonverbal (SLIDE) elements are underlined, and the verbal components (TREAD) are depicted in **boldface**. Both fonts **combined** show that a task can contain both nonverbal and verbal elements, such as students listening to the teacher during the demonstration of an experiment.

The second column points out which language skill is involved in the lesson step *from the point of view of the students* and gives a visual depiction of the size gap between the classroom communication and Edith's current beginning English proficiency. Finally, the third column depicts the nonverbal and verbal supports that best fit with the lesson tasks.

Final Thoughts

After reviewing the answers to the verbal assessment of the lesson she had conducted with Edith, Ms. Oliver is amazed how much of the concept Edith had understood and was able to express, even if the communication had been a bit taxing for the two of them. "I wonder if she entirely caught on to what causes day or night, or if I could have asked better follow-up questions to find out," she ponders. "In any case, thank goodness Ms. Montilla was early for our weekly meeting and looked over my lesson plan while I finished email responses. The illustration from her bilingual encyclopedia saved me from having to look up the terms in Spanish to label our textbook and sure freed up time to construct the sentence frames. I wouldn't even have thought of this resource without her suggestion. Everything worked more smoothly, and Edith was so much more engaged than at other times! I'll have to ask Ms. Montilla or the mentor ELD teacher about additional tips and better resources than the ones I printed off last week." It looks like the principal's hope for Ms. Oliver becoming the best teacher she can be for all students is off to a good start thanks to the assistance of her Spanish language colleague in Harveston Elementary's fourth-grade dual language program.

STOP AND REFLECT QUESTIONS

1. How can you engage your students in scientific inquiry while respecting their cultural beliefs about science, especially if their views rest on supernatural forces to explain scientific events? How would you approach the topic of scientific inquiry and the need for your MLs to participate in the activities? In other words, how would you begin the discussion on this topic?
2. We introduced the IRF (initiation/response/follow-up) approach. If you have never used it, what would impede you from trying it in your class (e.g., time required, fear of losing control of the class or having students add comments you may not be sure of). Write or reflect on anything that would stop you from implementing this approach. If you have used it, how did it encourage your students to engage in scientific discussions?

GO AND PRACTICE ACTIVITIES

1. To motivate your students toward scientific learning, you will need to conduct an informal study to determine their views on science. First, begin by exploring their attitudes toward science and how they define the study of science. Second, find out whether or not they want to work in a science-related area after high school or

college. Do not accept yes-or-no answers; have them provide detailed answers. If your MLs are at the beginning or intermediate stages of language proficiency, you will need to ask the questions in the students' native language for full comprehension. Use the information obtained to modify your lessons to motivate them toward science learning.

2. Click on the science lesson video links below and view the videos. Watch the language-intensive (TREAD-heavy) lesson first. Then watch the hands-on (SLIDE-dominant) lesson and compare how comprehensible the concepts are in each. What elements of the first lesson make it difficult for a beginning second language learner?
    a. This lesson contains a lot of verbal elements (TREAD heavy): https://player.vimeo.com/video/96802419.
    b. This lesson offers a lot of nonverbal support (SLIDE dominant): https://player.vimeo.com/video/96802417.

CHAPTER 5

Teaching Tasir to Map Data

Project-Based Learning and the Use of Technology

"Nope. That's not right! These things are for mines. Look at the website!" exclaimed Tasir. Ms. Parker could hardly believe it when she overheard Tasir's contribution to the group discussion. "Let me see, Tasir. What are you referring to?" she asked as she leaned over the worksheet and pointed. "Oh, these V shapes here, here, and here? What do the rest of you think they are? Are you sure? No? Well, if you're not sure, I suggest you look at the website Tasir found, and you can take the discussion from there," Ms. Parker said with a wink to Tasir as she walked over to the next group.

Before leaving for the day, Ms. Parker stopped by the media center to look for the English language development teacher. "Ms. Marlin, I'm glad I caught you. I wanted to let you know that I've seen some improvement in Tasir's level of engagement lately, especially since you encouraged me to try other forms of text with her. However, a week from today, we start a new unit that requires the students to sift through a lot of online text and data. Could we possibly meet this week to discuss more strategies?"

This was a really busy week for Ms. Marlin, with several faculty meetings and a baby shower she was hosting for another teacher, but she did not want to put her colleague off. Ms. Parker had really been trying to differentiate her instruction for Tasir. So, Ms. Marlin asked Ms. Parker to email her the lesson plans for the unit, promising that she would review them and get back to her in a few days.

In chapters 3, 4, and 6, we examine teaching academic subjects to multilingual learners (MLs) within self-contained academic subjects. Because Tasir is at the middle school level and project-based learning is very suitable for grades 6 through 8, we make the integration of academic subjects through project-based learning the focus of this chapter. Additionally, we address considerations for the use of instructional technology with MLs.

COMMUNICATION IN TEACHING AND LEARNING THROUGH PROJECT-BASED LEARNING

Throughout this book, we have shown that it is possible for teachers to make academic subject classroom instruction accessible for MLs, as long as teachers provide the necessary verbal and nonverbal support. In our work with multilingual learners of English (MLEs) like Tasir, we have seen repeatedly that developing English language proficiency and literacy interacts with developing knowledge and skills in academic subjects. Consequently, one of the key aspects of helping MLs meet grade-level standards is for teachers to create the instructional conditions under which the students can learn language and use language to learn content concurrently.

Project-Based Learning and Thematic Units

Originating from John Dewey's educational philosophy of solving real-life problems with hands-on activities, modern-day project-based learning (PBL) is an instructional method used with groups of students who focus on completing realistic projects that draw upon different disciplines.[1] Seen from a broad point of view, PBL both enhances students' achievement and engagement in learning[2] and offers an avenue for differentiation and student choice, which leads to increased intrinsic learner motivation.[3] It also provides an excellent means of integrating the teaching of literacy and content in the classroom because the learners engage with other students in a wide range of activities in groups while working on an authentic learning task that leads to the completion of an end product.[4] Thus, PBL also integrates various important skills such as teamwork and problem solving.[5] Teachers, acting as facilitators of learning rather than purveyors of knowledge, pay particular attention to scaffolding instruction in support of learners' investigations.

An additional advantage to PBL is that it lends itself to the use of thematic units. A thematic unit is organized around a central topic, idea, or theme and uses related activities and experiments across multiple content areas where language learning is integrated with the development of content knowledge.[6] The inherent collaborative nature of PBL and thematic units greatly benefits students as they solve real-world problem-solving scenarios, as opposed to practicing isolated skills. Because they are repeatedly exposed to a topic in different subject areas, students are afforded longer exposure to the academic content, and they profit from the in-depth learning experiences as various aspects of the academic content are put into meaningful association.[7]

Teachers can employ various communication technologies to offer opportunities for students to search for and interpret information and produce solutions in addition to delivering their lessons with the time-tried use of PowerPoint or Canva and utilizing the internet to download pictures, graphs, or videos to provide visual enhancements for their lessons, For instance, experts can be brought in through videoconferencing (e.g., a physicist can demonstrate how a Tesla coil produces high-frequency, alternating-current electricity or a civil rights leader can relate their experience in attending rallies), or classes across the nation (or internationally) can connect through social media as they research, observe, and report observations of bird migration. Technology-supported connections like these can serve as springboards for a thematic unit, research activities, and culminating events.

Project-Based Learning and Thematic Instruction with Multilingual Learners

There is a growing body of evidence that PBL is an effective means of promoting oral language and literacy development for MLs, especially for students learning English in non-English-speaking contexts.[8] Studies have found that these MLEs enjoy and are motivated by PBL, which increases their engagement and interaction in learning the academic subjects and language.[9] In one of the investigations on the use of technology for PBL, teachers saw value in pairing MLEs with English-proficient students because the ample opportunities for interaction led to increased curriculum-related conversation. Students became "language models and language brokers with their peers, relying on each other for help in revising and polishing."[10]

As we discussed in chapter 1, learning through language and learning language occur during meaningful interactions with content and with others. We submit that PBL and thematic instruction bring tremendous value in MLs' academic and personal growth *for this very reason.* The rich contexts PBL creates through the authentic, real-life application of content and language facilitate second language acquisition for the following reasons:

1. MLs get more time to recognize and practice using topic-specific academic vocabulary and phrasing from across content areas than would be possible in a single content-area unit.
2. MLs get to practice their listening and speaking skills as they collaborate with more advanced users of the target language when researching a topic, searching for a solution to the given problem, writing a report, and making an oral presentation that represents the group's end product.
3. MLs get to interact with the content and academic language in a safe environment as they complete projects in collaborative groups, which reduces the anxiety they might experience in whole-group discussions.

When implementing PBL and/or thematic units with or without the use of technology, it is valuable to remember that MLs may need access to a different set of resources than native speakers because the way the information is organized and conveyed has to be compatible with their second language (L2) proficiency levels, just like they would in traditional lessons.[11] At the same time, some native speaking students who encounter difficulty with reading and writing academic language may benefit from the same support given to MLs.

In dual language programs, PBL benefits instruction in both languages used in the classroom. One outstanding benefit that PBL offers dual language programs is its natural way of bridging academic language between the two languages used for instruction. For programs that alternate languages by blocks of time during a day, by day of the week, or even by weeks, an ongoing project can alternate from one language to the other as students work through each stage of its completion. This allows for transferring terminology and phrasing learned in one language to the other in an intentional way, rather than reteaching the discipline-specific language and concepts during blocks when the partner language is used or by leaving the transfer from one language to the other to chance.

The Use of Technology with Multilingual Learners

Technology offers myriad avenues to support MLs' specific needs. Many teachers use the internet to locate alternative sources of information for MLs who may not have developed high reading skills or download images to offer visual supports in text-rich lessons or use electronic translators in a variety of situations. Others may assign an ML to regularly complete grammar-based modules on the computer that are designed to address the particular developmental needs of the student at their proficiency level, or they may use a number of apps on mobile devices to provide on-the-spot tutoring, also geared toward the ML's particular language or background needs. Technology often plays a key role in PBL because it allows teachers to design learning experiences in multiple modalities and at different levels of complexity, thus creating conditions in which their students' various needs can be met.[12] When implementing technology with whole groups, however, teachers should take into account that not all tools that are appropriate for native speaking students are equally beneficial for MLs.

When considering the inclusion of technology in academic-subject classes with one or more MLs, teachers should keep in mind the distinction between synchronous and asynchronous technologies. Synchronous communication can be enticing for students because it involves direct social interaction with others through, for instance, a discussion platform or videoconferencing. MLs at beginning levels are unlikely to benefit from these interactions because they require quick comprehension of what is said and equally quick language production in response. MLs at higher levels, although more able to participate, may still feel reluctant to engage because the immediacy of the interaction does not allow them to carefully plan their responses so as to avoid miscommunication and errors. Asynchronous modes, such as email or the construction of a blog, a multimedia presentation on Canva, or a web page, remove the need for immediate reaction and language production, which can lower anxiety.

In chapter 1, we discussed optimal conditions for second language acquisition, referring to comprehensible input, interaction, and output. Within this framework, in table 5.1, we categorize some of the more common technological tools (by no means a complete list) that content-area teachers can consider.[13] It is imperative that the selection and implementation of technology tools be in tune with the ML's level of L2 proficiency.

TABLE 5.1
Useful Technology Tools for Content Instruction

Input	Interaction	Output
• Audio recording—lecture or read-aloud • Smartboard (with audio, glossaries, etc.) • Multimedia presentation (PowerPoint, Canva) • Web-based research • Information apps (e.g., TED, Night Sky) • Artificial Intelligence	• Web page creation • Email, texts • Online Discussion platforms (e.g., Yellowdig, Packback) • Videoconferencing (e.g., Zoom, FaceTime) • Digital storytelling • Smartboard • Artificial Intelligence	• PowerPoint, Canva • Online presentation tools (e.g., Nearpod, Flipgrid) • Blog entry • Video demonstration • Digital storytelling, with audio recording • Web page creation • Video creation apps

ESSENTIAL POINTS

1. PBL and thematic units are especially beneficial for MLs because they integrate language learning with academic content, promoting deeper engagement, critical thinking, and opportunities for students to practice academic language in context. Thematic units, where subjects are connected around a central theme, provide extended exposure to academic vocabulary and concepts, enhancing both language and content mastery.
2. Technology plays a key role in PBL because it offers multiple ways for students to engage with content. It also supports differentiated learning by allowing MLs to explore topics through various modalities, providing language skills (speaking, listening, reading, and writing) practice while reinforcing content knowledge in more motivating and relevant ways than traditional methods.
3. Asynchronous tools like blogs, video creation, and online presentations can reduce anxiety, giving students more time to process and produce language, which is key to their language development and academic success. Synchronous tools such as videoconferencing with experts or live chats foster direct social interaction with others while learning content and using academic language. Either way, technology tools need to be tailored to students' proficiency levels.

The following section describes a social studies/geography PBL unit and presents the details on how the Supportive Classroom Communication Protocol is applied to the unit with the needs of MLEs at Tasir's oral proficiency level in mind.

CLASSROOM APPLICATION

The district seventh-grade benchmark test results were low. The principal called an emergency meeting with all department chairs, instructional coaches, and guidance counselors. "I'm not interested in placing blame for these disappointing results. That won't change the reality that our seventh graders are not learning enough. All I am saying is we have *got* to try something different *now.* We can't afford to continue like this," said Mr. Phillips. After a deep breath, he stretched his arms out, holding them just above the tabletop, palms up, and continued, "I'm open to suggestions. Any and all ideas will be considered, as long as there is some evidence that whatever we're going to do has had success in other schools." After a long silence, a few ideas were brought up. An hour later, the team had reached consensus on what should and could be done but only after Mr. Phillips promised that he would support the changes by freeing up the seventh-grade teachers on a regular basis to collaborate on planning. Their goal was to implement thematic units across the content areas.

Excited yet equally unsure about how the switch to an integrated thematic instructional model would work out, the seventh-grade team chose the theme of renewable energy to begin. They settled on three essential questions: (1) How do households use renewable and nonrenewable energy sources? (2) How can the physical environment impact resource use? (3) And how does energy use impact economic decisions? Because all of the teachers were new to thematic units across a grade level, the team decided to implement individual smaller projects for each content area, each of which would inform at least one other area, rather than trying to produce one large project. The following list describes the main objectives for the project in each content area.

- Science—Identify renewable energy sources for noncommercial use in various geographic regions in the United States.
- Social studies/geography—Investigate geological formations and climate conditions, as well as energy consumption of rural and urban centers in the United States through geographic information system (GIS) mapping.
- Mathematics—Considering the cost of original investment and cost recovery, develop a budget for a household of five that converts to renewable energy.
- Language arts—Write a persuasive essay to a city council, county commission, or state legislature supporting or opposing incentives for converting to renewable energy sources (to be highlighted in chapter 10).

GIS MAPPING LESSON DESCRIPTION

Since attending a professional development workshop several years ago that introduced her to GIS mapping, Ms. Parker had used the new tool just a handful of times to show her students the difference between traditional maps and GIS. This would be the first time her students would create their own maps using this technology. Cognizant that general reading and communication skills would be necessary to complete the cross-disciplinary project, she decided to investigate the state standards for social studies and for literacy/language arts, as well as the national geography standards.[14] She then designed the lesson around pieces already in place from her prior lessons using GIS maps.[15]

OBJECTIVES

- The student will be able to research and collect data and visually display it through GIS mapping.
- The student will be able to identify and categorize existing or potentially available renewable energy sources based on geographic formations and locations.
- The student will be able to connect the availability of renewable energy sources to their utility for given population centers.

INTRODUCTION

Project a traditional street-level map of an area that has several lakes or rivers; ask what it is and what it is used for. Display side by side the same map, a satellite view of the area, and a GIS view with the area's flood zones, each with a caption explaining what it is. Solicit from the students the ways in which the maps are similar and different. Give an operational definition of GIS mapping. Tell the students to brainstorm what a GIS flood zone map could be used for. Inform the students that they will use GIS maps to investigate the current and potential future use of renewable energy in a county or city assigned to them.[16]

LESSON STEPS

1. Present the National Renewable Energy Laboratory website, spending some time on the Geospacial Data Science Data and Tools page to show various maps and review vocabulary from science and geography.[17]
2. Assign a mix of rural areas and urban centers in the United States to groups of four students.
3. Provide groups with various web-based and printed text resources to research assigned areas.[18] Each group designs a plan for researching needed data points (e.g., energy consumption, existing options for renewable energy sources), selects information sources, writes bullet summaries of findings to be used in presentation planning, and builds the GIS map.[19]
4. Each group creates a PowerPoint, Canva, or interactive whiteboard presentation and rehearses and reports their findings and conclusions to the entire class.

EVALUATION

Rubrics for (1) accuracy and details of the produced GIS map and (2) presentation.

APPLICATION OF THE SUPPORTIVE CLASSROOM COMMUNICATION PROTOCOL TO THE GIS MAPPING LESSON

Due to her recent interactions with the English language development (ELD) specialist regarding Tasir's affect during class time and her language growth needs, Ms. Parker was quite familiar with Tasir's proficiency levels. Thus, she skipped reviewing the WIDA proficiency level descriptors and started applying the Supportive Classroom Communication Protocol to her updated GIS lesson plan.

STEP 1

Analyze Communication in Lesson Tasks

This section describes the steps to analyze the language demands of the lesson tasks based on the underlined verbs and verb phrases in the lesson description as the basis to determining necessary verbal and nonverbal support for Tasir's successful participation in the GIS mapping lesson. Table 2.2 on page 56 provides sample verbs that indicate whether a lesson task is primarily completed through nonverbal (SLIDE) or verbal (TREAD) actions.

ANALYZE SLIDE

The hands-on portions of the lesson provide multiple opportunities for students and Ms. Parker to connect with the content through nonverbal means:

- Teacher: displaying maps
- Teacher: modeling how GIS software works
- Students: constructing their own maps
- Students: including visuals in the technology-based presentation

ANALYZE TREAD

There are numerous lesson tasks that require oral language communication (L = listening, S = speaking) between all classroom participants as well as literacy skills (R = reading, W = writing) for researching the assigned area and presenting the findings. *From their point of view*, the students will experience and use language as follows:

- Teacher: defining and explaining GIS maps (L)
- Teacher and students: discussing similarities and differences of the two map types (L/S)
- Student groups: brainstorming use of GIS flood zone map (L, S)
- Student groups: discussing how to design the research plan (L, S)
- Students: skimming written resources (R)
- Students: participating in research (R), interpretation (L, S, R, W), and discussion of information (L, S)
- Students: producing (L, S, R, W) and delivering (S) the presentation to the class

The SLIDE and TREAD analyses showed that although he lesson naturally contains many visual elements such as images and hands-on application, large portions of learning the subject of GIS mapping are language dependent. Ms. Parker knew right away that she would find several sizable gaps between these demands and Tasir's current level of English proficiency, and started to search for the precise locations.

Size the Gaps

Ms. Parker's familiarity with Tasir's linguistic strengths and challenges based on the WIDA ACCESS Report and her observations, as previously stated, would not necessitate her looking them over before deciding on appropriate nonverbal and verbal supports. We display the proficiency level descriptors in table 5.2 and examine them for those less familiar with WIDA or the process of second language acquisition.

TABLE 5.2
Tasir's WIDA Proficiency Level Descriptors (Grades 1–12)

Domain	Level	Students at this Level Generally can . . .
Listening	4	. . . understand oral language in English related to specific topics in school and can participate in class discussions, for example: • Exchange information and ideas with others • Connect people and events based on oral information • Apply key information about processes or concepts presented orally • Identify positions or points of view on issues in oral discussions
Speaking	5	. . . use English to communicate orally and participate in all academic classes, for example: • Discuss the causes and impact of events • Summarize and relate information • Present and justify ideas showing how or why • Express and defend opinions backed by examples and reasons
Reading	2	. . . understand written language related to common topics in school and can participate in class discussions, for example: • Identify main ideas in written information • Identify main actors and events in stories and simple texts with pictures or graphs • Sequence pictures, events, or steps in processes • Distinguish between claim and evidence statements
Writing	2	. . . communicate by writing in English using language related to common topics in school, for example: • Describe ideas or concepts using phrases or short sentences • Label illustrations describing what, when, or where something happened • State steps in processes or procedures • Express opinions about specific topics or situations

Tasir's advanced levels of oral proficiency will allow her to exchange information and ideas, verbally summarize information, express her opinion with her group members, and listen to the teacher's presentation. Her reading skill level, which is well below her oral proficiency, allows her to pull out important information on familiar topics and identify main ideas and events from *simple* text for the research phase.[20] Related to the presentation, Tasir's writing proficiency level, which is also well below her oral proficiency, enables her to place labels, describe concepts in short sentences, and state steps. Let us now consider the magnitude of the gap caused by the language-dependent tasks.

- No gap: Being assigned to a group is the only place in this lesson that does not present a challenge for Tasir.
- Small gaps: The whole-class discussion during introduction is manageable because not too many technical terms are used.

  The visual aspects of watching Ms. Parker present the renewable energy website and demonstrate tools on the GIS site facilitate the comprehension of what the class will be learning and doing.

  Tasir will likely have some difficulty with some of the recently acquired terms from the science portion of the thematic unit (e.g., geothermal, solar, wind turbine) or of geography-specific words (e.g., surface area, stream, shoreline, wind direction, mountainous, community) because she was not able to retain them well on those days when the instruction moved too quickly for her.
- Medium gaps: Learning new vocabulary specific to mapping (e.g., legend, layers, attribute, feature, coordinates) will be difficult for Tasir who expressed frustration at being rushed to the next point just as she started to catch on. If she does not get a good grasp on the vocabulary when first encountered, she will not apply it correctly while designing and constructing the map, and it will impact her participation in creating the presentation slides.

  To interact with her peers while deciding on research points to include and building the map in meaningful ways will require Tasir to hear and use new academic vocabulary.
- Large gaps: The research and selection of available resources will take place through websites and other reading materials supplied by Ms. Parker that are written at grade level and thus well above Tasir's level 2 in reading.

  Because her writing skills enable Tasir to apply labels to the map and write phrases and short sentences for the research summary points, writing a script for her part of the presentation will be demanding. Although Tasir will have rehearsed the script with her group members, she will still be nervous to deliver her part because of the academic terms and having all eyes on her instead of talking in the small group.

With this information in hand, Ms. Parker can move to narrowing the gaps by adding nonverbal and verbal supports.

Address the Gaps Between MLs' L2 Proficiency and Lesson Tasks

ADDING NONVERBAL SUPPORTS

Whether it is reviewing vocabulary from the science unit or her own geography class or teaching the new terms for GIS mapping, Ms. Parker should remember that MLEs at or below Tasir's proficiency level do better when they see what they hear. Therefore, she could write the words and short definitions on the board while going over them and accompany that with a quick drawing whenever possible. In a similar vein, if she pointed to the various map views and satellite image when brainstorming in the introduction phase of the lesson, she would connect spoken language with visuals. These *universal* supports benefit Tasir and her peers alike.

For the research component of the lesson that involves selecting information from web pages and magazine articles on geological formations and energy consumption in urban and rural areas, Ms. Parker decided that she would augment the textual information with graphics from textbooks or online images for Tasir, making this a *supplemental* support.

ADDING VERBAL SUPPORTS

The largest and most crucial undertaking in narrowing the verbal gaps in this language-heavy lesson is to facilitate Tasir's access to written materials. Without that, she won't be able to actively participate in researching and making decisions on the group's map design. Ms. Parker could create the following *supplemental* materials for Tasir:

- Highlight important vocabulary or phrases to draw attention to the portions of the text necessary to fully comprehend
- Reduce the amount of text by simplifying it in phrasing
- Augment text through graphics (as listed in the section above)

Ms. Parker could further aid Tasir's wading through the written materials by assigning her to a group of students who model good reading strategies. This strategic move is not a verbal support but one that, when done repeatedly, could help Tasir develop better reading comprehension in the long run.

To promote vocabulary retention and usage, Ms. Parker should also provide a list of the necessary terms and definitions for consultation during the research and design phases. Because this resource will be available to all students, it is *universal* support, but it is critical that Tasir be reminded to use the resource throughout the lesson.[21]

Of course, whether during whole-class instruction time or when checking in on the group's progress, leveled questioning targeted at Tasir's proficiency level (*supplemental* support) is critical. Furthermore by modeling where information can be found (in text or images and labels) and reminding Tasir to use the group's summary bullets as starting points to write her script, Ms. Parker can lay the foundation for helping her elaborate on the subject or make her sentences more complex, where appropriate, once they reach that point in the lesson because Tasir would have something to build on.

One additional *supplemental* verbal support Ms. Parker could provide for Tasir would be to find time and space for Tasir to practice the script away from the group so that she can concentrate on the text without the risk of getting distracted if she stumbles.[22]

Managing Grouping, Time, and Provider

All suggested nonverbal and verbal supports should be adequate to narrow the classroom communication gap during the whole-group lesson or while the groups work together. Other than Tasir's individual script practice prior to the presentation, there is no need to preteach any portions or follow up with support. Ideally, this would take place the day before the presentation, while Tasir's group members put finishing touches on the presentation slides.

If available, an aide or volunteer could help prepare the modified materials (e.g., adding graphics, highlighting important vocabulary/phrases, adding graphics, or simplifying some textual density). Another option would be the use of an artificial intelligence (AI) tool (see appendix C for suggestions). If a classroom aide with experience working with MLEs at an advanced oral language proficiency level was present on a given day, they could ensure that Tasir uses the verbal supports and also check on her understanding through leveled questioning, but Ms. Parker felt confident that she could successfully deliver these supports on her own.

TABLE 5.3

Support for Beginning and Intermediate Multilingual Learners

Oral Proficiency	**Providing Nonverbal Support**	**Providing Verbal Support**
Beginning	• Label social studies chart for climate conditions, geological formations, and energy consumption (with pictures) for the student to refer to throughout the project. • Point to maps and map features and use gestures when soliciting responses from students. • Provide illustrated instructions in chronological order for the project.	• Provide first language support through a bilingual aide, if available. • Reinforcement of science lesson concept: Show video of alternative energy sources or teacher-created PowerPoint slides with pertinent vocabulary highlighted. Student then completes sentence frames, such as "Power from [water] is called [hydro]." These sentences can then be used for creating the bulleted list and during the presentation. • Provide simplified text (with pictures) geared to proficiency level for research. • Student is not expected to speak in full sentences during presentation.
Intermediate	• Same as first and second supports listed above but to a lesser degree.	• Simplified (highlighted) and elaborated (with translated specialized terms) text geared to proficiency level • Graphic organizer to organize/condense information • Paired writing

INSTRUCTIONAL SUPPORT FOR OTHER MULTILINGUAL LEARNERS

Based on the SLIDE and TREAD analysis and the nonverbal and verbal supports Ms. Parker could select for Tasir, table 5.3 shows possible supports in the GIS lesson for assisting learners at a beginning or intermediate oral proficiency.

Lesson Summary

Table 5.4 provides an overview of the Supportive Classroom Communication protocol applied to Ms. Parker's original GIS lesson plan. The first column displays the nonverbal (SLIDE) elements underlined and the verbal components (TREAD) in **boldface** of the lesson's tasks. Both fonts **combined** show that a task can contain both nonverbal and verbal elements, such as reading or writing and referring to visual elements.

The second column lists the language skills associated with the tasks *from the point of view of the students* and gives a visual depiction of the size gap Ms. Parker discovered between the classroom communication in each lesson step and Tasir's current English proficiency. The third column shows the planned nonverbal and verbal supports.

Final Thoughts

Ms. Parker can expect a positive impact on Tasir's affect when looking over the changes she made to the original plan by adding the verbal and nonverbal supports. The actions set Tasir up for success first and foremost by her selection of the group membership and by providing modified written materials. By consulting a highlighted text with a few additional images and graphs that focus her attention on pertinent information and vocabulary and reading texts with simplified phrasing, Tasir is able to keep pace with the group while observing good reading strategies practiced by her peers. This, in turn, builds confidence to actively contribute to the discussion and the design of the map. Similarly, having access to the bulleted summary points from the research phase when writing her script facilitates Tasir's interaction with her group members, which reduces her apprehensiveness to share with the whole class. Such successes enhance a multilingual student's self-esteem and undoubtedly motivate them to take risks in the future.

At the conclusion of the team meeting during which all teachers debriefed their colleagues on the challenges and successes of the thematic unit on renewable energy, Ms. Parker composes a thank-you note to Ms. Marlin for her assistance in determining the best types of verbal support in preparation for the GIS lesson. "I'm sorry you had to fill in for a colleague on the day Tasir's group presented their map and didn't see her in action," she starts out. "Your suggestion to schedule time to rehearse the script as a group first made a big difference. I made a point of telling the other faculty today how that contributed to Tasir's self-confidence when speaking to the rest of the class and want you to know how much I appreciate your insights and collaboration." After putting the note

TABLE 5.4

The GIS Mapping Lesson at a Glance

Lesson Steps	Skills and Gap Size[1]	Added Supports[3]
Project a traditional street-level map of an area that has several lakes or rivers; **ask** what it is and what it is used for. Display side by side the same map, a satellite view of the area, and a GIS view with the area's flood zones, each with a caption **explaining** what it is. **Solicit** from the students the ways in which the maps are similar and different. **Give an operational definition** of GIS mapping. **Tell** the students to **brainstorm** what a GIS flood zone map could be used for. **Inform** the students that they will use GIS maps to **investigate** the current and potential future use of renewable energy in a county or city assigned to them.	L, S, R ↕	***Nonverbal Support:*** Point to images/maps. ***Verbal Support:*** Write an operational definition of GIS mapping on the board.
Present the National Renewable Energy Laboratory website, spending some time on Geospatial Data Science Data and Tools page to show various maps and **review** vocabulary from science and geography.	L, S, R Website presentation and vocabulary review: ↕ New vocabulary: ↕↕	***Nonverbal Support:*** Point to terms listed in verbal supports. ***Verbal Support:*** Write terms and definitions on board.
Assign a mix of rural areas and urban centers in the United States to groups of four students.	L Ø	No supports needed
Provide individual groups with various web-based and printed **text resources** to research assigned areas. Each group **designs a plan** for **researching** needed data points (e.g., energy consumption, existing options for renewable energy sources), **selects** information sources, **writes** bullet summaries of findings to be used in presentation planning, and **builds** the GIS map.	L, S, R, W Research and selection of resources: ↕↕↕	***Nonverbal Support:*** See simplified text in verbal support. ***Verbal Supports:*** • Provide a copy of the challenging terms and definitions of new vocabulary for the group. • Create simplified text, elaborated with images/drawings of some research materials (supplemental). • Highlight important vocabulary/phrases in some research materials (supplemental). • Make sure Tasir uses modified research texts to write summary bullets (supplemental). • Have check-ins with Tasir, using leveled questioning and referring to vocabulary lists, images, etc. (supplemental).

Continued...

TABLE 5.4

The GIS Mapping Lesson at a Glance *(Continued...)*

Lesson Steps	Skills and Gap Size[1]	Added Supports[3]
Each group **creates** a PowerPoint, Canva, or interactive whiteboard presentation and **rehearses** and **reports** its findings and conclusions to the class.	L, S, R, W Presentation creation: ↕↕ Script writing and delivery: ↕↕↕	***Verbal Supports:*** • Make sure Tasir uses summary bullets for writing script. • Have check-ins with Tasir to help elaborate sentences (supplemental). • Practice script without peers.
Evaluation: Rubrics for (1) accuracy and details of the produced GIS map and (2) presentation	R, S ↕	***Verbal Support:*** Small allowances for occasional hesitations or fillers (e.g., uhm)

Key:
1 Language Skills: L = listening, S = speaking, R = reading, W = writing
2 Gap sizes: No gap = Ø, ↕ = small gap, ↕↕ = medium gap, ↕↕↕ = large gap
3 Unless otherwise noted, all supports are considered universal.

into Ms. Marlin's mailbox, Ms. Parker writes herself a note to upload presentations to the class website and send the link to the parents. As she grabs her bag, she smiles. "I can't wait to talk to them about this project at the next parent-teacher conferences."

STOP AND REFLECT QUESTIONS

1. What is your perception of PBL? Do you think it is an effective approach for teaching MLs, or is it too heavily language based and time consuming to be implemented?
2. What are the benefits of engaging students in activities to solve real-world problems?

GO AND PRACTICE ACTIVITIES

1. Go to a project-based learning site. Explore the various projects students are engaged in at the elementary or secondary levels or create one on your own. Once you have decided on the guiding question, identify the areas where your MLs might need verbal and nonverbal support so that they can participate in the project, regardless of their current proficiency level.

2. Many MLEs come from countries where technology is not as readily available as in the United States, but they often possess a collection of technological knowledge and related language when they come to this country. Naturally, many terms experience phonological and morphological variations when spoken in other countries, but the resemblance to English remains obvious. For example, in Haitian Kreyòl, imèl is the same as email; Facebook enjoys the same spelling, but the emphasis is placed on the second syllable instead of the first. Despite minor differences in pronunciation, the words are easily understood by both speakers of English and Haitian Kreyòl. To determine just how much your MLEs know about technology terms and how to interact with multimedia, create a list of technology-related words used in English and have them circle the familiar words. This simple survey will allow you to assign tasks or assignments using technology with full confidence that your students know and understand those words and the devices.

Teaching Edgar Algebra

The Challenge of Word Problems in Math

"Paige . . . Jared . . . Marquise . . . Edgar . . . Edgar, where's Edgar?"
Mr. Leibniz peered over his reading glasses just as the door handle clicked. "Edgar, you're late." Engrossed by the impending confrontation, those in attendance watched the tardy student. "I just come from ELD. Ms. Myers want me for help new student." Edgar held up a folded slip of paper, set it on Mr. Leibniz's desk, and walked to his seat.

It wasn't the first time Edgar had been late, but not one second of the remaining forty-five minutes could be wasted on verifying the note. That would have to wait. Mr. Leibniz approached the whiteboard, uncapped a red marker, and began. "Bobby is four times as old as Sally. Twelve years ago, Bobby was seven times as old as Sally. How old is Sally now?"

Edgar leaned toward his classmate in the next row, squinting to see what he was writing. "So what's the unknown?" Mr. Leibniz asked as he pointed to Edgar. "Let's hear from Mr. Punctuality. Yes, you, Edgar. What's the unknown?"
"I dunno," said Edgar as the class started laughing. "I dunno what is unknow."
Mr. Leibniz approached Edgar's desk. "Very funny, Edgar. But you'd better get serious about doing your homework, getting to class on time, and paying attention when you're here or you'll never pass Algebra 1." Edgar looked straight ahead, silent and expressionless, lest he lock eyes with the math teacher instigating this confusing and aggravating exchange. "I can't waste any more time here," Mr. Leibniz said as he moved toward the front row. "Let's hear from someone who knows the unknown. Paige, what is it?" Edgar slid low in his chair, crossed his arms on the desk, and put his head down.

COMMUNICATION IN TEACHING AND LEARNING MATHEMATICS

In many ways, mathematics is a universal language; fundamental mathematical operations such as addition, subtraction, multiplication, and division are present in all languages regardless of culture or location. Even though fundamental principles may be universal, the way mathematics is taught and assessed varies widely across the globe. In many countries, subtraction is tested using simple math equations, such as 6 – 4= ___? However, in the United States, math assessment relies heavily on word problems. Word problems are short passages containing a question that requires working with numbers provided indirectly in the passage. In a study that looked at how language affects math problem solving, Walter Kintsch found that native English speakers performed 10 to 30 percent worse on mathematical tasks using words rather than numbers.[1] Scholars such as Huang and Normandia assert that the common practice of focusing on key words in word problems is inadequate because many problems lack key words, and for those that do include them, the actual meaning of the details that convey mathematical reasoning may be revealed through sentence structure and other grammatical features.[2] Let's look at a typical word problem for a tenth-grade student and then consider a few issues that teachers of multilingual learners of English (MLEs) like Edgar should keep in mind when they teach how to translate word problems into equations.

> If a tire rotates at 500 revolutions per minute when the car is traveling 81 km/h, what is its circumference?

First, to be able to solve this word problem, learners must be able to comprehend most if not all the words that make up the mathematical statement. Moreover, words often have multiple meanings, and MLE students must grasp the precise meaning used in the problem. These students know that they must be able to unlock the meaning of every key word, almost in a linear fashion, because there is little narrative context to help them figure it out. Therefore, unknown words will prevent MLEs from putting ideas together to form a story line. For example, the key word in the problem is *tire*. Depending on their levels of language proficiency and reading ability, some MLEs might be able to skip the unknown word and move forward in the problem, but most would lack the confidence to do this because they get hung up on the meaning of the word *tire*. The same applies to the other key words of the problem, *revolutions* and *circumference*, both academic terms.

Second, the question segment of the word problem itself (i.e., "what is its circumference?") may be confusing to some MLEs because the key word *tire* has been replaced by the possessive determiner *its*. Most native English speakers will not even notice that *tire* is not present in the question because they instinctively know what *its* relates to. MLEs, however, might have to work a bit harder to puzzle it out. Finally, it is worth stressing that word problems are predominant in math assessments. For example, Coombe, Folse, and Hubley analyzed the standardized assessment tests for grade 4 and found that none of the forty items were expressed as a simple numerical problem.[3] Additionally, 65 percent of the questions in the test were word problems accompanied by a map, a geometric figure, or a table of data. The other 35 percent of questions were word problems without any nonverbal support.

Focus on Vocabulary

Experienced mathematics teachers know that words have multiple meanings, which ultimately impacts the teaching and learning of mathematics to all students, native speakers included. They know that some of the words used in mathematics are also found in everyday language and across other academic subjects such as science and social studies. However, when conveying mathematical concepts, these polysemous words have specialized meanings that must be taught in the context of mathematics. For example, words such as *combine*, *describe*, or *analyze* are used in various subject areas, whereas mathematics involves words (e.g., *average*, *angle*, or *number*) that are often but not exclusively associated with mathematics concepts. Still other words (e.g., *asymptote*, *logarithm*, or *cosine*) are technical terms that have specific meanings in mathematics.[4]

One additional complexity of mathematics vocabulary is that similar mathematical concepts may be taught and used in assessments in different ways. For example, MLEs must know that the operation of addition can be signaled by any of these six words: *add*, *and*, *plus*, *combine*, *sum*, and *increased by*. MLEs often have difficulty understanding the use of prepositions when solving math word problems—for example, *divided by* as opposed to *divided into*.[5]

Language experts Lily Wong-Fillmore and Catherine Snow identified words that are challenging for MLEs.[6] These include terms that express various kinds of quantitative relationships as well as everyday words that provide logical connections in sentences found in typical math word problems. Words that indicate quantitative relationships include *hardly*, *scarcely*, *rarely*, *next*, *last*, *most*, *many*, *less*, *longer*, *older*, *younger*, *least*, and *higher*. Words that indicate logical relationships include *if*, *because*, *unless*, *alike*, *same*, *different from*, *opposite of*, *whether*, *since*, *unless*, *almost*, *probably*, *exactly*, *not quite*, *always*, and *never*. MLEs need extra support in comprehending the various meanings of these words, which may be nuanced and even change depending on the context. As with discipline-specific terms in other subjects, many of these words have one meaning for general use and a specialized meaning in mathematics.

Complex math expressions often contain words with specific meanings. The phrase *least common multiple* is an example of a problematic math phrase that MLEs might have difficulty comprehending. It is hard for MLEs to grasp the specialized math meaning of the phrase if they attempt to process it word by word using a dictionary, as they would normally do for isolated words. In this case, the math instruction should treat the phrase as an indivisible "chunk," meaning that when MLEs see it, they should not attempt to separate it into components and get the meaning of each element.

TEACHING MULTILINGUAL LEARNERS MATHEMATICS

The above examples illustrate the important role vocabulary plays in understanding mathematics and in doing well in mathematics assessments, especially for students like Edgar, whose language proficiency is still developing. We suggest that a mathematics classroom can be a rich environment for learning language as well as math, as long as teachers help ensure that MLs are supported with both nonverbal and verbal communication.

Clearly language is an essential part of mathematics. Even though the primary goal of disciplinary subject instruction for MLs is to master the content of the discipline, mathematics teachers play a critical role in these students' second language development through a focus on successful communication of mathematics. For instance, when teaching students to solve math problems using mathematical expressions that contain technical terms with specific meanings, teachers should provide verbal support that goes beyond word definitions. In fact, they can help make mathematical concepts much more comprehensible by incorporating nonverbal support such as visuals and gestures, and by providing adequate verbal support to make oral presentations, reading materials, and other relevant media accessible to MLs. In addition, mathematics teachers can help MLs interact with the teacher or other students, fostering their verbal exchanges with nonverbal support and language adjusted to their L2 proficiency. Finally, teachers may want to engage students in assessment activities that will help determine whether they have actually learned the mathematical concepts taught and to what extent they can solve the problems posed. These types of supported communication strategies are likely to advance students' mathematical knowledge while simultaneously improving their L2 development.

ESSENTIAL POINTS

1. Word problems in mathematics are a common challenge for MLs, particularly because they rely heavily on academic vocabulary and complex sentence structures. Students like Edgar must not only understand key mathematical terms but also interpret them in the context of the problem.
2. Mathematical terms often overlap with everyday language but carry specialized meanings, and words like *sum* or *divide* can differ in nuance when used in math. Teachers should explicitly teach the meanings of mathematical terms and expressions, such as *least common multiple*, that cannot be easily understood by breaking the phrase down word by word. Providing clear, context-specific explanations is crucial for MLs' success.
3. To teach the content and support language development, effective math instruction for multilingual learners involves nonverbal strategies, such as realia, visuals, and gestures, to aid verbal communication. Encouraging student interaction, supporting language during problem solving, and using assessments that evaluate both content knowledge and language proficiency will help students like Edgar succeed in math, improve their second language skills, and ensure they are not only learning math but also developing the language skills needed to express and understand mathematical concepts.

CLASSROOM APPLICATION

After reviewing the results from the chapter test on multistep equations, Mr. Leibniz walked into the teachers' lounge. "What's up, Mr. Leibniz?" asked Mr. Otto, the science teacher. "You don't look particularly happy today."

Mr. Leibniz let out a long sigh and started a rant: "My third-period kids are driving me nuts! They don't listen in class. They don't do homework. Heck, they don't even copy the solutions I write on the board. Look at these test results!" Mr. Leibniz held up a stack of papers. "Not even half of them are going to pass the end-of-course exam! Edgar in particular is a problem. Even when he does show up on time, he disengages the moment I start talking. And the attitude of that kid!" He saw his colleagues nodding with understanding. Only Mr. Otto, a second-year teacher who was new to Highpoint High, seemed doubtful. Although Mr. Otto had his own struggles with Edgar's lack of enthusiasm for school, he felt for him. "Well," he said, "I don't know what Edgar's issues are in your class, but I had a pretty similar experience with him in the first few weeks of the school year. My wife who is an instructional coach in middle school suggested that I start to break explanations, directions, and tasks into more digestible chunks." Mr. Leibniz turned toward his colleague. "Not only did several of my usual troublemakers start paying better attention," Mr. Otto continued, "but I've even caught Edgar making more of an effort. In my case, I found that occasional direct instruction mixes things up and works quite well. I'm not sure, but maybe the regular comprehension checks keep them engaged. Maybe it'll work for you." With twenty years of teaching experience, Mr. Leibniz was tempted to disregard the unsolicited advice from a newcomer, but then he said, "Maybe you're right. Maybe it's worth trying something different."

ALGEBRA WORD PROBLEMS LESSON DESCRIPTION

After Mr. Leibniz decided to give direct instruction a try, he did more than simply redesign his original lesson. Instead, he decided to start as far back as explaining necessary vocabulary, such as *variable*, *algebraic expressions*, and *algebraic equations*. Let's see how Mr. Leibniz put Mr. Otto's suggestions into action.

OBJECTIVES

- The student will be able to translate sentences into algebraic expressions with 85 percent accuracy.
- The student will be able to translate sentences into algebraic equations with 85 percent accuracy.
- The student will be able to correctly solve four out of five equations with two variables.

INTRODUCTION

Tell the students that because of yesterday's chapter test results, the class will have to repeat the entire chapter so that everyone can comprehend the material and clear up any misunderstandings.[7] Give the good news: by going back, they will do better on the chapter test retake and be better prepared to *successfully* move through the next chapters.[8]

LESSON STEPS

1. Display vocabulary on a projector (e.g., *variable, algebraic expressions, algebraic equations, formula, solve, evaluate, proof*).
2. Ask the students to define/explain the terms, elaborating upon their responses, correcting misconceptions, and explaining any terms they don't know.
3. Show several sentences (e.g., "five times a certain number," "five more than a certain number") and translate them into algebraic expressions.
4. Assign sentences similar to those in step 3 and direct students to translate them into algebraic expressions independently.
5. Tell the students to compare responses with a shoulder partner, and then display correct answers. Discuss and correct mistakes.
6. Show what happens when the variable (e.g., *x*, *y*, *n*) is given a number (e.g., 11) with the algebraic expressions used in step 3.
7. Tell the students to work with their shoulder partner to solve the expressions first with 7 and then with 23. Display the correct answers, discuss the results with the class, and correct mistakes.
8. Display several sentences (e.g., "9 less than a number equals 22," "The sum of 3 and a number is 34") and translate them into algebraic equations.
9. Assign ten similar sentences for students to translate as homework.

The reteaching of the chapter progresses in a similar manner for a few more days, moving from solving equations with one variable to equations with two variables, until the chapter is covered.

EVALUATION

Review daily homework for formative assessment. The end-of-chapter test is calculated into the final class grade.

APPLICATION OF THE SUPPORTIVE CLASSROOM COMMUNICATION PROTOCOL TO THE ALGEBRA WORD PROBLEMS LESSON

While Mr. Leibniz selected the mathematics vocabulary to include in the upcoming class sessions, he realized that he hadn't considered Edgar's language proficiency levels in a while and pulled out Edgar's folder. You will see Edgar's proficiency level descriptors in table 6.1 when we discuss the classroom communication gaps. For now, we're going to turn our attention to the nonverbal and verbal elements in Mr. Leibniz's new lesson plan.

STEP 1 Analyze Communication in Lesson Tasks

UNDERSTANDING THE TASK

To size up the gap between the language demands of each task in the lesson and Edgar's English proficiency, we first examine the degree of nonverbal communication (SLIDE)

TABLE 6.1

Edgar's WIDA Proficiency Level Descriptors (Grades 1–12)

Domain	Level	Students at this Level Generally can . . .
Listening	3	. . . understand oral language in English related to specific common topics in school and can participate in class discussions, for example: • Connect spoken ideas to own experiences • Find, select, or order information from oral descriptions • Identify the causes and effects of events or situations discussed orally • Classify pros and cons of issues in discussions
Speaking	2	. . . communicate ideas and information orally in English, using language that contains short sentences and everyday words and phrases, for example: • Share about what, when, or where something happened • Compare objects, people, pictures, and events • Describe steps in cycles or processes • Express opinions
Reading	1	. . . understand written texts that include visuals and may contain a few words or phrases in English, for example: • Interpret information from graphs, charts, or other visual information • Comprehend short text with illustrations and simple and familiar language • Identify steps in processes presented in graphs or short texts with illustrations • Identify words and phrases that express opinions and claims
Writing	1	. . . communicate in writing using visuals and symbols that may contain few words in English, for example: • Express ideas or concepts using text and illustrations • Share personal experiences through drawings and words • Label steps in processes presented in graphs or short texts • State opinions or preferences through text and illustrations

and then analyze the ways Edgar is required to listen, speak, read, and write (TREAD). Refer to table 2.2 (see page 56) for sample SLIDE/TREAD verbs.

ANALYZE SLIDE

If Mr. Leibniz conducted a cursory analysis of the instructional actions in this plan by looking at verbs that fall into our SLIDE and TREAD categories, he would think that the content is quite comprehensible for Edgar because he notices the verb *display* four times and *show* twice. Once he looked more closely, however, he would quickly realize that none of these actions do much to decrease the language load of the lesson for Edgar. This is because whatever he displays or shows is either text by itself (i.e., the vocabulary or sentences) or is accompanied by a verbal explanation (e.g., what happens when numbers are substituted for variables).

ANALYZE TREAD

There are a number of oral communication demands (L = listening, S = speaking) for all classroom participants, as well as literacy demands (R = reading, W = writing), in this lesson. *From the point of view of the students,* they will experience and use language as follows:

- Teacher: saying that they will have to redo the chapter (L)
- Students: reading the projected vocabulary (R)
- Students: defining and talking about the terms (L, S)
- Teacher: explaining the terms (L)
- Teacher: talking about how to translate projected sentences into algebraic expressions (R, L)
- Students: translating new sentences into algebraic expressions, discussing them with shoulder partner, and comparing them to projected answers (L, S, R, W)
- Teacher: explaining what happens with algebraic expression when a variable is given a number (L, R)
- Students: solving expressions with shoulder partner (L, S, W)
- Teacher and students: discussing correct projected results (L, S)
- Teacher: translating projected sentences into algebraic equation (R, L)
- Students: translating sentences into algebraic equations for homework (R, W)

This lesson is largely conducted through spoken and written language. A few examples illustrate this finding: students read a displayed vocabulary term and attempt to verbally define it, with Mr. Leibniz adding to their thoughts; the students are shown how to translate sentences into equations and then practice doing so with more sentences.

STEP 2

Size the Gaps

As we previously stated, once teachers are familiar with their MLEs' WIDA ACCESS Reports and have made observations of their linguistic strengths and challenges, they do not need to consult this information each time they plan instruction. Edgar's levels are shown in table 6.1 to explain the decisions Mr. Leibniz can make to support his learning in this algebra lesson.

Related to the lesson tasks, the proficiency level descriptors reveal that Edgar is able to connect with what his shoulder partner says fairly well and give his own opinion when they solve algebraic expressions or compare their results because he can relate the verbal exchange to his own working through the expressions. Defining the terms, however, is going to be quite challenging because MLEs at a WIDA speaking proficiency level 2 can state or compare events with short sentences using everyday words and phrases, whereas talking about mathematics vocabulary requires academic language.

At level 1 in reading, Edgar can comprehend short text (with illustrations) and familiar and simple language. Understanding the projected sentences will be difficult at times, although they are short. For instance, when encountering the word *decreased*, he might not know that it means *lessened* or *reduced* or that it is often used in word problems to indicate subtraction.

The SLIDE and TREAD analysis has exposed the number of verbal elements present in this lesson. Let us now consider the magnitude of the gap caused by the many language-dependent tasks.

- No gap: There is only one place in this direct instruction where Edgar won't encounter any gap—hearing that the class did poorly on the test and that they will redo the chapter and then retest.
- Medium gaps: Because Edgar's listening proficiency is level 3, he can follow some of Mr. Leibniz's description of how to translate the sentences into algebraic expressions and then into equations, if the teacher doesn't speak too fast, but he will not catch many of the necessary details to learn how to translate them independently.
- Large gaps: From reading the mathematical terms and defining them to listening to Mr. Leibniz translate the projected sentences into expressions and then equations to following suit while discussing the steps with a shoulder partner, each instructional instance in this lesson creates a large gap for Edgar to overcome, even though the class had previously covered the content.

Faced with this fact, Mr. Leibniz might start to wonder whether it is even possible to convey algebra to students whose native language is not English and who have not reached advanced proficiency.

Address the Gaps Between ML's L2 Proficiency and Lesson Taks

STEP 3

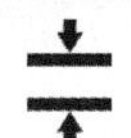

Based on the gap analysis, Mr. Leibniz is now ready to select the nonverbal and verbal supports that will enable Edgar to be more engaged.

ADDING NONVERBAL SUPPORTS

Is there anything Mr. Leibniz can do to lower the verbal demands of this lesson by adding nonverbal support? Of course there is! As a matter of fact, what he (rightfully) disregarded as SLIDE actions of his instructional plan in the analysis phase can easily be turned into nonverbal support. For instance, while rewriting or translating phrases such as "five times a certain number" into the algebraic expression $5 \, . \, x$ or $5x$, Mr. Leibniz should indicate through the use of colored pens or circles and arrows that "times" means multiplication and "a certain number" is the same as a variable—thus x, or whatever letter is given to the variable. He can apply the same strategy as he demonstrates the steps to solve an equation after a number has been substituted for a variable.

Although this *universal* use of graphics is accompanied by academic talk, it provides Edgar with a visual frame of reference.

ADDING VERBAL SUPPORTS

To provide substantial verbal support in this lesson, Mr. Leibniz does not have to look far. One of the advantages of direct instruction is its scripted nature. By thinking about what he will say at each step of the lesson, he can think about his intonation (i.e., *how* he can put emphasis on important words or phrases) and identify places where he restates what he illustrates both verbally and nonverbally. He could also institute a choral repetition of the signal word each time a sentence is translated into an expression or when an equation is written on the board. This is considered a *universal* support because all students benefit from hearing the emphasis and repetition of signal words and from participating in the choral repetition. Mr. Leibniz can ask Edgar leveled questions that allow him to respond in a short sentence or even a sentence fragment that shows he understands the process, which is categorized as a *supplemental* support.

Allowing the students to work in groups to discuss how they solve the math problems will help Edgar speak about math and use the terms in a safe environment, but he will need support to translate the sentences into expressions in a timely manner to keep up. One general recommendation we give secondary content-area teachers is to visit a primary school classroom in order to reacquaint themselves with the rich visual support that is closely tied to the development of academic language. For his algebra classes, Mr. Leibniz could create posters with "signal" words typically found in word problems that relate to addition, subtraction, multiplication, and division (see table 6.2). Ideally, Mr. Leibniz would start this list with his students each year, with the class adding to it whenever a new word that fits one of the categories appears in a word problem.

Because Mr. Leibniz must reteach the chapter and move ahead, he does not have the benefit of time to co-construct with the students a wall chart like the one shown below as he might do at the beginning of the school year and get them used to referring to it when they get stuck. For now, he should provide a copy of the table for Edgar to use. Because of Edgar's beginning proficiency, however, simply seeing these words or phrases organized by operation does little to help him make the connection once he sees them in word problems. Mr. Leibniz could either seek the assistance of a bilingual

TABLE 6.2

Signal Words in Word Problems

Operation	Signal Words
Addition	Increase, more, sum, combine, total, altogether, raised by
Subtraction	Less, fewer, minus, reduce, decrease, difference, take away
Multiplication	Times/times as much, double (two times)/triple (three times), etc., product, by
Division	Divided by/into, split, per, share, out of

aide to translate the words into Spanish or look them up in a bilingual glossary like the one created for students in the State of New York.[9]

Because Edgar has to pass state end-of-course exams or other standardized tests, he needs to be able to solve the same word problems in the chapter test as the mainstream students. However, although Edgar practices the translation of word problems into algebraic equations, Mr. Leibniz may want to give him the option of completing fewer homework problems. Although it is not a support that narrows the classroom communication gap, this nod to Edgar's special circumstance would place less pressure on him and might reduce his frustration level to a point that leads him to give homework a try. Reminding Edgar to use the bilingual resource and telling him that, even though he has faith in Edgar's ability to translate all ten sentences into equations, it's okay if he only does seven of them just might motivate Edgar to try harder than he otherwise would have.

Managing Grouping, Time, and Provider

Despite the language-intensive nature of this lesson and the large gaps between the tasks and Edgar's English proficiency in each lesson step, no alternative supports are needed. It would be best for Mr. Leibniz to go over the bilingual signal word list with Edgar prior to the lesson so that he can follow along while listening to the teacher demonstrates the translation of the sentences into expressions. Similarly, Mr. Leibniz should provide Edgar with a copy of the definitions the class goes over at the beginning of the lesson both in English and in Spanish just prior to the second step so that he can refer to it during the lesson and while doing homework.[10] Time permitting, the table of signal words in word problems is something that Mr. Leibniz or the English language development (ELD) teacher could reteach as a follow-up, giving Edgar extra practice.

Although Edgar may not require the assistance of a same-language peer in this lesson, he would benefit greatly from specific language-related instruction. Mr. Leibniz should consult with an ELD specialist regarding grammatical features of English that typically cause MLEs difficulty. Being at intermediate proficiency, Edgar may not have fully mastered comparatives and superlatives (i.e., *older, oldest, more, least*), for example. This can cause him to overlook or misinterpret important information in word problems, leading to him to incorrectly translate sentences into algebraic expressions or equations. Whether this instruction can be assumed by the ELD specialist during her language arts class or needs to be assumed by Mr. Leibniz himself naturally depends on the school's ELD programming resources.

INSTRUCTIONAL SUPPORT FOR OTHER MULTILINGUAL LEARNERS

Based on the SLIDE and TREAD analysis, table 6.3 shows suggested support for assisting learners at beginning or advanced oral proficiency for this lesson. These supports are in addition to leveled questioning appropriate for the MLs' oral proficiency to check for understanding and built-in repetition of vocabulary while the teacher explains, models, and so on.

TABLE 6.3

Support for Beginning and Advanced Multilingual Learners

Oral Proficiency	Providing Nonverbal Support	Providing Verbal Support
Beginning	• Frequent pointing to posters when referring to key vocabulary terms or explaining solutions • Diagrams/charts of word problems in simplified language, with pictures	• Provide written first language translations of a few word problems as a model (possibly preteach). They can also be utilized during assessment. • Select word problems that only use basic interpersonal communication skills (BICS) vocabulary at the start of the lesson. • Provide bilingual handout of important content vocabulary. • Offer first language support through bilingual aide, if available. • Allow students to write answers on individual whiteboard instead of asking them to vocalize answers.
Advanced	• No additional nonverbal support needed beyond what is supplied for intermediate-level student	• Include leveled questioning to confirm students' understanding. • Provide bilingual glossaries, where needed to prepare for use during homework.

Lesson Summary

An overview of the Supportive Classroom Communication protocol applied to Mr. Leibniz's Algebra lesson plan is provided in table 6.4. The nonverbal (SLIDE) elements are <u>underlined</u>, and the verbal components (TREAD) are depicted in **boldface**. Both fonts **<u>combined</u>** show that a task can contain both nonverbal and verbal elements, such as students listening to the teacher during the demonstration of an experiment.

The second column identifies the language skills involved in the lesson step *from the point of view of the student* and offers a visual illustration of the gap size between the classroom communication and Edgar's current intermediate of English proficiency. The final column lists the types of designed supports and how they are managed in the lesson.

Final Thoughts

A few days after the first direct instruction lesson:

"Alright, alright, everybody, settle down. Watch your backpack, Edmund. Let's see, Paige . . . Jared . . . Marquise . . . Edgar . . . Isabelle. Now to the good news. Everybody's homework looks much better than last week's. We still have a few things to iron out, but we'll get there. Today we're going to watch a short video to reinforce signal words and learn a few new ones that we will write on our chart. Then we'll do a short session similar to Monday's where

TABLE 6.4

The Algebra Lesson at a Glance

Lesson Steps	Skills[1] and Gap Size[2]	Added Supports[3]
Tell the students that because of yesterday's chapter test results, the class will have to repeat the entire chapter so that everyone can comprehend the material and clear up any misunderstandings. **Give the good news**: by going back, they will do better on the chapter test retake and be better prepared to *successfully* move through the next chapters.	L Ø	No supports needed.
Display vocabulary on a projector (e.g., *variable, algebraic expressions, algebraic equations, formula, solve, evaluate, proof*).	R ↕↕↕	***Nonverbal Support:*** Pointing while reading vocabulary term by term aloud ***Verbal Support:*** Choral repetition of vocabulary
Ask the students to **define/explain** the terms, **elaborating** upon their responses, **correcting** misconceptions, and **explaining** any terms they don't know.	L, S ↕↕↕	***Nonverbal Support:*** Pointing to terms while correcting and explaining ***Verbal Supports:*** • Writing definitions or phrases used by students on board • Repeating vocabulary • Leveled questioning for Edgar's proficiency level (supplemental)
Show several sentences (e.g., "five times a certain number," "five more than a certain number") and **translate** them into algebraic expressions.	R, L ↕↕	***Nonverbal Support:*** Circling, underlining, or using arrows with colored pens to make connection between signal words and symbolic expressions explicit ***Verbal Supports:*** • Bilingual terms/signal words • Emphasizing and repetition of signal words while adding nonverbal support • Leveled questioning (supplemental)
Assign sentences similar to those in step 3 and **direct** students to **translate** them into algebraic expressions independently.	R, W ↕↕↕	***Nonverbal Support:*** Not applicable ***Verbal Support:*** Providing bilingual terms/signal words (supplemental)
Tell the students to compare responses with a shoulder partner, and then display correct answers. **Discuss** and **correct** mistakes.	L, S, R ↕↕↕	***Nonverbal Support:*** Marking signal words and expressions with colored pens to make connections to expressions explicit while correcting errors ***Verbal Supports:*** • Emphasize signal words while correcting mistakes • Leveled questioning (supplemental)

Continued...

TABLE 6.4

The Algebra Lesson at a Glance *(Continued...)*

Lesson Steps	Skills[1] and Gap Size[2]	Added Supports[3]
Show what happens when the variable (e.g., *x*, *y*, *n*) is given a number (e.g., 11) with the algebraic expressions used in step 3.	L ↕↕	***Nonverbal Support:*** Circling, underlining, or using arrows with colored pens to show what happens while talking ***Verbal Support:*** Leveled questioning (supplemental)
Tell the students to work with their shoulder partner to solve the expressions first with 7 and then with 23. Display the correct answers, **discuss** the results with the class and **correct** mistakes.	L, S ↕↕↕	***Nonverbal Support:*** Circling, underlining, or using arrows with colored pens to explain errors while talking ***Verbal Support:*** Emphasize signal words while correcting mistakes
Display several sentences (e.g., "9 less than a number equals 22," "the sum of 3 and a number is 34") and **translate** them into algebraic equations.	R, L ↕↕	***Nonverbal Support:*** Circling, underlining, or using arrows with colored pens to make connection between signal words and symbolic expressions explicit ***Verbal Supports:*** • Emphasis and repetition of signal words while adding nonverbal support • Leveled questioning, repeating Edgar's responses (supplemental)
Assign ten similar sentences for students to **translate** as homework.	R, W ↕↕↕	***Verbal Support:*** Bilingual signal words list (supplemental)
Evaluation Daily homework review as formative assessment and the chapter test as a summative assessment that is calculated into the final grade for the algebra class.	R ↕↕↕	***Verbal Supports:*** • Option to translate fewer items for homework (supplemental) • Bilingual definitions and signal words list (supplemental)

Key:
1 Language skills: L = listening, S = speaking, R = reading, W = writing
2 Gap sizes: No gap = Ø, ↕ = small gap, ↕↕ = medium gap, ↕↕↕ = large gap
3 Unless otherwise noted, all supports are considered universal.

we are going to look at another way to solve the equations. Afterward, I'll let you work in small groups while you investigate how to do an algebraic proof."

While handing out the corrected homework papers, Mr. Leibniz casually leaned over Edgar's desk. "Uh-oh, what did I do now?" Edgar thought and immediately started to take a defensive posture. To his surprise, however, Mr. Leibniz actually smiled and said quietly, "I was thrilled to see that you decided to translate all ten sentences into an algebraic equation. Most of your solutions are correct. You did really well, Edgar. Estoy orgulloso de ti," he said hesitantly, aware of his midwestern accent when speaking these few Spanish words.

STOP AND REFLECT QUESTIONS

1. As you know, math is a discipline that builds on prior knowledge of concepts. This can be problematic for some MLs who have not learned certain concepts in earlier grades or in their native countries. Rather than describe students as having low math skills, have you considered assessing them to determine whether or not a gap exists between their background knowledge and the concepts you will be teaching in your math unit?
2. Reflect on the MLs in your math class. How often do they readily contribute to the classroom discussion when presented with word problems? Observe and describe their behaviors. Do they appear to be engaged in trying to solve the problems individually, or are most engaged only when working with classmates?

GO AND PRACTICE ACTIVITIES

1. Research how math symbols, calculations, and word problems are done in your students' native countries. This background information will help you understand how your MLs have been taught math in their respective countries.
2. Have your MLs create a list of math concepts that they believe to be represented in many different ways in their math textbooks and/or practice tests. For example, addition operations are signaled in many ways: add, plus, combine, and so on. Allow them to work as a group on this project. Once completed, review the list with your second language development specialist and add any missing concepts you believe they should know. Last, review the list with your MLs. Tell them they may refer to the list when needed.

PART III

Focusing on Language and Literacy

Targeted Language Arts and Literacy Instruction for Multilingual Learners

In chapter 1, we defined communication and described how it includes both verbal and nonverbal symbols to share meaning.[1] Throughout part II, we looked at communication broadly, considering its central role in the teaching and learning of disciplinary subjects. In part III, we zero in on the language side of communication, exploring how language, and more specifically a second language, is learned and taught.

Just as with classroom communication, we view adapting language and literacy instruction for multilingual learners (MLs) in terms of the distance between multilingual learners' L2 proficiency and grade-level language and literacy instruction. Distinct from how we approach classroom communication for MLs, however, we show how language and literacy instruction needs to be aimed at each ML's more precise proficiency levels in listening, speaking, reading, and writing.[2] Our term for this goal is *targeted language and literacy instruction*. In this chapter, we discuss the research and theory behind our approach, and in chapters 8 through 11, we provide practical examples and guidance to achieve this targeted goal for MLs at different grades and proficiency levels, explaining and applying our Targeted Language/Literacy Instruction (TLI) protocol—described beginning on page 173—through the classroom lenses of Gero, Edith, Tasir, and Edgar, our multilingual learners of English (MLEs).

DEVELOPING COMPETENCE IN SPOKEN AND WRITTEN COMMUNICATION: LANGUAGE AND LITERACY INSTRUCTION

It is difficult to overstate the importance of the role of language in teaching and learning. Yet, for educators and students alike, language can be the most imperceptible aspect of the classroom. Paraphrasing Marshall McLuhan, communication scholar James Carey once noted that just as the one thing of which a fish is unaware is water, for human beings, language and other symbolic systems of meaning compose the very environment of our existence. But these systems of meaning do not grasp our attention. Regular conversations, instructions, and other routine forms of communication become so familiar, so mundane and devoid of mystery, that they may no longer be perceived.[3]

Classroom Communication in Language and Literacy Instruction

Most people typically don't know much about the form and structure of their own first language.[4] They can understand and use the language, but they don't normally know how to explain its rules. For example, most native speakers of English don't know why they can say, "He gave me a dollar," but not, "He gave me a money," when both *dollar* and *money* are nouns. Native speakers of English don't need to consciously learn rules to understand *count* and *noncount* nouns.[5] They just "picked up" how to use them and never thought about how and why.

The same goes for how and why verbs should be sequenced in a sentence. For example, native speakers of English know the correct order of words in the sentence, "You are not playing here!" but probably were never taught the rule as *You* + second person singular form of the present tense copula [*are*] + not + present participle form of the main verb [*playing*] + *here*! Nor did they practice using that sentence in dialogue exercises with a classmate after having already learned and practiced conjugating present tense sentences using the verb *be*. When native speakers first utter that type of sentence, most likely the only instruction they receive is some type of correction from an adult (if they had said, for instance, "You not playing here!").

Because they acquired spoken language in a natural setting, without formal instruction, native speakers are often unable to explain the form and structure of their language.[6] Native speakers develop an ear for what sounds right, but a second language learner is still developing that ability to hear correctness versus error in grammatical forms and structures.

The variety of the language that is used and taught in the language arts classroom is known as *Standard* language, such as Standard English. This is a prestigious variety of the language, which is spoken and written in many social and academic contexts. Standard language is a given in academic language of all types. For children whose language environment outside of school closely matches that in school, there is a small to nonexistent gap between their own language use and grade-level classroom language use. When a real gap exists, such as with MLs who are still acquiring oral proficiency in their L2, it becomes more important to explicitly teach and practice using the form, structure, and conventions of the language these students are expected to use at school.

In any classroom, one responsibility of teachers is to make the hidden nature of language visible and the pathway to skillful language use accessible for all students. Unlike the main focus of, for example, math or science lessons, during which students learn *through* language, language and literacy instruction is focused primarily on what M. A. K. Halliday termed *learning the language* and *learning about the language*.[7] In learning the language, language is the *substance* of what is being learned. In learning about the language, language is studied as an *object* so that the learner can understand how it works. With instruction in math, science, economics, or other disciplinary subjects, communication that uses means other than language can enable MLs to master the course objectives; however, in language arts and literacy instruction, understanding and using language *is* the objective (or, at least, one of the objectives).

The traditional divisions between instruction in disciplinary subjects and instruction in language and literacy have softened, however.[8] Many disciplinary subject teachers we know are now including some degree of focus on the language of their disciplines, and language and literacy teachers are moving beyond teaching mostly literary texts and language skills in isolation.[9] In many cases, this is advantageous for MLs, but just as with any other instructional practice that is appropriate for non-MLs, different needs or issues may exclude MLs from gaining the same benefits. Multiple, complex factors are at play, perhaps the greatest of which is proficiency in the second language. We now turn to how a second language is learned, taught, and defined.

INSTRUCTED SECOND LANGUAGE ACQUISITION

Maybe you or someone you know learned another language by moving to a country or community where it is spoken. After being immersed in the new language environment for a while and having a need or desire to communicate, it's possible to pick up enough of the language to get by. Alternatively, maybe you or someone you know learned another language by studying it at school. Taking four or eight or twelve years of world language classes can lead to a basic ability to communicate as well.[10] Thus, unlike most other school subjects, a second language can be learned through informal or formal instruction. For language learning to occur in either case, three essential elements must be present: accessible input, interaction, and output. However, formal instruction offers something more: it provides practice with and explanation of grammar.

Acclaimed second language acquisition researcher Rod Ellis terms informal and formal second language learning *naturalistic* and *instructed second language acquisition*, respectively.[11] Typical world language classes, for example, are designed to provide *instructed second language acquisition*. Unlike a naturalistic learning environment, an instructed learning environment is structured around *teaching the language* but includes *teaching about the language*. This usually means that elements of language are isolated and taught in a variety of spoken and written exercises and activities. In addition, the complexity of language is gradually increased in the course sequence, beginning with simple grammar forms such as present tense and moving to more complicated constructions.

What Does Instructed Second Language Acquisition Look and Sound Like?

A common format for instructed second language acquisition is to begin a lesson with a dialogue or reading passage that uses a particular verb tense. You might remember dialogue from your middle or high school classes that goes something like this:

MIGUEL: Hola. *(Hello.)*

MARIA: Hola.

MIGUEL: ¿Donde está la biblioteca? *(Where is the library?)*

MARIA: La biblioteca está a la derecha. *(The library is on the right.)*

This dialogue uses the present tense of the verb *to be* and a noun that is common to students the world over (*library*). This is not real communication, as would occur in the naturalistic learning environment. It is contrived to include only the language that the world language student can learn at the beginning level. The technical term Ellis uses for a course organized by complexity of grammar points, such as the example above, is a *focus on formS*. Focusing on forms takes the overwhelming task of learning a world or second language and divides it into small, sequential pieces that become increasingly more complex. All exercises and activities are then based on the grammar point (also referred to as the form or structure) of focus.

Ellis refers to the other hallmark of instructed second language acquisition as a *focus on form* (using the singular term *form* rather than the plural used above, *formS*), which can also be considered learning about the language. This simply means that the course includes an explicit presentation of a grammar point, either deductively, by stating the rule and giving examples, or inductively, by presenting examples and requiring students to figure out the rule. No matter the language teaching approach that it's part of, a focus on form indicates that some part of the language used in the lesson will be highlighted and analyzed, whether or not technical grammar terms, such as *antecedent*, are mentioned. There will likely also be an exercise for students to practice using the form of focus correctly.

The preceding Spanish dialogue example illustrates a lesson that is part of a focus on formS. Now, let's look at how a focus on form could be added to the lesson. Because the verb used is the present tense of *to be*, the lesson might give an initial explanation that in Spanish there are two forms of the verb *to be*. To simplify the distinction, the lesson could explain that *ser* tells what something is and *estar* tells what something does or is at the moment. Then the lesson could provide conjugations of the verb *estar* (yo estoy, tú estás, etc.).

One other characteristic of instructed second language acquisition is a focus on language skill development—activities that focus on listening, speaking, reading, or writing, using the grammar and vocabulary of the lesson. For example, a short audio file of two Spanish speakers using the form of focus (the verb *be*) might be played in class, and students would be expected to answer multiple-choice questions (without English translations) about the details of the dialogue. This activity helps develop listening skills in a second language, isolating details that come from spoken discourse or text. The dialogue presents language that is pitched to or just beyond the learner's current level of proficiency, primarily in terms of grammatical competence, meaning the degree of complexity of the forms and structures that the learner knows and can use.

These exercises may remind many of us of our own instructed second language learning experiences with Spanish, French, German, or another world language. They are common practices in world language classes. Often these same techniques are used as part of teaching MLEs English language arts and literacy in an English-speaking environment, typically in what are called English language development (also known as English as a second language or English for speakers of other languages) classes. In English language development (ELD) classes, students do typically practice dialogues with formulaic language (chunks or phrases that are commonly used and memorized as whole units, rather than being created word by word) or use sentence frames focused on the give-and-take of academic subject-related conversations to improve their oral proficiency, especially for the beginning proficiency.[12] They also often study the form and structure of English and practice their listening, speaking, reading, and writing skills in English. Other things are going on in ELD classes, however, in addition to these stalwarts of world and second language instruction.

ELD teachers know a lot about their students' developing grammatical competence, often having specialized degrees and years of experience teaching and conversing with newcomers, exited MLEs, and everyone in between. Over time, these teachers also develop an ability to detect and match the communicative and grammatical level of their students' comprehension and expression in English. When they teach a student at a particular level of English proficiency (i.e., instructed second language acquisition), they engage them in understanding and using language pitched at and slightly above the student's current grammatical competence.[13] These ELD specialists are, in other words, attuned to their MLEs' language and literacy development needs. They regularly collect and reflect on their students' spoken and written language samples, pace their instruction appropriately, select the right amount of language to focus on, and add any support needed, be it grammatical, cultural, or anything else, to develop language skills and clarify meaning.

Being attuned to the level of their MLEs' communicative competence also enables ELD teachers to lead *instructional conversations*.[14] From the term itself, it is probably obvious that instructional conversations are more than haphazard, inconsequential chatter. Instead, they are very purposeful and powerful forms of language instruction, using conversations about the subject of focus or activity taking place (i.e., a real, rather than contrived or scripted, dialogue) to model and elicit forms and structures that a student is in the process of acquiring. Doing this allows ELD teachers to incorporate instructed second language acquisition into any subject or type of lesson. Using students' communicative and grammatical errors as cues for instruction, ELD teachers can recast errors with the correct wording and phrasing, giving the students new language input that is accessible through this interactive process. It takes an expert in second language acquisition to make these conversational moves instructional, but these intermittent, impromptu teachable moments can make a great difference in MLEs' language development.[15]

Why Do Multilingual Learners Need Instructed Second Language Acquisition and When Do They Need It?

Although it is possible to learn a language solely naturalistically, instructed second language acquisition has a number of documented benefits. Studies show that those who take part in instructed second language acquisition are better able to avoid making developmental errors permanent (known as *fossilization* or *stabilization*) and to reach higher levels of proficiency.[16] For example, for some MLs (especially adults who learned the language through exposure only), certain grammatical errors, such as "Why she couldn't come?" may persist even though the learners continue to be exposed to standard vocabulary and grammar through accessible communication. It has become increasingly clear that instructed second language acquisition can complement naturalistic second language acquisition and that preK–12 MLs, particularly at the secondary level, can benefit from the former.

You might be wondering how researchers track progress or measure language development in MLs. According to Ellis, second language acquisition can be considered as acquiring the form and structure of a language (among other aspects of language and its functions).[17] An important area second language acquisition researchers examine is the order in which learners acquire language forms, such as the added *s* on present-tense verbs, and the sequence of stages in acquiring a particular structure, such as the sentence structure of negative statements, beginning with placing *no* at the beginning of a sentence (No you talk here) and moving eventually to using *do* with the main verb (They didn't like the noise). Progression through these orders and sequences is constrained by various factors, many of which are considered developmental. This means that many developmental patterns are common to learners from different first language (L1) backgrounds, rather than determined solely by the influence of the learners' first languages, and should be expected for most students. Ellis surveyed a wealth of research showing that an explicit focus on these forms (e.g., the added *s* on present-tense verbs) can accelerate learners' rate of development and elevate their ultimate level of attainment of second language (L2) proficiency. There is less clear research, however, on the best way to sequence and teach the forms and structures. So, what do teachers have to go on in making those decisions?

Ellis points to Manfred Pienemann's Processability Theory as a successful attempt to predict the grammar development experienced by learners of a second language, beginning with single words or chunks, followed by simple subject/verb/object sentences and other structures, and moving eventually to embedded statements (e.g., "I see the spider suspended in its self-woven web").[18] Pienemann's theory can offer guidance for teaching and correcting learners' grammar because it has shown that certain forms or structures must be acquired before a given form or structure can emerge. For example, using the indefinite article *a* correctly can occur only if the learner has moved beyond the one-word-phrase stage. This finding has important implications for teaching. It shows that correcting an ML's grammatical error is important for future acquisition of the form or structure because the error can only be produced if the learner has developed some of the forms or structures required to utter it. However, most likely, the ML student will not use the corrected form accurately in spontaneous speech until later because it may be beyond processability for their stage of L2 development.

What does this mean for teaching MLs? Although some aspects of language can be taught without prerequisite knowledge or skills specific to the second language (e.g., spelling in English for adolescents or adults who can write in a language that uses the Roman alphabet—they don't need to learn how to spell *cat* before they can learn to spell *catastrophe*), some have to be learnable before they can be teachable (e.g., complex verb tenses—a learner won't be able to spontaneously produce "Why couldn't she have been fleeing from the scene at the time of the crime?" if they haven't acquired the ability to say "Why is she running?").

How Do Individual Factors Affect Instructed Second Language Acquisition?

We just spoke about developmental errors in second language acquisition, but they are not the only source of nonstandard (or incorrect) uses of an ML's new language. A major source of influence for second language development is the native language of MLs. In many instances, MLs use expressions or grammatical structures from their first language when they speak in their L2. For example, Edith, a native speaker of Spanish, may say, "I live in a house white" because in Spanish, the adjective may come after the noun, not before, as with English. In this case, first language interference may make the English expressions MLEs produce difficult to understand. It's important to note that this interference is more common at the early stages of second language acquisition and decreases as an ML becomes more proficient. This sort of influence from the first language can intermingle with the normal developmental patterns that MLs from various language backgrounds go through on their way to full proficiency. The spontaneous spoken and written utterances of MLs moving through the second language acquisition process follow a sequence and pattern of increasing complexity and common developmental errors.

There's a huge upside to native language influences on second language development, however. The transfer between two languages doesn't always cause grammatical or pronunciation errors. If the L1 and L2 have similar features, MLs might benefit from the transfer of knowledge from the first to the second language. One example is cognates, which are words in two languages that share a similar meaning, spelling, and/or pronunciation. Thirty to 40 percent of all words in English have a related word in Spanish, which makes cognates a great tool for Spanish-speaking MLEs. The similarity between the first and second language, including the number of cognates, affects the amount of exposure and study required to become proficient. Of course, the number of cognates varies greatly, depending on the second language. All things being equal, a speaker of Chinese, which has a totally different writing system and grammatical structure from English and shares virtually no cognates, would require more instructed second language acquisition and exposure to English than a speaker of Italian.[19]

Let's take a moment to add insights into the second language acquisition perspective that translanguaging, which offers a different vantage point on issues of language transfer, can offer. Generally coming from a more social than cognitive perspective on developing proficiency in a second language (viewed as becoming bilingual), translanguaging takes a more holistic position than second language acquisition's analytic stance, emphasizing the interconnectedness between the two languages that are part of a bilingual person's one linguistic repertoire and describing the process of becoming bilingual as a dynamic interrelationship between the two languages present in one person, instead of simply adding a second language to its predecessor (the first language).

Rather than anticipating L2 errors at certain stages of proficiency and organizing instruction around them, translanguaging collaboratively engages students and the teacher in critical and creative language practices, using both languages fluidly. The intention is to support students in comprehending complex content, developing linguistic practices for academic contexts, making space for bilingualism, and developing their bilingual identities.[20] This approach, which begins with the student and contextualizes their language use in purposeful interactions about academic topics, encourages moving between languages for thinking and expression, which, we believe, can be a powerful complement to the research and theory-driven way the field of second language acquisition addresses the topic of learner language.[21]

From a second language acquisition perspective, however, we can conceptualize MLs' developing grammatical competence in their L2 as *learner language* or what is termed *interlanguage*, a dynamic, internalized learner language that reflects the MLs' underlying developing knowledge of their new language, while still containing aspects of their native language.[22] Students' interlanguage may appear as error-filled spoken and written language. However, second language acquisition specialists view these errors as typical stages that are replaced with correct forms as the learner becomes more proficient in their L2. In other words, the interlanguage produced by learners in the early stages of acquiring their new language can reflect the sentence structure, vocabulary, and pronunciation patterns of their native language. These patterns then become increasingly similar to accurate forms of the second language, as the learner gains more experience hearing, speaking, reading, and writing it using already known vocabulary and sentence structure.[23]

In a review of decades of research on instructed second language acquisition environments, Ellis found that younger children, such as Gero, normally acquire a second language without as much need for instructed second language acquisition, in particular the part that organizes instruction by learning grammar (focus on formS).[24] However, instructed second language acquisition is especially beneficial for older students such as Edith, Tasir, and Edgar and, according to Ellis, has been shown to improve the rate of acquisition and the ultimate level of proficiency in the second language. This is certainly an important goal. Everyone wants ML students to reach grade-level proficiency in L2 listening, speaking, reading, and writing as soon as possible. It's not a simple one-to-one prospect, though. Quadrupling the amount of instructed second language acquisition doesn't guarantee reaching a language milestone in one-fourth the amount of time it takes to get there without instruction. But the positive effects of instructed second language acquisition are well established by research, and MLs in regular classes do benefit from this way of learning language. Even though research indicates greater benefits of instructed second language acquisition for older children, we have found it to be beneficial to some degree for MLs of all ages. So even simply pointing out the *s* on the end of present-tense verbs for *he*, *she*, or *it*—reminding Gero and Edith to pronounce and write that final letter—can help them acquire accurate forms and structures in English and perhaps do so a little more quickly.

When Does Instructed Second Language Acquisition Occur for Multilingual Learners in the Regular Classroom?

Instructed second language acquisition can be incorporated into lessons on any subject or topic. Teachers can do this through focusing on language/literacy skills that they sequence by increasing grammatical complexity (focus on formS) or focusing on the rules of language structure that are relevant to the lesson (focus on form). The ELD classes that Gero, Edith, Tasir, and Edgar attend generally provide that instructed second language acquisition environment, targeted to their levels of English proficiency, with an increasing focus on grammar as they move up the grade levels. However, under the right conditions, the instructed second language acquisition can be integrated into regular language arts and disciplinary subject instruction, especially when ELD and classroom teachers collaborate to support their MLEs. We will see examples of this in chapters 8 through 10.

LANGUAGE FORM AND STRUCTURE IN SECOND LANGUAGE LITERACY

So far, we have discussed how becoming proficient in an L2 involves the acquisition of words and grammatical forms and structures. Students acquiring a second language learn the meaning of the words, forms, and structures, as well as how each word is put together and the order in which words are assembled in phrases and sentences. Learning grammatical forms and structures is part of developing oral proficiency—using and understanding spoken language—and oral proficiency is a key factor in the ability to comprehend and compose written texts. We also know that being able to read and write in the native language means that an ML won't need to learn how to read and write all over again when learning to read and write in their L2. Together, oral proficiency in the L2 and first language literacy are powerful determiners of MLs' literacy skills in their new language.[25]

Learning to Read in English

The research available on MLEs who are learning to read (that is, learning to read, for the first time, in their L2) is quite limited in comparison to the research on native speakers of English learning to read (for the first time) in English.[26] It is also worth noting that of the research conducted with MLEs, the vast majority of studies have been conducted mostly with Spanish-speaking children in primary grades, with few studies of children in upper elementary grades. Nonetheless, research findings from these studies have provided valuable insights about the factors that influence language and literacy development across languages.

Studies comparing MLEs' reading development in their second language to that of their non-MLE peers have shown similarities and differences between the two groups.[27] For instance, in one major research study, Nonie Lesaux and her colleagues reported that primary grade MLE and non-MLEs typically perform at similar levels on measures of basic reading skills such as phonological processing, word reading, and spelling.[28] However, they conclude, "the findings of studies on reading comprehension paint a very different picture, yielding highly consistent results that, in comparison to their monolingual peers, reading comprehension is an area of weakness for language minority learners." They further report that in upper elementary grades, the effect of word reading skills on reading comprehension for MLEs becomes increasingly weak, whereas the influence of other skills such as vocabulary, listening comprehension, and oral proficiency becomes increasingly strong.

Although there is less definitive research on MLEs in middle and high school classrooms, we know from available cross-language research that for most MLEs, instruction in key components of reading, such as phonemic awareness, word recognition, vocabulary, reading fluency, and comprehension, is necessary but not sufficient for teaching them to read and write proficiently in English. Cross-language research indicates that oral proficiency in English is equally important, but it is often overlooked in instruction. In addition, this research has further shown that the development of literacy in English is a process that is influenced by individual differences in oral language proficiency, age, previous schooling, and cognitive abilities, as well as similarities between a student's native language and the language of instruction (English, in this case).[29]

How Vocabulary, Word Forms, and Sentence Structure Affect Multilingual Learners' Reading

Research has shown that language elements that are typically part of instructed second language acquisition, such as vocabulary development, are important to MLEs' reading and writing ability in English. In two studies, one of fourth-grade Spanish-English speakers and the other of eighth to tenth graders, high correlations were found between vocabulary knowledge and reading comprehension.[30] These findings show that given adequate word decoding skills, vocabulary knowledge is crucial for improved reading comprehension for MLEs (similar to many studies of the relationship between vocabulary knowledge and reading comprehension with non-MLEs).

There is also research showing that understanding the form and elements of words impacts students' ability to read and understand what they read. In other words, readers who "know" the internal structure of words have a distinct advantage in vocabulary and comprehension. In their influential report *Preventing Reading Difficulties in Young Children*, Catherine Snow and her colleagues maintain this type of knowledge is important because it helps readers connect word forms and meanings.[31] For example, children learn that past events use verbs with an *-ed* suffix. For children, awareness of these forms and elements of words may be an important support skill in reading and spelling.

A relatively small but growing body of research indicates that in addition to vocabulary and word formation skills, knowledge of other grammatical aspects of language contributes to proficiency in reading and writing in English. Language and literacy studies suggest that while below-grade-level vocabulary knowledge is at the core of reading problems among upper-grade students, a similar lack of grammar knowledge and skills, such as understanding and using correct sentence structure, likely plays a larger role in reading comprehension than originally assumed.[32]

Finally, understanding how information is organized in different types of texts (referred to as discourse structure) has been found to impact MLEs' reading (as well as non-MLEs' reading) across various grade levels. Research in this area is quite extensive, documenting positive effects of understanding discourse structure on students' reading, writing, and learning from text.[33]

We've discussed how acquiring the forms and structure of a second language is a major part of becoming proficient in oral language and literacy. In the next section, we look at how these building blocks of language are assembled to describe how proficient MLs communicate in listening, speaking, reading, and writing.

DESCRIBING AND MEASURING ENGLISH PROFICIENCY

"There should be nothing on your desk except a number 2 pencil. You may not open the test booklet until I tell you to. You may not move to the next section until you are told. You may not . . . ." Testing seems to involve a lot of negatives, nothings, and nots. This testing was different, however, for Gero, Edith, Tasir, and Edgar. It was English language proficiency testing time at their schools, and throughout the designated day, each MLE filed into the office where an ELD teacher led them through an oral proficiency interview. This was the type of test on which Gero, Edith, Tasir, and Edgar could feel successful, and its results gave their teachers great insights into their performance in language arts and literacy classes and their English language development. The ELD teachers carefully recorded and filed their test results, planning to meet with each MLE's classroom teachers to share ideas for supporting their progress.

L2 proficiency is evaluated in different ways. We've seen how researchers study the process of second language acquisition in terms of language forms and structure, but proficiency is also measured by the ability to use spoken and written language accurately for real purposes. Standardized tests such as ACCESS for English Language Learners and the English Language Proficiency Assessment for the 21st Century (ELPA 21) are one way to place MLEs' listening, speaking, reading, and writing skills at their appropriate levels, enabling teachers to provide the necessary targeted support.[34] These standardized language assessments correspond to national and state standards of English language development for MLEs. We look at the most widely used standards and descriptors in the next section.

English Language Development Standards

There are multiple sets of national standards for English language development in the United States, including the TESOL preK–12 proficiency standards, the K–12 English Language Development Standards published by the WIDA Consortium, and the ELPA21 standards.[35] Each set of standards describes the process of language acquisition through multiple levels. Because learners go through predictable stages as they acquire English, there are many similarities between the sets of standards, the notable distinction being that WIDA uses six levels of proficiency (the sixth representing grade-level proficiency) and TESOL and ELPA21 use five levels.[36]

WIDA LANGUAGE PROFICIENCY LEVELS

Related to these standards, which are organized by level of English proficiency, WIDA developed language proficiency level descriptors as well as performance definitions across the preK–12 grade continuum for their assessments of English proficiency. Because many states use this assessment to measure MLEs' progress, we summarize these descriptions in table 7.1 to show their increase in complexity from levels 1 to 6.

Back in chapter 2, we presented a sample WIDA Individual Student Report, and we focused primarily on oral proficiency for providing communication supports at three broad levels. As we look at teaching language and literacy to MLEs, aiming to provide targeted instruction, we need a more precise categorization of what they can comprehend and express in English. The WIDA Consortium language proficiency levels help us know what listening, speaking, reading, and writing behaviors to expect from a student at given levels, and by looking ahead, we can also see what we should be helping the student to reach as they progress to the next level.

When planning language and literacy lessons, teachers can refer to the WIDA language proficiency level descriptors (in the individual student reports) and performance definitions documents appropriate for the MLEs in their classrooms.[37] In the TLI protocol section of this chapter, we draw from these resources to develop language and literacy instruction for MLEs. With these more specific descriptors of MLE s' four skill levels of English proficiency, teachers can better support these students' listening, speaking, reading, and writing development. When learning any subject in English, MLEs face a gap between their English proficiency and classroom communication. In chapter 2, we described the teacher's goal as "narrowing the classroom communication gap." For language and literacy instruction, we describe the teacher's goal as providing targeted language/literacy instruction, the topic of the next main section, "Targeted Language and Literacy Instruction for Multilingual Learners."

A NOTE ABOUT UNDERSTANDING MLS' PROFICIENCY LEVELS

Although L2 language proficiency assessments that are used to satisfy state and federal mandates for MLs can tell you at which level(s) your MLs performed on the last test, we suggest that you also consider recent student language samples when designing new instruction. You can gather important information about your MLs' proficiency

TABLE 7.1

WIDA Performance Definitions for Expressive Domains (Grades K–12)

Proficiency Level	Linguistic Complexity	Language Forms and Conventions	Vocabulary Usage
Level 1 Entering	• Words, phrases, or chunks of language • Single words used to represent ideas	• Phrase-level grammatical structures • Phrasal patterns associated with common social and instructional situations	• General content-related words • Everyday social and instructional words and expressions
Level 2 Emerging	• Phrases or short sentences • Emerging expression of ideas	• Formulaic grammatical structures • Repetitive phrasal and sentence patterns across content areas	• General content words and expressions • Social and instructional words and expressions across content areas
Level 3 Developing	• Short and some expanded sentences with emerging complexity • Expanded expression of one idea or emerging expression of multiple related ideas	• Simple and compound grammatical structures with occasional variation • Sentence patterns across content areas	• Specific content language, including cognates and expressions • Words or expressions with multiple meanings used across content areas
Level 4 Expanding	• Short, expanded, and some complex sentences • Organized expression of ideas with emerging cohesion	• Compound and complex grammatical structures • Sentence patterns characteristic of particular content areas	• Specific and some technical content-area language • Words and expressions with expressive meaning through use of collocations and idioms across content areas
Level 5 Bridging	• Multiple, complex sentences • Organized, cohesive, and coherent expression of ideas	• A variety of grammatical structures matched to purpose • A broad range of sentence patterns characteristic of particular content areas	• Technical and abstract content-area language, including content-specific collocations • Words and expressions with various degrees of meaning across content areas
Level 6 Reaching	Language that consistently meets all criteria through Level 5, Bridging, without support.		

through collecting spoken and written language samples repeatedly throughout the school year. While listening to each recording, you can take notes on the words and phrases your ML uses and how well they can understand and contribute to the conversation. If you're feeling ambitious or if you have a classroom helper, you can even transcribe the conversation (artificial intelligence [AI] apps such as Otter.ai can be helpful), so you have a written document of your student's speech at given times in the year. When you read the transcript, you can compare the student's language use to descriptions of L2 development, such as WIDA proficiency descriptions and performance definitions, identifying where you think your student is on the oral proficiency (listening and speaking) continuum.

Giving your students recurrent open writing prompts can provide the same type of language samples (without your having to transcribe them), placing their written skills on the writing proficiency continuum. These sources of student language can give you a more complete understanding of where they are than a mere categorization from a standardized test. We will show what the combination of these two types of data looks like in practice in chapters 8 through 11.

TARGETED LANGUAGE AND LITERACY INSTRUCTION FOR MULTILINGUAL LEARNERS

Picture an archer at a competition—their left hand gripping the arc of the bow, all four bent fingers of their right hand at eye level, pulling the bowstring taut. Directly ahead of the bow stands a target, perfect concentric circles of red and white. The archer tilts their chin and left hand up slightly, releases the string, and the arrow shoots skyward, its trajectory rising well above the target and ending far beyond it.

Why would an archer miss the point of their goal, you might wonder? Why wouldn't they attempt a direct hit? Just think how odd it would be to hear the archer explain, "I was told to aim high. Anything less would not be acceptable." How useful would it be to aim high if this were nowhere near the goal?

So it is with language and literacy instruction for MLs. Their L2 proficiency in listening, speaking, reading, and writing is at a temporary place, a momentarily stable (yet incrementally rising) level of second language development. But just imagine that every time the target is hit, every time instructed second language development occurs, the target moves ahead, getting closer and closer to its ultimate destination—grade-level proficiency in listening, speaking, reading, and writing. Instructed second language development, what we call *targeted language and literacy instruction*, is a mark that any teacher of an ML needs to hit for that learner to progress steadily, promptly, and accurately toward grade-level proficiency in spoken and written language in their L2. What if the targeted proficiency for an ML is way below grade level? Some might say that's aiming too low. However, we believe it serves no purpose to insist that all students should meet grade-level language and literacy standards within a given lesson if some of them are still developing basic L2 proficiency. Setting the target high above MLs' proficiency, just to require the same rigorous standards of all, misses the point.

In discussing State English language arts standards, many English language development scholars have pointed to the benefit for MLEs because the explicit instruction in the four skill areas, as well as the incorporation of a focus on form, can greatly aid the second language acquisition process, as discussed earlier. Although we agree with this view, we do need to point out that these benefits disappear if the classroom communication involved in curriculum, instruction, and assessment is far beyond the ML's L2 proficiency level.

If, for example, a lesson on embedded phrases (e.g., "the person whose money was stolen") were part of grade-level English language arts instruction in Edith's class, Edith could not process it—as a beginning MLE, she produces only single words and chunks in English. As we discussed earlier, Pienemann's research about the internal processing constraints on the acquisition of language features shows that Edith would still need to acquire a number of grammatical forms before she could internalize the complex structure involved in embedding.[38] If she were participating in this fourth-grade English language arts lesson, Edith could copy examples of embedded sentences that were being taught in class, but exposure to and even explicit teaching of the grammatical features of embedded phrases would not prompt immediate acquisition. The grade-level language arts instruction would benefit Edith very little, if at all, because the distance between her proficiency in listening, speaking, reading, writing, and grammar and the classroom language and literacy instruction is substantial.

If language and literacy instruction were designed and offered exclusively for the needs of MLs (for example, a fourth-grade MLE like Edith, who is at level 1), it would likely include instruction specific to each of the six language skill levels in the WIDA ELD standards (often offered in multilevel ELD classes). Examining this second language instruction on the preK–12 continuum, there is a distance between the grade-level expectations in language and literacy lessons and instruction that is targeted to proficiency levels of the ML. This fits one defining characteristic of an ML—assessed second language skills that have not reached grade-level expectations yet.

Given the constructive, incremental nature of second language acquisition and the potential variation in proficiency across the different skill areas (listening, speaking, reading, and writing), teaching aspects of language that are well above the individual level of proficiency is not productive. Rather, language and literacy instruction should meet an ML just at or beyond their current level of proficiency—targeted language instruction—and move the target incrementally upward toward the grade-level language standards.

This is illustrated in figure 7.1, with Edith as an example. When Edith entered fourth grade, she was assessed at level 1 in listening, speaking, reading, and writing. As she progresses, on track, to more advanced levels of proficiency, something is holding her back from reaching grade-level expectations. At the same time she's advancing, the language demands are rising by grade level. To enable her to reach the challenging grade-level standards that prepare her for college or a career, her teachers need to provide targeted language and literacy instruction so she can proceed as swiftly as possible.

As seen in figure 7.1, language and literacy teachers must hold in mind two opposing forces when deciding about the right degree of challenge for MLs. This is especially true for MLs at the intermediate level, such as Edgar. On one end, there are developmental constraints to the student's ability to rise to grade-level language and literacy tasks at a given moment. On the other end is the urgent need to move the ML forward and upward on the language development continuum. If the ML is put in a position where the classroom language instruction is well beyond their current L2 proficiency, no learning of consequence occurs. Conversely, if the ML stays at their level, asked only to do what they can do effortlessly, or if their teachers accept language use that doesn't improve in complexity or accuracy, the student may plateau at a level of proficiency that won't reach college and career readiness. That is not acceptable for Edgar or for any ML.

Similarities and Differences Between First and Second Language and Literacy Instruction

Can targeted language and literacy instruction for MLs take place together with non-MLs? That depends on several factors, most important of which is likely grade level. Figure 7.2 shows how the learning targets for MLs and non-MLs could be close together or far apart. In this diagram, language arts and literacy taught in the native language of non-ML students (noted as L1 in the triangle) is contrasted with targeted second language and literacy instruction for MLs (noted as L2 in the circle).

FIGURE 7.1

Edith's Current (Fourth Grade) and Projected (Through Twelfth Grade) English Proficiency Compared to Grade-Level English Language Arts Instruction

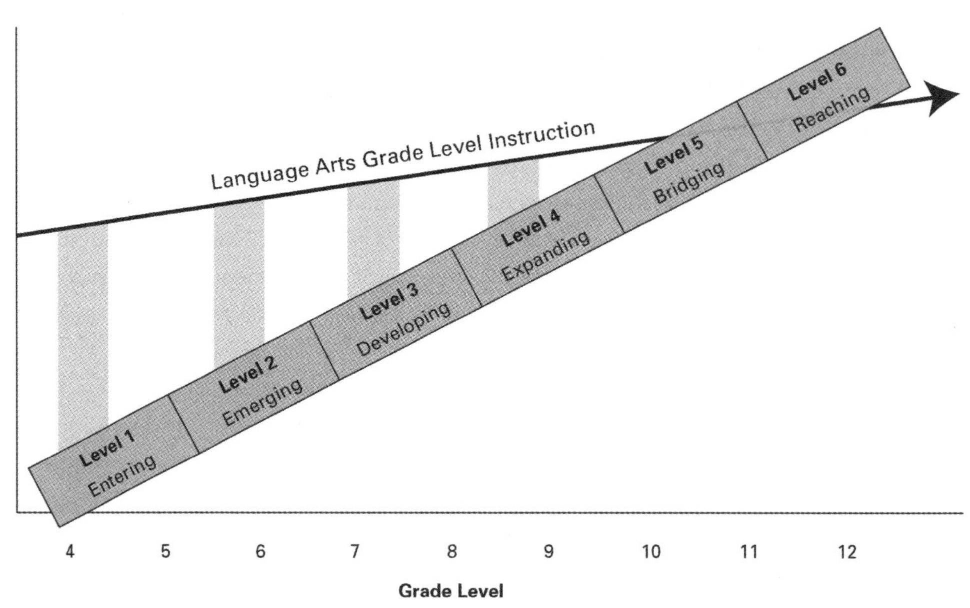

FIGURE 7.2

Native Language (L1) Language and Literacy Instruction Compared to Second Language (L2) Development Instruction at Kindergarten and Twelfth-Grade Levels

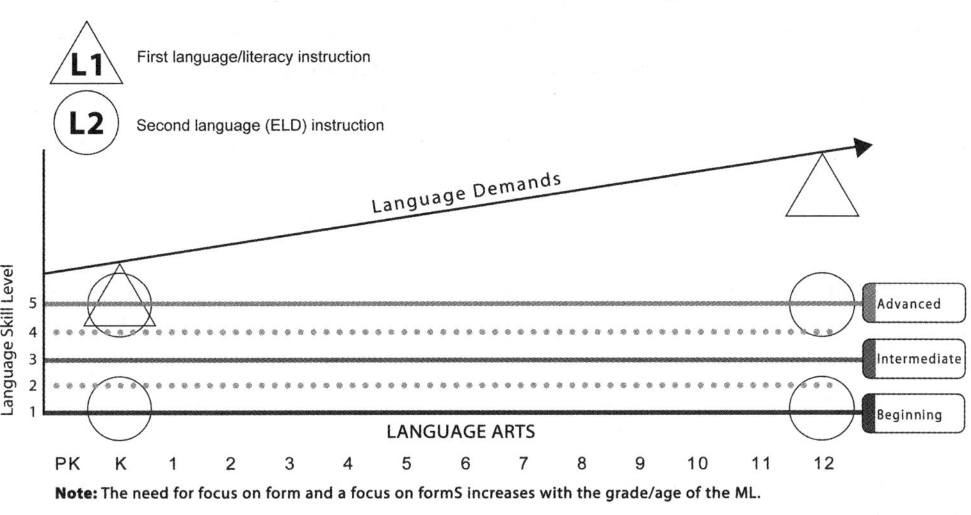

Let's take a closer look at the diagram, starting with the kindergarten side and then moving to the right for twelfth grade. In kindergarten, an advanced ML would need targeted language and literacy instruction that is overwhelmingly similar to grade-level language arts and literacy instruction for native speakers (or non-MLs). In this case, it is possible for the specific needs of this hypothetical advanced ML to be met through added verbal and nonverbal supports in the same classroom (although some research shows that separate ELD programs for MLEs even in early grades lead to greater gains in English oral proficiency).[39] You can see in the diagram that the L2 circle icon, which represents what would occur in instructed second language acquisition (or ELD) for that level of proficiency, overlaps significantly with grade-level first language arts and literacy instruction (represented by the L1 triangle icon). However, at the opposite end of the spectrum in twelfth grade, instruction for beginning-level MLs would have nothing in common with grade-level instruction for non-MLs, illustrated by the wide divide between the L1 and L2 instruction icons.

Why Second Language Development Classes Are Important for Multilingual Learners

Unlike formal instruction for MLs (which at beginning levels resembles what would be taught in a world language class), language and literacy classes for non-MLs typically focus primarily on developing skills in reading and writing. The assumption is that these students already possess oral language skills—they can comprehend spoken language and express themselves through speech. Teachers then help build literacy skills on students' already established oral language. But for MLs, oral language proficiency in their new language may be absent or much less developed due to second language acquisition processes and influences from the students' native languages.

In other words, the progression in the preK–12 language arts and literacy curriculum is based on the norm for native speakers, who were raised speaking the language of instruction. Grade-level expectations indicate where the average native speaker should be at a certain point in time, given grade-level oral language proficiency upon entering preschool (or kindergarten) and adequate yearly progress in language arts and literacy. MLs, however, can enter preschool with no oral proficiency in the language of instruction (i.e., their L2) or with less oral proficiency than native speakers. And preschool or kindergarten is not the only point of initial access to school conducted in an ML's L2. An ML with no oral proficiency in the language of instruction may enter school in any grade—kindergarten, fourth, seventh, or tenth.

MLs entering any of these grades may have already developed grade-level literacy in their native languages. Or they may have no literacy whatsoever. Clearly, L1 literacy skills help MLs develop literacy skills in their L2, but their oral language still needs to be developed for them to participate meaningfully in language arts and literacy instruction.[40] And if literacy needs to be developed for the first time in any language, in tandem with developing oral proficiency in an L2, the ML has a much more challenging course to follow.

Teaching language and literacy to MLs should be more akin to an instructed second language learning environment through targeting a focus on form (and, where possible and necessary, a focus on formS) to the ML's L2 proficiency levels. When the target can't be reached in the general classroom because of a large gap between grade-level expectations and the ML's current proficiency, then the ML should be learning language arts and literacy with an L2 development specialist (similar to a second language acquisition environment for a world language). In a synthesis of research on the value of ELD classes for preK–12, William Saunders and colleagues note that there is evidence for continuing this form of instructed second language acquisition from beginning through advanced levels of English proficiency.[41] They also assert that ELD instruction should be provided daily and be offered by proficiency levels, explicitly teach language structure and form, focus on academic and conversational English, emphasize listening and speaking in addition to reading and writing, balance a focus on meaning and form, provide corrective feedback on form, and include carefully planned interactive activities.

Other than the optimal learning environment of bilingual or dual language programs, instructed second language acquisition that takes place in separate second language development classes taught by specialists is the gold standard for meeting MLs' language arts and literacy instruction needs. But teachers know that optimal environments and gold standards aren't the norm everywhere. What can teachers do if ELD isn't provided at their school or if its scheduling doesn't coincide with their language and literacy block? When we know we can't give our students what's absolutely best for them, we don't have to be resigned to giving them nothing at all. We do our best with what we have to give our MLs as much as we can. The TLI protocol is a tool to help make this happen.

THE TARGETED LANGUAGE/LITERACY INSTRUCTION (TLI) PROTOCOL

We've discussed what second language acquisition research and theory tell us that MLs need in language and literacy instruction. So how do we provide that targeted, explicit instruction in the general classroom? Many teachers might respond, "Scaffolding!" But what does it mean to scaffold language and literacy instruction for MLs? And if we do this for one or two MLs in a class filled with non-MLs, how do we know if we're reaching them? Does the scaffolding we provide for non-MLs hold up for MLs as well?

It's easy to assume that language and literacy teaching techniques are universal. Articles in professional journals for L2 instruction specialists often include descriptions of teaching techniques and activities that are quite familiar to any language arts or literacy teacher (e.g., close reading), not just those who teach a second language. The steps might be the same, but something major is different. For MLs, it's not *what* you do (the technique or strategy), it's the *way* that you do it (and *why*).

The TLI protocol is a tool to help determine the way and the why of scaffolding language and literacy instruction for MLs. The TLI protocol can help teachers address an ML's language and literacy development needs within a lesson that is not specifically designed for MLs, keeping *the spirit* of the lesson's listening, speaking, reading, or writing objective(s) as the focus of instruction. This process involves adjusting four linguistic and instructional aspects that scaffold instruction to the student's current proficiency levels in listening, speaking, reading, and/or writing.

The TLI protocol guides classroom teachers in providing the most targeted language and literacy instruction for MLs possible, given available resources and time. At schools with lots of MLEs and plentiful resources to offer adequate ELD instruction, the TLI protocol would be applied in collaboration between classroom and ELD teachers. Because the available ELD class doesn't always coincide with the MLE's language arts block and because some schools don't have the minimum number of MLEs to provide specialized ELD instruction, we emphasize providing targeted language instruction through scaffolding in the general classroom, led by the classroom teacher or another school professional. For cases where there is no real possibility of doing this (as with Edgar in chapter 11), we show what would be done in the separate ELD class and how the ELD teacher could support Edgar's classroom teachers.[42]

Now it's time to take a closer look at the steps of the TLI protocol. We begin by looking generally at how the steps of the TLI protocol would apply for a very small distance between an ML's proficiency levels and the language/literacy focus of the lesson (Gero) and end with how the steps would apply for a very large distance (Edgar).

Path 1: Administer the Supportive Classroom Communication Protocol

As was discussed in chapters 1 and 2, the Supportive Classroom Communication (SCC) protocol is the first segment of applying the TLI protocol because the quality of classroom communication is an essential aspect of any type of lesson. Beginning with reviewing the student's proficiency level descriptors from their WIDA assessment data (Individual Student Report or Student Roster Report), we examine the language arts/literacy lesson by identifying SLIDE and TREAD. We then compare the SLIDE and TREAD to the student's oral language (listening and speaking) level, considering their literacy level (reading and writing) as well if there is a sizeable discrepancy between them. When we have sized the gap between the student's L2 proficiency and classroom communication (SLIDE and TREAD), we add verbal and nonverbal supports. Let's see how that looks for a read-aloud lesson in Gero's kindergarten classroom.

Looking at WIDA Kindergarten Screener results for Gero (level 1), we see that he (1) understands and uses general and everyday single words and chunks of language and (2) can match visual representations to words and phrases.[43]

Ms. Levin's read-aloud lesson will focus on reading skill development and expects her kindergarten students to:

1. Listen as the teacher reads a big book—*Brown Bear, Brown Bear* (by Bill Martin and Eric Carle)
2. Match printed words from the story to their pictures in the book
3. Answer questions about story details, such as "What was the second animal Brown Bear saw?"

Beginning with identifying SLIDE/TREAD, Ms. Levin sees that **listening** to the teacher **read** involves a lot of **TREAD**. Matching printed words to pictures includes **TREAD** (**printed words**) and <u>SLIDE</u> (<u>pictures</u>). **Answering questions** about the story is also a **TREAD** activity.

Knowing that Gero's oral proficiency in English is at a beginning level, Ms. Levin sizes the gap between the TREAD and Gero's English proficiency level. She knows that Gero can understand a few basic words in English, and she knows that the story uses a lot of repetition. This means that he will need support for understanding the names and colors of each animal as well as the overall meaning of "What do you see?" and "I see ____ looking at me."

Ms. Levin then addresses the gap by adding verbal and nonverbal supports, such as pointing to the pictures that show the words she is reading. So, when Ms. Levin says "Brown Bear," Gero should see the brown bear because Ms. Levin points to it, and when she says, "What do you see?" she will gesture to her own eyes followed by a questioning gesture with her elbows bent upward/palms raised and her face scrunched in a quizzical expression. For the matching activity, Ms. Levin pairs Gero with Merline, who can help him in their shared language, Haitian Kreyòl. While Gero and Merline are matching words and pictures, Ms. Levin comes by and uses leveled questioning to ask Gero story details, such as, "What color is the frog?" which is appropriate for a beginning MLE's level of oral proficiency, rather than asking the more linguistically complex questions she asked her non-MLEs, such as "What was the second animal Brown Bear saw?" Now that Ms. Levin has applied the SCC protocol, she moves on to path 2 in figure 7.3, the TLI protocol.

FIGURE 7.3

Targeting Language Arts/Literacy Instruction to MLs' Proficiency Levels

Referring to each ML's WIDA ACCESS* or Screener Individual Report Levels (L, S, R, & W Proficiency Level Descriptors), apply the following:

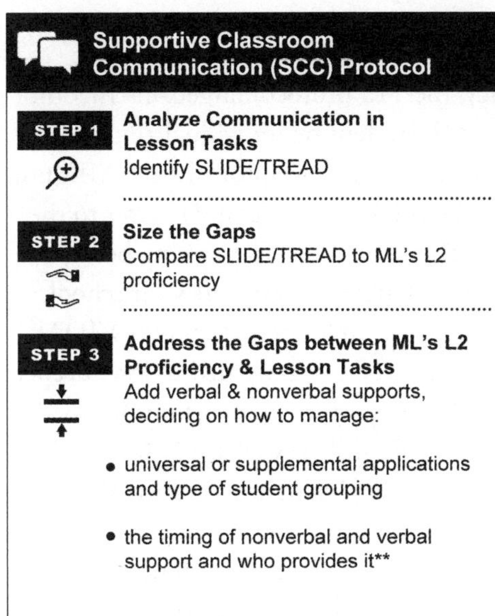

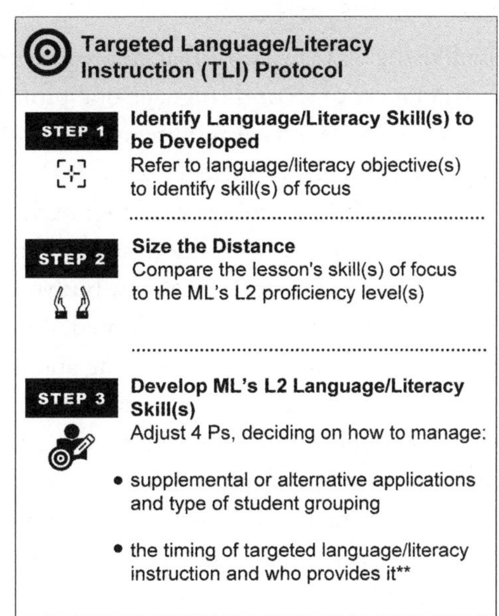

*Or other L2 assessment

**Possible variation of best fit of providers between Protocols

Path 2: Administer the Targeted Language/Literacy Instruction Protocol

Depending on the distance between a lesson's grade-level language and literacy skill of focus and the ML student's proficiency level in the skill, the TLI protocol will be implemented partially or fully. Partial implementation includes steps 1 and 2, and full implementation comprises all three steps. You can think of partial implementation as doublechecking whether implementing the SCC protocol, which adds verbal and non-verbal supports by L2 proficiency level, is sufficient for a small distance between the language skills of focus and the ML student's proficiency in those skills. Full implementation is necessary when that distance is large enough to require language and literacy scaffolding, in addition to the added verbal and nonverbal supports, to meet the ML student where they are in the skill of focus.

IDENTIFY LANGUAGE/LITERACY SKILL(S) TO BE DEVELOPED

Ms. Levin's SCC protocol-enhanced lesson required Gero to listen and watch while Ms. Levin read the book *Brown Bear, Brown Bear, What Do You See?*, a book that uses repeated language patterns with simple word substitutions, which limits vocabulary and grammar demands. Gero and Merline match written words to their pictures from the book. Ms. Levin sits with Gero and asks him leveled questions about story details.

The skills to be developed in the lesson are mainly matching the printed story words and their pictures (reading) and listening to the read-aloud. Although speaking is necessary for working in pairs on the matching activity and answering Ms. Levin's leveled questions, it is not a skill of focus in the lesson.

STEP 2

SIZE THE DISTANCE

Unlike the SCC protocol that categorizes verbal and nonverbal support into three broad ranges of second language oral proficiency, the TLI protocol targets instruction to the precise language and literacy levels of the ML student by individualizing according to their actual proficiency levels (on a 1–6 scale), using descriptors for the ML's proficiency levels in listening, speaking, reading, and writing. We suggest you refer to the WIDA performance definitions for listening, speaking, reading, and writing because of their detail, clarity, and simplicity, but you can use whatever descriptors your school, district, state, or country has adopted.[44] Because Gero is in kindergarten, his WIDA testing report only assessed listening and speaking, so Ms. Levin needed to look deeper into Gero's proficiency. She reviewed the level 1 WIDA performance definitions for details on what Gero understands and can express in English as well as her informal assessments of Gero's reading and samples she collected of his writing in English.

After using the SCC protocol to improve the lesson for its quality of communication, Ms. Levin found that the gap between the lesson's supportive classroom communication and Gero's oral proficiency level is small, so he will be able to comprehend and participate. Additionally, she noted that the distance between the lesson's reading skill focus (matching simple words with pictures) and Gero's current reading proficiency in English is also small, so step 3 of the TLI protocol is not necessary for this lesson. To illustrate how step 3 of the TLI protocol, developing MLs' language and literacy skills, would be put into practice, we will discuss how Edgar's ELD teacher, Ms. Myers, would scaffold instruction to his proficiency levels by adjusting the 4 Ps (pitch, pace, portion, and perspective/point).

STEP 3

DEVELOP MLS' L2 LANGUAGE/LITERACY SKILL(S)

We have worked with classroom language arts and literacy teachers for many years, and one of the biggest areas of confusion we've seen is what is different about teaching ML students, especially because a lot of the same terminology and techniques are used. As we have discussed in this chapter, what we think is most different, or what makes a real difference for MLs, is instructed second language acquisition, or what we refer to as targeted language and literacy instruction. In targeted language and literacy instruction, typically offered in L2 development classes (referred to as ELD classes if the MLs' L2 is English), teachers design language skill-building activities, facilitate instructional conversations, and focus on grammar at the level of L2 proficiency of their students. Teachers can provide these types of language development support, or scaffolding, in various settings. We identified qualities of scaffolding that set the instruction of MLs apart from that of non-MLs.[45] We termed these qualities of scaffolding for MLs *pitch*, *pace*, *portion*, and *perspective/point*. These qualities are the focus of the next section.

The third step of the TLIP presents the four scaffolding criteria for providing targeted language and literacy instruction in relation to grade-level language arts and literacy instruction. Combining our analysis of second language development (ELD in this case) teachers' language use and instructional practices in targeted language instruction for MLs, we developed the mnemonic device of the *four Ps*, which represent the language arts and literacy scaffolding qualities of **p**itch, **p**ace, **p**ortion, and **p**erspective/**p**oint. Let's look at what they represent.

Adjusting Pitch

Pitch pertains to classroom language use and expectations, specifically their degree of complexity, accuracy, and familiarity. We use the word *pitch*, which conveys a meaning similar to *level*, or something that can be made higher or lower, such as a high-pitched or low-pitched ramp or roof. We don't use the term *level* when discussing classroom language use or expectations to avoid confusion with the common use of *level* in describing MLs' assessed proficiency in listening, speaking, reading, and writing (in other words, a student's levels of L2 proficiency). In targeted language and literacy instruction, the pitch of classroom language is addressed at or just beyond the ML's level of L2 proficiency. For example, second language development teachers use the approach to developing composition skills known as process writing, but they gear it to their ML students' level of vocabulary and sentence structure. L2 development teachers know what their MLs' learner language, or interlanguage, should be at their specific level of L2 proficiency, so they work with that learner language to strategically correct each student's errors, focusing on those that are typical at the given level. Working with each ML's learner language where it is enables L2 development teachers to lead the student through the steps of process writing, but the language they use and the language they expect their students to use will be different.[46]

Second language development teachers also adjust the pitch of their language in their presentations and instructional conversations, using "foreigner" or teacher talk that involves careful selection of words, sentence structures, and nonverbal connections to promote comprehension. Similarly, students' oral language reflects their levels of proficiency, and teachers understand and expect corresponding second language developmental patterns.

Let's look at an example of pitch adjustments Ms. Myers made for Edgar in her grade-level disciplinary literacy lesson whose objective is for students to read and answer questions about a scientific text, which is the same objective that the regular English language arts class was addressing. After reviewing the lesson plan with the lens of the SCC protocol and adding nonverbal and verbal support such as diagrams, models, leveled questioning, and glossaries to the lesson, she knew that those supports alone would not reach Edgar at his current level of proficiency to build his language and literacy skills in English. To follow the spirit of the objective through adjusting the pitch of the language used in the tasks, Ms. Myers could select or adapt a text with less grammatically complex and more familiar language, such as Spanish-English cognates (substituting "composed," which is similar to "compuesto," for "made up" in "a cell is *composed* of the membrane, the nucleus, and the cytoplasm"). She decided to use a text she found in an ELD curriculum that was slightly above Edgar's current proficiency level in reading so that she could help him to build his reading skills. This will enable her to work within the space where Edgar can comprehend a reading independently and where he can comprehend a text with the help of an instructor, or what Lev Vygotsky terms his zone of proximal development. She still plans to use the added verbal and nonverbal supports from her earlier application of the SCC protocol with this pitch-adjusted text, which is slightly above where Edgar is now, to help him comprehend phrasing and vocabulary beyond his current proficiency.

Adjusting Pace

Pace refers to the rate of instructional practice, which is dependent on language. In targeted language and literacy instruction, the rate of instruction is slower, with more comprehension checks, expansion, and elaboration. For example, in a directed reading lesson, the L2 development teacher would rephrase and extend much of the language presented in the text or produced by the students, asking questions to ensure comprehension was achieved. Because MLs often need more time to phrase an answer in their L2, wait time can be longer than for non-MLs. There is also more interaction around language, with instructional conversations between teacher and student, using language pitched to their levels and frequent expanding and rephrasing of the ML's learner language. More interaction between students, with opportunities for negotiating meaning, is an important part of targeted language instruction for MLs.

Similar to the extent that pitch would be adjusted for Edgar's reading activity, the pace Ms. Myers would use to check his comprehension of the scientific text would be slowed down to allow for more instructional conversations and negotiation of meaning. Because Edgar's first response to most questions is typically brief and partial, with his tendency to begin a statement and trail off, Ms. Myers makes a point of asking follow-up questions to draw more language from Edgar. This not only checks Edgar's comprehension of the scientific text's details but also encourages him to use more complex and complete sentences to build his oral proficiency and literacy in English.

Adjusting Portion

Portion is the amount of spoken or written content in a lesson. In targeted language and literacy instruction, reading materials and other media beyond (even well beyond) the ML's proficiency level are used, but the amount of content is reduced, enabling unpacking for issues relevant to each ML at their level of proficiency. For example, ELD teachers often use a listening activity with a brief audio or video file and go through it sentence by sentence, even word by word, to clarify meaning. Extracting a smaller portion from an "authentic source" rather than one designed for a specific level of L2 proficiency is a technique that has been used successfully in ELD classes.

In Ms. Myers's lesson, instead of using the ELD curriculum text with less complex and more familiar language (adjusting pitch), the grade-level text could be broken down into short segments that Ms. Myers would unpack for Edgar. For example, the sentence, "Photosynthesis is the process by which plants, algae, and some bacteria convert light energy into chemical energy in the form of glucose," could be unpacked by breaking it down into three connected, brief sentences. Then, Ms. Myers could show other examples of the grammatical form "by which . . ." to help Edgar understand the meaning of this discipline-specific wording and even use it in sentences Ms. Myers guides Edgar to compose. This breaking down of the text would also affect the pace of instruction, as each segment could take as long to unpack as the regular classroom teacher's instruction for the entire reading passage. Ms. Myers could also encourage Edgar to take notes in Spanish to remind him of the meaning she conveyed while unpacking each segment.

Adjusting Perspective/Point

Issues of focus for MLs, or the perspective of instruction, often differ from what would be emphasized with non-MLs. For example, targeted language instruction often includes a presentation of first and second language form or structure contrasts and similarities, using the students' L1 as a resource but also pointing out when miscommunication or errors can occur in their L2 because of language differences.[47] Another illustration of difference in perspective or point is when the class tells a story based on a shared experience and the teacher records it on chart paper. With native speakers, it is common for the teacher to write what they say and to focus on the spelling and composition of the dictated passage, primarily to help develop emergent reading and writing skills in primary grades. For example, "Yesterday we went on a field trip to the science museum. We saw the planets in the planetarium." In contrast, MLs can benefit from a literal transcription of their speech for teacher-led reflection on the grammatical accuracy of the sentences, with the teacher writing them as spoken but then correcting them together with the class. They might dictate, "Yesterday, we go to field trip at science museum. We see the planet in planetarium." Using these written sentences, the teacher would begin by asking, "Yesterday, we *go*. Is that correct?" leading the children to reflect on the verb and its tense. The issues of perspective/point that are generally different for MLs tend to address *meaning* (extra support needs to be provided for infrequent and unusual terms or idioms like "piece of cake" whose meaning isn't apparent by understanding its words), *language form and structure* (a focus on form or forms that are appropriate for the ML's level can clarify meaning or help develop accuracy of expression), and *cultural background knowledge* (MLs often lack background knowledge related to culture, such as references to baseball or American history for MLEs).

Ms. Myers knows that phrasal verbs, which are verbs plus prepositions such as "made up of" whose meaning do not equal the sum of their parts, are confusing for MLEs. Because the grade-level scientific text uses a number of phrasal verbs, she explains what they are and asks Edgar to find them in the text. They then discuss the meaning of each phrasal verb that he found and add those terms to his vocabulary notebook.

These examples show how language arts and literacy teachers can attune the 4 Ps of targeted language instruction to each ML's proficiency level during an individualized or small-group process of scaffolding.[48] When working one on one with an ML or with pairs or small groups of ML students at the same levels of L2 proficiency, teachers can carefully lead the conversation by prompting students to respond to questions and tasks that are appropriate for their L2 proficiency. They can extract a short segment of text or audiovisual media to unpack. They can also teach a mini grammar lesson on a point of relevance that is learnable at the students' current proficiency level.[49] All of these adjustments to the language and instruction enable MLs to address language and literacy standards in language arts and literacy, using common teaching and learning practices but scaffolded for MLs' proficiency levels in the language skill(s) of focus.

MLs in general classrooms may not be afforded instruction that includes these qualities of scaffolding during teacher-led whole-class instruction. Obviously, for the teacher to present new information using instructional or "foreigner talk" and reading materials whose pitch is geared to the proficiency of a beginning ML would not be ideal for the non-MLs in upper grades. Likewise, a pace and portion of instruction adjusted for the MLs would be too slow and cover too little for non-MLs. And the entire perspective of a lesson for MLs could be completely different from what non-MLs need. To help determine how scaffolding can be provided under these circumstances, we move to the logistical aspects of implementing the TLI protocol.

MANAGING ADJUSTMENTS, GROUPING, TIME, AND PROVIDER

Application. As with the SCC protocol, application involves assessing the type of scaffolding needed (which of the 4 Ps you need to adjust for MLs) and whether that scaffolding can be applied as a supplement or should be an alternative to language and literacy instruction for non-MLs. In Edgar's case, the distance between his listening, speaking, reading, and writing levels and general classroom language and literacy instruction is so large that instruction should be an alternative to what non-MLs are doing.

Grouping. Because the TLI protocol zeroes in on individual MLs' proficiency in listening, speaking, reading, and writing, providing scaffolding that supports language and literacy development requires individualization. Depending on the enrollment of MLs at the school, there may be groups of students in a class that are close to the same levels in various skills, so working with small groups would be appropriate in that case. In cases where, for example, there is only one student at a particular skill level, such as an ML student who experienced years of interrupted schooling and is well below grade-level literacy in their L1, individual instruction may be most appropriate. In Edgar's case, there are other MLs at his proficiency levels who could work on the same alternative activities with Ms. Myers, so targeted language and literacy instruction could be provided for him through group or individual instruction.

Time. The timing of targeted language and literacy instruction will likely be affected by available personnel and resources. Supplemental targeted language and literacy instruction could occur before, during, or after a grade-level lesson when the distance between the skill instruction and the ML's proficiency level isn't too large for the ML to be engaged in targeted language and literacy instruction. If instruction needs to be alternative to what occurs in the general language arts and literacy classroom, ideally it would take place while general language and literacy instruction is scheduled. For the elementary level, this would likely be during the language arts/literacy block. For Edgar at the secondary level, the ELD class could be taken in lieu of a general English language arts or literacy class, but it must address the same standards so Edgar has access to the core curriculum.

Provider. The people best suited and available to scaffold instruction are largely dictated by the resources at a school, the ML program model used, and the degree of collaboration that instructional and other school professionals practice. We designed the TLI protocol to be used in collaboration, wherever possible. Depending on the distance between the student's proficiency and the lesson's grade-level skill focus, as well as resources at the school, the provider could be the classroom teacher, an L2 development teacher, a qualified bilingual aide, a literacy specialist, or a technology-assisted resource. Edgar is fortunate that his school has enough MLEs to justify Ms. Myers's full-time ELD teacher position.

A NOTE ABOUT USING TECHNOLOGY FOR SCAFFOLDING

Technology can be a great way to provide the specific scaffolding that MLs need. Tools such as grammar apps and online tutorials and practices such as creating and sharing podcasts and videos allow for individualization that can provide any of the 4 Ps that would not be feasible to provide otherwise. For instance, Gero might benefit from using an iPad or other electronic tablet to develop basic concepts of print, decoding, and word identification skills. Gero, Edith, Edgar, and Tasir can use iPads to listen to stories through e-books, thus seeing the print being read, which can improve their word recognition and reading fluency skills. They can also monitor and improve their reading fluency by listening to themselves reading by using the voice-over function to record themselves reading a book and then replaying their recording. Recent research has shown that tablets have the potential to reduce many social and behavioral barriers by providing tools and applications that allow students with and without learning difficulties to communicate and learn.[50] Adolescent MLs like Tasir and Edgar who are developing reading skills in their L2 might benefit from text-to-speech software that enables them to simultaneously read and listen to any kind of digital or scanned printed material and provides a host of online reference and study tools, such as online bilingual dictionaries, to strengthen listening, speaking, reading, and writing skills. Finally, students with advanced oral proficiency in social language but below grade-level proficiency in academic language and literacy, like Tasir, can benefit from web-based instruction aimed at enhancing new literacy skills and strategies such as asking questions, locating and synthesizing information, and communicating information to others. There are also many promising AI tools that can adjust the pitch of a text or point out and explain grammatical errors in student writing that can be incorporated into lessons and activities.[51]

Don't worry if the TLI protocol is still a bit abstract at this point. As you read chapters 8 through 11, the protocol's specifics will become more concrete. Each chapter shows samples of and more details about each of our four MLEs' developing listening, speaking, reading, and writing skills in English. We will also discuss research and theory on second language acquisition issues related to each MLE's language development and the grade level they are placed in. And on the very practical side of the upcoming chapters, we will show four different language arts and literacy lessons and how we used the TLI protocol to provide targeted language and literacy instruction for Gero, Edith, Tasir, and Edgar. Once you get to the conclusion, you'll know what targeted language and literacy instruction looks, sounds, and feels like.

ESSENTIAL POINTS

1. Language and literacy instruction for MLs should be tailored to or slightly above their current language proficiency, focusing on gradual progress toward grade-level expectations in speaking, listening, reading, and writing.
2. Instructed second language acquisition helps MLs accelerate their L2 proficiency and helps prevent errors from becoming ingrained, with an emphasis on grammar and academic language structures.
3. Effective instructional scaffolding (the 4 Ps) involves adjusting pitch (complexity of language), pace (speed of instruction), portion (amount of content), and perspective/point (alignment with L2-specific developmental needs) to support language development.
4. Teachers should differentiate instruction for MLs by addressing language structures, comparing L1 and L2, and using students' native language as a resource to enhance learning and engagement.
5. Technology tools such as grammar apps, text-to-speech software, and e-books help personalize instruction, support literacy, and assist MLs in overcoming communication barriers.

STOP AND REFLECT QUESTIONS

1. How important are listening activities in second language acquisition? What specific role do they play in assisting learners to acquire a language?
2. Review your state's (or country's) L2 proficiency levels for the main language of instruction and assessment that your ML students learn in (e.g., English in the United States, Italian in Italy). Identify where your MLs would be placed on this continuum. How can you help your learner progress to the next level?

GO AND PRACTICE ACTIVITIES

1. Devote a class session to listening and recording verbal interactions among your MLs. You should record interactions between MLs and/or between MLs and non-MLs. Analyze the interactions. How are your MLs demonstrating progress toward obtaining oral academic language proficiency?
2. Develop a plan to sequence the teaching of affixes to your MLs. Review your list. Is your sequence for affixes in line with current research on this topic? Review at least three research-based articles on the teaching of morphological development of multilingual learners.

Teaching Gero to Write About "My Favorite Pet"

Language and Literacy in the Primary Grades

"Krik!" exclaimed Grand-mère, the burst of the final *k* shaping her smile. "Krak!" replied Gero, ever ready for the call to respond. *[In Kreyòl]* "Grandmother, tell us another story about Bouki and Malice!" Grand-mère continued *[In Kreyòl]*, "One day, Malice . . . ." Grand-mère spoke slowly, pausing at dramatic turns. Her voice, throaty for Malice and creaky for Bouki, carried clear into the living room, where Gero's mother and father had sought quiet to read. Gero, along with his brothers and sister, stayed at the table, sweet-talking Grand-mère into one more tale of the notorious characters' antics.

Every evening Gero and his family sat snug around the dinner table, nimbly moving from French to Haitian Kreyòl and back.[1] As they ate, Papa singled out the children, round-robin style, until everyone answered each of his daily questions. *[In French]* "Gero, what was your favorite part of school today?" Gero loved telling about Ms. Levin's storybooks and bulletin boards. *[In Kreyòl]* "I learned about *kayiman*. In English, it's al-li-ga-tor." Mama clapped her hands together and said, *[in French]* "Gero, it's alligator in French, too! So you know how to say alligator in three languages!" Gero turned toward his older brother, who nodded in agreement. *[In French]* "Ms. Levin will be so happy when I tell her all the ways I can say alligator!"

Before Gero began kindergarten, his first school had been their home, filled with picture and chapter books and weighty discussions in both Haitian Kreyòl and French. Outside of school, Gero continues to converse with adults and is building emergent literacy and conversational skills in his home languages. At school, Ms. Levin knows the importance of using these skills in developing Gero's literacy in English, and she is quickly learning how to teach to his unique language and literacy needs.

GRADE-LEVEL EXPECTATIONS FOR LANGUAGE AND LITERACY IN KINDERGARTEN

Like many schools around the United States, Pine Woods Elementary implemented their state's latest standards in English language arts that *all* students are expected to meet. The following sections outline the language demands these expectations establish for reading, writing, speaking, listening, and language.

Reading

In developing specific skills for reading, kindergartners are taught how to follow words on a page, name all upper- and lowercase letters of the English alphabet, identify syllables in spoken words, isolate and substitute sounds in one-syllable words, and read high-frequency words such as *the*. As they develop the broader skills involved in comprehending texts, kindergartners are taught how to identify details, main topics, and major events; connect illustrations and the text they correspond to; identify book components such as the cover, author, and illustrator; and read grade-level texts with purpose and understanding of characters, settings, events, and points of view.

The following passage gives a sense of grade-level text for kindergarten[2]:

> I went to a pet store. I saw big dogs. I saw little dogs. I saw dogs with long hair. I saw dogs with short hair. I got a little dog.

Writing

In the related area of writing, kindergartners can draw, dictate, or write their opinion on a book topic or a series of events. The language category includes many skills that are necessary for writing (rather than solely relying on drawing or dictating), such as printing upper- and lowercase letters, capitalizing the first word in a sentence, knowing letters for most consonant and short vowel sounds, spelling simple words phonetically, expressing opinions, and giving supportive reasons. With the support and guidance of an adult, kindergarten students are also tasked to improve drawing and writing by planning and revising.

Speaking, Listening, and Language

Speaking and listening are part of all language use, so kindergartners are taught to converse about grade-level topics and texts, confirm comprehension of others' speech, and describe people, places, things, feelings, and thoughts. Similar to the speaking and listening standards, language standards apply to all other language skills. This involves using frequent nouns and verbs, adding *-s* or *-es* to make spoken words plural, ensuring subject-verb agreement, using possessives and prepositions, and expressing thoughts in full sentences. Lastly, kindergarten students must be able to identify common words and use grade-level-appropriate vocabulary in speaking and writing.

This brief overview summarizes the general expectations in language and literacy for kindergarten students who are native speakers of English. It is also important to understand which parts of these grade-level expectations a multilingual learner of English (MLE) at Gero's level of proficiency can reach—the topic of the next section.

RESEARCH ON TEACHING LANGUAGE AND LITERACY TO MULTILINGUAL LEARNERS OF ENGLISH IN PRIMARY GRADES

Some children arrive in kindergarten with the crucial set of skills needed to begin reading. Other children may not have been taught those skills in preschool or at home. Children who routinely observe literary practices at home, such as parents reading the newspaper, leaving notes on the refrigerator door, and making grocery lists, have already become socialized into literacy. Those who haven't developed these understandings of literacy need to be taught them. Research has shown, however, that with MLEs, the teaching of foundational literacy skills, while necessary, is insufficient because oral language proficiency influences the ability to learn to read and write.[3] This finding is important for two reasons. First, learning to read in a second language (L2) depends on having good oral language proficiency in that language, a key point that will be discussed in the following section. Second, it echoes a crucial disclosure contained in the National Literacy Panel Report,[4] which asserts that research available on acquiring literacy in English as a second language is quite limited in comparison to the vast research available on learning to read in English as a first language (L1).[5] These findings suggest that when teachers read about best practices in teaching literacy skills, they should not assume that the same practices work equally well or should be implemented in the same way for MLEs. However, research does indicate that primary-grade MLEs and non-MLE students typically perform at similar levels on measures of basic reading skills such as processing sounds, word reading, and spelling.[6] As will be discussed in more depth in chapter 9, the greatest differences in MLE students' reading performance pertain to reading comprehension.

Of the research conducted with MLEs, the vast majority of studies have been conducted with Spanish-speaking children in the primary grades, with few studies representing upper elementary grades. Nonetheless, research findings from these cross-language studies and neurolinguistics have provided valuable insights about the factors that influence language and literacy development across languages. Given these caveats, there are key findings from the National Literacy Panel that can help guide teachers of L2 students in primary grades:

- Instruction in the five areas described by the National Reading Panel—phonemic awareness, phonics, fluency, vocabulary, and text comprehension—helps MLEs develop literacy skills.[7]
- Instruction in oral proficiency for MLs is critical for their acquisition of literacy skills.

- Oral proficiency and literacy in the native language can facilitate literacy development in the L2.
- Individual differences such as general language competence, age, cognitive abilities, previous learning, and similarities between the native language and English greatly affect English literacy development.
- Home language experience can positively affect literacy development.

Oral Proficiency in English

One accommodation that research has found effective for expanding literacy in MLEs is developing oral proficiency in the "context of literacy instruction."[8] Children whose oral language is limited in their L2, and whose literacy in any language is emergent, lack the ability to self-monitor and self-teach because they may not comprehend the meaning of words they decode.[9] Catherine Snow explains that learning to read (for the first time) in an L2 is different from learning to read an L2 (after learning to read in at least one other language) and suggests that more research is needed to illuminate the different processes involved. Snow agrees with other researchers that "language and literacy skills in either the first or second language have a transactional relationship with one another [see figure 8.1]: The development of each depends on and contributes to the other."[10]

Transfer of Basic Literacy Skills and Strategies from the L1

There is a general consensus among researchers that once a learner has acquired a given level of phonemic awareness in one language, it is possible to transfer that understanding to any other language. Research has shown, for instance, that in kindergarten and first grade, students' ability to isolate initial sounds in their L1 significantly predicted their ability to do the same in the L2.[11] Children learning languages whose spelling systems have close and consistent sound/symbol correspondences (called transparent orthographies), such as Spanish, Greek, Finnish, German, Italian, and Haitian Kreyòl, rapidly acquire phonemic awareness. Conversely, children learning nontransparent orthographies, where the same sound can be represented by many different symbols

FIGURE 8.1

Transactional Relationship of L2 Literacy Development

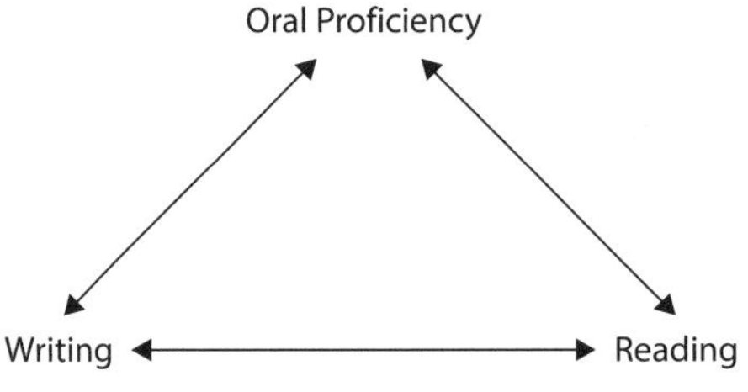

and spelling patterns, such as English, Danish, and French, acquire phonemic awareness more slowly.[12]

Other literacy skills and strategies transfer from L1 to L2 reading and writing. The greater the similarity in the writing systems of the two languages, the greater is the degree of transfer, thus reducing the time and difficulties involved in learning to read the L2.[13] Through our experiences as teacher educators, we have concluded that the more teachers are aware of the students' underlying interlanguage and the common contrasts between students' first and second languages, the better prepared they are to address their language and literacy needs.

LEARNER LANGUAGE CONSIDERATIONS FOR HAITIAN MULTILINGUAL LEARNERS OF ENGLISH

To understand the support needed for MLEs with a Haitian Kreyòl language background like Gero, it is important to know a few pertinent contrasts between the native language(s) and English.

General Similarities and Differences in English, French, and Haitian Kreyòl

As soon as he joined her kindergarten class, Ms. Levin started to search for information to understand Gero's interlanguage and cross-language transfer between his native Haitian Kreyòl language and English to better assist him in developing English language and literacy skills.[14] In regard to orthography, she discovered four fundamental principles: one sign for each sound, the same sign for the same sound, no silent letter, and each letter has its own function.[15] She further found out that, for example, the Kreyòl lexicon and phonology (sounds) are formed on French, whereas syntax (word order) and morphology (way words are formed) are based mainly on West African languages.[16] This means that verbs and nouns are not inflected in Haitian Kreyòl like they are in French or English in order to indicate gender, tense, number, person, or mood. For example, in Haitian Kreyòl, nouns are not feminine or masculine, as they are in French. In French, *le livre* (*the book*) is masculine, but in Haitian Kreyòl, *liv la* is gender neutral. In English and French, nouns carry an *-s* to demonstrate plurality. In contrast, Kreyòl uses *yo* as a plural marker; *the books* are thus *liv yo.* Furthermore, in English, both the definite (i.e., *the*) and indefinite (i.e., *a/an*) articles precede the noun. In Kreyòl, the indefinite article precedes the noun and definite articles follow the noun.[17] These are but a few contrasts that could affect Gero's understanding and use of English. However, because word order for affirmative and negative statements and also for yes-no questions is the same in both languages, following the subject-verb-object sequence, Ms. Levin won't need to pay much attention to how Gero forms sentences.

Cultures across the world have developed different ways to organize thoughts and texts.[18] Although kindergarten students don't have to compose long narratives, Ms. Levin realizes that Gero has likely started to internalize rhetorical structures different from English as a result of the family reading French children's books and engaging in rich Haitian Kreyòl storytelling time. Proverbs are widely used in Haitian Kreyòl conversations, and essay introductions often open on a philosophical note or are flowery in style due to the French influence, but this is not a concern for Ms. Levin because Gero is only starting to acquire literacy skills in English.

Moving from the birds-eye view of how words and sentences are formed in Haitian Kreyòl, we now turn our attention to Gero's developing literacy skills in English.

Analyzing Gero's Language Samples

My favorite anim an a ligator. It HA sHrp tetH ta Lev In tagwater.

"Do you like alligators, Gero?" asked Ms. Levin. Gero smiled as he looked down at the ruled paper, the tops of his scribbled letters just clearing the bold lines that alternated with the dotted ones. "Look at that word, *favorite*. You copied it perfectly, and you wrote the letters so neatly." Gero looked up for a second. Ms. Levin bent down next to him. "Favorite means the one you like the most. *My* [pointing to her chest] favorite animal is a rabbit. A bunny rabbit," Ms. Levin made bunny ears with her index and middle finger, hopping back and forth across the table.

"Let's look at the word you wrote after *favorite*. I see A-N-I-M, and that sounds like *an-im*, but there is something missing at the end. How do we say that word, Gero?" She waited, and waited some more. "Gero, finish this word, *an-im . . . .*" "Ah! ah-nee-máhl!" Gero exclaimed. "An-i-mal, right, animal!" confirmed Ms. Levin. "So, how do we write the whole word? How do we write the missing letters? A-N-I-M-*uhl*. Can you write the letters for the sound *uhl*?" She pointed to the chart paper on the whiteboard, and read its first two sentences, "My favorite animal is an alligator. It has sharp teeth and lives in the water." Ms. Levin pointed to a poster behind them, an alligator lounging on a riverbank. Gripping the number 2 pencil with his thumb and all four fingers, Gero wrote *al* to the right of the letter *m*.

Gero is working hard to print. Although some of the letters are the wrong case and are not written neatly on the lines, he is doing very well. In Haiti, students are not taught to print. It is believed that very young children begin to write by drawing scribbling lines and round shapes with one consistent line. Therefore, Haitian educators see no need to break up this skill by introducing print during the early grades and then reintroducing cursive after the primary grades. Haitian students begin to use cursive writing as soon as they enter school, even as prekindergarten students, and by the fourth or fifth grade, they have perfect penmanship. Knowing that printing is very new to Gero, Ms. Levin plans to provide him with many opportunities to practice.

Gero is using inventive spelling to spell the words unfamiliar to him. He is also using his understanding of the sound system of the English language, an indication of his developing phonemic awareness in English. Because Haitian Kreyòl enjoys a one-to-one sound-to-letter correspondence, Gero is also transferring his limited knowledge of spelling of Haitian Kreyòl to writing in English. Gero knows that words are written left to right, he has a general idea of word boundaries, and he knows some sight words in English. Ms. Levin is ready and willing to provide him with the support he needs to assure success in writing.

One aim of early writing is to develop the ability to form the letters and order them properly. For example, by copying sentences, Gero is learning and practicing writing letters, words, and words in a sentence. A second aim of early writing is to list, restate, or paraphrase information rather than express original thoughts. These two goals are not considered composition. In Gero's writing sample above, his only original contribution to the writing is selecting the animal in the first sentence; he copies the second sentence, which describes a physical feature and habitat of the animal.[19]

Gero is progressing well in all language arts and literacy skills, having been assessed at level 1 a few weeks earlier by the district English language development (ELD) testing supervisor. Ms. Levin took Gero's test data into account, along with her observations of his performance in class, her spoken interactions with him, an informal reading assessment she conducted, and samples of his writings in and out of class. These various types of data have informed her approach to scaffolding instruction so that it is targeted to Gero's needs at his current level of English proficiency.

ESSENTIAL POINTS

1. MLEs need L2 oral language instruction *in addition to* phonemic awareness, phonics, fluency, vocabulary, and text comprehension to develop literacy skills in the new language.
2. Gero's literacy development is shaped by his multilingual background, speaking Haitian Kreyòl, French, and English. His family's language practices, like storytelling and switching between languages, help strengthen his literacy skills in his home languages, which are crucial as he learns English. Ms. Levin understands the importance of using Gero's cultural and linguistic strengths to support his English development.
3. Gero struggles with English writing, particularly with spelling, letter formation, and proper use of capitalization and punctuation. Coming from a Kreyòl-based phonetic system, he uses "inventive" spelling, applying his understanding of sounds to write words in English. While he faces challenges with writing, he is slowly improving his phonemic awareness and understanding of English writing rules, with support from Ms. Levin.
4. Ms. Levin uses Gero's language assessment data and classroom observations to guide her teaching. She tailors her lessons to address his needs, such as letter formation, matching sounds to letters, and basic sentence structure. With verbal support, like copying sentences and focusing on one skill at a time, Gero is making steady progress in learning to write in English

CLASSROOM APPLICATION

Ms. Levin likes to initiate writing with her kindergartners by getting the students to put their thoughts on paper first before helping them make their text better, which she accomplishes by modeling how to improve spelling through the familiar phonics skills the children use to decode text when reading. She often uses shared writing experiences to accomplish this. Therefore, while she makes sure to include teaching language conventions, she focuses her instruction on having the students name what they are writing about and supply some information about the topic.

MS. LEVIN'S WRITING LESSON

The lesson described here connects English language arts to life science. Ms. Levin, like many teachers in elementary school, regularly introduces or reinforces science concepts through reading. After a series of lessons on animals' physical aspects, behaviors, habitats, and other characteristics, she wants her students to reflect on the animals they encountered by means of children's books and grade-level informational texts and decide which would make good class pets.[20]

OBJECTIVE

The students will be able to explain through descriptive writing why their chosen animal should become the class pet.

LESSON DESCRIPTION

1. Display the books on animals that the class has been reading. Students share with their shoulder partners what they remember about them. List the animals on the whiteboard as students report out.
2. Add a column labeled *adjectives* next to the list of animals. Pick an animal and ask the students to describe it (e.g., furry, soft, cute), and write down these words. Repeat until the number of animals up for choice is reached.
3. Assign specific animals to shoulder partners, who must think of three new adjectives that describe the animals.
4. Add the adjectives to the column as students report back. When done, students read the list aloud.
5. Explain the writing prompt, and then reveal the sentence frame "A/An [animal] because it is _____." Point to an animal and an adjective and tell students to say the completed sentence frame out loud, writing as they say it. Repeat twice more.
6. Remind students to use the lists of animals and adjectives for ideas and spelling to fill in their own sentence frames. Students write and then draw the animal.
7. Collect the papers. Shoulder partners tell each other about their choice and reason.
8. Discuss editing using a previous year's first draft. Model how to improve writing by adding more adjectives (expand the sentence frame to "A/An [animal] because

it is _____ and _____") and by checking for missing words and spelling mistakes. Rewrite the corrected sentence.

9. Encourage students to say each word out loud as they reread and correct their sentence and add to their sentence based on the frame. Students rewrite and then enhance their drawing.

EVALUATION

Use writing accuracy and representation of animal drawing as a formative assessment to inform future instruction.

APPLICATION OF THE TASLL FRAMEWORK PROTOCOLS TO THE WRITING LESSON

In chapters 3 to 6, we described the steps and decision-making points of the Supportive Classroom Communication (SCC) protocol in detail. In this chapter, we summarize each step and concentrate on explaining the Targeted Language/Literacy Instruction (TLI) protocol steps to scaffold Gero's language and literacy development for this lesson. The at-a-glance table (table 8.2) in the last section of this chapter will show the entire protocol realized.

Analyze Communication in Lesson Tasks

STEP 1

Other than two SLIDE elements, namely displaying the book on animals and the students drawing the animal, every lesson task uses TREAD when the students speak and listen to each other or the teacher, when they read the adjectives and sentence frames written on the board, and when they write and revise their sentences (see table 2.2 on page 56 for sample SLIDE/TREAD verbs).

Size the Gaps

STEP 2

Gero's proficiency level as a newcomer allows him to follow short spoken messages and produce a few familiar words while using nonverbal communication means. In writing, he's able to communicate with drawings, so the fact that Ms. Levin has been working with him on copying sentences will facilitate his completing the sentence frame with support.[21] There are no places in this plan where Gero would encounter no gap or a small one. Only four lesson tasks represent a medium gap: the introduction when the students discuss what they remember about animals from the books, the two-part adjective vocabulary-building activity, and the students telling a partner about their sentence. Everything else will prove greatly challenging for Gero.

Address the Gaps Between ML's L2 Proficiency and Lesson Tasks

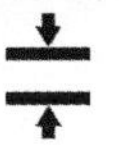

Ms. Levin can apply many of the same verbal and nonverbal supports that proved to be successful in Gero's social studies lesson (see chapter 3) to this writing lesson. She can demonstrate instructions, gesture adjectives, use images, and point out and draw attention to written text with arrows. By placing Gero nearby, Ms. Levin ensures that he can better hear the directions while she can hear his pronunciation of the sentences during choral repetition. Furthermore, pairing him with a Haitian Kreyòl peer when he talks about his text attends to his affective needs. As in each lesson, Ms. Levin should use leveled questioning to help him understand her comprehension checks and to respond at his proficiency level.

MANAGE APPLICATION, GROUPING, TIME, AND PROVIDER

Most supports can be implemented universally because the vocabulary is concrete, the sentences are short, and kindergarteners must acquire literacy skills close to those of a beginning-level MLE who already has L1 literacy awareness. Leveled questioning to check on Gero's comprehension and to gently elicit from him animal names and adjectives, as well as the bilingual glossary, are supplemental because his non-MLE peers would not benefit from them. They do not need a modified sentence frame that reduces the amount to write. Even though the gaps are all medium to large, Ms. Levin can manage the supports. If a volunteer were available, they could closely monitor Gero's draft writing. With the SCC protocol put in place, we can move on to those parts in the lesson where the TLI protocol is indispensable for developing his L2 skills.

STEP 1 Identify Language/Literacy Skill(s) to Be Developed

The lesson objective requires students to explain their choice of a classroom pet through descriptive writing. Therefore, writing is the skill to be developed.

STEP 2 Size the Distance

The TLI protocol calls for sizing the distance with the granular WIDA performance definitions. As you learned in chapter 3, Gero's school only screens for newcomers' listening and speaking skills. Because those skills are both at level 1 and oral language typically is developed before literacy, the ELD specialist and Ms. Levin can reasonably assume that the reading and writing levels would also be at level 1. The language samples and formative assessment results they obtained over the previous weeks certainly support this assumption. Therefore, we show his assumed writing WIDA performance definitions at that level in table 8.1 to highlight the adjustments needed for this lesson.

The lesson objective and the associated state standard that calls for using "a combination of drawing, dictating, and writing to express opinions about a topic" align with what an MLE at level 1 of English proficiency can do.[22] However, the distance between the demands to meet the objective and Gero's proficiency level is wide enough that targeted language andliteracy instruction is warranted. Gero is not yet able to check independently for accuracy in his own writing through sounding out. Reading many words one letter or sound at a time, he is unable to tell if the word "sounds right," and he's still some distance from being able to comprehend and construct longer sentences. It is more essential for Gero's continued L2 language and literacy development to build vocabulary and learn to pronounce the words than to concentrate on minor spelling errors or missing connecting words. After consulting the ELD teacher for advice, Ms. Levin decides to work with Gero by practicing the pattern of the sentence frame.

TABLE 8.1

Gero's Assumed WIDA Performance Definitions in Writing (Grades K-12)

Skill and Level	Linguistic Complexity	Language Forms and Conventions	Vocabulary Usage
	At each grade, toward the end of a given level of English proficiency, and with instructional support, English language learners will process (L/R) or produce (S/W)		
W 1	• Words, phrases, or chunks or language. • Single words used to represent ideas.	• Phrase-level grammatical structures. • Phrasal patterns associated with common social and instructional situations.	• General content-related words. • Everyday social and instructional words and expressions.

Develop ML's L2 Language/Literacy Skill(s)

STEP 3

This section describes Ms. Levin's plans to provide Gero with individualized instruction that reinforces adjectives and enhances his favorite class pet sentence, two actions that will move him forward in English language and literacy developments.

ADJUSTING PACE

Ms. Levin circles back repeatedly to the sentence frame to elicit more oral language from Gero, expanding and recasting his phrasing in an instructional conversation. Gero might mentally translate some words during these interactions. Depending on the time he takes before speaking or depending on his responses, she asks probing questions on language that is new to Gero in a risk-free manner.

ADJUSTING PERSPECTIVE/POINT

Non-MLEs have already acquired simple English sentence patterns and basic vocabulary in spoken language, but Gero hasn't acquired them in English yet. Although formal grammar lessons aren't appropriate for early childhood, showing a pattern template (example sentence) and working with a sentence frame based on it act as an inductive grammar lesson to advance Gero's English proficiency.

Managing Grouping, Time, and Provider

Grouping. At this time, Gero is the sole WIDA level 1 in the class, so Ms. Levin will conference with him individually to focus on his acquisition of English vocabulary.

Time and Provider. There is no need to preteach or postteach anything to meet Gero's needs. The time spent on vocabulary and sentence pattern practice, while the non-MLE students spend time on revising and expanding their sentences perfectly, matches the duration required for Gero's scaffolded instruction.

Lesson Summary

Table 8.2 provides an overview of both the SCC protocol and the TLI protocol applied to the kindergarten writing lesson. We display the lesson tasks in the SCC

TABLE 8.2

The Writing About My Favorite Pet Lesson at a Glance

Instructional Steps	**Skill[1] and Gap Size[2]**	**Added Supports[3]**
<u>Display</u> the books on animals that the class has been reading. Students **share** with their shoulder partners what they remember about them. **List** the animals on the whiteboard as the students report out.	L, S, R ↕↕	***Nonverbal Supports:*** • Pointing to the books and gesturing instructions • Attaching images of the animals next to the words ***Verbal Supports:*** • Placing Gero nearby to better hear teacher language (supplemental) • Connecting oral and written language: tracking the animals with a wand while the students read the words
Add a column labeled *adjectives* next to the list of animals. **<u>Pick an animal</u>** and **ask** the students to **describe** it (e.g., furry, soft, cute) and **write** down these words. Repeat until the number of animals up for choice is reached.	L, S, R ↕↕	***Nonverbal Supports:*** • Pointing to the animal image • Gesturing adjectives ***Verbal Supports:*** • Leveled questioning (supplemental) • Connecting oral and written language: tracking the adjectives with a wand while the students read them
Assign animals to shoulder partners, who must **think of** three new **adjectives** that describe them. **Add** the adjectives to the column as students **report back**. When done, students **read** the list aloud.	L, S, R ↕↕	***Nonverbal Supports:*** • Sitting by Gero and partner to help with bilingual glossary (supplemental) • Pointing to animals' pictures before writing adjectives • Gesturing adjectives ***Verbal Supports:*** • Leveled questioning (supplemental) • Connecting oral and written language: tracking the adjectives with a wand while the students read them

Explain the writing prompt and then **reveal** the **sentence frame** "A/An [animal] because it is _____." Point to an animal and an adjective and **tell** students to **say** the completed sentence frame out loud, **writing** as they **say** it. **Repeat** twice more.	L, S, R	***Nonverbal Support:*** Drawing arrows from each animal image and the chosen adjective to correct place on sentence frame ***Verbal Supports:*** • Connecting oral and written language: tracking the sentences with a wand as the students reread them • Leveled questioning (supplemental)
Remind students to **use the lists** of animals and adjectives for ideas and spelling to **fill in** their own **sentence frame**. Students **rewrite** the sentence frame and then draw the animal.	L, S, R	***Verbal Supports:*** • Assisting Gero to pick an animal by pointing to an animal and ask, "Is this your *favorite* class pet?" until he says "Yes." Pointing to blank and watch him write the word. Repeating process with adjective: "Is your [animal] soft? Is it cuddly?" • Modified sentence frame for rewriting: "A _____ because it ___________." (alternative)
Collect the papers. Shoulder partners **tell** each other about their choice and reason.	L, S	***Verbal Support:*** Partnering with Merline to assist with L1, if needed (supplemental)
Discuss editing, using a previous year's first draft. **Model** how to improve through **adding** more **adjectives** (expand sentence frame to "A/An animal because it is _____ and _____.") and by checking for missing words and spelling mistakes. **Rewrite** corrected sentence.	L, W, R	***Nonverbal Support:*** Underline incorrect words on sample draft in same color as corresponding animal, adjective, or other words on the whiteboard. ***Verbal Support:*** Tracking the corrected sentence with the wand as students read it.
Gero needs dedicated instructional assistance through the **TLI** protocol to shore up his understanding of the vocabulary and to augment and improve his writing. He will work with Ms. Levin for his sentence pattern practice while the other students are writing their second draft independently.		

Continued...

TABLE 8.2

The Writing About My Favorite Pet Lesson at a Glance *(Continued...)*

Instructional Steps	Nonverbal and Verbal Supports	4 P Adjustments
Model a variation on the sentence frame pattern with a picture: "A sloth, because it is slow and happy." Gero reads the sentence alongside Ms. Levin as she tracks each word. Showing two more pictures of animals, elicit from Gero their names and their qualities while pointing to the printed list of adjectives and the sentence pattern template/sentence frame. Write what he says, and then have him read the sentence. Assist Gero in breaking down the segments of his sentence frame while checking on his work. Point out missing words and have him repeat and correct the words. Gero then adds "and [chosen adjective]."	***Nonverbal Support:*** Pictures of different animals ***Verbal Support:*** Recast spoken errors	***Pace:*** • Eliciting more oral language by repeatedly returning to the sentence and expanding and recasting his phrasing. • Adjusting time spent on new language, asking probing questions depending on his responses. ***Perspective/Point:*** • Practicing new vocabulary (animals and adjectives). • Working with sentence frame based on pattern template (example sentence).

Key:

1 Language skills: L = listening, S = speaking, R = reading, W = writing

2 Gap sizes: No gap = Ø, ↕ = small gap, ↕↕ = medium gap, ↕↕↕ = large gap

3 Unless otherwise noted, all supports are considered universal.

protocol portion with nonverbal (SLIDE) elements <u>underlined</u> and the verbal elements (TREAD) in **boldface**. Both fonts **<u>combined</u>** show that a task can contain both components. The second column lists the language skills *from the point of view of the students* alongside the gap size that exists between the classroom communication and Gero's current beginning level of English proficiency. Finally, the added verbal and nonverbal supports are depicted in the third column.

You will see a brief explanation just above the lesson tasks where the TLI protocol is applied, which situates the need for the language/literacy development portion. The columns then show how Ms. Levin targets Gero's instruction through actions. The second column contains the nonverbal and verbal supports finely tuned to his needs for the student-teacher interaction, and the 4 P adjustments are presented in the last column.

Final Thoughts

While making copies of each student's picture and their text to take home, Ms. Levin stopped for a moment to look at Gero's writing. She was happy to see how many adjectives he had retained from the whole-class instruction and their one-on-one session. She would need to identify a way to reinforce these words several more times so that he could internalize them for good.

The next day, at the end of her morning meeting, Ms. Levin flipped the whiteboard around. "Let's see how fast you can count the tally marks next to each picture. How about the hamster? How many do you count?" After writing the number the children called out next to each picture, she told them that these are how many votes the animals got in the writing lesson. "So, that means the winner is the *pig*! Second place? Yes, the *bunny*. And who takes third place—the horse? No? Oh, you're right, the *toad* is in third place," Ms. Levin said amid the children's laughter and cheers. Well, next week we'll start decorating this side of the classroom with their pictures and learn more about these animals. But now it's time for PE. Everybody quickly line up. We're leaving in one minute."

On her way back after handing off the students, Ms. Levin shared her success with another teacher in the hallway: "They sure were excited! I'm not surprised Elijah asked if he could add the chicken to the list. He's so proud of his big sister's win at the poultry show and he had the biggest smile on his face when he told me about it. And sweet Gero, I wonder whether he picked the bunny because I told him that it is *my* favorite animal? Hmh. I'm definitely curious to see their reaction on Monday when I lift the sheet off the fishbowl."

STOP AND REFLECT QUESTIONS

1. Do you know whether rhyming activities or songs are common educational practices in the cultures of your MLs? Speaking with a bilingual aide or a parent volunteer could help bridge their L1 educational practices with common practices in your classroom.
2. Do you simply correct the writings of your multilingual learners, or do you analyze them to identify areas of strength and/or weakness? If you mainly correct, you might consider keeping a running list of errors by student so you can begin to select areas on which to focus.

GO AND PRACTICE ACTIVITIES

1. List at least five activities you have created or designed to specifically focus on oral language development of your MLs.
2. Obtain a copy of the WIDA or other English language proficiency standards and your state (or national/regional) language arts/literacy standards. Evaluate both documents and determine how the ELP standards will assist your MLEs to meet the state standards.

Teaching Edith How Words Are Formed

Language and Literacy in the Intermediate Grades

Some time had passed since Ms. Oliver first sat down to talk with Edith. Knowing Edith had difficulty participating in Wednesday's science lesson, Ms. Oliver thought it would be helpful to get a better understanding of Edith's reading and writing skills in English and maybe even in Spanish. The test scores in Edith's folder didn't explain much, so Ms. Oliver invited Edith to be this Friday's weekly "Lunch with Ms. Oliver" companion.

"I can already see that your English is better than when I met you," said Ms. Oliver, slowly and clearly, as she opened her lunch bag. "I'm happy you can understand more now." Edith nodded and poked a straw into her juice box. Taking a sip, she looked around the room. Empty chairs were pushed under scratched and dented tables, and there was no one else for Ms. Oliver to pay attention to but Edith. It felt like her birthday. Or was she in trouble? She felt nervous, not understanding why Ms. Oliver was meeting with only her.

After they finished eating, Ms. Oliver handed Edith a blank page and a pencil. "Edith, would you write something for me in English? Would you please write two or three things about yourself?" Edith put her head down. She did not understand what Ms. Oliver was asking her to do. Ms. Oliver knew Edith liked the character Moana, so she wrote on the paper, "Edith likes Moana." Ms. Oliver read the sentence out loud and nodded and smiled saying "likes." Then she repeated, "Edith likes Moana." Edith was feeling less nervous because Ms. Oliver was helping her understand the words. Ms. Oliver took the pencil and acted like she was writing on the paper, and she said, "Edith, write two or three [holding up two fingers and then three fingers] things you [pointing at Edith] like. "I no . . . I no . . . ," Edith whispered. "Edith, it's just for me. Write what you can. Tell me about yourself." "No puedo escribir en ingles," Edith explained. "Just two or three things," Ms. Oliver gently pleaded, "English or Spanish." Edith took the pencil and began:

Ma na se Edith. [My name is Edith.]
I es 10. [I am 10.]
Ilo vien de Mexico. [I come from Mexico.]
Mi comida feborita es la pizza. [My favorite food is pizza.]

"Thank you, Edith," Ms. Oliver said as she reached for the paper. "For our next lunch, I'll bring a pizza." Edith was happy. Ms. Oliver helped her feel comfortable, and she wasn't nervous anymore.

The dialogue presented in this transcript shows that conversations between Edith and Ms. Oliver have been steadfast, yet strenuous, with each grasping for words that make sense to the other. It is easy to see that although Edith seemed to understand most of what Ms. Oliver was saying, her current level of English proficiency doesn't allow Edith to express all that she's thinking and feeling.

GRADE-LEVEL EXPECTATIONS FOR LANGUAGE AND LITERACY IN FOURTH GRADE

In recent years, many states have put into place directives to incorporate literacy skills throughout different disciplines, encompassing social studies, mathematics, and science from kindergarten through twelfth grade. With a focus on essential literacy skills like reading comprehension, writing proficiency, effective communication through speaking and listening, and adept language usage in varied subjects, rather than only in English language arts, this shift aims to furnish students with essential abilities and proficiencies needed to excel in a multifaceted and interconnected global landscape. The following sections summarize the language demands established by these expectations in the skills of reading, writing, speaking, and listening.

Reading

By fourth grade, students are anticipated to have cultivated most of the specific language and literacy proficiencies and competencies essential for proficient reading. These proficiencies encompass:

- Decoding and fluently reading multisyllabic words
- Possessing a fundamental grasp of the morphemic structure of words and their meanings
- Using prefixes and suffixes, with the capability to contemplate and manipulate their structure
- Comprehending the structural arrangement of sentences at a basic level, demonstrated by the ability to scrutinize and adjust the arrangement

At this grade level, increasing emphasis is given to comprehending and explaining literary and informational texts. Drawing inferences from details in the text, students are also expected to summarize the theme or main idea, describe key elements in detail, and refer to the structure of various types of texts when discussing their differences. In addition, they are required to integrate information across two or more texts on the same topic.

The following passage gives a sense of grade-level text for fourth grade[1]:

> Outside of the station, the astronauts must wear special suits because there is no air to breathe in space. But inside the space station, people can breathe because there is air. People stay at the station and do experiments. Some of these experiments show how plants grow and act in space. Staying at the space station can be fun. It can also be dangerous.

Writing

In upper elementary grades, students like fourth grader Edith are expected to produce increasingly longer and more complex texts, such as:

- Compositions with multiple sections and paragraphs
- Arguments based on facts and reasoning, using precise language
- Narratives that include descriptions of situations, narrators, and characters, as well as dialogue

The language category includes many skills specific to writing, such as avoiding fragmented and run-on sentences and correctly using homophones such as *to*, *too*, and *two*. The students are also expected to use punctuation and capitalization for quotes and compound sentences accurately, spell grade-appropriate words, and use terms and punctuation to convey ideas precisely.

The following passage provides a sense of the expectations for satisfactory writing at the intermediate grades. It is an excerpt from a fourth-grade writing sample graded a 3-2-3 (purpose/structure–development–language) on a four-point scale[2]:

> There are things you can both do in the digital world and hands on. Kids can find hobbies. When kids do hands-on play can discover hobbies by building. They can build forts and discover they like to build or can-do art or the outdoors. Hobbies can also be transferred to digital play. You can look it up on the internet or download a game on your hobbies. Only difference is hands on reality, so with you. This can power the imagination for kids. Hands on play sparks kids' imagination.

Speaking, Listening, and Language

In preparation for speaking, students are expected to read texts on specific discussion topics. They ask and answer relevant questions, paraphrase information, and explain their ideas in relation to key points. They are expected to use formal registers (how they would speak with adults in authority) when appropriate and be able to paraphrase orally presented information. They also use descriptive details in telling stories and recounting experiences.

Language skills are implicit in reading, writing, speaking, and listening. Students are expected to correctly use:

- Relative pronouns such as *who*, *whose*, *whom*, *which*, *that*, *where*, *when*, and *why*
- Past, present, and future progressive verb tenses
- Auxiliary verbs such as *can*, *may*, *must*, *might*, and *could*
- Proper order of adjectives in a sentence
- Prepositional phrases

Additionally, fourth-grade students can use context, frequently used Greek and Latin prefixes, suffixes, and roots, and reference materials to understand a term; explain the meaning of simple similes, metaphors, idioms, adages, and proverbs; and relate words to their antonyms and synonyms. The following section briefly highlights the definition and features of morphology.

A FEW WORDS ABOUT MORPHOLOGY

Because fourth graders are expected to use prefixes, suffixes, and root/base words, the lesson in this chapter focuses on teaching morphology in a dual language program. We will touch on the most important elements here.[3]

Overview of Morphology

Morphology is the study of how words are constructed within a language. Morphological awareness refers to children's conscious understanding of the structure of words and their ability to manipulate that structure effectively.[4] Morphological awareness is essential for proficient reading comprehension, especially with complex texts. Explicit instruction of morphology becomes more important in the fourth grade.

Morphemes are the smallest unit of language that conveys meaning. A word such as *cat* is a free morpheme because it can stand alone, and the *-s* in the word *cats* is a bound morpheme because it has no meaning unless attached to a free morpheme. Bound morphemes are divided into two main components: inflectional and derivational. Inflectional morphemes do not change the meaning of root or base words or parts of speech/lexical category but provide important information about agreement (e.g., the *-s* in *she likes*), tense (the *-ed* in *he walked*), and plurality (the plural suffix *-s* in *dogs*).[5] In English, there are eight inflectional morphemes, and all of them are suffixes:

- Plural *-s* (dogs)
- Possessive *-'s* (Mary's)
- Third person singular present *-s* (he sings)

- Past tense *-ed* (she wanted)
- Past participle *-ed/-en* (we have walked/they have eaten)
- Present participle *-ing* (I am speaking)
- Comparative *-er* (bigger)
- Superlative *-est* (biggest)

The other type of morphemes are called derivational morphemes, which in English are prefixes and suffixes. They alter word meanings, such as *happy* to *unhappy* or *functional* to *dysfunctional*, and syntactic class (e.g., an adjective that changes to an adverb by adding *-ly*), as seen in transformations such as *magic* to *magician*, *teach* to *teacher*, *clever* to *cleverly*, *work* to *worker*, and *agree* to *agreement*.[6]

When teaching about morphology, the interconnectedness between the form of words and the structure of sentences must be addressed. Developing awareness of syntax, the structure of sentences, involves understanding the structural organization of sentences and the ability to analyze and modify that structure.[7] It encompasses children's implicit grasp of sentence structure and their ability to manipulate it, which significantly influences reading fluency and comprehension.[8] Research shows a direct correlation between students' ability to identify and correct syntactic errors and their comprehension of written material.[9] Less proficient readers often struggle with various syntactic processing tasks, such as sentence correction and grammaticality judgments, indicating challenges.[10] As will be seen in the lesson application, when teaching inflectional morphology, it is common to also teach related syntactic elements, such as using the present participle *-ing* at the end of the base verb (e.g., **walk**ing) in a sentence that requires a subject and an auxiliary verb before it, as in "I am walking."

Similarities and Differences Between Prefixes and Suffixes in English and Spanish

Prefixes and suffixes play similar roles in English and Spanish grammar. In both languages, they affix to base words to alter their meaning or function. However, there are some fundamental differences in their usage between the two languages. Recognizing these similarities (cognates) and differences helps learners use prefixes and suffixes correctly in both English and Spanish. Table 9.1 depicts the fundamentals of prefixes and suffixes in both languages.

To lead multilingual learners of English (MLEs) like Edith to develop metalinguistic awareness, teachers can introduce similar, or cognate, prefixes in English and the students' home language, such as *autonomy* in English and *autonomía* in Spanish. Subsequently, less similar derivational morpheme cognates such as *-ity* (nationality) and *-idad* (nacionalidad) can be presented.

In table 9.2, we summarize the main differences between English and Spanish suffixes by types, origins, and specificity. By being aware of these differences, schools can systematically provide support to help Spanish-speaking MLEs in upper elementary grades meet grade-level language expectations and succeed academically.

TABLE 9.1

Bound Morphemes: Prefixes and Suffixes in English and Spanish

	Features and Function	**English**	**Spanish**
Prefixes: Bound morphemes before the base morpheme	Prefixes typically change the meaning of the base word they are attached to and are considered derivational morphemes.	"un-"—negation or reversal: unhappy "re-"—to do again: rewrite	"des-"—opposite or lack of something: desorden (disorder) "re-"—to do again: reconstruir (rebuild)
Suffixes: Bound morphemes after the base morpheme	Derivational morpheme suffixes change the grammatical function or meaning of the base word.	"-ly"—changes adjectives to adverbs: quick ➔ quickly "-able" changes nouns to adjectives: comfort ➔ comfortable	"-mente"—changes adjectives to adverbs: fácil ➔ fácilmente (easily) "-ción" changes verbs to nouns: explicar ➔ explicación (explanation)
	Inflectional morpheme suffixes are grammatical markers.	"-s"—changes singular nouns to plural nouns: dogs	"-s"—changes singular nouns to plural nouns: perros (dogs)

LEARNER LANGUAGE CONSIDERATIONS FOR SPANISH-SPEAKING MULTILINGUAL LEARNERS OF ENGLISH

Spanish-speaking MLEs encounter several challenges when reading, writing, and using English in educational settings because of important differences in the sound system, grammar, and rhetorical organization. Edith's language samples will be analyzed and explained in terms of her developing proficiency in English and its relation to her first language (L1; Spanish) knowledge.

General Similarities and Differences in English and Spanish

Unlike Haitian Kreyòl, which contains elements from the Romance group of Indo-European languages and influences from various African languages, Spanish is

TABLE 9.2

Main Differences Between English and Spanish suffixes

Types	English has a wider variety of suffixes than Spanish, especially for forming adverbs and altering grammatical functions.
Origin	Some English suffixes come from Old English, such as *-ness*, whereas Spanish suffixes predominantly have Latin roots.
Specificity	English suffixes, such as *-ed* for past tense (walked), are more specialized in function compared to Spanish suffixes, which have broader applications across different word types, for example, *-o* in gender marking (caro—expensive) and *-o* in verb endings (hablo—I speak).

essentially a Romance language. We indicate a few cross-language differences often encountered by native speakers of Spanish when learning English next before explaining Edith's current grammatical and pronunciation challenges based on her language samples.

The Spanish vowel system is much simpler and consistent than the English vowel system. Each of its five vowel sounds (a, e, i, o, u) has a clear, predictable sound. In contrast, the English vowel system contains more vowel sounds, including diphthongs (combined vowel sounds), and word meaning can vary depending on whether a vowel sound is long or short. For example, the words "ship" and "sheep" might sound similar to Spanish speakers, but they are very different in English.

English consonant sounds are less problematic for Spanish speakers, but some notable differences exist, making pronunciation more difficult. Sounds like "th" (as in "this" or "think"), which do not exist in Latin American Spanish, are often replaced with a "d" or "t" sound, saying "dis" instead of "this" or "tink" instead of "think." Also, because the difference between "v" and "b" is minimal in Spanish, native Spanish speakers often do not hear the difference between pairs of words like "bent" and "vent," which makes vocabulary acquisition tougher. Because of the close correspondence between pronunciation and spelling in Spanish, learning to spell in English before having had a chance to acquire the subtleties of the English sounds system can be challenging for MLEs like Edith.

The grammar systems of Spanish and English differ in several ways. One major difference is the placement of adjectives. For example, in Spanish, adjectives usually follow the noun (e.g., "casa blanca" = "house white"), whereas in English, they come before the noun ("white house"). Spanish also uses articles that change based on the gender and number of the noun (e.g., "el" for masculine singular, "la" for feminine singular). In contrast, English uses "the" for all nouns, regardless of gender.

Verb systems in the two languages also differ. Spanish verbs change based on tense (yo caminé—I walked), subject (tú caminaste—you walked), and mood (yo caminaría—I would walk). English verbs are simpler and don't change as much, using auxiliary verbs like "do," "have," and "will" to indicate tense and subject and "would" for mood. Also, prepositions in Spanish and English don't always match. For example, the Spanish "en" can mean "in," "on," or "at," depending on the context. Spanish also uses articles more often than English, as seen in "Voy a la escuela" (I'm going to school), where the article "la" is necessary in Spanish but not in English.

Spanish and English organize ideas differently in writing. Spanish often uses longer, more complex sentences, allowing for detailed explanations. In contrast, English often uses shorter, clearer sentences, presenting ideas in a more linear way.

Analyzing Edith's Language Samples

To get a general sense of Edith's reading and writing ability, Ms. Oliver asked Ms. Montilla, the dual language Spanish language arts teacher, to join her at the kidney table while Edith read aloud. Ms. Oliver sat nearby as Ms. Montilla handed Edith a book entitled *The Book About Me*, asking her in Spanish to read the book for her. Edith spoke very softly, slowly, and hesitatingly, watching for cues and confirmation from both adults.

Edith: I em [pauses] em [hesitates]

Ms. Montilla: Sound it out.

Edith: D . . . [hesitates] d . . . er [hesitates] dring [pauses] drin . . . k

Ms. Montilla: ing [pronounces emphatically]

Edith: Drink

Ms. Montilla: Drinking

Ms. Montilla and Edith: [very slowly] Drinking

Ms. Montilla: I am

Edith: Drink . . . ing

Ms. Montilla: Perfect! I am drinking. Do you know what that means?

Edith: [hesitates] Um . . .

Ms. Montilla: What? In Spanish. Pero, dímelo en español.

Edith: Um . . .

Ms. Montilla: ¿Estoy que?

Edith: Uh . . . Tomando.

Ms. Montilla: ¡Tomando! ¡Perfecto! Okay.

Edith: I . . . I . . . ea . . . [hesitates] um . . . ea . . .

Ms. Montilla: Same ending. I am eat [exaggerates the *t* sound at the end of the word while Edith softly repeats eat] ing. I am eating [pronounces normally]. What's that?

Edith: Come [in Spanish].

Ms. Montilla: Está comiendo. ¡Perfecto!

Edith: I am try—

Ms. Montilla: Talk [emphasizes this syllable] ing.

Edith: Talking.

Ms. Montilla: ¿Que es eso?

Edith: Habla.

Ms. Montilla: Hablando. Okay. ¿Ves todas las palabras con ing? Talk—ing, cry—ing, laugh—ing. Okay? So, let's see what the next one is.

Edith's interaction with Ms. Montilla clearly demonstrates Edith's language challenges with pronunciation, suffixes, and consonant clusters and shows her attempt to understand the text using her native language, Spanish. It also highlights how Ms. Montilla capitalizes on the use of the native language to scaffold Edith's English language acquisition.[11] Let's now look more closely at Edith's attempts to read the text.

After quickly reading "I em" (her pronunciation reflecting her native language), Edith has difficulty decoding the last word of the sentence. It takes her several tries to say the word *drink*, at which point she stops reading. The fact that she does not produce the *-ing* can be explained in two ways. First, Edith probably recognized the verb after decoding *d-r-i-n-k*. She stopped to translate the sentence's meaning back to Spanish. Second, the grammatical feature of *-ing* added to a verb is unfamiliar. Even after Ms. Montilla supplies the ending and asks Edith to repeat "drinking" after her, Edith hesitates to put the verb and the ending together. She has not yet acquired the *-ing* tense in spoken English. However, although she struggles to read these verb patterns because they are slightly above her current proficiency, repeated exposure through visuals will help accelerate their acquisition.

Edith's challenges in decoding are evident in her difficulty reading "eat" and "talk" because the irregular spelling of English does not allow her to consistently pronounce each letter to form words as is possible in Spanish, the language in which Edith learned to read when she was in first grade. English, in contrast to Spanish, does not enjoy one-to-one sound-letter correspondence. As recounted in the introduction, Edith began learning to read in Mexico, but her schooling was interrupted, and as a result, her reading skills in Spanish are below grade level. In her dual language class, Edith also has access to reading materials in her L1, Spanish. The English text Edith is reading, a book students wrote and illustrated as a group project in last year's class, meets all these parameters. The sentences are short, simple vocabulary is used, and there is a lot of repetition of the very basic morphological and syntactic features of the present progressive tense (I am ______ ing). Now, as Edith is developing proficiency in English listening, speaking, reading, and writing, she will be expected to read fourth-grade texts in English. However, her emerging oral proficiency in English has not yet reached a level allowing comprehension of the more complex texts required in intermediate grades.

Edith's writing sample also shows her attempts to combine her Spanish language and literacy skills with her developing English vocabulary. Beginning multilingual learners (MLs) often shift to their native language when they are required to express something in their L2 that is beyond their current proficiency. For example, Edith mixes Spanish and English in simple sentences, such as "I es ten," and she uses Spanish sentences exclusively for more complex expressions, such as "Mi comida feborita [sic] es la pizza." Her spelling in Spanish shows an understanding of its sound-symbol correspondences, with errors where two different symbols could represent the same sound (the letters *b* and *v*, as in fe*b*orita).

Although Edith knows the formulaic phrase in English, "My name is . . . ," she hasn't yet learned the spelling of the individual words and writes "Ma na se Edith." She is using inventive spelling according to her developing understanding of the sound-symbol correspondences, such as "na" to represent "name." As her English develops from one-word expressions and formulaic phrases to more complex sentences, she will need to learn English spelling conventions to write accurately and precisely. Listening activities can assist Edith in hearing the final sounds in words and applying them to writing.

The WIDA standards for listening, speaking, reading, and writing state that students at level 1 of English proficiency, such as Edith, are expected to process and produce simple sentences or questions, basic grammatical constructions and sentence patterns, and general content words and expressions. At Edith's level of English proficiency, students need a great deal of verbal, visual, graphic, and interactive support to enable them to process and produce the language needed for effective listening, speaking, reading, and writing. As the analysis of her writing and reading samples has shown, the exchanges between Edith and Ms. Oliver began to form an initial strong basis for tailoring instruction to Edith's language and literacy learning needs. From interactions such as these coupled with information gathered from other assessment data, educators working with MLs in general classrooms can gain an understanding of what a beginning MLE like Edith can say and do in a second language.

ESSENTIAL POINTS

1. In many states, educational standards are emphasizing integrating literacy skills across disciplines to help all learners navigate a complex and interconnected global landscape.
2. As higher reading objectives are set for all students and the shift from learning to read to reading to learn occurs, understanding morphology becomes crucial for effective reading comprehension.
3. Morphology allows readers to analyze and manipulate words to determine their meanings, often by breaking them into prefixes, suffixes, and root/base words. Readers must also differentiate between inflectional morphemes, which do not affect syntax or sentence structure, and derivational morphemes, which do influence them.
4. Because Edith's native language is Spanish, it was necessary to examine the similarities and differences between prefixes and suffixes in Spanish and English to understand how she applied her morphological knowledge to both languages. For instance, in both languages, prefixes modify the meaning of the base words they attach to, whereas suffixes (excluding inflectional morphemes) alter the grammatical function or meaning of the base words.
5. It is important to use varied assessments to evaluate ML students' language and literacy levels. Analysis of classroom interactions among students and with the teacher and texts written by the ML provide valuable insights that help target instruction to meet the student's specific language development needs. Collaboration between dual language teachers (e.g., English-medium and Spanish-medium class teachers) leads to a better understanding of what a beginning ML like Edith can express and accomplish in both languages.

CLASSROOM APPLICATIONS

Ms. Oliver recently observed many of her students leaving off word endings when writing. Knowing that understanding and using morphology features is a foundational reading and writing skill, she set aside small blocks of time in the coming weeks to teach her students about morphology. For a moment, she was unsure whether she was equipped to adjust her instruction to support Edith's needs, but after reminding herself of Edith's WIDA proficiency levels, having observed Edith's English word formation skills through interactions, and being tapped into Edith's full linguistic repertoire in the English language arts class through her regular collaboration with Ms. Montilla, Ms. Oliver felt amply prepared to teach morphology to her fourth-grade class.

MS. OLIVER'S INFLECTIONAL MORPHEMES LESSON

Ms. Oliver used an app to generate a fourth-grade lesson plan introducing inflectional English morphemes. For this first of two lessons on inflectional morphemes, she selected *-s* (plural), *-ed* (regular past tense), *-ing* (present participle), and *-er* (comparative) and a dozen base words to attach.[12] The lesson plan included objectives, a description, and an evaluation.[13]

OBJECTIVES

1. Identify inflectional morphemes and root words in grade-appropriate examples across content areas.
2. Explain the functions of adding inflectional morphemes to base words.
3. Use inflectional morphemes correctly in paragraph-length writing.

LESSON DESCRIPTION

1. Give pairs of students a set of index cards with the words *pens, papers, singing, laughing, taller, backpacks, walking, happier, smaller, hopped, cooked,* and *greeted.* Tell pairs to discuss patterns they notice in parts of the words and to group the words by the patterns they find.
2. Partners share their word patterns and rationale for grouping the words with the class.
3. Give the definitions of a morpheme and an inflectional morpheme. Discuss the meaning of each of the four inflectional morphemes with students, encouraging them to explain what the word endings signify.
4. Hand out a four-column table with headings of the *-s*, *-ed*, *-ing*, and *-er* suffixes and their grammatical functions (*-s* = more than one, *-ed* = past tense, etc.). Give pairs of students a list of words from an upcoming chapter in their textbook and tell them to copy them in the correct columns.
5. Discuss the word definition and why partners placed words in each column. Give examples of spelling patterns that are used for each morpheme (e.g., add an e

before the *-s* if the word ends in the letters s, sh, ch, x, or z; for words ending in a consonant and a y, change the y to i and add *-es*).

6. Using each of the four morpheme suffixes, students write a paragraph about one of the following topics: favorite sport, special family member, or fun school event. Students underline each inflectional morpheme in their paragraph.

EVALUATION

Written paragraph using the four inflectional morphemes with correct form (morphology), phrasing (syntax), and meaning (semantics).

APPLICATION OF THE TASLL FRAMEWORK PROTOCOLS TO THE INFLECTIONAL MORPHEMES LESSON

The lesson adaptations to ensure supportive classroom communication for Edith begin with the Supportive Classroom Communication (SCC) protocol. They are discussed in condensed form, whereas the considerations for applying the Targeted Language/ Literacy Instruction (TLI) protocol are elaborated. The at-a-glance table (table 9.4) in the last section of this chapter shows both protocols realized.

STEP 1

Analyze Communication in Lesson Tasks

There are virtually no SLIDE verbs (see table 2.2 on page 56 for sample SLIDE/ TREAD verbs) in the lesson. *Give* could be one if the index cards had images, but in this case, they only include words (TREAD). In addition to Ms. Oliver's repeated questioning and explaining, much of the lesson centers around verbal (spoken and written) interactions: the students *discuss* patterns of words, *categorize* them, and *talk* about their rationale, and the teacher and students *discuss* morphemes. The students also *read* the definition of morphemes, and they *write* a paragraph.

STEP 2

Size the Gaps

At level 1 at which she was assessed, Edith can understand familiar words and phrases, match pieces of oral descriptions to visual representations, name common items or people, answer short, simple questions, and state personal preferences.[14] Comparing the grade-level language skills required to participate in this language-intensive lesson to her current abilities, it becomes evident that all tasks represent large gaps.

STEP 3

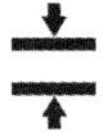

Address the Gaps Between ML's L2 Proficiency and Lesson Tasks

To aid comprehension through nonverbal support, Ms. Oliver can enhance Edith's index cards by glueing graphics of a pattern to explain the concept and images that depict the meaning of each word on the backside (lesson stop 1). The same images can be placed next to each base word on the handout (lesson step 4). To provide verbal support during the partner discussions, Ms. Oliver can pair Edith with a Spanish-speaking peer and provide her with bilingual sentence frames, allowing Edith to tap into her full linguistic repertoire. These measures, in addition to using exaggerated gestures and movements, speaking more slowly, and enunciating root words and inflectional morphemes, will afford Edith a chance to understand what Ms. Oliver says and make connections based on her L1 literacy skills.

Understanding the foundational concept of morphemes through definitions and discussion in English is too abstract an undertaking at Edith's current proficiency level. Therefore, we recommend support through a technology-based Spanish language arts presentation that she can view while the class completes lesson steps 3 and 5. Using all four selected inflectional morphemes in writing a personal story remains beyond Edith's English language ability and would leave her feeling lost and anxious. Ms. Oliver must thus determine when the lesson targeted language instruction that will build her reading and language skills and allow her to meet the language objectives should occur.

MANAGE APPLICATION, GROUPING, TIME, AND PROVIDER

With the exception of the Spanish language arts morpheme lesson presentation, which is alternative in nature due to the large gap size, and the universally applied support of gestures and clear enunciation, all supports are supplemental. Ms. Oliver can seamlessly implement them while she teaches the whole class. If available, a volunteer could prepare the modified index cards and sentence frames, while a bilingual aid could identify the appropriate technology-based Spanish-medium morpheme lesson and/or monitor Edith's comprehension with leveled questions or through translanguaging.

Identify Language Skill(s) to Be Developed

STEP 1

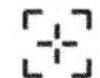

The objectives of Ms. Oliver's lesson plan require students to identify inflectional morphemes and their functions and to use them correctly in writing. This means that reading (identifying morphemes in print) and writing are the skills to be developed.

Size the Distance

Knowing Edith's listening, speaking, reading, and writing proficiency level descriptors and having applied the SCC protocol to improve classroom communication, Ms. Oliver consults the WIDA performance definitions for the two skills of focus in her morphology lesson at Edith's current assessed level (shown in table 9.3) and sees that Edith can read small statements and grammatically simple sentences and recognize written everyday words. Some parts of the morphology lesson are grammatical features that Edith can grasp and manipulate correctly, such as adding an *-s* to a simple noun to make it plural (dogs). It helps that the same feature exists in Spanish (perros). She could also apply the spelling rules to make nouns plural because there is no L2 developmental constraint on spelling and she wouldn't need to understand the word to spell it.

TABLE 9.3

Edith's Assessed WIDA Performance Definitions in Reading and Writing (Grades K-12)

Skill and Level	Linguistic Complexity	Language Forms and Conventions	Vocabulary Usage
	At each grade, toward the end of a given level of English proficiency, and with instructional support, English language learners will process (L/R) or produce (S/W):		
R 1.1	• Single statements or questions • An idea within words, phrases, or chunks of language	• Simple grammatical constructions (e.g., commands, wh-questions, declaratives) • Common social and instructional forms and patterns	• General content-related words • Everyday social and instructional words and expressions
W 1.1	• Words, phrases, or chunks of language • Single words used to represent ideas	• Phrase-level grammatical structures • Phrasal patterns associated with familiar social and instructional situations	• General content-related words • Everyday social and instructional words and expressions

Ms. Oliver next consults her notes on Edith's recent reading and writing samples and notices that Edith sometimes uses the correct present progressive form (I am walking), leaves out the auxiliary verb *be* (I walking), or uses the incorrect form of the verb be (I es walking). She also tends to use the simple present form in English to express an action that is occurring, likely due to her internalized knowledge of talking about what is happening *now* in Spanish where both simple present or present progressive tenses can be used to express that time and duration aspect. This leads Edith to sometimes state "I eat now" instead of "I'm eating now" because both are correct in Spanish.

Although the spelling conventions for using each suffix are important for MLEs and non-MLEs alike, Edith will mostly need help with understanding when to use certain inflectional morphemes, and non-MLEs will not likely need explanation for that. To accelerate Edith's process of developing accuracy in the use of present progressive and acquiring new English forms, Ms. Oliver realizes that explicit grammar explanation is indispensable and starts to design the instruction, which will take place while the non-MLEs write their stories with the four inflectional morphemes because that part of the lesson presents too wide a gap for Edith to overcome.

STEP 3 Develop ML's L2 Language/Literacy Skill(s)

With the language skill identified (step 1) and the distance between Edith's current proficiency level and the lesson part gauged (step 2), we begin with the last step of the TLI protocol. When targeting instruction to Edith's precise English proficiency level, Ms. Oliver needs fewer nonverbal and verbal supports than during whole-class instruction to ensure successful interaction, but she fine-tunes the techniques.

ADJUSTING PITCH

Because the *-ing* suffix is recognized as an early-acquired morpheme, it is processable and acquirable for Edith. Ms. Oliver chooses short, simple sentences with demonstrable actions (I am smiling, she is singing, etc.). The sentences also use common words, such as paper, pencil, and sandwich.

ADJUSTING PACE

Slowing the pace of instruction by using leveled questioning both checks comprehension and application and provides an opportunity for correction of error forms through recasting. During the first time asking "What . . . are . . . you . . . DOING?" the question is asked while slowing the pace of speech. From then on, stating the question is done with natural pacing.

ADJUSTING PORTION

As a beginning MLE student, Edith has not acquired most of the forms yet in spoken English. Choosing to focus on only the present progressive inflectional morpheme is an appropriate decision based on errors and omissions in Edith's reading and writing samples.

ADJUSTING PERSPECTIVE/POINT

Knowing when to say "I go to school" versus "I am going to school" is something that more likely needs pointing out to an MLE than to a non-MLE because non-MLEs would know when to use each tense without being able to state the rule. Grammatical rule explanations can help MLEs in the intermediate grades and above because they have a level of cognitive development that enables them to consider more abstract constructs such as tense (past, present, or future action) and aspect (ongoing, completed, habitual, or repetitive action). In terms of form and structure, additional emphasis linking the spelling and pronunciation of the word elements would help Edith learn the new word-building blocks. For example, it would be helpful to reinforce that *-ing* is pronounced with the tense sound /ng/at the end rather than /n/, as that sound isn't used at the end of words in Spanish.

Manage Grouping, Time, and Provider

In Edith's departmentalized two-way dual language class (meaning certain subjects are taught in one language by one teacher and other subjects are taught in the partner language by the other teacher), there are ample opportunities for students to translanguage individually and collectively, for the curriculum to bridge instruction in both languages, and for the teachers to collaborate to reinforce and extend knowledge and skills gained in one language to the partner language. The variations of grouping, timing, and providers are too many to include, so we focus on common ones that are feasible for teachers to implement.

Grouping. Because Edith is the sole newcomer who is a beginning MLE in the class, Ms. Oliver will work with her alone at the kidney table to meet her exactly where she is in her acquisition of English morphology and syntax.

Time and Provider. The ideal circumstance would be to have coteaching support during the lesson. To further support Edith's L2 development, it may be possible for the Spanish language arts teacher to preteach the Spanish cognates of the prefixes, root/base words, and suffixes and their English counterparts. In this case, that teacher could also prepare a supplemental handout with word elements supplied for Edith's reference as she participates in the pair activities and discussion in the English language arts class. However, given the program's departmentalization, Ms. Oliver decides that a follow-up in Ms. Montilla's Spanish language arts class would be the better option to ensure Edith fully understands the difference between the use of the two verb tenses in English and Spanish.

During the class discussion and pair activities and discussion, Edith could work independently with an English language development (ELD) or bilingual education teacher, or if there were other beginning MLs in the class, they could be gathered in a small group for this portion of instruction. Through small-group and one-on-one assistance, Edith can gain increasing confidence and encouragement.

Lesson Summary

Table 9.4 depicts the lesson plan with the Teaching All Subjects, Language, and Literacy (TASLL) Framework protocols applied. In the SCC protocol portion of the lesson, the lesson tasks are displayed with nonverbal (SLIDE) elements underlined and the verbal elements (TREAD) in **boldface**. Both fonts **combined** indicate that a task can contain both components. The second column lists the language skills from the point of view of the students and illustrates the gap size that exists between the classroom communication and Edith's current beginning level of English proficiency. The added verbal and nonverbal supports are depicted in the third column.

In the TLI protocol section, we first list the instructional steps. We elaborate on how Ms. Oliver targets Edith's instruction, showing both her actions and Edith's anticipated responses. The second column contains the nonverbal and verbal supports applied to the steps, and the 4 P adjustments are presented in the last column.

Final Thoughts

After dismissal, Ms. Oliver reflects on Edith's engagement during this initial morphology lesson. She believes that Edith has gained the awareness that both English and Spanish use suffixes similarly to alter the meanings or functions of base words so she pulls out another book for Edith to read that would reinforce the progressive form. She also makes a note in Edith's folder to include occasional activities in the near future in which she would teach the remaining three suffixes that were covered in today's lesson. She would then add vocabulary activities that would focus on prefixes to enhance Edith's ability to use them effectively in understanding and producing English. Mrs. Oliver's goal is to systematically strengthen Edith's grasp of morphology and syntax,

TABLE 9.4

The Inflectional Morpheme Lesson at a Glance

Lesson Steps	Skill[1] and Gap Size[2]	Added Supports[3]
Give pairs of students a set of **index cards with the words** *pens, papers, singing, laughing, taller, backpacks, walking, happier, smaller, hopped, cooked*, and *greeted*. **Tell** pairs to **discuss** patterns they notice in parts of the words and to **group the words** by the patterns they find.	R, L, S ↕↕↕	***Nonverbal Supports:*** Graphic of a pattern to explain concept and images on back of each card for Edith (supplemental) ***Verbal Support:*** Pair Edith with a Spanish-speaking partner at higher English proficiency (supplemental).
Partners **share** their **word patterns** and **rationale** for grouping the words with the class.	L, R ↕↕↕	***Verbal Support:*** Bilingual sentence frames for giving a rationale ("These words are similar because they have ________") (supplemental)
Give the definitions of a morpheme and an inflectional morpheme. **Discuss** the meaning of each of the four inflectional morphemes with students, encouraging them to **explain** what the word endings signify.	L, R, S ↕↕↕	***Verbal Supports:*** Tablet with Spanish language arts morpheme lesson presentation including the definition in Spanish (alternative)
Hand out a four-column table with headings of the *-s*, *-ed*, *-ing*, and *-er* suffixes and their grammatical functions (*-s* = more than one, *-ed* = past tense, etc.). **Give** pairs of students **a list of words** from an upcoming chapter in their textbook and **tell** them to **copy** them in the correct columns.	L, R, W ↕↕↕	***Nonverbal Support:*** Images next to the words on the list to depict the base word's meaning (supplemental)
Discuss the word definitions and why partners placed words in each column. **Give examples** of spelling patterns for each morpheme.	L, S, R ↕↕↕	***Verbal Support:*** Spanish explanation of the four inflectional morphemes' purposes on Edith's tablet (supplemental)
Edith is not able to complete the whole-class task of writing a paragraph using each of the four morphemes. Because she is in the process of acquiring the *-ing* progressive form, the **TLI protocol** is needed to help her develop proficiency-level-appropriate language.		

Continued...

TABLE 9.4

The Inflectional Morpheme Lesson at a Glance *(Continued...)*

Instructional Steps	Nonverbal and Verbal Supports	4 P Adjustments
Pantomime various *actions* while *saying them* (e.g., "I am smiling, I am laughing, and I am crying," etc.). Read simple present progressive statements aloud from a handout *with corresponding images.* Show Edith *cards with images of actions* with the base verb written underneath, such as playing the piano. As Edith *pantomimes* the action, ask, "What are you doing?" If Edith makes an error in response, *recast* the statement correctly.	***Nonverbal Supports:*** • Pantomiming while saying the actions • Handout and cards with images ***Verbal Support:*** Repeated question patterns with recasting Edith's answers	**Pitch:** Simple present progressive sentences with demonstrable actions and common words, such as paper, pencil, sandwich, etc. **Pace:** • Leveled questioning to check for comprehension/application and to provide opportunities for correction of error forms through recasting. • Slowing pace of speech, asking "What . . . are . . . you . . . *doing?*" at first and then stating the question with natural pacing from then on
Show Edith a handout with the base verbs *walk, talk, speak, go,* and *read* and ask her to write complete sentences for each using the *sentence frame,* "I am _____" and to read each of her sentences aloud. Show Edith a *timeline diagram* indicating the time and duration of the simple present and the present progressive tenses for the two sentences "I go to school every day" and "I am going to school now."	***Nonverbal Support:*** Timeline diagram ***Verbal Support:*** Sentence frame	***Portion:*** Focus on only one inflectional morpheme, -ing, because Edith has not acquired most of the forms yet in spoken English. ***Perspective/Point:*** • Grammatical rule explanations of difference between "I go to school" and "I am going to school." • Emphasize the pronunciation of /ng/ at the end of words so Edith will say and spell them correctly.

Lesson Follow-Up		
The Spanish language arts teacher will follow up with Spanish and English contrasts for the two verb tenses.	No supports needed	***Perspective/Point:*** Spanish-English translanguaging and cross-linguistic comparisons to help understand how and when the two tenses are used in English

Key:

1 Language skills: L = listening, S = speaking, R = reading, W = writing

2 Gap sizes: No gap = Ø, ↕ = small gap, ↕↕ = medium gap, ↕↕↕ = large gap

3 Unless otherwise noted, all supports are considered universal.

supporting her ability to comprehend and manipulate English vocabulary and phrasing more proficiently over time.

Almost out the door, Ms Oliver sent Ms. Montilla a text message saying how much progress she was seeing since they had discussed how they could support Edith's L2 development.

STOP AND REFLECT QUESTIONS

1. Reflect on the conversations of your MLEs. Do you recall any evidence of your learners using various inflectional morphemes? If so, when did they use them? Were they speaking with you, other teachers, non-MLE classmates, or other MLEs?
2. Do you have a general idea of the grammatical structures of the different languages spoken in your class?

GO AND PRACTICE ACTIVITIES

1. Make a list of derivational morphemes that change meaning (e.g., *un-*, *pro-*) that you would like your MLEs to know and use. Create sentence strips of those morphemes printed in English in one color and in their L1 in a different color, and share them with the entire class. Give the class time to practice combining these prefixes and suffixes with base words with each other. Observe the demeanor of your MLEs as they become the experts in teaching the morphemes in their native language!
2. Google or ChatGPT the different languages spoken in your class. Familiarize yourself with differences in grammatical structures between your students' language and English. Think of it as detective work—have fun with it! Your students will deeply appreciate your interest in their language.

Teaching Tasir to Write a Persuasive Argument

Language and Literacy in Middle School

"Listen carefully, Tasir. You wrote, 'That was so mean. How they *could* have *did* that?' Does what you wrote sound right? You just need to hear the sentences to know if they're correct."

"Sounds okay to me. I don't hear anything wrong." Tasir shifted to the right, moving about an inch away from Mr. Grant, who had bent down to the left of Tasir's desk.

"Really? Don't you hear it?" Mr. Grant raised his voice. "Don't you hear the mistakes?"

"I hear the words. I know what they mean. Everything's right." Tasir half-smiled and inched away a bit more.

As he stood up, Mr. Grant gripped the back of Tasir's chair. Once steady, he let go and rested his hand briefly on Tasir's shoulder. "That's okay, Tasir. That's okay for now. I'll correct it when you turn in the paper."

Tasir looked down at her composition, nowhere near the required five paragraphs. It told the story of her family's move to the United States, how she and her mother, father, brother, and sister boarded the plane with passports, visas, and their most valuable possessions. They packed what they could carry and shipped a few things they couldn't. But they left so much there.

Tasir's last recollection of Egypt was her grandmother's face, crestfallen and cradled in her hands. "But, Nanna, why can't *you* come, too?" "I tried, Tasir," her grandmother said. "I did everything I could, but my application was rejected. I can't come now, but don't worry. I promise I will join you soon." Tasir imagined her grandmother walking toward her at the airport terminal, picked up her pencil, and continued writing.

GRADE-LEVEL EXPECTATIONS FOR LANGUAGE AND LITERACY IN SEVENTH GRADE

Like all colleagues in South Carolina, Mr. Grant has been studying the newly approved College and Career Readiness Standards to ensure he prepares his seventh-grade students to meet the expectations.[1] The following sections summarize the language demands established by these expectations.

Reading

By middle school, foundational reading skills are no longer addressed, and seventh graders are expected to use skills in a variety of reading functions, such as:

- Cite evidence in analyzing and making inferences from a text
- Determine, analyze, and summarize a theme or central ideas within and across texts
- Analyze literary elements and stylistic aspects of various text types
- Critically analyze and evaluate author's choices within and across a variety of literary, expository, persuasive, and informational texts, as well as multimedia formats
- Apply critical thinking to investigate, evaluate, and synthesize a variety of sources

The language knowledge and skills pertaining to reading include using context, background knowledge, word knowledge (e.g., synonyms and antonyms, nuances of words, word relationships), morphology, and reference materials to comprehend terms. By the end of seventh grade, students are expected to demonstrate proficiency of the grade-level indicators with independence.

The following passage gives a sense of grade-level text[2]:

> The United States has lagged behind other countries in developing fast, convenient rail travel. Instead more attention has been given to travel by air and by car. The United States has one high-speed rail line, the Acela Express, which runs between Washington, D.C., and Boston via New York City. Although the Acela trains are capable of running up to 150 mph (241 km/h), they average around 78 mph. More rail lines need to be built in the United States to have high-speed trains. This is because passenger trains share tracks with freight trains and the tracks are too crowded to allow high-speed trains to run.

Writing

Seventh-grade writers are expected to:

- Produce a variety of narrative, informative/expository or argumentative texts
- Use data and statistics to support claims and acknowledge counterclaims
- Use words, phrases, and clauses for cohesion and clarification of relationships

- Use formal style, provide a conclusion supporting their argument
- Use precise language
- Improve clarity and enhance text through revising
- Organize ideas using rhetoric and use transitions for cohesion

The language skills that pertain to writing include explaining the function of phrases and clauses, using compound and complex sentences to convey relationships, using phrases and clauses in sentences, avoiding dangling modifiers, using commas to separate coordinate adjectives, spelling correctly, and using language precisely and concisely, avoiding wordiness and redundancy.

The following paragraph provides a sense of the expectations for satisfactory writing at the middle school level. It is an excerpt from a seventh-grade writing sample graded a 3-2-3 (purpose/structure–development–language) on a four-point scale:[3]

> Building an average home can cost thousands of dollars, and produce an excessive amount of harmful waste. What's more? Once you build it, it's stuck there for as long as it's still standing. This is not the case with "Prefab", or "Prefabricated" homes. According to the article, prefabricated houses "don't create as many extra pieces of material that have to be thrown away." Prefab houses are also easier to customize, and can teach the home owner to learn to manage smaller spaces. On top of all this: They're easier to clean as well!

Speaking and Listening

The speaking and listening requirements placed on seventh-grade students include reading to prepare for and participate in discussions, eliciting elaboration from others and reacting to information, acknowledging others' new information, analyzing main and supporting ideas and explaining how they clarify the topic being discussed, evaluating a speaker's argument and effective delivery, presenting claims using clear pronunciation, and adapting speech to contexts and tasks, demonstrating a command of formal English and evaluating and using appropriate presentation skills.

RESEARCH ON TEACHING LANGUAGE AND LITERACY TO MULTILINGUAL LEARNERS OF ENGLISH IN MIDDLE SCHOOL

In describing the Teaching Language/Literacy Instruction (TLI) protocol in chapter 7, we noted that instruction in language arts and disciplinary literacy should focus primarily on developing multilingual learner (ML) students' language skills (i.e., listening, speaking, reading, and writing) in English. We suggested that given the dynamic, incremental nature of second language acquisition and potential variation in proficiency across the different skill areas, instruction must be targeted to the individual student's precise level of proficiency in each skill area. In other words, the goal of second language instruction is to move the target successively upward toward the grade-level language standards, which requires significant shifts in instructing MLs.[4] The following findings are particularly relevant to middle school multilingual learners of English (MLEs), who vary in terms of language proficiency as well as first and second language literacy development.

First Language Influences on English Literacy

An interesting yet controversial issue related to MLE students' writing relates to how different languages organize thoughts. During the past several decades, a great deal of contrastive and error analysis research has focused on comparing and contrasting various aspects of language, reading, and writing across languages.[4] Teachers of MLEs have used findings from this research to help anticipate areas of divergence across language systems, which are likely to cause their students difficulty, and those of convergence, where one could expect positive transfer.

Second language researchers have found that cultural differences in the rhetorical organization of text affect how students from different first language (L1) backgrounds compose written work in English. For example, in Haitian Kreyòl, proverbs, which are inherently indirect, are added to communication to provide support or verbal evidence to strongly emphasize a particular point. For example, "*yon sel dwèt pa manje kalalou*" literally means that "one cannot eat okra with one finger," implying that people must work together to accomplish tasks. Robert Kaplan classified language groups according to cultural thought patterns.[5] For instance, in Germanic languages such as English, German, Dutch, or Norwegian, communication is direct and linear and doesn't digress or go off topic. In Semitic languages such as Arabic and Hebrew, thoughts are expressed in a series of parallel ideas, both positive and negative. In Asian languages, communication is indirect. Topics are not addressed head on but viewed from various perspectives, whereas in Romance languages such as French, Italian, Romanian, or Spanish, communication often digresses to introduce extraneous material. In languages such as Russian, communication is often digressive and includes a series of parallel ideas.

The main premise behind Kaplan's assertions is that, to communicate effectively across cultures, one needs to understand the cultural thought patterns behind the language of communication. These thought patterns influence how native speakers of a language express themselves and how particular individuals expect to hear information presented. Although this study has had a fair amount of positive and negative criticism, its insights have helped inform the teaching of reading and writing to MLEs, especially at high school and college levels.[6]

Transfer of Basic Literacy Skills and Strategies

Second language (L2) learners may display difficulty in writing, especially in spelling, depending on the writing system of their L1. Various writing systems map out and represent spoken language in very different ways.[7] In alphabetic writing systems, such as Korean, English, and Romance languages, letters must be arranged according to their individual sounds to form syllables. Conversely, in writing systems that use graphic symbols, such as Chinese, these symbols represent an entire unit of meaning (i.e., a word or part of word, such as *un*, that has meaning) and not just the symbol's sound.[8] Thus, research demonstrates that L2 writers from L1 systems like Chinese may not be as sensitive to sounds in the alphabetic system of English.[9] Therefore, the writing system of ML learners' L1 can affect their spelling ability in their L2.[10]

Teachers of MLEs need to understand the issues unique to L2 writing and how to appropriately address them. Because high-stakes assessments for *all* students have moved beyond multiple-choice formats to include short, extended, and essay-response questions, it is imperative that teachers are able to identify and respond to errors made by MLEs when learning to read and write in English.[11] Experts in literacy instruction for MLEs agree that errors are a normal part of language acquisition, that the acquisition of particular language structures may be delayed or even halted when these students do not receive pertinent feedback and appropriate instruction, and that targeted mediation can help them improve their writing skills over time.

The types of errors MLE writers commonly make range from improper use of parts of speech (e.g., use of articles, pronouns, and verbs) to errors in number (i.e., use of plural endings), word choice, sentence structure (e.g., use of tenses, word order, and subject-verb agreement), and language mechanics (e.g., use of punctuation, capitalization, spelling, and related conventions). Many mistakes involve sound-letter correspondences, more precisely concerning the "uh" sound, which can be represented by every vowel in English or with the letters *s* and *c*. Pronunciation mistakes often transfer to the written language, such as the Japanese use of the letters *l* and *r*.[12] For Romance and Germanic language speakers, pronunciation of the short *i* sound (bit) as a long *e* sound (beet) can cause errors in spelling and reading. Sound-linked errors often reflect MLE students' conceptual knowledge of the sound system of the L1, as letters with matching sounds are substituted and transposed, especially when English letter sounds and blends don't correlate or exist within the native language. For instance, beginning MLEs who are native speakers of Arabic often substitute the sound /b/ for /p/ in words such as *park* because the phoneme /p/ is not a phoneme per se in Arabic. Similarly, studies indicate that a large proportion of errors can be attributed to the user's native language phonological system.[13] Permissible combinations and variations in letter and sound placements may also be responsible for difficulties in pronunciation that can be reflected in student writing.

Experts recommend addressing these errors at beginning, intermediate, and advanced stages of writing development, focusing primarily on significant errors that are likely to pose reading comprehension problems. Teachers of MLEs can and should integrate effective strategies for treating errors in writing. Depending on whether teachers provide error correction feedback to students individually, in small groups, or in classroom settings, instructional strategies might range from explicit and direct feedback (e.g., teacher corrects errors and explains the rationale for doing so) to indirect but guided input (e.g., teacher points out the error, asks student to make the correction, and assists as needed) to selective feedback focused on specific error types (e.g., teacher marks patterns of several specific error types by underlining or highlighting these errors).[14]

As we indicated in previous chapters, a majority of the research available pertains to learning to read in English as a first language. We urge teachers of MLEs in intermediate grade levels and middle school to carefully interpret those insights when designing and implementing instruction because these students greatly vary in age, language proficiency, literacy development, and schooling. In other words, deciding what and how to teach MLEs should be informed by the relevant research as well as the insights gained by working directly with these students.

LEARNER LANGUAGE CONSIDERATIONS FOR ARABIC MULTILINGUAL LEARNERS OF ENGLISH

There are well-established contrasts between Arabic and English that cause cross-language interference errors or challenges in acquiring different language skills that native speakers of Arabic often experience when learning English. This section first highlights a few of these challenges in a general sense. Others are then shown through an analysis of Tasir's language samples. Finally, we show some of her specific learner language based on the language samples.

General Similarities and Differences in English and Arabic

The more teachers are aware of cross-language contrasts and MLE students' underlying learner language, the better they are prepared to address these students' language and literacy needs. Pertaining to grammar, these contrasts include, but are not limited to, use of articles, gender, number, personal pronouns, prepositions, question formation, verb tenses, and word order. For example, a native speaker of Arabic might make errors in the use of subject-verb-object word order because they follow the Arabic verb-subject-object order.

As a Semitic language, Arabic differs from English in terms of script, orthography, and directionality. The Arabic script is written from right to left in a cursive style. In most cases, the twenty-eight letters of Arabic transcribe consonant rather than vowel sounds. When transcribed, vowel diacritics (symbols similar to accent marks) are placed above and below consonants to indicate pronunciation and meaning differences. Because the writing system prioritizes consonants, meaning that vowels can be inferred in a word by their surrounding consonants, vowels are rarely used in written Arabic texts above third-grade level. In most cases, starting in fourth grade, normally developing readers and writers are expected to be able to read and produce writing materials without vowel diacritics.

When teaching adolescents who are literate in Arabic before learning English, like Tasir, to address language and literacy challenges, researchers and practitioners agree on a needed equilibrium between instruction that focuses on meaning and some degree of targeted attention paid to language form or discrete aspects of language development.

When second language instruction is entirely communication driven or meaning focused, important grammatical or lexical features of the L2 may not develop to targeted levels. Ultimately, those aspects of L2 acquisition that learners need to notice, but for whatever reason do not, will need to be addressed through appropriate instructional intervention that meaningfully integrates the teaching of communication and language skills. (Anecdotally, when one of this book's coauthors, Kouider Mokhtari, was learning English as a foreign language, his language classes focused mostly on language forms. He had very few opportunities to practice speaking inside or outside the classroom. Consequently, for some time, he felt "grammatically competent" but "communicatively incompetent." His experience learning English in Morocco was markedly different from Tasir's experience learning English in South Carolina.)

Analyzing Tasir's Language Samples

The following classroom language samples shed some light on Tasir's strengths and areas that are currently challenging for her with a view to potential cross-language interference. The first sample represents a transcription of a read-aloud by Tasir followed by Mr. Grant's reaction and thought process. The second is a brief written paragraph in which the students had to write a personal statement and back it up with reasoning. Together, they reveal much about Tasir's instructional needs in view of reaching grade-level expectations.

> "As she watched . . . the top of . . . of tall . . . sky . . . [sigh] scrappers disappeared from view . . . and and . . . her mind began to der [pause] derft . . . to the mountains . . . in . . . Montana. Uh, Grandma [pause] and Grandfather lived . . . on the small ranch near Great . . . Great Falls." Tasir paused for quite some time before going on to read the following passage.
>
> "The whole piece . . . of land . . . was actually . . . actually only ten . . . uh uhsss [long pause] uh . . . curs [acres] but [flat intonation] . . . to . . . Melissa [descending intonation as with ending a sentence] . . . who lived in [rising intonation as with beginning a sentence] in an apartment with her mother . . . it was . . . as big as . . . Central Park."
>
> Tasir continued reading aloud in spurts, clear to the end of the story, alternating between word-by-word and small chunk bursts, sometimes expressionless and other times dramatically expressive. Mr. Grant was working individually with his students, helping them with text-dependent questions. "So, Tasir, what was the reason Melissa went to Montana?" "I think it was because she really missed her grandmother," Tasir replied. "Her grandmother couldn't come to New York, so Melissa had to go to Montana." Mr. Grant scrunched his eyebrows and pursed his lips. "Are you sure about that, Tasir? Does it say that in the text?" "Yeah, I think so. Melissa is thinking about her grandmother. She's far away, in Montana." Mr. Grant thought he had explained how to extract meaning from the text, but Tasir didn't seem to catch on. Getting

> his MLEs used to the close reading required of state standards could take some time. At the last grade-level meeting, Ms. Parker said the English language development (ELD) teacher had given her some instructional tips to help Tasir better understand text. "Maybe I should touch base with her as well," he thought. After all, the required district training course was quite a while back, and he could use some fail-proof pointers for reaching Tasir.

In the read-aloud sample and text discussion above, it is easy to see that despite her advanced English conversation skills, Tasir clearly has difficulty reading text with adequate fluency. Her reading is marked with frequent pauses, hesitations, corrections, repetitions, and mispronounced words.[15] Because fluency errors or miscues affect speed, accuracy, and expression, Tasir's reading comprehension is affected. In other words, she appears to have some basic word decoding problems that force her to devote most of her cognitive resources to decoding and less of them to comprehension. Language arts and literacy teachers have an array of evidenced-based fluency-oriented reading strategies (e.g., repeated readings, reader's theater, echo-reading) for addressing reading fluency problems. These strategies also work well for teaching MLEs who are just below a level of 3 of 6 in reading and writing like Tasir.[16]

Given that Tasir had relatively well-developed reading and writing skills in Arabic at the end of second grade when she moved from Egypt to the United States, it is likely that her academic writing in English reflects some of the ways texts are structured in Arabic. This late (third grade) start in learning to read and write in English affected her composition skills. The following writing sample points to a few problems related to content, organization or ideas, and mechanics, which are likely due to cross-language interference (i.e., awareness of audience and general awareness of writing conventions in English).

> "My gramna is the oldest person in my relatives, she's nice and really cares about every one she gives me presnt and gets me out of trouble. She read to me and explains me everything. When i come to her house she cooks food. When im not happy she trys to make me feel better. I love my granma she is the Best Older Person in my family."

When it comes to mechanics, her writing shows that Tasir sometimes uses the *-s* at the end of present tense verbs when needed (my granma cares, gets me out of trouble), and other times she doesn't (she read to me). Because she alternates between the correct and incorrect forms, this would be a good area to focus on to improve grammatical accuracy in writing. Her writing also demonstrates that she is still developing accuracy with verbs that use indirect objects (she explains me everything), so focusing on this aspect might also help advance her competence in correct word order.

Another point of cross-linguistic transfer is Tasir's use of prepositions. Although there are about twenty prepositions in Arabic, only five or six are used most of the time. For example, Arabic uses the preposition *fii*, roughly the equivalent of *in* in

English, in instances where English uses several other prepositions, such as *into*, *among*, *at*, and *on*. The use of the preposition *in* in the first sentence ("My gramna is the oldest person *in* my relatives") is likely transferring the use of the preposition *fii* from Arabic into the closest preposition equivalent in English.

A further error relates to the use of punctuation (e.g., "My granma is the oldest person in my relatives, she's nice and really cares"). Arabic often uses commas rather than periods to separate sentences with complete thought units. A third instance of possible native language interference is the lack of capital letters or incorrect use thereof, as in the phrases, "When i come to her house," "When im not happy," and "Best Older Person," because Arabic does not make a distinction between capital and lowercase letters.

Teachers of native Arabic MLEs might consider discussing how text structures (e.g., textbook chapter, narrative, expository texts) differ across both languages.[17] Direct instruction will help develop an awareness of how messages are communicated in English. Specific strategies might include teaching awareness and production of different organizational patterns such as stories, directions, comparison-contrast, cause and effect, and description, along with the appropriate language structures that support the reading and production of these text types.[18]

In literacy, Tasir finds herself at a point that many MLEs encounter. Toward the top of one proficiency level (2.8 in writing and 2.9 in reading) and close to moving to the next level, she risks getting stuck and plateauing, which would lead her to become a long-term ML.[19] Therefore, it is important for teachers of MLs to occasionally look ahead and consider the next proficiency level(s) while scaffolding literacy instruction. This supports the students' current needs while helping them move toward the next level.

ESSENTIAL POINTS

1. Teachers should be mindful of what grade-level expectations for language, literacy, and content learning mean for MLs across their current levels of L2 proficiency in the domains of reading, writing, speaking, and listening.
2. Understanding MLE students' home language is paramount when addressing students' language and literacy strengths and needs. Differences between students' home languages and English can lead to errors due to cross-language interference as can be seen in Tasir's language samples.
3. MLs need tailored instruction to help them meet grade-level expectations for language, literacy, and content learning. Strategies for addressing these challenges should focus on meaning-making with attention to language form, developing awareness of text structures in the L2, and providing direct instruction in academic vocabulary and reading comprehension.

CLASSROOM APPLICATION

"When it's our turn, I want to offer a cool project like they do in geography and mathematics. What could that be?" Mr. Grant taps his fingers on the desk for a while before an idea comes to him. "The city council has been talking about renewable energy. The students could develop an argument in support of or in opposition to providing local or state funding to businesses and private households that switch to renewable energy sources. By ending with a mock city hall meeting, I can even add in the career readiness standards for which I've been having difficulty finding time. This is going to be epic!"

MR. GRANT'S PERSUASIVE WRITING LESSON

Because the students had learned about the various types of renewable energy available in the United States in science, conducted research on current energy usage and available renewable energy sources in various regions in geography, and worked out budgetary consideration of conversion to renewable energy in mathematics, Mr. Grant feels confident that the students can fully concentrate on the construction of an argument and the writing process rather than having to spend time locating materials to support their viewpoint. After consulting the new state standards and checking on the desired thematic unit outcome, he constructs the lesson plan.[20]

OBJECTIVES

- Create and orally present a written argument in support of or in opposition to a given topic.
- Participate in peer editing of written argument.

INTRODUCTION

- Hook: Project five choices (e.g., "diet soda OR regular soda?," "basketball OR baseball?"). Each member of a pair chooses one option and explains in three sentences why it is the better choice.
- Project the statement "Principal Phillips: We should have more time for lunch." Complete a T-chart of main points and benefits/evidence that the students offer to convince the school principal.
- Construct an anchor chart to review the common features of persuasive arguments (i.e., claims and evidence) and how to present one (i.e., sequence, consideration of the audience) and then introduce the project.

LESSON *DESCRIPTION*

- Groups review the research texts from the geographic information system (GIS) mapping lesson and the financial calculations conducted in mathematics. They brainstorm which elements from their discoveries support arguments for the initiative placed before the city council and which could be a counterargument.

- Sequentially lead the students through writing the first draft, offering guidance:
  a. Choose the position to support or oppose the initiative and select three pieces of supporting evidence from the brainstorm.
  b. Write the first draft, including an opening statement, three supporting paragraphs, and a concluding statement.
- Sequentially lead the students through revising:
  a. Student reads their draft argument aloud, and partner listens.
  b. Based on the checklist, partners make suggestions for improvements to introduction, argument evidence and sequencing, and conclusion.
  c. Each student revises their first draft.
  d. Students read a partner's argument and make suggestions for improvement of language conventions.
  e. Each student revises their second draft.
- Argument delivery:
  a. Show short video clips of good speeches.[21] Hold class discussion of posture, eye contact, voice projection, and pace.
  b. Students rehearse their speeches with two new partners.
  c. Conduct mock city hall meetings in small groups (one student from each geographic region in the social studies and mathematics projects). Students rate each argument for effectiveness.

EVALUATION

One rubric to assess the written product including a rating component of each peer's engagement in providing feedback and one rubric for the presentation delivery.

APPLICATION OF THE TASLL FRAMEWORK PROTOCOLS TO THE PERSUASIVE WRITING LESSON

Based on observations of Tasir's interactions in the classroom, Mr. Grant is ambivalent about Tasir's challenges during the grade-level whole-class discussions and instruction. However, he knows that writing her own arguments, providing feedback, and revising her text present big hurdles. This is a classic situation where supporting classroom communication can make a big difference in enabling MLEs to participate alongside their peers but attention to their language/literacy development is required in small, specific segments.

As in chapters 8 and 9, we summarize the Supportive Classroom Communication (SCC) protocol application and elaborate on the TLI protocol considerations to scaffold language and literacy development—this time for Tasir's needs in writing instruction. The at-a-glance table (table 10.2) in the last section of this chapter shows the two protocols realized.

STEP 1

Analyze Communication in Lesson Tasks

Based on the analysis of underlined verbs and verb phrases in the lesson plan (see table 2.2 on page 56 for a list of the verbs that indicate SLIDE/TREAD), only three portions of the original lesson plan provide opportunities to connect visual aspects (SLIDE) to classroom discussions (TREAD): the T-chart construction, the anchor chart construction, and viewing the video clips of good speeches. However, these activities involve a fair amount of disciplinary language as well. All remaining lesson tasks are entirely language dependent.

STEP 2

Size the Gaps

Tasir's WIDA assessment shows the split between her oral language and literacy development. With support, Tasir's oral proficiency levels of 4 (listening) and 5 (speaking) would make most of the class discussions and the small-group portions of the lesson accessible. Her literacy skills are in stark contrast to her oral language skills, with both reading and writing assessed at level 2. This indicates that she can understand text and communicate in writing about common topics, identifying main ideas and describing them in phrases or short sentences, but these abilities do not reflect seventh-grade expectations for this writing lesson. Mr. Grant needs to carefully consider how to help her overcome the following medium and large-sized gaps:

- The whole-class review of persuasive writing features
- The group review of research texts and financial calculations from geography and mathematics and brainstorming which elements support or do not support the initiative
- Writing the first draft, providing feedback through listening and reading, and revising two drafts
- Rehearsing the argument and listening to her peers' arguments

STEP 3

Address the Gaps Between ML's L2 Proficiency and Lesson Tasks

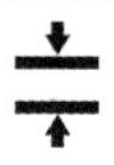

While modeling how to construct an argument with the T-chart and while completing the anchor chart for the persuasive features review, Mr. Grant should implement already familiar supports. By pointing (nonverbal support) to frequently repeating signal words, sentence starters, and grammatical features (e.g., conditional mood), placed on the anchor chart with emphasis through intonation (verbal support), he can draw Tasir's attention to the linguistic features she needs to use to write and revise her argument. He can also facilitate Tasir's small-group interaction and selection of arguments for or against the proposal by providing her with the same reading materials she consulted in geography. Leveled questioning (verbal support) makes her verbalize disciplinary language before she must use it in writing.[22]

To narrow the gap to provide meaningful feedback and to receive actionable feedback for her revisions, Mr. Grant should pair Tasir with strong writers. She may read her own argument more slowly than the peers, but because her own argument will be shorter, no extra time will be needed. Hearing and reading well-developed texts aid her comprehension, do not create objectionable delays in giving feedback, and allow Tasir to comment on argument development and strength of wording. Furthermore, by selecting and highlighting items on the checklist that make sense for Tasir and the partners to focus on, Mr. Grant can lower Tasir's apprehension in the task.

MANAGE APPLICATION, GROUPING, TIME, AND PROVIDER

All supports can be implemented during the lesson with Tasir participating in the whole-class discussion or in her group/pair work, and they are easily assumed by the teacher. Except for leveled questioning and the adapted feedback checklists, which are supplemental supports, all supports are universal and benefit everyone.

Knowing that classroom communication would be addressed in many places, Mr. Grant turned his attention to checking whether that is sufficient for Tasir to meet the lesson's language objectives.

Identify Language/Literacy Skill(s) to Be Developed

STEP 1

Writing and speaking stand out as potential skills to be developed through the TLI protocol based on the lesson objectives, but because Tasir will learn about good delivery strategies in the video and class discussion and will deliver the argument she wrote, edited, and rehearsed, no targeted instruction to build her speaking skills is necessary. However, Mr. Grant immediately recognized argument construction, providing peer feedback, and editing tasks as areas of focus for Tasir to meet the lesson objectives.

Size the Distance

After applying the SCC protocol to improve classroom communication based on Tasir's oral proficiency as an intermediate MLE, Mr. Grant consults the WIDA performance definitions at the current assessed level for the skill of focus in the writing lesson (see table 10.1). He also considers the writing sample shown above, which, given Tasir's difficulty in reaching the required length of a personal narrative, foreshadows the upcoming struggle in expressing her opinion through a persuasive argument. Tasir's inability to make self-corrections because she does not recognize her mistakes presents an equally challenging obstacle for her to give meaningful feedback to partners.

At a 2.8 in writing, Tasir currently lies at just below intermediate level. When comparing this proficiency in writing to the grade-level standards, it is clear that she can support her claims in writing with evidence, even if her phrasing is formulaic and simple. The access to sources and notes from the geography, mathematics, and science portions of the thematic unit and having the two-sided notes from the brainstorming session for consultation allow her to work with familiar materials to identify evidence for her claims. The language provided on the anchor chart gives her frames of reference while writing and editing. However, her learner language includes numerous grammatical and mechanical errors that would be marked as unacceptable in a

TABLE 10.1

Tasir's Assessed WIDA Performance Definitions in Writing (Grades K-12)

Skill and Level	Linguistic Complexity	Language Forms and Conventions	Vocabulary Usage
	At each grade, toward the end of a given level of English proficiency, and with instructional support, English language learners will process (L/R) or produce (S/W):		
W 2.8	• Phrases or short sentences • Emerging expression of ideas	• Formulaic grammatical structures • Repetitive phrasal and sentence patterns across content areas	• General content words and expressions • Social and instructional words and expressions across content areas

native English-speaking student's writing. The opportunity to become aware of her errors through peer editing might help, but the remaining gap still needs considerable attention.

STEP 1 Develop ML's Language/Literacy Skill(s)

The supports provided through the SCC protocol allow Tasir to actively participate in all whole-class activities. In the at-a-glance table (table 10.2), you see that Mr. Grant will go back and forth between the SCC protocol and the TLI protocol a few times to facilitate Tasir's argument writing and draft revisions. This takes place when he stops by her desk to offer guidance, like he does with all students during individual writing times. These encounters require fewer nonverbal and verbal supports, but to ensure successful communication, he integrates them in a deliberate fashion alongside the 4 P adjustments.

ADJUSTING PITCH

To aid Tasir in writing more complex sentences, Mr. Grant discusses combining sentences and co-constructs one example. He also encourages Tasir to add adjectives or adverbs that make the argument more telling and to look up synonyms both on the anchor chart and in the tablet dictionary to reduce repetitive phrasing.

ADJUSTING PACE

Tasir's developing academic language skills require a slight adjustment to the pace, which Mr. Grant provides with wait time between pointing out mistakes in Tasir's argument and when he expects her to respond. Step-by-step grammatical rule explanations may need to be restated or rephrased for Tasir to understand fully.

ADJUSTING PORTION

Because Tasir is developing proficiency in using academic language, she takes longer to compose and revise her work. To compensate, her assignment will require a shorter composition, which also helps with having fewer errors to focus on for feedback and revisions.

ADJUSTING PERSPECTIVE/POINT

It is difficult to anticipate which errors will show up in Tasir's drafts. The best strategy is to prevent mistakes from occurring. While checking in slightly more frequently than with his non-MLEs students to check grammar and word choice, Mr. Grant addresses easily fixed spelling and grammatical errors as he notices them. He explains some terms that native speakers would know and assists with making sentences more complex. He decides on the spot which grammatical errors that are still visible in the second-draft revision are level appropriate to help correct (e.g., mistakes such as "By next year, I am living here 5 years") and also answers questions Tasir has regarding the areas of improvement of the signal words and closing statement her partner pointed out.

Manage Grouping, Time, and Provider

Grouping. Tasir is the only MLE student at an assessed high level 2 in writing, so Mr. Grant consults with her individually during the built-in writing and revision times all students have.

Time and Provider. Grammatical features common to persuasive writing that Mr. Grant will likely need to address during consultations, such as conditional mood, would ideally be explained before the lesson through a brief preteaching session or a short online grammar tutorial.[23] In this case, he provides his input and checks on Tasir's output during each writing and revision phase. He could also refer Tasir to a pertinent tutorial following the lesson to reinforce the grammar points Tasir struggled with during editing.

Given the built-in consultation times for all students and his knowledge of grammar and armed with the information on feedback for MLEs he recently read in the book given to him by the ELD specialist, Mr. Grant can provide the necessary scaffolding by adjusting the 4 Ps in the grade-level lesson himself. [24]

With the classroom communication supports during whole-class instruction and the scaffolding afforded through the TLI protocol and in place, Tasir will be able to meet the language and literacy expectations of the lesson objectives.

Lesson Summary

Table 10.2 depicts the lesson plan with the Teaching All Subjects, Language, and Literacy (TASLL) Framework protocols applied. In the SCC protocol portion of the lesson, the nonverbal (SLIDE) tasks are <u>underlined</u> and the verbal elements (TREAD) elements are in **boldface**. The <u>**combined**</u> fonts show that a task can contain both components. The second column lists the language skills from the point of view of the students and illustrates the gap size that exists between the classroom communication and Tasir's current intermediate level of oral English proficiency, and the third column lists the added verbal and nonverbal supports.

TABLE 10.2

The Persuasive Argument Writing Lesson at a Glance

Lesson Steps	**Skill[1] and Gap Size[2]**	**Added Supports[3]**
Hook: **Project five choices** (e.g., "diet soda OR regular soda?," "basketball OR baseball?"). Each member of a pair **chooses** one option and **explains** in three sentences why it is the better choice.	L, S, R Ø	No supports needed
Project the statement "Principal Phillips: We should have more time for lunch." **Complete a T-chart** with main points and benefits/evidence the students offer to convince the school principal.	L, S, R ↕	***Nonverbal Support:*** Pointing during modeling ***Verbal Supports:*** • Modeling of two-sided note-taking strategy • Repeatedly asking in which columns claims and reasons/evidence go as students state them
Construct an anchor chart to review the common features of persuasive arguments and how to present one, and then introduce the project.	L, S ↕↕	***Nonverbal Support:*** Pointing to features under discussion on chart. ***Verbal Supports:*** • Creation of anchor chart with frequent repetition of grammar features (e.g., personal pronouns, verb tense and mood, adverbs, subordinate clauses) and use of rhetorical questions • Leveled questioning to engage Tasir's participation
Groups **review** the research texts from the GIS mapping lesson and the financial calculations conducted in mathematics. They **brainstorm** which elements from their discoveries support arguments for the initiative placed before the city council and which could be a counterargument.	L, S, R ↕↕	***Verbal Supports:*** • Tasir uses modified reading materials from GIS unit (i.e., less text and more graphics) (supplemental) • Leveled questioning during check-in, referring to group's T-chart (supplemental) • Check that Tasir's T-chart is complete (aupplemental)
Tasir is able to select her position and three pieces as evidence based on the group brainstorm, but **the TLI protocol** is crucial to help her put the evidence into her own words and write both a catchy opening and a strong closing statement.		

Lesson Step/How	Nonverbal and Verbal Supports	4 P Adjustments
• **Choose** the position to support or oppose the initiative and **select** three pieces of supporting evidence from the group brainstorm. • **Write** the first draft: an opening statement, three supporting paragraphs, and a concluding statement.	***Verbal Support:*** Check that Tasir's T-chart from group discussion is complete, and ensure she uses it for writing.	***Pitch:*** Conference with Tasir, and discuss how to use longer, more complex sentences. ***Portion:*** Shorter composition is acceptable because it takes Tasir longer to write. This will also reduce the number of errors to focus on for feedback. ***Perspective:*** Explain word usage or glaring grammatical errors.
End of the TLI protocol application		

Lesson Steps	Skill1 and Gap Size2	Nonverbal and Verbal Supports[3]
Sequentially lead students through revising: • Students **read** their draft aloud, and partner **listens**. • Based on checklist, partners **make suggestions** for improvements to introduction, argument evidence and sequencing, and conclusion.	L, S, R ⇕⇕⇕ L, S ⇕⇕⇕	***Verbal Supports:*** • Select a partner who is a strong writer and patient and encouraging. • Highlight partner's checklist to focus on argument evidence as well as basic grammatical errors (i.e., subject-verb agreement) (supplemental). • Highlight Tasir's checklist to give partner feedback about argument evidence (supplemental).
Tasir requires focused attention to improve her draft. Mr. Grant needs to point out and help correct wording and grammatical mistakes that non-MLEs would not make, which is why the TLI protocol comes back into play.		

Continued...

TABLE 10.2

The Persuasive Argument Writing Lesson at a Glance *(Continued...)*

Lesson Step/How	Nonverbal and Verbal Supports	4 P Adjustments
Each student **revises** their first draft.	***Verbal Supports:*** • Make sure Tasir uses the dictionary on her tablet to reword the areas the partner suggested to improve. • Refer Tasir to the anchor chart for signal words, sentence starters, and variations of topic sentences.	***Pitch:*** Co-compose a few of Tasir's simple sentences with more complexity and suggest stronger wording. ***Pace:*** Provide sufficient wait time between grammatical rule explanations or suggestions of wording change and be prepared to restate or rephrase. ***Perspective:*** • Model importance of signal words and transitions in Tasir's current sentences. • Explain grammatical rules if Tasir is not able to self-correct basic mistakes.

End of the TLI protocol application. The following section returns to the SCC protocol because it does not require targeted instruction for Tasir.

Lesson Steps	Skill1 and Gap Size[2]	Nonverbal and Verbal Supports[3]
Students **read** a partner's argument and **make suggestions** for improvement and language conventions.	R, W ↕↕↕	***Verbal Supports:*** • Select a partner who is strong writer and patient and encouraging. • Highlight partner's checklist to focus on word choice (i.e., synonyms, signal words) and formulaic/repetitive phrasing (supplemental). • Highlight Tasir's checklist to give partner feedback about unclear parts, signal words, and strength of closing statement (supplemental).

Changing wording, even when precise locations are given, are largely beyond Tasir's current language ability. She needs Mr. Grant's focused attention both to accomplish the task and to fix grammatical errors that likely occurred during the previous revision. Therefore, the **TLI protocol** comes back into play.

Lesson Step/How	Nonverbal and Verbal Supports	4 P Adjustments
Each student **revises** their second draft.	***Verbal Supports:*** • Make sure Tasir uses the dictionary on her tablet to fix spelling errors the partner highlighted. • Refer Tasir to the anchor chart to revise for variation of transition phrasing and strong closing statements.	***Pitch:*** Discuss how to use longer, more complex sentences. ***Pace:*** Provide sufficient wait time between grammatical rule explanations or suggestions of wording change and be prepared to restate or rephrase. ***Perspective:*** • Explain the grammatical rules in sentence-level errors that are proficiency-level appropriate to correct. • Answer questions regarding the areas of improvement of signal words and closing statement her partner pointed out.

End of the TLI protocol application. The following section returns to the SCC protocol because it does not require targeted instruction for Tasir.

Lesson Steps	Skill1 and Gap Size[2]	Nonverbal and Verbal Supports[3]
Argument delivery: • **Show** short video clips of good speeches. **Hold class discussion** of posture, eye contact, voice projection, and pace. • Students **rehearse** their speeches with two new partners. • **Conduct** mock city hall meetings in small groups. Students **rate** each argument for effectiveness.	L, S, R ↕ ↕ ↕ and ↕↕[25]	No supports needed.

Key:
1 Language skills: L = Listening, S = Speaking, R = Reading, W = Writing
2 Gap sizes: No gap = Ø, ↕ = small gap, ↕↕ = medium gap, ↕↕↕ = large gap
3 Unless otherwise noted, all supports are considered universal.

In the TLI protocol section, we first list the instructional steps. Without knowing what Tasir will write, we cannot elaborate on *how* Mr. Grant will target his consultations to her argument writing and revisions. Therefore, we do not give detailed instructional steps, but the nonverbal and verbal supports in the second column and the 4 P adjustments presented in the last column give a clear picture of *what* he is planning on doing and at which point in the lesson.

Final Thoughts

Mr. Grant's attention to the 4 Ps of scaffolding reduced the gaps between Tasir's current English proficiency in the four language skills and the specific language skills required to engage successfully in the lesson. By adjusting the 4 Ps, Mr. Grant helped Tasir feel less anxiety, which, in turn, enabled her to focus more on developing writing skills and less on worrying about her performance. Tasir's collaboration with her peers went more smoothly than previously because she didn't feel intimidated by her groupmates' suggestions for editing after she and Mr. Grant had conferred about her draft. His judicious selection of grammatical errors to address, as well as setting the goal for Tasir to write longer, more complex sentences based on her current and subsequent literacy proficiency levels, targeted the instruction to exactly where Tasir is on her journey to reaching the highest levels of proficiency in literacy.

After the completion of the thematic unit in Mr. Grant's language arts class, Principal Phillips called a meeting of the faculty involved. He brought refreshments as a thank-you for their trailblazing efforts in constructing the school's first problem-based learning unit. After a few minutes of socializing, he asked each teacher to discuss challenges and successes and share a few samples of the end products.

Mr. Grant was last to speak. He concurred with the geography teacher's comment that Tasir had become an active participant during the unit: "Yes, Tasir was more engaged, even though, as you all know, writing poses rather large challenges for her. The recycling of information from the other content areas and the close peer work surely benefited her. I would like to thank Ms. Parker for suggesting we take advantage of our ELD specialists to obtain teaching tips for helping MLEs grow academically. I haven't had a chance to do that given the extra work this new thematic unit required, but I intend to contact her soon. I did read a short chapter on sentence-level error correction that Ms. Marlin put in my mailbox when she heard about this project. It helped me understand and attend to Tasir's writing needs better. I do need to refresh my knowledge in second language acquisition and related topics. Does anybody else agree that our professional learning community should request a workshop from her? It seems our MLE population is growing every year."

"Before I close this meeting," said the principal, "I want to let you know that I will highlight your excellent work at the opening session of next week's grade-level meetings. I think this way we could get other faculty's creative juices flowing, and I would like to ask you to encourage other grade levels to try now. More importantly, though, I am soliciting your thoughts about adding a second thematic unit in the last grading period as well. Think of it as an inspiration for your peers. This way, our seventh grade would already have two thematic units in place for next academic year."

STOP AND REFLECT QUESTIONS

1. Reflect on the MLs in your class. Which students do you think would consider themselves to be "grammatically competent" and which ones would describe themselves as being more "communicatively competent"? Which students would say they are equally balanced between the two? In other words, how do you think your students would categorize their acquisition strengths?
2. How would you rate your knowledge of grammar? Would you say you are (a) very knowledgeable, (b) somewhat knowledgeable, or (c) you don't remember grammar rules very well but you get by. If you selected b or c, what should you do to improve your knowledge of grammar?

GO AND PRACTICE ACTIVITIES

1. Review a book on grammar to refresh your knowledge on the rules that govern the language. Then, in simplified language, explain to your MLs some of the grammatical features of the language that are described as being most problematic to L2 learners in general.
2. Write feedback reports for each student. Select three of the major errors committed and write possible reasons for those errors. Include exercises/activities that would help your MLs to edit their writing by recognizing their own errors. Then give your ML students a copy of your report and place another in their portfolio. The feedback forms demonstrate progress over time as you document the reduction in errors made each week.

Teaching Edgar to Analyze a Text-Based Argument

Language and Literacy in High School

On the table were a lidded glass quart jar, half a quart of milk, and a plastic cylinder filled with pH strips. Edgar approached the objects and immediately began pouring. "Hold on there, Edgar," said Mr. Otto. "I can see you are excited to get started, but we need to follow the correct procedures." Edgar set the milk down and turned toward the front of the room. A girl who sat in the first row began handing out copies of a data table with three columns, one for listing the day, one for recording the pH, and one for noting the appearance of the jar of pasteurized milk in a 37°C incubator. Mr. Otto called Edgar back to help set up while he stated the directions for the weeklong experiment.

Every day, Edgar entered his observations, carefully noticing the changes. The activity objective was to help students understand ecosystems and their functions, and Edgar was working steadily toward this end. Now that he had developed a sense of the changes over time, Edgar had to show his comprehension. Today the front-row girl handed out another paper, but this time, it wasn't a data table. It was a quiz, with questions such as, "What might happen to an ecosystem if all the decomposers were to die?" and "Explain how the flow of energy contributes to and overlaps with the steps of the carbon cycle." Edgar's biology class was implementing the state standards for disciplinary literacy with a science writing assessment, and he had no idea how to respond. After Edgar handed his teacher a blank page, Mr. Otto decided to contact Ms. Myers for help.

You might have expected to find Edgar in his language arts class like our other multilingual learner of English (MLE) students in chapters 8 through 10. However, because his assessed overall English proficiency level is just shy of level 2, which presents too vast a gap to the language demands of tenth-grade language arts instruction, he was placed in a separate English language development (ELD class.[1] The classroom application presented in this chapter details Edgar's experiences in this specialized classroom for MLEs, showing in detail what type of language is used. We also show how his ELD teacher supports his use of academic language in other subjects and classes.

GRADE-LEVEL EXPECTATIONS FOR LANGUAGE AND LITERACY IN TENTH GRADE

The State of Illinois, where Edgar lives, has implemented the Common Core State Standards in English Language Arts (ELA) that *all* students are expected to meet. The following sections summarize the language demands established by these expectations for reading, writing, speaking, listening, and language.

Reading

Analysis of complex, grade-level narrative and informational texts is the focus of most of the reading standards. Tenth graders are expected to cite evidence; analyze and summarize the central theme, character interaction, and plot development; comprehend figurative and connotative meanings and the impact of word choice on tone; and analyze text structure and order, development of ideas, rhetoric, and argumentation. The language standards impacting reading include comprehension of unknown words by using context, parts of speech, and reference materials; interpretation of figures of speech; and analysis of nuances in word meaning.

The following passage gives a sense of grade-level text for tenth grade:[2]

> When two people speak the same first language, they occasionally misunderstand each other. Imagine the difficulties that interpreters have when they must first understand what the speaker of one language has said and then translate the message into another language. Translators are challenged when the speaker makes a reference to an event or story character that is not known to listeners from another country. A speaker may refer to someone as a "Cinderella," meaning that a person was once poor and is now wealthy, but if the listeners do not know the story, the meaning is lost.

Writing

In writing, tenth graders are required to make claims and counterclaims; supply evidence; write cohesively; use formal style and objective tone; introduce, develop, and conclude an argument using facts and details; use transitions and precise language; use dialogue, pacing, description, reflection, and multiple plot lines; and use appropriate style for the task. The language standards pertaining to writing include the use of parallel structure and various types of phrases (noun, verb, adjectival, adverbial, participial, prepositional, and absolute) and clauses (independent, dependent, noun, relative, and adverbial) as well as accurate use of academic and discipline-specific terms. They are also expected to use semicolons and colons and spell correctly.

The following paragraph provides a sense of the expectations for satisfactory writing at the high school level. It is an excerpt from a tenth-grade writing sample graded a 3-2-3 (purpose/structure–development–language) on a four-point scale:[3]

> Many people will assume that planning out your free time can make you exreamly unmotivated. According to Selin A Malkoc, he states "When scheduled, leaisure tasks feel less free-flowing and more forced." Selin is trying to say hat the reward at the end of the work day will not feel as rewarding if it is planned. While his opinoin is respectible, he is ultimently wrong. Infact it is way more rewarding to plan out your leisure time becasue anticipation makes hard work rewarding. Instead of not planning your leisure time, you should plan it for the thrill of anicipation.

Speaking, Listening, and Language

Students in tenth grade read in preparation for discussions; sustain conversations; respond thoughtfully; present information clearly, concisely, and logically, using substance and style that is appropriate to the audience; adapt their speech to the context; and use formal style.

RESEARCH ON TEACHING LANGUAGE AND LITERACY TO MULTILINGUAL LEARNERS OF ENGLISH IN HIGH SCHOOL

Supporting MLE students' literacy development at the high school level is multifaceted. Effective reading requires proficiency in three interrelated sets of factors pertaining to language, literacy, and world knowledge.[4] Linguistic factors relate to knowledge of textual elements such as word, sentence, and text structures. Literacy factors pertain to cognitive and metacognitive awareness and use of reading strategies such as setting a purpose for reading, monitoring one's understanding, solving reading comprehension difficulties during reading, and monitoring comprehension. Knowledge factors consist of the background information that readers already possess and may use to fill in gaps in the explicit linguistic elements in a text.

Oral Proficiency in English

As noted in previous chapters, oral proficiency in English is necessary for reading comprehension and writing proficiency, but the degree of oral proficiency necessary for most multilingual learners to participate in class is not sufficient for successful reading in a second language (L2). Indeed, significant numbers of students have a great deal of proficiency in conversational English and yet read very slowly and with poor comprehension. In other words, good oral language proficiency skills are a necessary but not sufficient condition for fluent reading and comprehension because disciplinary reading requires proficiency in academic English, which even students with advanced conversational English skills need time and support to develop[5]. MLEs with no prior schooling or support in their first language (L1) may take seven to ten years to catch up to their native English-speaking peers.[6]

Language arts and literacy teachers in high school often face the challenge of working with L2 learners who have adequate oral language proficiency but below-grade literacy skills. When MLEs, like Edgar, experience difficulty in reading and text understanding, it is common for teachers to focus on vocabulary knowledge as a major source of difficulty. However, language arts and literacy teachers also know that although vocabulary knowledge is crucial to reading, writing, and content learning, effective reading comprehension requires much more. Research indicates that almost any kind of vocabulary instruction can improve students' performance on vocabulary tests. Unfortunately, many commonly used methods of vocabulary instruction do not reliably increase students' reading comprehension.[7] MLEs, even those with high levels of oral proficiency in English, may be less sensitive to certain types of information supplied by context, particularly details supplied by morphological (word structure) and syntactic (word sequence) components of language. In fact, for struggling MLE and non-MLE readers and writers in upper elementary, middle, and high school classrooms, morphological and syntactic aspects of language have been shown to play more important roles in reading development than previously assumed.[8]

By tailoring their literacy instruction to the unique needs of their MLs, teachers can attend to specific linguistic needs and help move them toward reaching the required standards. Furthermore, because reading comprehension requires more than being able to decode words and knowing word meanings, we encourage language arts and literacy teachers to incorporate in their teaching both formal and informal instruction by focusing on (1) what readers need to know about language and text features to apply reading and learning strategies effectively and (2) what good readers do when they engage in text reading and understanding.

For example, teaching students how certain aspects of language such as morphology and syntax work might include information about important prefixes, suffixes, and root words. It is helpful for developing L2 readers and writers to know, for instance, that inflectional morphemes such as the plural suffix *-s* or the past tense *-ed* do not change the meaning of the words, but they convey information about agreement, tense, and plurality. However, derivational morphemes change word meanings and parts of speech, as in the words *read–reader*, *magic–magician*, *teach–teacher*, and *clever–cleverly*.[9] Teachers can help students like Edgar develop morphological knowledge and skills by incorporating instruction that focuses on prefixes, suffixes, and root words while emphasizing that words are related in meaningful ways (e.g., *create*, *creation*, *creativity*). This type of instructed second language acquisition, or focus on form, helps students decode morphologically complex words, understand word meanings, and comprehend what they read. It can also help MLEs develop grammatical competence in all four skills—listening, speaking, reading, and writing—as well as further their acquisition of new forms in English and avoid fossilization or stabilization of errors. Pointing out that the added *s* in, for example, *she likes* is required can help MLEs notice that feature and develop competence in using it correctly over time.

In addition to teaching MLEs about important morphological and syntactic aspects of language, language arts and literacy teachers should help students develop strategic or metacognitive knowledge about reading. Examples of this type of knowledge might include strategies for unlocking the meanings of unknown words, using what they already know about a topic to make sense of what they read, restating the meaning of a text or passage using one's own words, and evaluating what one reads in a critical way. To help students develop this type of knowledge, it is best for teachers to first explain the strategic processes involved in reading, model these strategies using different types of texts, and provide students opportunities to practice these strategies, first with teacher guidance and then on their own using self-selected texts.

First Language Influences on English Language Literacy

Students like Edgar possess a wealth of knowledge about their native languages. Edgar's language arts and literacy teachers should take advantage of the similarities and differences between Spanish and English when designing instruction to support his language and literacy development. There are well-established similarities and differences between L1 and L2 reading. We suggest that teachers consider integrating in their teaching explicit instruction in how languages are different and similar in terms of sound structure, word and sentence formation, vocabulary, and text structure. Differences and similarities across languages can then be reinforced by engaging Edgar and his peers in reading sample texts that address similar topics in Spanish and English and in comparing the texts to see how they differ in their expression of ideas in writing and their use of vocabulary, grammar, and text structure. These activities will help Edgar expand his knowledge of how both languages work and ultimately use what he knows about his own language to advance his listening, speaking, reading, and writing skills in English.

Students need to know that writing is used as a means of communication to express ideas, thoughts, and feelings across all human languages. Writers in all languages use a variety of genres (e.g., essays, poems, stories), formats (e.g., narrative, descriptive, explanatory texts), and styles (e.g., formal, casual). Students should know that all languages have conventions, guidelines, and procedures for writing and that, developmentally, the process of learning to write in any language takes greater time and effort than learning to speak it.

When learning to write in a second language, students should know that different languages apply different conventions, guidelines, and procedures in their writing systems. These conventions, which encompass, among others, word order in sentences, script and directionality, and spelling, vary a great deal depending on the linguistic distance between any two languages.[10] As we did in the previous chapters, we highlight a few distinguishing features between English and the L1 of the case study student who is the focus of this chapter, Edgar.

LEARNER LANGUAGE CONSIDERATIONS FOR SPANISH MULTILINGUAL LEARNERS OF ENGLISH

In chapter 9, we discussed some considerations in cross-language transfer from Spanish to English that might impact how a learner at beginning proficiency like Edith approaches pronunciation, spelling and grammar, or longer text. The following points typically come into focus with MLEs at an intermediate or higher proficiency.

General Similarities and Differences for English and Spanish

Given the close correspondence between Spanish pronunciation and spelling, many MLEs with Spanish as their L1 struggle with decoding words in English and when writing newly acquired vocabulary. For instance, Edgar tends to reduce double letters in English, such as in *communicate*, to only one consonant (*comunicate*), especially when spelling cognates.

One aspect of English grammar that Ms. Myers often points out to her Spanish-speaking MLEs is word order. English grammar is less flexible than Spanish, with subject-verb-object being the norm in declarative sentences and adjectives being placed before the noun they modify. In Spanish, however, sentences commonly start with a verb or an object, and adjectives are placed after nouns. Questions can be formed in several ways, but none of the options include the required addition of the auxiliaries "do/does" or "am/are/is" as in "Does that make sense?" or "Is she running late?" in English.

High school students like Edgar are expected to write to inform, to persuade, to compare and contrast, to propose solutions, to show cause and effect, and so on. Although English usually focuses on one main idea per paragraph and tends to prioritize clear, concise arguments and logical reasoning, Spanish allows for more repetition and emotional appeal, especially in persuasive writing. Spanish-speaking MLEs who possess high literacy skills in their L1 need to be explicitly taught how to organize text in English. Even though the message of disciplinary text in English can be understood, writing in the same manner requires awareness of similarities and differences, targeted instruction, and practice.

Edgar's Language Sample Analysis

Nearing the end of the school year, Ms. Myers possesses information from numerous formative and summative assessments and some diagnostic assessment data and has collected several language samples for each student. If asked by an administrator or a teacher in another discipline, she can talk about her students' challenges and growth patterns and propose instructional strategies that work for them. Despite Edgar's steady progress in vocabulary acquisition and formation of more complex phrasing, however, she is not noticing much growth in his reading fluency and comprehension. She decides to make another attempt at pinpointing the stumbling block and calls him to one of the designated classroom small-group conferencing tables while the rest of the students learn about and practice passive voice exercises on their laptops.

> "I don't like read." "Yeah, Edgar, I know," Ms. Myers said, laughing a bit as she let out a shallow sigh. "Let's go ahead and try this story. Edgar, please do your best for me." Ms. Myers reached under the table and pulled up a plastic-wrapped hardcover book, already open to the first page. She set it in front of Edgar, holding her palm in the crease until Edgar gripped the sides. Now that it was in Edgar's hands, Ms. Myers put her cupped hand to her ear, raising her eyebrows. Edgar half-smiled and rolled his eyes, unapproving yet obliging Ms. Myers, and began:
>
> "Um . . . William . . . um . . . we are going out. Um . . . We will be, um, at the movies . . . uh . . . and . . . we go out to dinner." Edgar read word by word flatly. There was no rise and fall in tone—just monotone expression, virtually meaningless.
>
> "Uh . . . 'We will not be out late. Please be good for the baby sister. Miss Lane may will be coming over,' says Mom. 'Okay, Mom,' say William. He was not ha . . . happy. He did not like, not like it, when Mom and Dad went out. They left h-him at home. William did not like having a babysit . . . sitter." One syllable, one syllable, one syllable, two. One syllable, one syllable, two syllables, two. Edgar read like a typewriter—a typewriter with Spanish accents on the vowels.
>
> "Miss Lane made him eat all his dinner. She did not let him play outside. She was afrai William wo get hurt. Miss Lane was no fun. She never play . . . play any games with William. Miss Lane walk-ed in the door, 'Hello, William, how are you?' say Miss Lane. 'Okay, (I don't know how to say that)' say William. He walk he walk-ed back to his room. He decide to read for (I don't know that). He like to read books."
>
> Edgar read the way he spoke, with final consonants dissolving like his confidence. Often he had been told to pronounce all the letters at the end of words, so he made sure to pronounce *walked* not as *walkt* or *walk*, but *walk-ed*. When he came across words he didn't know, he just said so. He was trying to read a story many grade levels below his own, and he was trying his best.
>
> "That's good, Edgar," said Ms. Myers. "That's enough for now. Thank you for reading for me." "Uh-huh," replied Edgar, as he shut the book and pushed it toward the edge of the table.

This language sample makes clear that Edgar is reading far below tenth-grade level and struggling with a third-grade story. He clearly needs targeted instruction in learning to read English. And because so much of the new content in his academic classes is transmitted through reading, he also needs to make as quick a transition to reading to learn as possible. Ms. Myers's ELD class is exactly what he needs.

Classroom teachers in upper elementary, middle, and high school should be mindful of all students, including MLEs, who appear to struggle when reading disciplinary content materials. It is evident that although Edgar seems to be doing fairly well and enjoys being in Ms. Myers's ELD class, he is clearly not doing as well in his subject-area classes like mathematics, science, and social studies. The intriguing thing is that he finds these classes "boring," most likely because he does not feel he is getting the same level of attention and help from his teachers or fellow students. Edgar has relatively good conversational skills in English, which are helpful when communicating with his teachers and peers. However, he doesn't have the requisite academic language skills (e.g., depth and breadth of academic vocabulary, understanding of the structure of words, sentences, and textual materials) to read and understand academic materials. As we indicated in previous sections of this book, the learning demands for reading, writing, and comprehending texts in grades 4 through 12 are far greater than in the earlier grades, in part due to text complexity, conceptual density, and arduous language demands. MLEs such as Edgar may have difficulties with one or more of these issues, which contribute in different and yet complementary ways to their ability to read and write.

Ms. Myers regularly requires her MLEs to write, giving them both structured and open assignments. For a free-writing assignment about his little brother's birthday present, Edgar wrote these lines:

> The TriCycle is good for childrens Like 3 or 2 year because the tricycle has wheel and the childrens don't fold wen The are playing.

The brevity of Edgar's composition shows a number of areas that he is struggling with. First, he was able to write only one sentence during the ten-minute writing activity. He has difficulties with basic language conventions in English such as capitalization, plural forms (childrens, 3 or 2 year, wheel), and spelling of vowel sounds that he hears and pronounces according to his native language sound system, causing the confusion between the spelling of *fall* and *fold*. Because his variety of Spanish often eliminates final consonant sounds, he is confused about when a consonant is pronounced in English word endings. It can't be overemphasized how much Edgar needs targeted English language instruction, which, given the gap between his current English proficiency and the expectations for tenth-grade ELA instruction, must take place in a separate instructional environment with a qualified ELD teacher.

ESSENTIAL POINTS

1. Edgar's experiences show the challenges faced by MLEs, especially in high school, where understanding complex texts and academic language is tough. While he's good at conversational English, he struggles with reading and writing for subjects like science, math, and social studies, which require more advanced skills.
2. Ms. Myers's ELD class helps Edgar improve his academic language skills. This targeted support is crucial for him to move from basic conversational English to more complex academic language, preparing him for the expectations in all subjects.

3. Language demands increase for high school students, especially in grades 9–10. Students need to analyze difficult texts, use academic vocabulary, and write clearly. For MLEs like Edgar, these tasks are harder because of their limited academic English skills. This highlights the need for language instruction provided by specialists to meet the high educational standards.

CLASSROOM APPLICATION

As described in the first section of this chapter and as demonstrated through Edgar's reading and writing samples, it is clear that there are a number of grade-level ELA standards that Edgar cannot currently meet. For example, CCSS.ELA-LITERACY.L.9-10.6 (*Acquire and use accurately general academic and domain-specific words and phrases, sufficient for reading, writing, speaking, and listening at the college and career readiness level*) is a standard that Edgar can work toward, but he does not yet have the English proficiency to attain this standard. However, many ELA standards are broad enough for Edgar to meet with targeted language instruction in an ELD classroom. This lesson reaches toward the ELA knowledge and skills that Edgar needs to develop to be college and career ready, but it is targeted to Edgar's skills at this point in time.

MS. MYERS'S TEXT MESSAGING LESSON

The lesson described here is one lesson in a unit framed around the topic "Does all communication serve a positive purpose?" that Ms. Myers has used for many years.[11] It is designed to address a number of grade-level ELA standards for reading informational text as well as listening and speaking. Specifically, the lesson concentrates on reading with the goal of identifying a main idea and supporting details.

The lesson description provides transcripts of teacher and student speech to give insights into how this lesson is different from grade-level language arts instruction. We then discuss these specifics using our 4 Ps of language arts differentiation for MLEs in high school. You will also see how verbal and nonverbal supports, which are applied through the Supportive Classroom Communication protocol in all general classroom lessons, is naturally woven into Ms. Myers's instructional moves.

OBJECTIVES

- The students will be able to support their opinion about a topic in discussion (if they use text messaging and whether it is good or harmful for teens)
- The students will be able to analyze a text for its main idea and the details that support it

LESSON DESCRIPTION

Ms. Myers holds up her smartphone and says, "Raise your hand [raises her hand] if you like to text [mimes texting on her phone] with your friends [points to the class]." After students raise their hands, she asks two complex questions, chunking each sentence segment and pausing to gauge comprehension and engagement. She clearly states her first question:

> Is texting different [pauses, looks at class]
> from how we communicate [pauses]
> when we talk? [pauses]
> How?

"I talk like text," Edgar answers as he smiles at the girl sitting beside him. "Why you so DDG [drop dead gorgeous]?"

"Okay, Edgar," says Ms. Myers, "we get what you mean. Some people text more than they talk. Maybe texting has influenced the way we talk now. Texting's influence could be big, or it could be a drop in the bucket. *A drop in the bucket* is an idiom that means a small influence. It comes from adding water to a bucket, or pail. We can add a cup [she mimes holding a cup and tilting it upside down], or we can add a drop [she mimes pinching an eye dropper pointed downward]. A drop is a small amount." She writes *drop in the bucket* on the Idiom of the Day wall chart.

Ms. Myers follows up with another chunked question:

> Is texting different [pause]
> from how we communicate [pause]
> when we write at school? [pause]
> How?

A student replies, "Is different. For write at school, we use word. For texting, we say thing like LOL." Everyone nods and smiles knowingly.

"Yes, that's right," says Ms. Myers. "When we write [pauses and scans the class for comprehension], we use full words [holds hands out at waist level, about two feet apart]. Full words like *laughing out loud.* When we write, we don't use [shakes head] abbreviations like *LOL.*" She then writes *abbreviations* on the board, saying the word slowly, syllable by syllable, and asks the students to repeat each syllable and then the entire word in chorus.

"An abbreviation is a short way of saying something. What examples of abbreviations can you think of?" Students offer more examples, yelling out terms like BFF (best friend forever), F2F (face to face), and JK (just kidding), as the teacher writes the abbreviations and their full forms on the board. Ms. Myers goes on, "When we write, we use correct grammar. When we text, we break a lot of grammar rules. The topic of our lesson today is why some people think text messaging is a bad form of communication. Let's read this article [points to copy of the article in the students' notebooks]."

The students follow silently as she expressively reads the article the first time, paragraph by paragraph.

> Do you like to send text messages? Text messaging through cell phones is popular among teens, but it can be controversial among adults. People who think it's harmful have put texting on trial.

Ms. Myers pauses after each point: "Text messaging through cell phones [pause] is popular among teens [pause] but it can be controversial [pause] among adults." After reading the short paragraph, she tells students to pair up and state in their own words what the paragraph means. She also asks them to identify any words or phrases that they don't understand. Once they have discussed the paragraph, she asks for a volunteer to paraphrase the paragraph. She then asks if anyone needs a definition for any words or clarification of any information in the paragraph. The students ask what *put on trial* means, and Ms. Myers explains that it means to examine the evidence to determine whether something is *right/good* or *wrong/bad*, like in a courtroom. Another question is the meaning of the word *among*, to which Ms. Myers not only offers *between* or *with* but also mentions that these words are synonyms.

Once everyone states that they understand the paragraph, Ms. Myers moves on, reading the following text with appropriate pauses:

> The first argument against text messaging is that the constant use of abbreviations takes away from a student's ability to write clear and well-organized papers. Supporters of texting say that language happens on a continuum, from very casual to very formal, and that it's unlikely that teens will confuse the two.

As they work together on paraphrasing the paragraph, some students ask what *takes away from* means. Does it mean steal or subtract? Ms. Myers happily notices that the students make a connection to mathematics with their second guess. She responds that another way to say *takes away from* is *detracts*, and it means to weaken or lessen something. This word is a cognate of *detractar* in Spanish, which helps some students gather its meaning. When students ask what a *continuum* is, Ms. Myers draws a horizontal line on the whiteboard and writes "very casual" on one end and "very formal" on the other.

After two more paragraphs that repeat the process, Ms. Myers explains that now each student will complete the daily table for this article, and she holds up the blank table her class uses each day to identify main ideas and supporting details (see table 11.1). She reminds them that they write each main idea in the left column (as she points to the left column) and each of the main idea's supporting details in the right column (as she point to the right column).

Once all students have completed the table, Ms. Myers uses a student selector app on her iPad to identify individuals to answer questions. Her first question is, "What is an argument the article presents against text messaging?" The selected student refers to

TABLE 11.1
Sample Daily Table

Main Idea	Supporting Details

the table he completed to respond, and Ms. Myers summarizes the reply with bullet points on the whiteboard. She continues the process, and then changes the question to, "How do people who support text messaging respond to these arguments?"

Now Ms. Myers asks the students to take turns in their groups, expressing their personal opinion by completing the following sentence frame:

"I think text messaging is/is not harmful for teens because ____________________."

When the students are done writing, she asks them to stand up, pick up their completed sentence frame handout, and line up according to their opinion on text messaging. One side of the room has a label that says "very harmful"; the opposite side's label says "not harmful at all." After they are situated, she asks each student to state their opinion as she moves from one side of the issue to the other.

EVALUATION

Ms. Myers conducts formative assessment through a journal entry, "My opinion on text messaging and teens." Summative assessment is conducted through a unit test.

APPLYING THE TASLL FRAMEWORK PROTOCOLS TO THE TEXT-BASED ARGUMENT LESSON

With this being a self-contained ELD class with all students in Edgar's proficiency range, there is no need to show the Supportive Classroom Communication (SCC) protocol portion of the Teaching All Subjects, Language, and Literacy (TASLL) Framework protocols because the instruction is geared to the students' linguistic needs already. In addition, Ms. Myers does not conduct steps 1 and 2 of the Targeted Language/Literacy Instruction (TLI) protocol —she's well aware of the linguistic skill to be developed and knows the distance between grade-level instruction and these MLE students' proficiency by heart. Her instructional planning starts with step 3 of the TLI protocol—determining where and how to implement the 4 Ps to meet the students where they are and develop their language. However, we show Edgar's performance definitions in table 11.2 for your consideration because it will help you better connect to the output that Edgar and his peers produce while examining the lesson transcript.

TABLE 11.2

Edgar's Assessed WIDA Performance Definitions (Grades K–12)

Skill and Level	Linguistic Complexity	Language Forms and Conventions	Vocabulary Usage
	At each grade, toward the end of a given level of English proficiency and with instructional support, English language learners will process (L/R) or produce (S/W):		
L 3.3	• Discourse with a series of extended sentences • Related ideas specific to particular content areas	• Compound and some complex grammatical constructions • Sentence patterns across content areas	• Specific content words and expressions • Words or expressions with common collocations and idioms across content areas
S 2.7	• Phrases or short sentences • Emerging expression of ideas	• Formulaic grammatical structures • Repetitive phrasal and sentence patterns across content areas	• General content words and expressions • Social and instructional words and expressions across content areas
R 1.4	• Single statements or questions • An idea within words, phrases, or chunks of language	• Simple grammatical constructions (e.g., commands, Wh-questions, declaratives) • Common social and instructional forms and patterns	• General content-related words • Everyday social and instructional words and expressions
W 1.3	• Words, phrases, or chunks or language • Single words used to represent ideas	• Phrase-level grammatical structures • Phrasal patterns associated with common social and instructional situations	• General content-related words • Everyday social and instructional words and expressions

As you examine the following description of the 4 Ps and management considerations for application, grouping, time, and provider that make up step 3 of the TLI protocol, you may want to occasionally move back to the preceding detailed lesson description, which shows what these features look like when put into action.

Developing ML's L2 Language/Literacy Skill(s)

STEP 3

As an ELD specialist, Ms. Myers has extensive experience in identifying specific challenges the English language poses for L2 learners and how to scaffold her instruction so that her students can move toward attainment of the grade-level ELA standards and simultaneously move up in language proficiency. If this lesson were taught in a regular tenth-grade language arts classroom with one or more MLEs at Edgar's proficiency, the targeted language instruction for these students would have to be an alternative to what is being taught to the native speakers because it would be below grade level. Given the ELD setting with all students at the same proficiency level 3, however, all adjustments described below are *universal.*

ADJUST PITCH

A number of elements in this lesson reflect research and theory on second language acquisition and literacy development. Ms. Myers's word and phrase choices are geared toward MLEs at Edgar's proficiency level. She paraphrases and defines idiomatic expressions (*drop in the bucket*) and phrasal verbs (*take away from*) and uses sentence structure that they comprehend. She is mindful of "processability" when setting expectations for Edgar's comprehension and production of grammatical structures.[12] She has in-depth knowledge of Edgar's proficiency in listening, speaking, reading, and writing through continuous assessment, using regularly collected samples of his spoken and written work as well as performance assessment and paper and pencil tests of his listening and reading skills. When speaking, Ms. Myers chunks long sentences, adding nonverbal support when introducing terms or phrases she believes are unfamiliar to the students. She also selected a reading passage that is just slightly above what students at this level can read independently in terms of grammatical complexity, vocabulary, and infrequent or unusual structure and form. The text uses present tense sentences, either in simple present (*parents also complain*) or present continuous form (*when kids get bored, they start sending messages*).

ADJUST PACE

Ms. Myers's pace is markedly slower than what a grade-level language arts teacher would use. She breaks up long sentences, even in oral presentation and discussion, and pauses between clauses and phrases, checking for comprehension through attentiveness to students' expressions as well as frequent questions directed at her MLE students' level of proficiency. In addition, her frequent elaboration of unfamiliar terms to further clarify meaning, as described under pitch, slows the pace of instruction and the amount of content she can address. Her associated nonverbal support and her frequent transcription of new terms and definitions on the whiteboard also slow the pace of instruction.

ADJUST PORTION

The topic of the lesson and the required reading are restricted to a manageable amount for MLEs at Edgars level. Although there is likely new terminology and phrasing for Edgar, there is ample time for Ms. Myers to discuss, expand, and explain it because the content is limited. The amount of writing is also kept to a reasonable task for the allotted time.

ADJUST PERSPECTIVE/POINT

There are a number of perspective aspects in the lesson for MLEs. The meaning of terms and phrasing is frequently expressed, with definitions, cognates, paraphrasing, and nonverbal support used. On the following day, Ms. Myers follows up this lesson with a focus on form, looking at the difference in when simple present and present continuous tenses are used and analyzing how they are formed in affirmative and negative statements and questions. This follow-up lesson for MLEs is an example of language arts instruction that has an entirely different point than it would if designed for native speakers.

Managing Grouping, Time, and Provider

Grouping. With all students at the same English proficiency level, the lesson takes place in whole class.

Time. This lesson is in a self-contained, dedicated ELD class that is held during Edgar's language arts period.

Provider. As the specialist teaching this ELD class, Ms. Myers is clearly the provider of the lesson. However, she also coordinates with Edgar's academic subject teachers to provide support for the language demands of those courses.

Lesson Summary and Final Thoughts

In addition to not seeing the SCC protocol and the first two steps of the TLI protocol applied to this lesson's debriefing, we have not transferred the lesson plan into an at-a-glance table, as done in chapters 8 to 10 because that would be senseless. Everything you read about in this chapter was geared toward the specific needs of MLEs at the same proficiency level, taught by an ELD specialist. We're certain that you are curious about how Ms. Myers reflected on her interaction with Edgar prior to the lesson, though, and will close out the chapter with a vignette as usual.

"Woah, Edgar *really* hates reading aloud. He does have some holes in foundational skills, but he's been filling this steadily. Something else must be going on. He still hesitates before words he uses conversationally on a daily basis, and he does not seem to understand what he reads *while* he reads it. I should ask him to bring a Spanish-language book or an article of interest, even if it is his mother's *People en Español* magazine, and read it to me and ask one of our Spanish teachers to sit in during their planning period. I do wonder whether Edgar exhibits similar difficulty reading in his L1."

Ms. Myers recalled writing in her notebook that Edgar's mother had told of his struggles in mathematics and reading back in Puerto Rico when the three of them met after the family moved to Chicago. Given that Edgar had progressed less on reading fluency and comprehension than she would have anticipated at this point in the school year, Ms. Myers wonders whether she should record him reading in both English and Spanish and share that information with the school's literacy specialist. "Maybe he needs some additional support? We'll find out. I sure am lucky to work at a school where I can count on administrators and all team members, be they in or out of the classroom. If I think of what Carol tells me about her school . . . . Ugh!"

STOP AND REFLECT QUESTIONS

1. What resources do you have at your school for ELD instruction? Talk with your colleagues about the support they provide for MLEs and any resources they have identified.
2. Can you recall a time when an MLE in your class demonstrated visible frustration from an inability to pronounce a word or read a sentence correctly? How was their frustration displayed? As the teacher, what did you do?

GO AND PRACTICE ACTIVITIES

1. Research the specific differences between narrative and expository (informational) text. Create a chart comparing the two. Simplify the chart and share it with your MLEs. Discuss which aspects of each they find to be easy or difficult.
2. Identify the various writing systems of the languages spoken in your class. Collect writing samples from your MLEs and determine which syntactical structures from your students' writing systems are being transferred into their writing in English.

Moving the Tassel

A Call for Collaboration

We've spent the previous chapters building a framework for multilingual learner (ML) success.[1] We looked at the process of becoming proficient in a second language (L2) from beginning levels to advanced, spanning kindergarten to high school. Grade-level expectations keep rising, and MLs keep striving to reach them in their new language. Thankfully, teachers can help. If MLs receive the highest quality and quantity of accessible communication and targeted language and literacy instruction, their language development and academic achievement will increase.

The reality is that most MLs—who have varying life and school experiences and different levels of L2 proficiency—are placed in regular classrooms for at least part of the day. This has implications not only for their teachers but also for the entire school. This means that all educators have the responsibility, and the privilege, of supporting MLs' achievement. We can all share their struggles, help shoulder their burdens, rejoice in their successes, and broaden and brighten our outlook through experiencing the newness of our own language and culture through their eyes.

In this concluding chapter, we focus on the Teaching All Subjects, Language, and Literacy (TASLL) Framework's collaborative aspects, illustrating how classroom teachers can partner with other school team members, as well as MLs' families and communities, to address MLs' academic and affective needs. As discussed in chapter 1, the TASLL Framework is built upon the foundation of sociocultural theory, which places interaction at the center of teaching and learning. Considering the various contexts of MLss in regular classrooms, the two TASLL Framework protocols (SCC and TLI) rely on solid, time-tested research derived from multiple perspectives on developing multilingual proficiency—but each perspective centers interaction at its core. Accordingly, interaction that is purposeful and coordinated, in the form of collaboration, is our framework's operational principle at all levels. In the following sections of this chapter, we lay out the TASLL Framework's approach to collaborative instruction and assessment as well as professional learning, and we conclude by asking you to get to know your MLs, just as you have come to know Gero, Edith, Edgar, and Tasir, so you can help shape your ML students' stories for the better.

SCHOOLWIDE COLLABORATION FOR MULTILINGUAL LEARNER SUCCESS

We have outlined our approach to raising the achievement of MLs in the general classroom, showing how educators can share expertise and combine efforts to improve classroom communication and language instruction for MLs. In describing and applying both the Supportive Classroom Communication (SCC) protocol and the Targeted Language/Literacy Instruction (TLI) protocol we offered many suggestions for planning and delivering curriculum, instruction, and assessment that are linked to the sharing of expertise among disciplinary subject teachers, language arts and literacy teachers, and L2 development (English language development [ELD] for multilingual learners of English [MLEs]) and bilingual education specialists.[2] All school-based educators have important contributions to make in ensuring that the ML population in our preK–12 schools receive the attention they deserve and require to reach their highest potential, because it raises the effectiveness of the school. Each educator in the school building performs essential duties consistent with their areas of expertise and experience. This means that they shouldn't be expected to have the same knowledge and skills to work effectively with MLs. It is the implementation of everyone's duties in a *coherent, collaborative manner* that leads to the academic achievement of MLs in the general classroom.[3] Educators often refer to effective schools as "communities of learners." Rooted in that description is the belief that these communities experience deep interpersonal connections that encourage teachers, administrators, noninstructional personnel, volunteers, and parents to address and openly communicate the needs of all students, including MLs. Creating such a culture of commitment and interconnectedness through communication promotes success for all.

Educator Roles

Schools are multidimensional centers of activity that run best when there is cross-disciplinary consultation, collaboration, and teamwork. Classroom teachers are undoubtedly the most visible educators working with students. In a typical week, most MLs, depending on their age and grade level, spend a significant portion of their school time in general classrooms with disciplinary subject teachers (e.g., science, mathematics, or social studies), language teachers, and/or literacy teachers. Second language development (L2D) specialists facilitate MLs' learning in various amounts of direct instructional time, depending on the school's program model for L2D. Occasionally, MLs also interact with various other noninstructional school personnel such as school psychologists, speech-language pathologists, counselors, and school administrators. And for MLs who have the advantage of being in dual language classes, a teacher who speaks their native language and who is well versed in bilingual education will lead a portion of their instruction.

MLs in elementary schools that do not offer dual language classes spend most of the day with the same classroom teacher who teaches most of the disciplinary subjects, as well as language arts/literacy. Like the classroom language and literacy teacher, the

L2D specialist focuses on second language (i.e., English for ELD specialists) development, but both the depth of involvement and the amount of time they interact with MLs vary greatly. Some L2D specialists have their own classrooms where they teach self-contained L2D content, as with the ELD teachers in Gero's and Edith's cases, to kick-start the second language acquisition process. Others go from classroom to classroom where they teach MLs in small groups for fifteen to thirty minutes while the classroom teacher continues instruction with the rest of the class.[4]

In secondary schools, where the students have a different teacher for each subject, L2D teachers may conduct self-contained classes that MLs attend in addition to their general language arts/literacy class, or they may provide targeted language instruction in place of the general class, which is designed to catch MLs up to grade-level instruction in their L2. This was the case with Edgar, whose English language proficiency was not compatible with grade-level language arts instruction.[5] Therefore, MLs at the secondary level typically spend about one class period per day with L2D teachers.

Noninstructional personnel have mostly intermittent contact with MLs, which doesn't add up to a lot of time throughout a school year. Nonetheless, they perform essential functions *in support of classroom teachers*, who depend on these professionals' knowledge of the intersection of L2 learning issues and ML students' home cultures and languages with their specialized expertise. For example, school psychologists follow up on requests from teachers to test for giftedness or assist in determining and carrying out interventions for MLs who don't meet national, state, or district benchmarks for reading instruction, while school counselors or administrators help families of newly arrived immigrants to navigate the school system in their new country.[6]

Because of their deep knowledge of second language acquisition, L2D specialists are best equipped to assist all instructional and noninstructional personnel in meeting their respective responsibilities of educating MLs. By collaborating with each other and with L2D specialists through cycles of examining student work and by creating and implementing instructional supports focused on students' language and content needs, classroom teachers can find effective ways of helping all students reach these learning goals while still maintaining their individual teaching styles and flexibility.

Working Together to Support ML Student Achievement

Few school districts have an ML programming framework that provides substantive support for L2 experts, such as a formal process for collaboration with classroom teachers that includes cotaught or coplanned content classes.[7] Nevertheless, some schools without this support have found ways to implement coteaching principles where L2D and classroom teachers work closely together on planning, teaching, or assessing student learning. Often these teams have adapted models previously developed by exceptional education specialists and classroom teachers. More common than coteaching, however, is the situation where the various instructional personnel work quite independently of one another. Our SCCP and TLIP protocols both encourage L2 specialist assistance in planning and implementing curriculum, instruction, and assessment, reflecting our assumptions that models providing backing for L2D are valuable. However, the protocols also allow for real, but less than ideal, circumstances, such as when there are too few MLs to warrant a school-based L2 specialist and classroom teachers rely on a different provider of support. Nonetheless, if schools want to provide the necessary support for MLs to reach their full academic potential, continued communication and collaboration between classroom teachers and the L2 specialist are most beneficial.

Although the implementation of a truly collaborative schoolwide model may have challenges at the outset, it has tangible benefits for school administrators, teachers, and students. We believe that all schools should be able to find ways in which some level of L2 specialist–classroom teacher collaboration can occur. To that end, we have designed a three-level joint effort model (table C.1) that schools can adapt. The three levels range from a coordination of efforts where the teacher of MLs and the L2

TABLE C.1

TASLL Framework Continuum of Systemic Instructional Support for Multilingual Learners

	Commitment to Working Together **Lower → Higher**			
	Coordinated Efforts	**Cooperative Efforts**	**Collaborative Efforts**	
Who and what	• Classroom teacher shares information on upcoming lesson concepts. • L2D teacher assists with language objectives and suggests supports and scaffolds for MLs in class. • L2D teacher continues teaching own curriculum in push-in or separate L2D class.	• Classroom teacher shares information on upcoming lesson concepts. • L2D teacher assists with language objectives and suggests supports and scaffolds for MLs in class. • L2D teacher adjusts push-in or separate lessons to preteach and/or reteach.	• L2D teacher in classroom assists MLs in supportive role part time or full time.	• L2D teacher coteaches in classroom with content teacher part time or full time.
Means and frequency of communication	• Intermittent lesson plans or notes in box or via email	• Weekly/monthly meetings for planning • Notes in box or email when needed	• Weekly meetings for planning • Daily debriefing	

specialist coordinate lesson planning, with the L2 specialist acting as a resource while still pursuing their own curriculum, to slightly more cooperative efforts in which the L2 specialist adjusts their own instruction to assist the classroom teacher through pre- or reteaching of difficult concepts, to two types of collaborative efforts where coteaching takes place. Schools and individual teachers can adapt the model to their specific contexts.

Research shows that the collaboration between L2 specialists and classroom teachers is a complex process that is highly dependent on mutual understanding and willingness to take ownership of the model. On the one hand, classroom teachers need to understand that the L2 specialist's expertise is not limited to methodology or strategies for teaching an L2, but it extends into teaching the language of various subject areas. On the other hand, the L2 specialist must be willing to understand the subject area well enough to support the classroom teacher by teaching the subject's academic language.[8] Table C.1 shows that the *coordinated effort level* requires the fewest scheduling changes. In settings where the ML goes to the L2 specialist for part of the day, the ML's two teachers can communicate in writing, simply coordinating their lessons. Similarly, if the teacher who provides L2D push-in services starts to coteach with the classroom teacher, no schedule change is needed because the specialist is already in the classroom for the fifteen to thirty minutes they would otherwise spend at the back of the room in small-group ML instruction.[9] Time commitment on the part of both teachers for the coordinated effort is relatively low because each can accomplish the planning of tasks at a time that is convenient for them.

Moving from coordinated to cooperative efforts and then to collaborative efforts calls for an increasing amount of commitment to work together as a team. This cannot be accomplished without the school principal's commitment to facilitating this journey. While individual classroom teachers and L2 specialists can enter into coordinated-effort relationships on their own, a principal's suggestion for forming such partnerships sends the message that the administration encourages teachers to share expertise and pay close attention to ML students' academic achievement. The schoolwide adoption of a teacher collaboration model requires tangible administrative support and resources. Classroom teachers and L2 specialists need to be afforded opportunities to meet outside of their "spare" time or during faculty meetings and/or professional development time, and noninstructional personnel should be encouraged to attend planning sessions or debriefings with the teams on a regular basis.

SUGGESTIONS FOR TEACHER-INITIATED TEAMWORK AND COLLABORATION

Educators reap great benefits when they regularly collaborate with colleagues in their own school—or beyond, in their district—to brainstorm new ideas or exchange best practices. Building relationships with other teachers, collaborating, and sharing best practices are critical for enhancing instruction and improving student achievement outcomes. Teacher consultation and collaboration contribute significantly to the improvement of school climate, teacher retention, career satisfaction, and student achievement, according to findings published in the "Collaborating for Student Success" report.[10]

The reality is that even though schools are multidimensional centers of activity, they may not always provide the structures and conditions under which teachers feel prepared to engage in meaningful interaction. One obstacle to starting systematic collaboration is lack of time for the effort that productive consultation, collaboration, and teamwork require. When teachers do have time to consult with colleagues, it's likely to be during professional development sessions, but these are often highly structured and too short for meaningful interaction. However, individual classroom teachers of MLs who want to at least approach others to work collaboratively need not feel alone in a school that lacks the appropriate structures.

For these teachers, we offer the following simple suggestions:

- Reach out. Teachers are very busy and typically hesitate to ask for or offer help without being invited because they don't want others to think that they aren't good teachers or that they believe other teachers aren't doing a good job. If you aren't sure what L2D specialists do when they teach MLs or how they determine the students' needs, ask them! Classroom teachers should not wait for expert colleagues (e.g., L2D teacher, reading specialist, bilingual teacher, speech-language pathologist, school psychologist, librarian) to come knocking on the door. Alternatively, L2 specialists, especially at the secondary level, are rarely subject-matter experts and may be uncertain about teaching dense, content-specific text in their L2D classes. The goal of all teachers is the academic achievement of their students, and at times, a little encouragement from colleagues is all that's needed to start collaborating.
- Build rapport first. Before reaching out to ask for assistance, show interest in your colleagues' work and expertise. A social studies teacher may want to start a conversation with the L2 specialist right before or immediately following a faculty meeting simply by asking how many children at which proficiency level they teach. By and large, all they need to do after that is nurture the relationship and move to the next step by making simple yet specific requests. For example, the social studies teacher could ask their L2D colleague for some tips on chunking reading assignments for an ML at intermediate proficiency.
- Clarify the purpose of your call for assistance. Classroom teachers shouldn't assume that colleagues they're reaching out to automatically know what kind of help is wanted. For example, suppose you are teaching a science unit on water cycles and discover that your ML has difficulty answering questions about the text relating specifically to key concepts of evaporation, condensation, and precipitation. In such a case, you may want to share a copy of the water cycle text with the student's L2 specialist and discuss how the specialist might help the ML advance their academic vocabulary in science. Understanding the classroom teacher's needs will help the L2 specialist provide focused advice.
- Reassure colleagues that their time and energy are well spent. When teachers reach out to expert colleagues for assistance, they should give a compelling reason to respond to the call for collaboration and teamwork. The key is to offer value to

colleagues by helping them see the benefits of working together to meet the language, literacy, and content needs of MLs in all classrooms.

- One general tip for working well together is to reach out to your colleagues and not just when you need something. Remember to stop by their room now and then just to see how they're doing, or consider putting a little note in their box or sending an email congratulating them for something good you heard about them or their class. Building good relationships creates a solid foundation for effective collaboration. All in all, as we have experienced, the time you spend collaborating to help your MLs will be repaid exponentially by their resulting progress.

Approaching Professional Learning in Your School

All educators need to know basic information about MLs and the context in which they learn. This entails a general understanding of the factors affecting second language acquisition, especially those over which educators have some control, such as the comprehensibility of classroom communication. Other factors, such as age and native language of the learner, are important to be aware of, especially in how they affect second language development, regardless of whether they are outside the teacher's sphere of influence. The learning context spans issues such as the program model and family and community support and their roles in ML language development and academic achievement. Teachers, principals, counselors, and so on need a foundational degree of understanding of these important topics.

In addition to these foundational topics, all teachers need to know how to ensure supportive classroom communication for MLs. Beyond ensuring supportive classroom communication, teachers who focus on language and literacy development also need expertise in teaching language, a deep understanding of the second language acquisition process, awareness of the influence that the first language has on the acquisition of students' L2, and skill in using instructional practices for second language and literacy development.

Specialized knowledge and skills are required of L2D and bilingual education teachers. These teachers are experts who coteach with and serve as resources for classroom teachers of MLs. Accordingly, their depth and breadth of knowledge and skills regarding teaching and assessing MLs are greater than what other types of teachers need.

Research has shown that collaborative approaches to professional learning improve school performance and student achievement beyond what teachers can accomplish on their own.[11] In a study aimed at examining what research and practice reveal about engaged, school-based teacher learning teams, the National Commission on Teaching and America's Future showed that teachers who collaborate in learning teams hold themselves to a higher standard, improve their practice, and accelerate student achievement.[12] Studies reviewed in this report further showed that "when teachers are given the time and tools to collaborate, they become life-long learners, their instructional practice improves, and they are ultimately able to increase student achievement far beyond what any of them could accomplish alone."

Our view is that job-embedded professional learning is key to advancing instructional practices and enhancing MLs' language, literacy, and content achievement. We advocate a broad-based approach to professional development that (1) is framed around local school district–specific needs; (2) integrates research-based language, literacy, and content instructional practices for MLs; and (3) is focused on increasing these students' achievement in language, literacy, mathematics, science, and other subjects.

Initiating this type of professional learning depends on various factors, such as the school's ML population, available programming and specialized personnel, the model adopted for in-service professional development, and the individual commitment of school personnel to collaborate. Rather than waiting for a district- or principal-led initiative, we encourage you to take the first steps. Look around for existing relationships and common interests. Approach your closest colleagues and inquire whether they would be willing to start an informal study group or undertake some research on how you can better serve your MLs. As soon as your group shows success in moving MLs forward, others will likely want to go on the journey with you!

COMMUNITIES OF PRACTICE

The notion of student learning communities extends to faculty, staff, and administration at a school, and school-based educators can support each other's exploration and application of new approaches to serving MLs by establishing a community of practice. Simply put, a community of practice is a group of practitioners that learns about a field they share interest in. Three elements are necessary for a community of practice to operate: (1) the domain (or field) they are committed to learning; (2) the individuals who choose to come together to help each other do their best work; and (3) the shared practice they engage in, drawing upon the repertoire of resources the members have developed and collected.[13] A community of practice can be organized around a goal, such as improving classroom communication or literacy development for MLs. In this case, the domain would be second language learning and teaching/bilingual education (participating in a book study of *Educating Multilingual Learners* would be a great way to review essential information in this domain). The individuals of the community could be teachers from a variety of disciplines who have MLs in their classrooms, or they could be a more focused group of teachers who teach the same subject, such as biology. Their shared practice could be enhancing their teaching for MLs by incorporating the TASLL Framework, including the stories of their own challenges and successes with MLs, which would be the repertoire from which they share their pedagogical expertise with each other.

An example of a participatory process of improving instruction comes from Japan and is called lesson study. It is a powerful way of guiding educators through a shared examination of the outcome of professional learning that took place within a community of practice. Lesson study begins by engaging the community of practice in identifying a focus and planning a lesson, and then one member of the community teaches the lesson while the other teachers observe and collect data. After the lesson, there is individual and group reflection and analysis, followed by optional revision and reteaching of the lesson. The results of the lesson study process are then shared with the whole school community.[14] We suggest trying lesson study to plan and teach one or two lessons enhanced with the SCC and TLI protocols within a community of practice seeking to improve instruction for MLs. Group-enhanced lesson plans, as well as the resulting data collection and analysis of their effectiveness, can be shared with the school community and may serve as a basis for professional development for new faculty and staff as they become accustomed to the school's approach to ensuring supportive classroom communication and targeted language and literacy instruction for their MLs.

Lesson study can be a productive and engaging way to spark a community of practice to engage in professional learning. In addition to this collaborative, lesson-by-lesson analysis that equips teachers to adjust their lessons to their ML students' L2 proficiency levels, the TASLL Framework encourages collaboration between classroom and L2D teachers to monitor the impact of their instruction for MLs over time. Regular monitoring of each ML student's language and literacy development, beginning with baseline standardized assessments and adding ongoing classroom language samples, informal inventories of reading skills in the first and second language, and computer-based assessment in learning management platforms (preferably those offering bilingual curricula and assessment), can show progress during the school year in between annual formal testing. This variety of student language assessment data, in turn, guides the type and degree of classroom communication support and targeted language and literacy instruction needed to meet MLs where they are as their language and literacy proficiency increases throughout the school year. Collaboratively examining these multiple sources of data for insights into ML students' progress can be a motivating focus for communities of practice, fueling their learning with real issues that they and their MLs face every day. Mapping individual students' progress with these data points is an important way for teachers to learn more about who their students are. But MLs are so much more than their test scores! Now, let's look at the many facets of your MLs and how discovering them will make you an even better teacher.

KNOWING WHO YOUR MULTILINGUAL LEARNERS ARE

It's not enough to know which students in your class are classified as MLs. As was shown in previous chapters, knowing the stories as well as the scores of your MLs gives you insights into *who* they are, not just *what* they are (i.e., their classification as MLs). Are they newcomers at beginning levels of L2 proficiency who have a strong academic background in their home language (Gero), or are they newcomers at beginning levels of their L2 who had interrupted schooling in their home country and now have resulting gaps in their L1 literacy (Edith)? Do they sound like they're proficient in their L2 speech but lag behind in their L2 literacy because of the timing of their family's move to a new country (Tasir), or does their L2 oral language and literacy include frequent grammatical errors and incomplete utterances but they can understand and express more than they think they can with teacher encouragement and support (Edgar)? What is their proficiency in their home language, and if they attended school in another country before entering your school, what are their academic skills in that language? Did they like school there? Do they like school here?

The answers to these and many other questions about your MLs *can* be found. The TASLL Framework's two protocols begin with reviewing individual L2 proficiency assessment data to determine what levels of support your MLs need during instruction. But these scores are just one of many available sources of information about your MLs, so we recommend supplementing proficiency-level descriptions from standardized assessments with your own informal observations of ML students' interaction with you and with other students, paying attention to how they express themselves and respond to questions and directions and in which languages. In addition, collecting ML students' writing samples and conducting informal reading inventories over time will complete a fuller portrait of their L2 acquisition process. This can complement other formal recurrent district assessments, many of which are computer based, such as Istation, i-Ready, and ELLevation.[15] Classroom teachers can monitor these indicators of ML student progress together with the ELD and bilingual teachers and specialists to determine if more individualized targeted language and literacy instruction should be provided for students whose progress has stalled.

Beyond knowing your ML students' L2 proficiency indicators, recognizing their strengths and assets opens up a wider and brighter view of their potential. MLs' primary assets and overall strengths are their developing bilingualism, biculturalism, and biliteracy. These are their burgeoning superpowers. No matter how MLs attain these hard-earned assets, their value is beyond measure. As the teacher of MLs, you can fuel the process of achieving this communicative triple crown by valuing and encouraging your ML students' multilingual identities and creating a learning environment that envisions bilingualism, biculturalism, and biliteracy for all—what the TASLL Framework calls a multilingual mindset. To know more about your MLs' collective assets and individual strengths as well as areas of need, gaining awareness of their lives at home and in their communities can offer further insights into who they are.

Suggestions to Get to Know Your ML Students

Although L2 test scores represent only one small part of who your ML student is and what they can do, obtaining previous testing information can be helpful. If the student was enrolled in your school the previous school year, you can access testing data through school records or by talking with the L2D teacher or the student's previous grade teacher. If the student was enrolled in your class for the first time in the United States, a screener L2 assessment should have been given by a trained test administrator shortly after the student began school. As mentioned previously, you can also supplement these standardized testing data with informal assessments, observations, and language sample collection to gauge where the student's L1 and L2 proficiency is over time because the standardized testing scores may be from many months prior. Completing a self-inventory of L2 proficiency in their L1 allows students to share their levels of confidence about their L2 skill areas.

To obtain student and family information, translated family surveys can be sent home,[16] or bilingual aides can chat with parents during drop-off or pick-up times or by contacting them by phone or WhatsApp. Helpful information to find out includes the following:

Student Information

- Prior schooling experiences (where, when, in what language, which subjects they did well in or struggled with, any previous identification of giftedness or disabilities)
- Languages the student speaks and is literate in, and if multiple languages, which language is their strongest
- Whether the student enjoys learning (now or before moving to the US mainland) and in what ways they learn best
- Individual degree of confidence about succeeding academically and becoming bilingual, bicultural, and biliterate
- Whether the student is extroverted or introverted in their home language and culture
- Whether the student feels they belong in the new school and class

Family and Home Information

- What language(s) are spoken at home
- Whether anyone at home is fluent in English
- How families prefer to communicate with the school
- Cultural practices, such as holidays, that the family engages in
- Who lives in their household and who the primary caregivers are (Does the student have caregiving responsibilities?)
- Whether the student has a place to study, school supplies, and internet access at home
- How stable access to housing and food availability is
- Parents' level and country of education
- Parents' educational aspirations for the student
- Parents' availability to attend school meetings and activities and ability to help with homework
- Any special needs or medical conditions in the family

In addition to knowing your students, connecting with your MLs' families and communities can be a way to connect the dots to their success. Encouraging family and community engagement is one important way you can do that.

Encouraging Family and Community Engagement

MLs whose families come from different parts of the world often have divergent experiences of education from those of typical US schooling, including educational policies, practices, and expectations. What parents born and raised in the United States know to do from their experiences in school may be quite different from what parents who were born and raised abroad know to do, and if that difference is complicated by not speaking English, trying to engage with the school can be challenging. Together with their school and district colleagues, classroom teachers can collaborate to learn more about the educational systems in their MLs' home countries as well as develop outreach initiatives for engaging their students' families and communities in their success at school.

The US Department of Education Office of English Language Acquisition offers suggestions for the design of family and community engagement programs for MLs, focusing on three areas: (1) supporting academic success through increasing family awareness of ways to support their children's learning; (2) increasing advocacy for their children and participation in decision-making for their children as well as others at the school; and (3) building awareness of school and community resources and how to access them to increase family well-being and personal growth.[17]

To put these core components into action, why not ask your school leaders about creating a "parent university" course, a family resource center, or a parent ambassador program? Your district administration may also have resources to help establish these options, so it's worth requesting funding or personnel to make this happen. They might even say yes! Welcoming parents of MLs to your school takes more than inviting them to open house and providing an interpreter. Just as with your students, you need to know the parents and communities to understand how to reach them. We have seen parent event turnout go from an empty room to standing room only after involving MLs' communities and their leaders in planning and announcing gatherings. Find out which stores, places of worship, amateur sports leagues, and community centers your MLs' families frequent and who leads or manages them, and ask them to help you spread the word about family events at your school. Perhaps the best way to get to know your students and their families is to meet with them in person, at school or in their communities, so take the first step and venture out! As we have come to know our four MLE student cases throughout the chapters of this book, we will now see where the end of the school year finds them in their journey to bilingualism and academic success.

END-OF-YEAR EVENTS FOR GERO, EDITH, TASIR, AND EDGAR

Nearly nine months have passed since we first met Gero, Edith, Tasir, and Edgar, and their lives have changed in many ways. They live in different parts of the country and their families come from different places, but they have one thing in common. They have teachers who care about them and are trying to help them succeed.

✦ Gero—Pine Woods Elementary School

"Bienvenus, Mr. and Mrs. Jantiy! Come have a seat next to Mrs. Confidante. She will interpret for me." Gero's parents moved in unison toward Ms. Levin, but before sitting, Mr. Jantiy said, "Thank you, Ms. Levin. I understand English, but my wife is still learning." They huddled on the miniature chairs as Ms. Levin handed them a stack of papers. "I want you to see what Gero has accomplished this year," she said, pausing to allow the interpreter to speak. "This is his writing from last August." Ms. Levin pointed to the first page. "Alligator!" exclaimed Mrs. Jantiy. "I remember when he told us he could say alligator in three languages!" Ms. Levin gently held each page as if she were a white-gloved archivist and explained how each piece showed Gero's progress. "And look at what he's writing now!" Ms. Levin boasted. She went on to show them Gero's reading assessments and other measures of his achievement. Mrs. Jantiy, dabbing the corner of her eye with a pressed linen handkerchief, whispered, "I thought that Gero would be lost and would fall behind. I was so . . . I was so afraid to come here tonight." Mrs. Jantiy took a deep breath, reached out her hand, and said, "Ms. Levin, thank you for teaching our son." Speaking directly to Gero's mother, Ms. Levin replied, "Merci pour votre fils. Il est un cadeau pour notre classe."[18]

✦ Edith—Pine Woods Elementary School

As she reflected on the events of the past school year, Ms. Oliver thought back to early spring, when she first felt Edith was ready to reply to a question requiring a full sentence. Her class was discussing career and college readiness, so she asked Edith what career she would like. Everyone leaned in to hear Edith state softly and slowly, "I want to be a teacher. I want to teach at this school." Ms. Oliver looked up to the left, took a short breath, and acknowledged Edith with a nod before going on to the next student. It wouldn't be until later, when the room was empty and private, that she could experience the magnitude of that moment. She kept a journal in the middle drawer of her desk for such occasions. It was a place she could deposit the intangible rewards of teaching. She pulled the bottom of the ribbon holding her place from the last entry and placed her pen on the remaining empty space. Then she lifted her hand and turned to a new page.

✦ Tasir—Freedom Middle School

"You know, Ms. Marlin, sometimes I feel like I can't pass the state test because my other teachers don't help me understand. But I mostly wonder whether it's just me. Maybe I'm not very smart. Maybe I *don't* try hard enough. I don't know why I'm having so much trouble passing." Ms. Marlin stopped erasing the whiteboard and walked over to Tasir. "Learning a second language isn't easy. If it were, everyone would be bilingual, at least. Also, it's not a quick process. It takes time." Tasir slumped in her chair. "I've had a lot of time, four years, and I'm still behind." "Look here, Tasir," Ms. Marlin said. "Let me show you something about learning second languages."

Ms. Marlin took out a diagram showing a steep slope rising from left to right across the page. "See, this is the grade you entered school here, the third grade." Tasir put her finger on the x-axis. "You were at this beginning line. As you learned English, you were expected to use your new language in more and more complex ways. You had a moving target, and you are getting caught up now." Ms. Marlin traced her finger up the slope to the seventh grade and indicated the gap between that point and the horizontal line representing advanced MLs. "You still have a little gap, and now that our school is writing learning goals for ELD, you'll start to see exactly what you need to accomplish to pass the test." Tasir peered at Ms. Marlin's new planner with sample scales. "So, what does *complex sentence* mean, Ms. Marlin?" Tasir and Ms. Marlin sat side by side, looking over Tasir's current English language proficiency assessment descriptors and those of the top level. Seeing where she was headed and the breakdown of how she would get there made passing the state test begin to seem possible. "Can I have a copy of the top level?" Tasir asked. Realizing her copy quota had long been exceeded, Ms. Marlin replied, "C'mon, Tasir, let's walk to the office and I'll buy a booklet for you."

✦ Edgar—Highpoint High School

"Hey, whatcha listenin' to?" Edgar asked as he walked into the classroom. The unmistakable *búh-buh-duhm-buhm, búh-buh-duhm-buhm* beat of reggaeton rattled the speakers connected to Mr. Otto's computer. "I just got into reggaeton," Mr. Otto replied. "Remember the students who performed at the cultural festival last month? Well, now I'm really hooked. It makes grading during my planning period a lot more fun."

"Ms. Myers, she teaches us with reggaeton. We're writing our own song and reading the words of a lotta reggaeton singers." Mr. Otto set aside his red pen and looked squarely at Edgar. "Do you think you could teach me about reggaeton? Like what the music is about and who the coolest artists are?" he asked. "Yeah, I can teach you," Edgar replied as he sat down and began scrolling through his playlist.

Ms. Myers had been working reggaeton into her reading and writing lessons since the day of the school festival. From the very first lesson, she had seen how her students related to the songs' themes. For someone who refused to write during the first weeks of school, Edgar was now writing daily, making up new lyrics and discussing the meaning of his favorite songs. Above the whiteboard, prominently displayed, was Edgar's latest composition:

I Write/Yo Escribo

I write because
I want to say
Who I am
Yo soy orgulloso
I am bilingual
I am Edgar.

YOUR TURN TO ACT

Perhaps just as important as what sets MLs apart from other students is what holds true for MLs and native speakers of the language of instruction alike. MLs can be just as lovable or incorrigible as any other student. Sometimes they try their best; sometimes they don't. They make good choices and irreparable mistakes. But there's something special about their connection with teachers who go above and beyond for them, who take the time to learn about how they learn, and who try to better understand and address their needs. You can be that teacher.

We have stressed that all MLs, no matter who they are or where they attend school, deserve educators who are competent in meeting their needs. In our view, only when those who work directly with MLs think and act in interdisciplinary ways can their broad and varied goals and needs be addressed effectively. Educator collaboration guides support for MLs, but most importantly, it advances professional learning and educator best practices, which in turn improves student achievement. In other words, learning to effectively teach these students is no longer preparation for the job. It *is* the job.

We believe that close interdisciplinary collaboration is critical to advancing academic achievement and access to college and careers for all students and MLs in particular. Our collective experiences over the past three decades indicate that working across the disciplines may not be easy, but it has tremendous benefits for teachers and their students. Interdisciplinary collaboration and teamwork require extraordinary commitment, intense determination, and a forward-looking vision, all of which are key characteristics that define effective teaching of all students, not just MLs. This is consistent with the recommendation by teacher effectiveness and student achievement experts that learning organizations should promote long-term and continuous professional learning that takes into account new teacher roles and that creates new structures for advancing student learning and engagement.[19]

Now that we have presented the principles and practices of our TASLL Framework and the research and theory behind it, we can affirm that whatever good comes from this book is due to collaboration. We talked through every issue together as a group, or sometimes one on one as time and place allowed, and then we wrote, read, and tried out each other's ideas with teachers in regular, imperfect schools. And so, it is fitting that a book about the importance of communication for, between, and of MLs was only made possible through communication between educators who want to help improve MLs' education.

Each of this book's authors has experienced being lost in an unknown language and culture. With the right circumstances and with the type of support we detailed in this book, each of us found our way. Wishing the same for every ML, we urge you to act. You have read this book. You understand your role in supporting MLs' needs, and you know what your colleagues can do to support MLs as well. Now it is your turn. We believe you now have the knowledge to *take action* to advance the academic achievement of the MLs in your school or district. We urge you to do all you can within your own classroom and to reach out to your colleagues, administrators, and families and their communities to work together for the success of all MLs at your school. *Yon sel dwèt pa manje kalalou.*[20]

ESSENTIAL POINTS

1. The Teaching All Subjects, Language, and Literacy (TASLL) Framework for Multilingual Learners emphasizes the importance of schoolwide collaboration among teachers, L2D specialists, school administrators, and families to support ML students' language and academic development.
2. Different educators, including classroom teachers, L2D specialists, and noninstructional personnel, have distinct but complementary roles in supporting MLs. Their coordinated efforts can significantly impact students' achievement.
3. Ongoing, job-embedded professional learning is crucial for educators to effectively teach MLs. Collaborative learning communities and lesson studies can help improve instructional practices.
4. Teachers should understand not only students' proficiency levels but also their backgrounds, experiences, and strengths. Building strong relationships with MLs and their families fosters better educational outcomes.
5. We encourage schools to actively engage ML families and communities, providing them with access to resources and opportunities to participate in their children's education. This fosters stronger connections between home and school, bridging cultural and linguistic gaps.

STOP AND REFLECT QUESTIONS

1. The TASLL Framework has four tenets (see chapter 1 for details). Looking back at this and previous chapters, identify examples of how the tenets are put into practice.
2. The TASLL Framework was designed to address the TESOL organization's Six Principles for Exemplary Teaching of English Learners: (1) know your learners; (2) create conditions for language learning; (3) design high-quality lessons for language development; (4) adapt lesson delivery as needed; (5) monitor and assess student language development; and (6) engage and collaborate with a community of practice. Looking back at this and previous chapters, identify how what you learned in this book addresses each of the principles.

GO AND PRACTICE ACTIVITIES

1. Schedule a time to meet with the L2D specialist (ELD or other L2 teacher) at your school to find out what they do when working with MLs. Prepare a list of questions you wish to ask before your meeting. Be sure to include topics such as what research-based strategies are appropriate to use at varying levels of English proficiency in the general classroom.
2. Assist in the creation of a quality professional development activity at your school. Be sure to invite the many professionals at your school to provide input, suggestions, and ideas in the spirit of true collaboration.

Terminology Used in the Book

STUDENTS

English learner (EL), the federal term in the United States, describes a student from age three to twenty-one who is enrolled or preparing to enroll in an elementary or secondary school and who (1) was not born in the United States or has a native language other than English and (2) whose difficulties in speaking, reading, writing, or understanding the English language may prevent the student from meeting challenging state standards.[1] Typically, a student is classified as an English learner after a process beginning with a questionnaire that parents complete to indicate whether a language other than English is spoken in the home. If so, the student is screened with a test of English proficiency, and if it is determined that their scores are within a designated range of proficiency in English oral and/or literacy skills, they are classified as an English learner, and they will be tested at least annually for growth in their English proficiency until they meet the state English proficiency requirements for reclassification to non-EL status. In this book, we focus on students who are currently classified as ELs, not those who have been reclassified to non-EL status or those who are balanced bilinguals with grade-level proficiency in each language (English and another language).

Multilingual learner of English (MLE) is the term we use in this book to recognize that ELs are becoming bilingual or multilingual, while specifying the new language they are learning in addition to their native/home language. For our student cases—Gero, Edith, Edgar, and Tasir—we use the term *multilingual learner (ML)* when we describe aspects of their experience common to all multilingual learners, and we use *multilingual learners of English (MLE)* when we focus on use or development of their specific second language (L2) (English). In the same manner that we specify the new language that MLs are acquiring for MLEs, we refer to students in two-way (Spanish/English) dual language education programs who are proficient in English and are learning Spanish as their new language as **multilingual learners of Spanish** (MLSs). Unless we are referring to federal, state, or local government classifications of English learners, we no longer use the term *English* *learner* because the term *multilingual learner* is increasingly used in the literature to highlight that learning an L2 is developing the asset of multilingualism.

Multilingual learner is a term that is increasingly used in publications and is preferred in multiple contexts because it acknowledges that students learning a new language (also known as an additional language) already know another language and are in the process of becoming bilingual. Similar to WIDA's definition of multilingual learners—"students who come in contact with and/or interact in languages in addition to English on a regular basis. This includes students who are learning English as an additional language in school, as well as students who speak multiple languages"—we include English learners, emergent and balanced bilinguals, and heritage language learners when using the umbrella term multilingual learner.[2] These multilingual learners may be served in regular classroom instruction, content and language integrated learning (CLIL), English language development (ELD) or English for speakers of other languages (ESOL)/English as a second language (ESL), or world languages education (such as English as a foreign language [EFL] or any second language), from prekindergarten through secondary education, as well as postsecondary and adult education.

Non-multilingual learners are students who have never been classified as multilingual learners or who were previously multilingual learners and have exited, also known as being reclassified. Native speakers of English are the largest group of non-MLs in the United States. We tend to use the term *non-ML* or *non-MLE* rather than *native speaker* because the notion of native speaker is not as appropriate in contexts where two or more languages are part of an individual's upbringing and because data reported on MLEs can include exited or reclassified former MLEs. Whenever we use the term native speaker, we intend those who were raised speaking the language of instruction and were never classified as MLs.

First language means the first language that a person learned, sometimes also called the mother tongue or home language. The abbreviation for first language is L1. In bilingual communities or households, the notion of first language is not as relevant because many children are brought up speaking two languages. In some cases, a student is more proficient in one language than the other, which we refer to as the dominant language. In other cases, students are balanced in their proficiency in both languages.

Second language means a language learned after learning the L1. The abbreviation for second language is L2. Other terms for second language learning are new language and additional language, such as English as a new language or English as an additional language. As with the term first language, in the bilingual education field, the meaning of second language is less relevant because many children grow up speaking and learning in two languages simultaneously.

INSTRUCTION

Regular classroom is the term the authors of this book use to refer to classes composed of students who are and who are not MLs and whose curriculum and instruction are not specially designed solely for MLs. These classes are sometimes known as ML integrated to indicate that MLs are included among other students.

English language development (ELD)/English for speakers of other languages (ESOL) classes, as a complement to the regular classroom, are provided for MLE students only. In contrast with regular education classes, which integrate MLE with non-MLE students, ELD/ESOL classes are sometimes known as MLE-dedicated classes to show that they focus solely on MLE students' listening, speaking, reading, and writing needs. We use the term second language development (L2D) to include all contexts of second language learning and English language development (ELD) to specify that the second language is English. We also specify other language development classes, such as Italian language development (ILD) and so on.

Dual language education is a program model that uses two languages of instruction. The proportion of instruction in each language can vary, but the most predominant models use either 50 percent English and 50 percent of the partner language in all grade levels (a 50/50 model) or will begin in kindergarten with 90 percent in the partner language (usually the home language of the majority of enrolled MLE students) and will taper off the partner language for each rising grade until a 50/50 proportion is reached by grade 4 (a 90/10 model). Many dual language programs also are known as **two-way immersion**, which means that each class comprises MLEs as well as multilingual Spanish (or Chinese, Japanese, etc.) learners. Edith's dual language program uses a two-way model (Spanish/English), which has the benefit of all students learning in a language that is new to them and striving to becoming bilingual, bicultural, and biliterate.

Second language acquisition and **bilingual development** are terms that describe many common processes in learning more than one language. However, elements of each perspective on this process are framed differently and originate from different theoretical and practical standpoints. See chapter 1 for more details.

Heritage language education aims to teach languages related to students and their family heritage, such as Spanish for students of Latin American heritage, but in which the students have varying levels of proficiency. It is common for heritage language instruction to focus on minority or immigrant languages to maintain their use across generations.

World languages education refers to teaching languages other than the dominant language in the community, such as teaching German in the United States.

Teaching classical and less commonly taught languages is also part of world languages education.

Content and language integrated learning (CLIL) is a program model in which second, or additional, languages are taught through disciplinary subjects. For instance, science or mathematics is taught in the language that students are learning as an additional language (often referred to as the target language), thus enabling students to learn the content of the subject as well as the language. CLIL is part of the language policy of the European Union and is used in other parts of the world as well. This book's TASLL Framework is well suited for CLIL instruction, especially with the Supportive Classroom Communication protocol.

English as a foreign language (EFL) programs are used in environments where English is not the main language of communication in daily life. In many ways, EFL is a type of world languages education, with English being the world language that is taught. Because of English's status as a major world language that has academic and career implications for learners, EFL is taught worldwide. This book's TASLL Framework is well suited for EFL instruction, especially with the Targeted Language/Literacy Instruction protocol.

The TASLL Framework Protocols and Theoretical Rationale

Language and Learning in School

The flowchart in figure B.1 provides a visual summary of decision points for planning and providing instructional adaptations for multilingual learners (MLs) under the two Teaching All Subjects, Language, and Literacy (TASLL) Framework protocols. We suggest you keep it in your planner and refer to it when developing or adapting lessons that are suitable for your MLs. A full explanation of each phase of the Supportive Classroom Communication (SCC) protocol is provided in chapter 2, and the Targeted Language/Literacy Instruction (TLI) protocol, in conjunction with the SCC protocol, is described in chapter 7.

Figure B.2 depicts the theoretical underpinnings of the TASLL Framework, and the details are explained in the narrative that follows it.

Philosophical Orientation

Both James Carey's Ritual View of Communication, which we suggest underlies all aspects of classroom communication, and Lev Vygotsky's notion of the Zone of Proximal Development, which we assert illuminates how targeted language and literacy instruction can lead to individual second language (L2) development, are rooted in sociocultural theory. As applied in the field of communication, sociocultural theory emphasizes the interconnectedness of social and cultural contexts, which not only shape the way we communicate but also create and maintain shared understandings among social groups. From this standpoint, the definition of communication, in the classroom and elsewhere, is the construction and maintenance of shared cultural meaning. As applied to the field of learning science, sociocultural theory posits that learning is fundamentally a social process, wherein individuals construct knowledge and develop skills through meaningful interactions with others, mediated by cultural tools and practices within their specific sociocultural contexts.

FIGURE B.1

TASLL Framework Protocols

TASLL Framework Protocols

Referring to each ML student's WIDA ACCESS* or Screener Individual Report Levels (L, S, R, & W Proficiency Level Descriptors), apply the following:

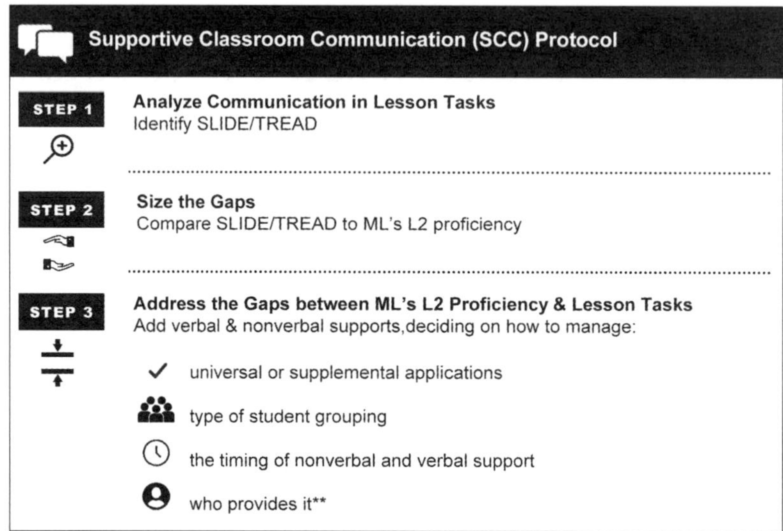

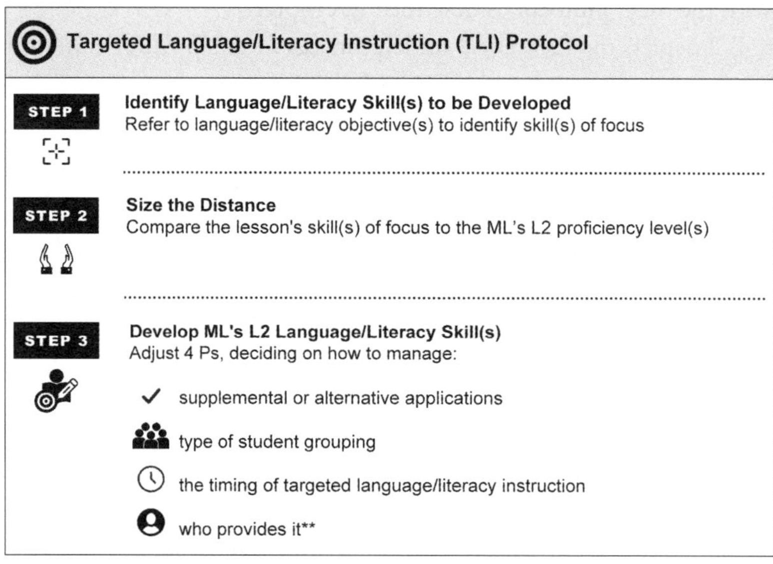

* Or other L2 assessment

** Possible variation of best fit of providers between Protocols

FIGURE B.2

Theoretical Underpinnings of the TASLL Framework

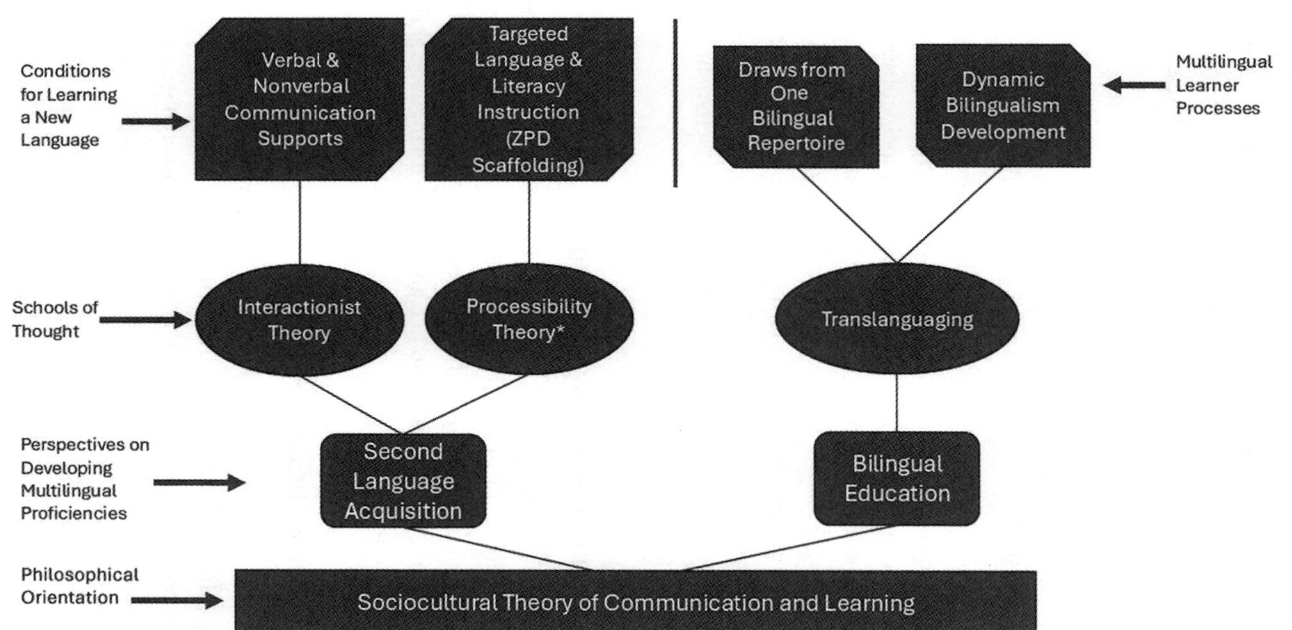

* Interactionist Theory originated from a psycholinguistic perspective but has since developed variations that are sociocultural in nature. Processability Theory (PT) is a psycholinguistic theory of learner internal competencies and constraints, but as with sociocultural theory, PT considers the learner's precise developmental stage and social interaction in its application.

Perspectives on Developing Multilingual Proficiencies

The fields of second language acquisition and bilingual education have similarities and differences in how they view multilingualism. They share the view that social and cultural factors are significant in second language learning (or in becoming multilingual), but each emphasizes different aspects. For example, second language acquisition has dedicated substantial focus to learners' stages of L2 acquisition, whereas bilingual education has focused much attention on how the connections between students' first and second languages impact their academic achievement. The TASLL Framework values the contributions to understanding the process of becoming multilingual that each perspective provides.

Schools of Thought

Although the schools of thought that the TASLL Framework draws upon in the field of second language acquisition are psycholinguistic in origin, both interactionist and processability theories can be successfully applied within a sociocultural approach to L2 learning, as is elaborated in chapters 2 (interactionist) and 7 (processability). The translanguaging school of thought, whose academic home is in the field of bilingual education, is woven throughout the TASLL Framework and is emphasized in Tenet 1. It is present both in forms of first language (L1) verbal support in the SCC protocol, as well as in the TLI protocol through expanding the perspective element of individual student scaffolding to students' L1.

Conditions for Learning a New Language

Along with an interactionist perspective that underlies the SCC protocol for MLs, the TASLL Framework's TLI protocol promotes MLs' second language development through identifying and working within students' Zone of Proximal Development by providing individualized, guided assistance and targeted language and literacy instruction (explicit instruction).

Multilingual Learner Processes

The TASLL Framework for MLs endorses using ML students' full linguistic repertoire to foster bilingualism, biculturalism, and biliteracy, valuing the linguistic and cultural assets that MLs possess. The framework shares translanguaging's focus on the learner, positioning the learner's experience of becoming multilingual as a dynamic process rather than a solely linear one.

Useful AI Tools for Multilingual Education

By Nirmal Ghimire

In today's diverse classrooms, artificial intelligence (AI) offers transformative potential for bridging gaps, enhancing personalized instruction, and reducing administrative burdens. This appendix provides a structured outline of AI tools that support multilingual learners (MLs) and their teachers. The recommendations are organized by function and include practical guidelines for responsible AI use, aligning with inclusive educational practices.

For Creating Nonverbal Supports (*essential visual aids for fostering comprehension, particularly when language barriers exist*)

- ***AutoDraw*:** Free drawing tool that transforms rough sketches into polished images, allowing teachers to quickly create culturally relevant visual supports
- ***DALL-E Mini (Craiyon)*:** Free text-to-image, picture-to-picture generator that creates custom illustrations from simple prompts, helping produce context-specific visuals that clarify complex content
- ***Microsoft Image Creator*:** Creates customizable visuals to illustrate academic concepts and vocabulary for visual learners

For Creating Verbal Support (*tools that simplify and scaffold academic texts, making them more accessible for multilingual students*)

- ***Rewordify*:** Free text simplification to replace challenging vocabulary with more accessible alternatives while preserving meaning
- ***Quillbot*:** Refines sentence structure and clarity through paraphrasing; ideal for creating scaffolded sentence frames and word banks
- ***ChatGPT*** **(free version):** Generates customized language scaffolds, elaborated definitions, leveled questions, and concept explanations on demand
- ***Perplexity AI*:** Combines AI with search capabilities to provide explanations with citations, supporting academic language development

For Developing Core Language Skills (*supporting listening, speaking, reading, and writing is crucial for language acquisition*)

- ***Speechify*** (free version)**:** Converts digital texts into natural-sounding audio in multiple languages, supporting auditory comprehension
- ***Elsa Speak*:** Provides immediate, personalized feedback on pronunciation, helping ML students develop speaking confidence
- ***Read&Write*:** Offers text-to-speech, dictionaries, and translation tools to support reading comprehension across content areas
- ***Grammarly*:** Provides real-time writing feedback on grammar, clarity, and word choices to develop writing skills

For Family and Community Engagement (*building effective communication for strong home-school connections, especially in multilingual contexts*)

- ***Google Translate*:** Real-time translation supporting over 100 languages through text, voice, and camera functions
- ***Microsoft Translator*:** Features conversation mode allowing multiple participants to communicate in different languages simultaneously
- ***Talking Points*:** Two-way communication platform offering translation between teachers and families in over 100 languages
- ***Seesaw*:** Digital portfolio platform with built-in translation for sharing student work with families who speak different languages

For Adaptive Learning and Personalized Instruction (*platforms offering personalized instruction and real-time feedback tailored to individual student needs*)

- ***Khan Academy Khanmigo*:** Tutor for personalized support across subject areas
- ***Duolingo*:** Adjusts difficulty based on student performance
- ***Newsela*:** News articles at five reading levels with built-in supports for ML students
- ***ThinkCERCA*:** Personalized reading and writing lessons that adapt to students' language proficiency levels

For Assessment and Feedback (*these platforms streamline grading and provide personalized feedback to enhance student learning outcomes*)

- ***GotFeedback*:** Delivers personalized feedback aligned to learning criteria, making assessment more accessible for ML students
- ***Quizlet*:** Creates interactive study sets with audio pronunciation support in multiple languages
- ***Edji*:** Allows embedding of comprehension questions and voice notes within digital texts for scaffolded reading experiences

Additional Tools for Content Creation and Lesson Planning (*empower teachers to develop instructional materials quickly and effectively*)

- ***Adobe Express*:** Creates videos, graphics, and presentations with built-in accessibility features
- ***Flipgrid*:** Video discussion platform with caption generation and transcript features to support comprehension
- ***WeVideo*:** Cloud-based video editor with caption and subtitle capabilities in multiple languages
- ***Curipod*:** Creates interactive lessons with built-in accessibility features from simple topic prompts
- ***Canva Magic Write*:** Combines visual design with AI text generation to create multilingual classroom materials
- ***Wakelet*:** Organizes diverse learning resources in customizable, shareable collections with translation capabilities

Guidelines for Responsible AI Use in PreK–12 Education

1. **Verify AI Outputs:** Ensure that AI-generated content is reviewed by educators or language experts to maintain accuracy and cultural appropriateness.
2. **Supplement; Don't Replace:** Use AI tools as supportive resources that enhance teacher-led instruction rather than replace it.
3. **Prioritize Data Privacy:** Confirm that all tools comply with relevant data privacy regulations (e.g., Family Educational Rights and Privacy Act) to protect sensitive student information.
4. **Maintain Transparency:** Communicate clearly with students, families, and staff regarding how and why AI tools are used in the classroom.
5. **Teach Critical AI Literacy:** Help students understand how AI works, its limitations, and how to evaluate AI-generated content.
6. **Promote Accessibility:** Choose tools that are free or low cost to ensure equitable access for all students, regardless of socioeconomic status.

Integrating AI tools thoughtfully can transform classrooms into engaging and efficient learning environments for all students. By leveraging both established and emerging technologies, educators can personalize instruction for MLs, reduce administrative tasks, and foster stronger home-school connections. Embracing AI with a commitment to ethical practices and ongoing professional development has capacity to empower every learner to thrive in the digital age.

Notes

Introduction

1. We use the term *multilingual learner*, or *ML*, broadly, referring to MLs when the discussion pertains to MLs of any language and in any context, such as with explanations of general principles of second language (L2) learning and teaching. When the context or issue being discussed is specific to understanding, using, or learning *English* in particular, we use the TESOL organization's term *multilingual learner of English*, or *MLE*, for clarity. For example, when referring to MLs in preK–12 two-way dual language classes, we use MLE for those learning English as a new language (meaning that they are classified by US federal definition as *English learners*) and MLS for those learning Spanish as a new language. When discussing our four student cases, we use the term *multilingual learner* when what we are addressing applies to MLs of any new language and the term *multilingual learner of English* if what we are discussing is specific to the English language or to an English-speaking educational context. We also use MLE when referring to research focused on students who are developing proficiency in English. It is important to point out that when we use the term *multilingual student*, we mean a student who is proficient in two languages, but when we use the term *multilingual learner*, we mean that the student is still developing proficiency in one of the languages of instruction.
2. Statistics are for fall 2021. US Department of Education, National Center for Education Statistics, "English Learners in Public Schools," The Condition of Education 2023, https://nces.ed.gov/programs/coe/indicator/cgf/english-learners-in-public-schools; The US Department of Education uses the term English learner (EL) to refer to the students we call multilingual learners of English (MLEs).
3. Statistics for 2020–21. Of these teachers, 42 percent did not have any coursework on how to teach MLs prior to their first year of teaching. Cristobal de Brey, Anlan Zhang, and Sarah Duffy, "Digest of Education Statistics, 2021 (NCES 2023009)," US Department of Education, National Center for Education Statistics (Washington, DC: US Government Printing Office, 2023).
4. Wendy Grigg, Patricia Donahue, and Gloria Dion, "The Nation's Report Card: 12th-Grade Reading and Mathematics 2005 (NCES 2007-468)," US Department of Education, National Center for Education Statistics (Washington, DC: US Government Printing Office, 2005).
5. US Congress, No Child Left Behind Act of 2001, § 6319: 2008; US Congress, Higher Education Opportunity Act, Public Law 110-315, 110th Congress (2008). Our queries on the National Education Achievement Program's Data Explorer have shown that this achievement gap has not changed significantly in reading and mathematics for students in grades 4, 8, and 12 since the program started (National Center for Education Statistics, NAEP Data Explorer, Institute of Education Sciences, http://nces.ed.gov/nationsreportcard/naepdata/). Margaret Heritage, Aída Walqui, and Robert Linquanti, *Moving Toward Equity in English Learner Education: Examining the Implementation of Common Core Standards* (San Francisco, WestEd, 2020).
6. Although this book's examples and student cases focus on the US context, the research and theory it draws upon, as well as the protocols that apply the research and theory, are relevant to any teaching or learning context and language.
7. When we discuss MLEs, their L2, or new language, is assumed to be English, which is the language of instruction that they are learning through and learning about. In many instances, we state *L2* rather than

specifying *English* to indicate that the theories and practices we explain are applicable to different L2s and school contexts (e.g., learning through French in content and language integrated learning [CLIL] classes).

8. See appendix A for a list or terms.
9. For reading clarity, we present dialogues in English when our case students communicate with their families, although in most cases, they would actually use their native language(s).
10. There are many different program models to support MLs' language development and academic achievement. Most of those models include an ELD (sometimes referred to as ESL or ESOL) or bilingual specialist who works with the classroom teacher to help MLEs, either in the regular or dual language class during instruction or in a separate class composed of MLEs only.
11. Mary Ellen Good, Sophia Masewicz, and Linda Vogel, "Latino English Language Learners: Bridging Achievement and Cultural Gaps Between Schools and Families," *Journal of Latinos and Education* 9, no. 4 (2010): 321–39; Suzanne Panferov, "Increasing ELL Parental Involvement in Our Schools: Learning from the Parents," *Theory Into Practice* 49, no. 2 (2010): 106–12.
12. Gero is a bilingual French/Haitian Kreyòl speaker, but because of his dominance in Haitian Kreyòl, we use it as the primary language of discussion when referring to Gero's native language.
13. Those who build a new life in a different culture are said to go through four stages of cultural adjustments: honeymoon, hostility, integration/acceptance, and home stage. Gregory J. Trifonovitch, "Culture Learning/Culture Teaching," *Educational Perspectives* 16, no. 4 (1977): 18–22; Seth J. Schwartz et al., "Rethinking the Concept of Acculturation: Implications for Theory and Research." *American Psychologist* 65, no. 4 (2010): 237–51.
14. Jim Cummins, "Rethinking BICS and CALP: Directions for Research and Practice," *TESOL Quarterly* 55, no. 3 (2021): 678–99; Jim Cummins, "The Role of Primary Language Development in Promoting Educational Success for Language Minority Students," in *Schooling and Language Minority Students: A Theoretical Framework*, ed. Charles F. Leyba (Los Angeles: California State University, Evaluation, Dissemination and Assessment Center, 1981), 3–49; Jim Cummins, *Bilingual Education and Special Education: Issues in Assessment and Pedagogy* (San Diego, CA: College Hill, 1984).
15. Virginia P. Collier and Wayne P. Thomas, "Why Dual Language Works for Everyone, PK-12," *Multilingual Educator*, California Association for Bilingual Education (2020 annual edition): 2–6; Wayne Thomas and Virginia Collier, *School Effectiveness for Language Minority Students* (Washington, DC: National Clearinghouse for Bilingual Education, 1997).
16. Patsy M. Lightbown and Nina Spada, *How Languages Are Learned* (Oxford, UK: Oxford University Press, 2013); Rod Ellis, *Understanding Second Language Acquisition* (Oxford, UK: Oxford University Press, 2008); John Schumann, *The Pidginization Process: A Model for Second Language Acquisition* (Rowley, MA: Newbury House, 1978).
17. Zoltan Dörnyei and Stephen Ryan, *The Psychology of the Language Learner Revisited* (New York: Routledge, 2015); Robert C. Gardner and Wallace E. Lambert, *Attitudes and Motivation in Second Language Learning* (Rowley, MA: Newbury House, 1972).
18. Henry Lemana II et al., "Affective Filters' Extent of Influence on Oral Communication: L2 Learners' Perceptions." *International Journal of Educational Management and Development Studies* 4, no. 1 (2023): 88–108.
19. James Soland and Lia E. Sandilos, "English Language Learners, Self-Efficacy, and the Achievement Gap: Understanding the Relationship Between Academic and Social-Emotional Growth," *Journal of Education for Students Placed at Risk (JESPAR)* 26, no. 1 (2021): 20–44.
20. Tamara G. Halle et al., "The Social–Emotional Development of Dual Language Learners: Looking Back at Existing Research and Moving Forward with Purpose," *Early Childhood Research Quarterly* 29, no. 4 (2014): 734–49.
21. Helen Fann, Patrick Pieng, and Lisa M. Soederberg Miller, "A Review of the Cognitive and Social-Emotional Correlates of Multilingualism: Implications for Policy and Practice," *Early Childhood Education Journal* 52, no. 1 (2024): 1–10.
22. David Singleton and Simone E. Pfenninger, *The Age Factor in Second Language Acquisition* (Clevedon, UK: Multilingual Matters, 2019); Lightbown and Spada, *How Languages Are Learned.*
23. Other terms that have been used to describe this population include English as a second language (ESL) students, English for speakers of other languages (ESOL) students, and English language learners (ELLs).

Another commonly used term, culturally and linguistically diverse (CLD) students, broadly describes students whose language or culture differs from the dominant language or culture, but this does not necessarily mean that they are not yet fully proficient in English. Similarly, a subset of these students is termed "language minority" students—those for whom a language other than English is the first or heritage language, but this group may include individuals who are balanced bilinguals or who have been exited from the English learner classification because they have attained full proficiency in English. The US Department of Education term *English learners* (whom we refer to as multilingual learners of English or MLEs) describes a subset of language minority students because their heritage or first language is not English and they are not yet fully proficient in English. Mistakenly, Hispanic or Latino students are sometimes conflated with MLEs. However, although the majority of MLEs in the United States are Latinos, a Latino student may not be an MLE, and an MLE may not be Latino. Our definition of MLE is based on the descriptors for English learners found in federal legislation and includes the following characteristics: a student who communicates in a language other than English exclusively or in addition to English and who has not yet developed adequate English proficiency for successful written and spoken communication in academic and/or social settings. MLEs' language proficiency can range from non-English-speaking newcomers to long-term multilingual learners of English (those who are classified as MLEs for approximately seven years or more).

24. Joyce W. Nutta et al., *Show, Tell, Build: Twenty Key Instructional Tools and Techniques for Educating English Learners* (Cambridge, MA: Harvard Education Press, 2018).
25. Michael A. K. Halliday, "The Notion of 'Context' in Language Education," in *Text and Context in Functional Linguistics*, ed. Mohsen Ghadessy (Amsterdam: John Benjamins, 1999), 1–24.
26. TESOL International Association. *The 6 Principles for Exemplary Teaching of English Learners: Grades K-12* (Alexandria, VA: TESOL Press, 2024).

Chapter 1

1. James Carey, *Communication as Culture: Essays on Media and Society* (New York: Routledge, 2009); John Dewey, *Experience and Nature*, vol. 1 (New York: Dover, 1958).
2. Carey, *Communication as Culture.*
3. Michael A. K. Halliday, "The Notion of 'Context' in Language Education," in *Text and Context in Functional Linguistics*, ed. Mohsen Ghadessy (Amsterdam: John Benjamins, 1999), 1–24.
4. Lev Vygotsky, *Mind in Society: The Development of Higher Psychological Processes* (Cambridge, MA: Harvard University Press, 1978).
5. Many educators lack sufficient understanding of what the state standards demands are, how they impact learning, and how they can be assessed in ways that will help teachers track student attainment of these skills and competencies. Researchers such as Sato and colleagues (Edynn Sato et al., *Accommodations for English Language Learner Students: The Effect of Linguistic Modification of Math Test Item Sets* [NCEE 2009-4079], US Department of Education, Institute of Education Sciences, National Center for Education Evaluation and Regional Assistance [Washington, DC: US Government Printing Office, 2010]) have developed criteria to enable measurement of academic language demands in receptive, or listening and reading, and productive, or speaking and writing, skill areas. Issues such as length, repetition, detail, abstraction, visual aspects, familiarity, complexity, sophistication, text structure, and style of discourse can be considered when examining the language demands placed on students in academic subjects.
6. Kenneth Goodman and Yetta Goodman, *Making Sense of Learners Making Sense of Written Language: The Selected Works of Kenneth S. Goodman and Yetta M. Goodman* (New York: Routledge, 2014).
7. With the integrated language and disciplinary subjects approach that state standards require, language arts teachers increasingly use texts from academic subjects as a focus for skill development in listening, speaking, reading, and writing. This, in turn, will raise students' achievement in disciplinary subjects, whose instruction and assessment depend largely on language.
8. Douglas Fisher and Nancy Frey, "Releasing Responsibility," *Educational Leadership* (November 2008): 32–37.
9. Rod Ellis, *The Study of Second Language Acquisition*, 2nd ed. (Oxford, UK: Oxford University Press, 2008).

10. We use the term *nonverbal communication* to mean any way of communicating other than primarily through language. We use the term *verbal communication* to mean primarily language-based (both oral and written language) communication.
11. Stephen D. Krashen, *The Input Hypothesis: Issues and Implications* (New York: Longman, 1985).
12. Merrill Swain, "Communicative Competence: Some Roles of Comprehensible Input and Comprehensible Output in Its Development," in *Input in Second Language Acquisition*, ed. Susan M. Gass and C.G. Madden (Rowley, MA: Newbury House, 1985), 165–79.
13. An audience evaluating output at a later time could also be a group of listeners, as with a speech or broadcast.
14. Michael H. Long, "The Role of Linguistic Environment in Second Language Acquisition," in *The New Handbook of Second Language Acquisition*, ed. William C. Ritchie and Taj K. Bhatia (San Diego, CA: Academic Press, 1996); Michael H. Long, *Second Language Acquisition and Task-Based Language Teaching* (West Sussex, UK: Wiley, 2015).
15. We speak mainly about the school environment because that is what the classroom teacher has influence over, but for MLEs in the US mainland, input, interaction, and output have an impact on their acquisition of English outside of school. Availability of English media at home, including technology such as television, computers, and the internet, as well as participation in community and extracurricular activities, such as fellowship at places of worship or playing on local sports teams, provide opportunities for exposure to English to which those who study English only at school (such as students of English as a foreign language in China) lack access. In addition, trips to the store, driving along the streets and highways, and many other places outside the home provide exposure to spoken and written English and opportunities to interact with native and more proficient speakers.
16. Michael H. Long, *Problems in SLA*, Second Language Acquisition Research Series (Mahwah, NJ: Lawrence Erlbaum Associates, 2006).
17. The constructs of input, output, and interaction are part of the theory of second language acquisition known as the interactionist perspective.
18. Jim Cummins, "The Role of Primary Language Development in Promoting Educational Access for Language Minority Students," in *Schooling and Language Minority Students: A Theoretical Framework*, ed. California State Department of Education (Los Angeles: Office of Bilingual Bicultural Education, Evaluation, Dissemination, and Assessment Center, California State University, 1984).
19. For more discussion on this discrepancy, we recommend research on systemic functional linguistics or on corpus-based linguistics.
20. Thomas W. Stewart and Nathan Vaillette, eds., *Language Files: Materials for an Introduction to Language and Linguistics*, 8th ed. (Columbus: The Ohio State University Press, 2001).
21. Although nonverbal communication can imply body language, our use of this term is broader and includes any means of communication using something other than or in addition to listening, speaking, reading, or writing to deliberately convey messages. One of the definitions of *verbal* implies oral expression (as in a verbal, or spoken, contract), but our use of the term is based on the definition that encompasses both spoken (oral) and written (print) language.
22. We believe that the communication environment in the early grades is more conducive to comprehensibility of instruction and L2 development for MLs than that in the upper grades. We are not suggesting that tenth-grade classrooms should resemble kindergarten classrooms. Instead, we are comparing a highly contextualized classroom to one with very limited context. Moving from highly contextualized to less contextualized instruction allows native speakers to develop academic proficiency in and through the use of their native language over a twelve-year span. However, a newcomer L2 learner placed, for example, in a tenth-grade classroom with little to no contextual support never had access to this progression from a highly contextualized environment to low or limited context. This poses unique challenges for MLEs entering US schools beyond the primary grades.
23. James Asher, *Learning Another Language Through Actions: The Complete Teachers' Guidebook* (Los Gatos, CA: Sky Oaks Publications, 1977).
24. Jim Cummins, *Bilingual Education and Special Education: Issues in Assessment and Pedagogy* (San Diego: College Hill, 1984).

25. Diane August and Timothy Shanahan, *Developing Literacy in Second-Language Learners: Report of the National Literacy Panel on Language-Minority Children and Youth* (Mahwah, NJ: Lawrence Erlbaum Associates, 2006).
26. TESOL also has published standards for MLEs' language use in specific academic subjects. The framework for the standards is available at https://www.tesol.org/media/fuwijiu4/bk_prek-12elpstandards_framework_318.pdf.
27. Another common categorization of MLs' proficiency levels comes from a second language teaching method called the natural approach. See Stephen D. Krashen and Tracy D. Terrell, *The Natural Approach: Language Acquisition in the Classroom* (Oxford, UK: Pergamon,1983). This approach uses four levels: preproduction, early production, speech emergence, and intermediate fluency. We have found that experienced classroom teachers of MLs are able to individualize instruction following these four general stages or levels, but because the first two stages tend to blend together fairly rapidly and the means of supporting communication at this level are very similar, we have adapted its classification of proficiency levels for our approach to supporting classroom communication for MLs. We combined preproduction and early production into beginning level, called speech emergence the intermediate level, and termed intermediate fluency the advanced level for clarity and simplicity of expression. From our research with teachers of MLs in regular classes, dividing the process of second language acquisition into these three categories for supporting communication in curriculum, instruction, and assessment balances feasibility of implementation with successful instruction for MLs.
28. In a research synthesis study, Genesee and colleagues reported on the relationship between first language literacy, background knowledge, and conceptual knowledge: Fred Genesee et al., "English Language Learners in U.S. Schools: An Overview of Research Findings," *Journal of Education for Students Placed at Risk* 10, no. 4 (2005): 363–85. They found that L1 oral proficiency and reading comprehension skills, in combination with MLEs' general knowledge about the topic of study, enabled MLEs to successfully transfer academic skills and conceptual knowledge from their L1 to English.
29. August and Shanahan, *Developing Literacy in Second-Language Learners.*
30. In a study conducted by García-Vázquez and colleagues, Spanish-speaking MLEs' standardized achievement test scores for tests administered in English were significantly related to Spanish language proficiency in reading and writing. See Enedina García-Vázquez et al., "Language Proficiency and Academic Success: Relationships Between Proficiency in Two Languages and Achievement Among Mexican American Students," *Bilingual Research Journal* 21, no. 4 (1997): 395–408. Moreover, writing proficiency in Spanish was significantly related to their mathematics achievement test, which was administered in English.
31. Stephen D. Krashen, *The Power of Reading: Insights from Research* (Portsmouth, NH: Heinemann, 2009).
32. Robert T. Jiménez, Georgia E. García, and P. David Pearson, "The Reading Strategies of Bilingual Latina/o Students Who Are Successful English Readers: Opportunities and Obstacles," *Reading and Research Quarterly* 31 (1996): 90–112.
33. These bilingual glossaries and cognates, provided by the New York State Statewide Language Regional Bilingual Education Resource Network, exist in a variety of languages represented in US classrooms and can be downloaded for different content areas and grade levels. They are available at https://steinhardt.nyu.edu/metrocenter/language-rbern/resources/bilingual-glossaries-and-cognates.
34. Philip Kerr, *The Use of L1 in English Language Teaching*, Cambridge Papers in ELT Series (Cambridge, UK: Cambridge University Press, 2019).
35. Ofelia Garcia, *Bilingual Education in the 21st Century: A Global Perspective* (Malden, MA: Wiley, 2011).
36. Eman Barri and Florin Mihai, "Translanguaging and Second Language Acquisition: A Brief Look at the Available Evidence," *Sunshine State TESOL* 16, no. 1 (2023): 5–12.
37. Garcia, *Bilingual Education, 45.*
38. Ofelia Garcia, Susana Ibarra Johnson, and Kate Selzer, *The Translanguaging Classroom: Leveraging Student Bilingualism for Learning* (Philadelphia: Caslon, 2017).
39. Appendix A provides definitions of various program models for MLs.
40. The US Government Accountability Office (GAO-24-106360) Q & A Report to Congressional Requesters, dated July 25, 2024, entitled *K-12 Education: Student, Teacher, and School Characteristics Associated with English Learners' Academic Performance*, available at https://www.gao.gov/assets/gao-24-106360.pdf,

provides correlational research findings regarding which elements are associated with MLEs' academic performance.

Chapter 2

1. Here we mean that unless a student has literacy skills in their L2 that diverge greatly from their oral proficiency, e.g., more than one level below (possibly due to below-grade-level literacy in their L1), we recommend using the types and degrees of support that are appropriate for the student's oral proficiency. This keeps implementation simple and straightforward. When an ML's literacy skills are more than one level below their oral proficiency, we recommend stepping down an oral proficiency category of support (e.g., from intermediate to beginning) because the lower the category of support, the more the types of support provide nonverbal elements, which help comprehension regardless of literacy skills.
2. Although the verbs encompassed by SLIDE and TREAD are quite clearly linked to more or less verbal student or teacher actions, there is a third group teachers should keep in mind when analyzing established lessons or designing their own. The language load of this third group of verbs depends to a large extend on the context. For example, when students are directed to "find" something, it could be a place in a text where something specific happens (i.e., demanding language use), or it could involve finding a visual clue in a picture or around the classroom (i.e., nonverbal). Similarly, the verbs provide and give could mean an opinion or proof (i.e., language use) or literally to hand something to a person. The important point to keep in mind is not the literal meaning of the verb but what it is asking the teacher or students to do.
3. Cummins refers to this nonverbal communication as context-embedded instruction; Krashen uses the term extralinguistic cues. Jim Cummins, Bilingual Education and Special Education: Issues in Assessment and Pedagogy (San Diego: College Hill, 1984); (Stephen D.Krashen, The Input Hypothesis: Issues and Implications (New York: Longman, 1985).
4. See http://dailyinfographic.com or http://www.easel.ly or http://pinterest.com/officialascd/education-infographics/ for information on infographics.
5. Many topics' complexity can be represented through diagrams, graphic organizers, and interactive media with associated verbal explanations slightly above the current L2 proficiency of the ML, promoting not only comprehension of the subject but also L2 development.
6. Other examples of verbal support are provided in the lessons presented in chapters 3–6.
7. It is important to note that reading materials developed for MLs at beginning, intermediate, and advanced levels of L2 proficiency are not the same as graded readers for native speakers of the language.
8. If our goal is to help MLs learn the academic content, such as history, while they are learning the language, the language used to present the content must be comprehensible. Reading passages that unpack embedded phrases and clauses (simplified text) and that expand details and build in redundancies that help define terms that less-proficient MLs may not know (elaborated text) can help promote comprehension. In a classroom environment where there may be only one or just a few MLs, providing unpacked (rephrased or elaborated) texts to supplement more complex texts is more feasible than expecting the classroom teacher to individually unpack each grade-level text with MLs of varying proficiency levels during whole-class instruction. Of course, unpacking complex texts for native speakers likely will be close enough to advanced MLs' level of proficiency to benefit their comprehension as well.
9. Jamal Abedi, Carol Lord, and Joseph R. Plummer, National Center for Research on Evaluation, Standards, and Student Testing, Center for the Study of Evaluation, Final Report of Language Background as a Variable in NAEP Mathematics Performance (Los Angeles: Graduate School of Education & Information Studies, University of California, 1997).
10. Margaret Heritage, Formative Assessment in Practice: A Process of Inquiry and Action (Cambridge, MA: Harvard Education Press, 2013).
11. See https://www.magibook.co for information about this resource and appendix C for a detailed list of AI tools.

Chapter 3

1. National Council for the Social Studies, "What Is Social Studies?," https://www.socialstudies.org /about/definition-social-studies. Furthermore, social studies "helps students examine vast human experiences through the generation of questions, collection and analysis of evidence from credible sources,

consideration of multiple perspectives, and the application of social studies knowledge and disciplinary skills. As a result of examining the past, participating in the present, and learning how to shape the future, social studies prepares learners for a lifelong practice of civil discourse and civic engagement in their communities. Social studies centers knowledge of human rights and local, national, and global responsibilities so that learners can work together to create a just world in which they want to live."

2. Erin Hogan et al., "Instructional Practices for Secondary Social Studies Teachers: Describing a Curricular Program Designed to Improve Language, Content Knowledge and Literacy Outcomes for Emergent Bilinguals," *TESOL Journal*, September 2024, https://doi.org/10.1002/tesj.866.
3. Ter Marlies Beek et al., "Relationships Between Adolescent Students' Reading Skills, Historical Content Knowledge and Historical Reasoning Ability," *History Education Research Journal* 19, no. 1 (2022), https://doi.org/10.14324/herj.19.1.02.
4. McGraw-Hill Education, *TimeLinks: Third Grade, Communities* (Columbus: Macmillan McGraw-Hill, 2007).
5. Priscila López-Beltrán et al., "The Effects of Information Structure in the Processing of Word Order Variation in the Second Language," *Second Language Research* 38, no. 3 (2021): 639–70, https://doi.org/10.1177/0267658321992461; Silvia Sánchez Calderón and Raquel Fernández Fuertes, "The Acquisition of English Active and Passive Monotransitive Constructions by English-Spanish Simultaneous Bilingual Children," *International Journal of Bilingualism* 26, no. 4 (2022): 502–26, https://journals.sagepub.com/doi/10.1177/13670069211056740.
6. For a thorough description, see Joyce W. Nutta et al., *Show, Tell, Build: Twenty Key Instructional Tools and Techniques for Educating English Learners* (Cambridge, MA: Harvard Education Press, 2018).
7. Jim Cummins, "The Role of Primary Language Development in Promoting Educational Success for Language Minority Students," in *Schooling and Language Minority Students: A Theoretical Framework*, ed. Charles F. Leyba (Los Angeles: California State University, Evaluation, Dissemination and Assessment Center, 1981): 3–49; Jim Cummins, "Empowering Minority Students: A Framework for Intervention," *Harvard Educational Review* 56, no. 1 (1986): 18–37; Jim Cummins, "BICS and CALP: Empirical and Theoretical Status of the Distinction," in *Encyclopedia of Language and Education*, ed. Nancy H. Hornberger (Boston: Springer, 2008), 487–99, https://doi.org/10.1007/978-0-387-30424-3_36.
8. Even children and families from Western countries who arrived during the early waves of immigrants and whose values contributed to the formation of those in the United States might refer to different frames of reference. For example, a Swiss middle school student would likely view democracy differently from American children, as Switzerland is a direct democracy as opposed to the American representative democracy. The greater the socioeconomic, cultural, and political differences between American norms and those of other countries, the more teachers need to consider background building prior to lessons so that students can learn the subtle differences.
9. Drishti Pillai, Akash Pillai, and Samantha Artiga, *Children of Immigrants: Key Facts on Health Coverage and Care* (KFF, January 15, 2025) https://www.kff.org/racial-equity-and-health-policy/issue-brief/children-of-immigrants-key-facts-on-health-coverage-and-care/.
10. Carlos J. Ovando and Mary Carol Combs, *Bilingual and ESL Classrooms; Teaching in Multicultural Contexts*, 6th ed. (New York: Rowman & Littlefield Publishers, 2018).
11. Evelyn Marino Weisman and Laurie E. Hansen, "Strategies for Teaching Social Studies to English-Language Learners at the Elementary Level," *The Social Studies* 98, no. 5 (2007): 180–84; Cheng-Ji Lai, "Examining the Impact of Multimodal Task Design on English Oral Communicative Competence in Fourth-grade Content-language Integrated Social Studies: A Quasi-experimental Study," *Asian-Pacific Journal of Second and Foreign Language Education* 9, no. 1 (2024), https://doi.org/10.1186/s40862-024-00289-7.
12. An argument is any expression or syntactic element that completes the meaning of the verb in a sentence.
13. Robert J. Marzano, *Building Background Knowledge for Academic Achievement* (Alexandria, VA: Association for Supervision and Curriculum Development, 2004). See the Tennessee Department of Education's 2009 Tennessee Vocabulary Project, at https://content.schoolinsites.com/api/documents/1b17a254cd0647ce89999c4a2749f2e8.pdf.
14. To be precise, the hierarchy of this example is actually individual food items that are grouped under the generic terms vegetables, fruit, or meat before they get grouped under food, which in turn is part of the actual social studies concept that is to be taught: "basic needs."

15. The types of services offered depend on factors such as the number of MLEs in a given school or district and the availability of appropriately trained personnel, and services vary greatly throughout the United States. When there are only a handful of MLEs per class, an ELD specialist or bilingual paraprofessional moves from class to class to provide small-group instruction for MLEs (typically twenty to thirty minutes per day during any content-area instructional time) with push-in, whereas in the pull-out model, the MLEs leave their regular classroom to join an ELD specialist for a specific period of time each day, preferably during English language arts time.

    The instructional model Specially Designed Academic Instruction in English (SDAIE), also referred to as sheltered instruction, falls under the umbrella of content-based language instruction. With a focus on content instruction for MLEs, there is a strong emphasis on language development. A widely used model of SDAIE is the Sheltered Instruction Observation Protocol (SIOP). See Jane M. Echevarría, Mary Ellen Vogt, and Deborah Short, *Making Content Comprehensible for English Language Learners: The SIOP Model* (Boston: Pearson, 2022).
16. Diane August, Lauren Artzi, and Christopher Barr. "Helping ELLs Meet Standards in English Language Arts and Science: An Intervention Focused on Academic Vocabulary," *Reading and Writing Quarterly* 32, no. 4 (December 21, 2015): 37396, https://doi.org/10.1080/10573569.2015.1039738; Dustin S. J. Van Orman et al., "Examining the Impacts of Extended Vocabulary Instruction in Mixed-English-Proficiency Science Classrooms," *The Journal of Educational Research* 114, no. 1 (2021): 74–88, https://doi.org/10.1080/002267.
17. Neelima Wagley et al., "Contributions of Bilingual Home Environment and Language Proficiency on Children's Spanish-English Reading Outcomes," *Child Development* 93, no. 4 (2022): 881–99, https://doi.org/10.1111/cdev.13748; Valeria M. Rigobon et al., "Does Spanish Knowledge Contribute to Accurate English Word Spelling in Adult Bilinguals?," *Bilingualism Language and Cognition* 26, no. 5 (2023): 924–41, https://doi.org/10.1017/s1366728923000093.
18. C. Patrick Proctor and Elaine Mo, "The Relationship Between Cognate Awareness and English Comprehension Among Spanish-English Bilingual Fourth Grade Students," *TESOL Quarterly* 43, no. 1 (March 1, 2009): 126–36, https://doi.org/10.1002/j.1545-7249.2009.tb00232.x; Elena Tribushinina, Elena Dubinkina-Elgart, and Pim Mak, "Effects of Early Foreign Language Instruction and L1 Transfer on Vocabulary Skills of EFL Learners with DLD," *Clinical Linguistics and Phonetics* 37, no. 8 (2022): 683–700, doi:10.1080/02699206.2022.2076261.
19. Specifically, we recommend the "Bilingual Glossaries and Cognates" for language arts, math, and science for elementary, middle school, and high school grades. These lists are published in over thirty languages and are made available through the Statewide Language Regional Bilingual Education Resource Network at https://steinhardt.nyu.edu/metrocenter/language-rbern/resources/bilingual-glossaries-and-cognates.
20. The best way to start with the protocol is to underline the verbs that indicate what the teacher and student(s) are doing during the activity. The verbs and verb phrases are already underlined in the lesson description for illustration purposes.
21. One symbol is explored each day. The lesson starts with the American flag. The tasks are always the same.
22. For example, see http://www.superteacherworksheets.com/patriotic-symbols/flag-fitb_FLAGS.pdf. Modifications for the students' grade and preparation levels should be made.
23. This can be done in PowerPoint, through an interactive whiteboard presentation, or by using a whiteboard app to be viewed on tablets; for example, ShowMe for the iPad (http://www.showme.com) or myViewBoard for Android devices (https://myviewboard.com/).
24. The writing spaces will be used during independent daily journaling time. A sample of such a worksheet can be seen at Mrs. Williamson's blogspot: http://mrswilliamsonskinders.blogspot.com/search/label/presidents.
25. The symbol from another country is preferably from a nation that is represented in the student body. The World Factbook, maintained by the Central Intelligence Service, lists a few national symbols for each country: https://www.cia.gov/the-world-factbook/field/national-symbols/. Some printable foreign flags can also be found at https://www.education.com/worksheets/kindergarten/national-symbols/.
26. All teachers should learn about the surface and deep cultural elements of their English learners' origins.
27. Placing MLs of the same heritage language in the same groups is one of the recommendations made by proponents of translanguaging, which we described in chapter 1. We always remind teachers that this verbal support should be employed with a specific purpose. The ML at the higher proficiency level has to

learn the content and practice the academic vocabulary just as much as the lower-proficiency-level peer. In this case, it takes Merline little time to assist Gero when he gets stuck and helps her make connections to their common L1, but does not distract her from fully engaging in the activity.

28. If their pronunciation is such that it makes the word/phrasing almost incomprehensible, the teacher can take a short moment to model it again with the second language learner while the rest of the students moves to their respective stations.
29. According to Herrell and Jordan, read-aloud strategies are especially useful to MLEs because the mixture of gestures, change in intonation patterns, questioning, and so forth reduce anxiety and allow the students to focus on the verbal and nonverbal elements of the activity. Adrienne L. Herrell and Michael Jordan, *Fifty Strategies for Teaching English Language Learners*, 6th ed. (Hoboken, NJ: Pearson, 2019).
30. Several ideas for this unit were taken from Erika Crowder's blog: http://sprinklestokindergarten.blogspot.com/2012/02/american-symbols.html.

Chapter 4

1. National Science Teachers Association, *Scope, Sequence, and Coordination of Secondary School Science* (Washington, DC: National Science Teachers Association, 1991).
2. Their findings hold true for many other languages. Zhihui Fang and Mary Schleppegrell, *Reading in Secondary Content Areas: A Language-Based Pedagogy* (Ann Arbor: Michigan University, 2010).
3. Fang and Schleppegrell, *Reading in Secondary Content Areas.*
4. Fang and Schleppegrell, *Reading in Secondary Content Areas*; Suzanne Eggins, *An Introduction to Systemic Functional Linguistics*, 2nd ed. (London: Pinter, 2004).
5. Okhee Lee and Sandra H. Fradd, "Science for All, Including Students from Non-English Language Backgrounds," *Educational Researcher* 27, no. 4 (1998): 12–21.
6. Lee and Fradd, "Science for All."
7. Trish Stoddart et al., "Integrating Inquiry Science and Language Development for English Language Learners," *Journal of Research in Science Teaching* 39, no. 8 (2002): 664–87.
8. Another resource science teachers whose language of instruction is English can consider is the "Bilingual Glossaries and Cognates" for elementary, middle school, and high school grades. These lists are published in over thirty languages and are made available through the Statewide Language Regional Bilingual Education Resource Network at https://steinhardt.nyu.edu/metrocenter/language-rbern/resources/bilingual-glossaries-and-cognates.
9. Joyce Nutta, Nazan Bautista, and Malcolm Butler, *Teaching Science to English Language Learners* (New York: Routledge, 2011).
10. Additional cognate examples among English, Spanish, and Haitian Kreyòl, respectively, are accident—accidente—aksidan and addition—adición—adisyon.
11. Positive feedback that emphasizes students' efforts, progress, and areas of improvement fosters stronger teacher-student connections and is especially critical for an ML to feel safe to learn and speak up in the classroom. Further, this positive communication can boost an ML's confidence in their ability to try more output of the new language, which will increase their second language abilities.
12. They also learn about the centrality of verbs and discover how sentences in English grow from the position of the verbs to construct the remainder of the sentence.
13. Lee and Fradd, "Science for All."
14. In 2019, the latest year of reported science scores, MLs (or English learners in federal documents) scored lower than their non-ML peers in grades 4 (by 34 points), 8 (by 46 points), and 12 (by 53 points). Irwin V. De La Rosa et alt., "Report of the Condition of Education 2022 (NCES 2022-144)," US Department of Education, National Center for Education Statistics (Washington, DC: US Government Printing Office, 2022).
15. Eleanor L. Babco and Nathan E. Bell, *Professional Women and Minorities: A Total Human Resources Compendium* (Washington, DC: Commission on Professionals in Science and Technology, 2008); Alberto J. Rodriguez, *Turning Despondency into Hope: Charting New Paths to Improve Students' Achievement and Participation in Science Education* (Greensboro, NC: Southeast Eisenhower Consortium, 2004).
16. Emily Gallmeyer's original lesson plan on the earth's rotation from 2007 can be found on her website under the portfolio section, curriculum, C5: http://users.manchester.edu/student/ekgallmeyer

/ProfWebpage/default.htm. The lesson teaches students to use critical-thinking and problem-solving strategies. We slightly changed the lesson objective, standards, and evaluation.

17. As an inquiry approach, the 5E Learning Cycle Model is attributed to the category of constructivist learning. The 5Es represent a sequence of five steps: engaging or exciting (the learner), exploring or investigating (the topic), explaining (students report what they have learned), extending (allowing the students to use their new knowledge by making connections to other related concepts and the world around them), and evaluating (the understanding—by both teachers and students). The 5E Learning Cycle Model was first developed by a team of the Biological Science Curriculum Study: Rodger W. Bybee et al., *Science and Technology Education for the Elementary Years: Frameworks for Curriculum and Instruction* (Washington, DC: National Center for Improving Instruction), 1989.
18. The best way to start with the protocol is to underline the verbs that indicate what the teacher and students are doing during the activity. The verbs and verb phrases are already underlined in the lesson description for illustration purposes.

Chapter 5

1. John Dewey, *Democracy and Education* (New York: Macmillan, 1916); William H. Kilpatrick, "The Project Method: The Use of the Purposeful Act in the Educative Process," *Teachers College Record* 19 (1918): 319–35.
2. Robert Geier et al., "Standardized Test Outcomes for Students Engaged in Inquiry-Based Curricula in the Context of Urban Reform," *Journal of Research in Science Teaching* 45, no. 5 (2008): 922–39; Mehmet Gültekin, "The Effect of Problem Based Learning on Learning Outcomes in the 5th Grade Social Studies Course in Primary Education," *Educational Sciences: Theory and Practice* 5, no. 2 (2005): 548–56
3. Stephanie Bell, "Project-Based Learning for the 21st Century: Skills for the Future," *The Clearing House* 83 (2010): 39–43.
4. Phyllis C. Blumenfeld et al., "Motivating Project-Based Learning: Sustaining the Doing, Supporting the Learning," *Educational Psychologist* 26 (1991): 369–98; Cindy E. Hmelo-Silver, "Problem-Based Learning: What and How Do Students Learn?," *Educational Psychology Review* 16 (2004): 235–66.
5. Bell, "Project-Based Learning for the 21st Century"; Linda Torps and Sara Sage, *Problems as Possibilities: Problem-Based Learning for K–12 Education* (Alexandria, VA: ASCD, 2002).
6. Phap Dam and Melinda T. Cowart, *Understanding the English Learner* (Denton, TX: Texas Woman's University Library, 2006).
7. J. Emmett Gardner et al., "Enhancing Interdisciplinary Instruction in General and Special Education: Thematic Units and Technology," *Remedial and Special Education* 24, no. 3 (2003): 161–72, https://doi.org/10.1177/07419325030240030; Betty Shoemaker, "Integrative Education: A Curriculum for the Twenty-First Century," *Oregon School Study Council* 33, no. 2 (1989).
8. Azadeh Shafaei and Hajar Abdul Rahim, "Does Project-Based Learning Enhance Iranian EFL Learners' Vocabulary Recalll and Retention?," *Iranian Journal of Language Teaching Research* 3, no. 2 (2015): 83–89.
9. Michael Joseph Ennis et al., "A Pilot Course with Project-Based Learning in An Intensive English Program," *Language Learning in Higher Education* 12, no. 1 (2022): 57–85, https://doi.org/10.1515/cercles-2022-2047; Raida Asfihana et al., "Students' English Learning Experiences on Virtual Project-Based Learning Instruction," *International Journal of Language Education* 6, no. 2 (2022): 196–209, https://doi.org/10.26858/ijole.v6i2.20506.
10. Teresa S. Foulger and Margarita Jimenez-Silva, "Enhancing the Writing Development of English Language Learners: Teacher Perceptions of Common Technology in Project-Based Learning," *Journal of Research in Childhood Education* 22, no. 2 (2007): 115.
11. Many MLs underestimate their abilities because they feel lost for much of the day while engaging in tasks that require academic language skills. Therefore, we suggest that teachers compile a list of resources appropriate for the MLs' proficiency level from which the students can choose. When unsure whether an alternative website, text, or personal contact is appropriate for MLs, teachers should consult with a second language development specialist.

12. We acknowledge that the term *technology* encompasses a whole array of tools teachers can employ to scaffold instruction for students that may or may not be computer based. For the purpose of this discussion, however, we limit ourselves to multimedia and computer technologies.
13. Although many of these tools are also beneficial for focused language and literacy development (e.g., language conventions, organization of text, fundamental reading skills), we list these tools here with a focus on academic content instruction. For explanations and examples of specific considerations in using technology for language acquisition, the reader may want to refer to Mary Ellen Butler-Pascoe and Karin M. Wiburg, *Technology and Teaching English Language Learners* (Boston: Pearson, 2003) or Denise E. Murray, "Technologies for Second Language Literacy," *Annual Review of Applied Linguistics* 25 (2005): 188–201.
14. Available at https://ncge.org/teacher-resources/national-geography-standards/.
15. The best way to start with the protocol is to underline the verbs that indicate what the teacher and student(s) are doing during the activity. The verbs and verb phrases in the instructional steps are already underlined in the lesson description for illustration purposes.
16. Several government and university sites offer mapping tools free of charge. See, for example, the National Map by the US Geographic Survey (https://www.usgs.gov/programs/national-geospatial-program/national-map) or Iowa University's GIS Online Mapping Tools (https://guides.lib.uiowa.edu/c.php?g=132116&p=2713587). Other free GIS software options are reviewed by GIS Geography (https://gisgeography.com/free-gis-software/).
17. Available at http://www.nrel.gov/gis/data-tools.html. The US Geological Survey also provides several free maps, data, and webtools: https://www.usgs.gov/.
18. Some MLs may need one-on-one support while reviewing online resources. Some students may need more assistance with computer literacy to select and interpret maps, whereas others may encounter some technological difficulties in creating the map.
19. The early part of the design phase could take place in the computer lab with no more than two students sharing a computer to familiarize them with the software. Later, smaller questions about the tool's function can easily be addressed in the classroom. There are many free mapping tools available, such as National Geographic MapMaker (https://www.nationalgeographic.org/society/education-resources/mapmaker-launch-guide/) or the open-source GIS software tool QGIS2 (https://qgis.org/en/site/about/index.html). Other free software options can be reviewed at https://gisgeography.com/free-gis-software/.
20. In chapter 10, you will see that Tasir's reading and writing scores are 2.9 and 2.8, respectively. Most of the time, it is enough for disciplinary subject teachers to know the whole number score, which is provided on the individual student ACCESS Report. In Tasir's case. it is beneficial to know the decimal, however. Tasir's reading and writing scores are within reach of the intermediate level (what WIDA calls *developing*) rather than at the beginning or the middle of *emerging*. This means that when the reading and writing tasks are intended to teach and show understanding of content rather than developing language skills, Ms. Parker's supports can be selected to more closely match Tasir's level 4 in listening. However, the language arts teacher would be targeting instruction of the language and literacy skills to Tasir's exact levels with the decimal points when applying the Targeted Language/Literacy Instruction protocol.
21. Experts in content-based language instruction typically point to the benefits of bilingual glossaries, but that is not necessary in Tasir's case because she would not have acquired any of the academic terms in her native Arabic, having moved to the United States in elementary school.
22. This allowance lowers her affective filter, and telling her classmates about the group's GIS map becomes less of a chore and more of an occasion to shine in a setting where she often does not perform well.

Chapter 6

1. Walter Kintsch, "Understanding Word Problems: Linguistic Factors in Problem Solving," in *Language and Artificial Intelligence*, ed. Makoto Nagao (Amsterdam: Elsevier, 1987), 197–208.
2. Jingzi Huang and Bruce Normandia, "Comprehending and Solving Word Problems in Mathematics: Beyond Key Words," in *Reading in Secondary Content Areas: A Language-Based Pedagogy*, ed. Zhihui Fang and Mary J. Schleppegrell (Ann Arbor: Michigan Teacher Training, 2008), 64–83.
3. Christine A. Coombe, Keith S. Folse, and Nancy J. Hubley, *A Practical Guide to Assessing English Language Learners* (Ann Arbor: University of Michigan Press, 2007).

4. To illustrate the nature of vocabulary in mathematics, we extracted an example of specialized vocabulary used in algebra from the Tennessee Vocabulary Project, available at http://www.tn.gov/education/ci/doc/VOCABULARY.pdf.
5. JoAnn Crandall, ed., *ESL Through Content-Area Instruction: Mathematics, Science, Social Studies. Language in Education: Theory and Practice*, no. 69 (West Nyack, NY: Prentice Hall, 1987).
6. Lily W. Fillmore and Catherine E. Snow, *What Teachers Need to Know About Language* (Washington, DC: US Department of Education, Office of Education Research and Improvement, Education Resources Information Center, 2000.
7. The best way to start with the protocol is to underline the verbs that indicate *what the teacher and student(s) are doing* during the activity. The verbs and verb phrases are already underlined in the lesson description for illustration purposes.
8. Note that *give* at the start of this sentence is a "TREAD" word because Mr. Leibniz will "give" the news verbally.
9. "High School Level Integrated Algebra Glossary English - Spanish," available at https://steinhardt.nyu.edu/metrocenter/language-rbern/resources/bilingual-glossaries-and-cognates.
10. Many states allow the use of bilingual glossaries during standardized testing. MLEs who have a habit of using them during class time know better when and how to use them during assessment than those who are given a glossary just before testing.

Chapter 7

1. By verbal symbols, we mean language; by nonverbal symbols, we mean graphic images and diagrams, real objects and models, hands-on experiences, gestures and expressions, and so on.
2. WIDA provides performance definitions for five levels: level 1, Entering, through level 5, Bridging. At level 6, Reaching, the MLE is presumed to have mastered all criteria of the lower levels.
3. Marshall McLuhan was a Canadian scholar on communication theory. James Carey, *Communication as Culture: Essays on Media and Society* (New York: Routledge, 2008).
4. We believe that the still undefined status of the language demands of schooling is a testament to this general lack of language awareness. With a few notable exceptions (such as Courtney Cazden's research on classroom discourse), educators typically pay little mind to the structure, form, and function of *spoken* discourse, nor do they necessarily sense how these linguistic aspects affect the listeners' comprehension of intended meaning. Likewise, when teachers design tasks that require students to communicate to and with others about disciplinary subjects, they often fail to identify how these activities require a certain facility with language. Although there is a sounder record of attentiveness to the structure, form, and function of language used in written texts than in oral communication, much of it has been limited to literary analysis or language study, or it has been oversimplified into formulas of informational text complexity that are not substantiated by strong research and theory.
5. Count nouns can be stated in plural form (most commonly by adding an *s*) and can therefore be counted. Noncount nouns cannot be stated in plural form, so they cannot be counted. If noncount nouns can't be counted, then they also can't be preceded by the indefinite article *a*, which indicates there is one of them.
6. Keith S. Folse, *Keys to Teaching Grammar to English Language Learners: A Practical Handbook,* 2nd ed. (Ann Arbor: University of Michigan Press, 2016.)
7. M. A. K. Halliday, *Language as Social Semiotic: The Social Interpretation of Language and Meaning* (London: Arnold, 1978).
8. With the implementation of state standards, English language arts teachers have become acquainted not only with the strands of reading, writing, listening, speaking, and language but also with the individual standards at each of the grade levels they teach. In the area of reading, the standards expect all students to build knowledge, gain insights, explore possibilities, and broaden their perspective through reading relevant and diverse selections from classic and contemporary literature as well as challenging informational texts in a range of subjects. Certain critical types of reading materials, including classic myths and stories from around the world, foundational US documents, seminal works of American literature, and the writings of Shakespeare, are required. In writing, the standards aim to develop students' ability to write logical arguments based on substantive claims, sound reasoning, and relevant evidence. The writing standards provide annotated samples of student writing in order to help establish adequate performance

levels in writing arguments, informational or explanatory texts, and narratives. The speaking and listening standards emphasize gaining, evaluating, and presenting increasingly complex information, ideas, and evidence through listening and speaking as well as through media. These standards emphasize academic discussion in one-on-one, small-group, and whole-class settings. They aim to develop necessary skills for formal presentations as well as the more informal discussion that takes place as students collaborate to answer questions, build understanding, and solve problems. The language standards emphasize language accuracy and vocabulary development. Vocabulary and language conventions are treated in their own strand not because skills in these areas should be handled in isolation but because their use extends across reading, writing, speaking, and listening.

9. See Corey Humphrey, "What Is Disciplinary Literacy and Why Is It Important?," Carnegie Learning Blog, June 3, 2024, https://www.carnegielearning.com/blog/what-is-disciplinary-literacy/.
10. We use the term *second language learning* according to its broad meaning to encompass both foreign language learning, which takes place in environments where the language studied is not the language spoken in the country or region of the school, and second language learning, which takes place in environments where the language studied is the language spoken in the country or region of the school.
11. Rod Ellis, *The Study of Second Language Acquisition*, 2nd ed. (Oxford: Oxford University Press, 2008). These are not either/or propositions, as an instructed environment could incorporate naturalistic features, such as requiring French 1 students to converse one-on-one with native speakers, and naturalistic environments may include instructed second language acquisition, such as living in a second language community while taking an online grammar course to help understand the mechanics of the language.
12. See https://online.stanford.edu/courses/xeduc201xb-effective-classroom-conversations for a great resource on supporting constructive classroom conversations.
13. What Stephen Krashen calls i + 1, or comprehensible input, focuses on understanding input. Stephen D. Krashen, *The Input Hypothesis: Issues and Implications* (New York: Longman, 1985).
14. The term *communicative competence* was extended to language pedagogy by Michael Canale. For more information, see Michael Canale, "From Communicative Competence to Language Pedagogy," in *Language and Communication*, ed. Jack Richards and Richard Schmidt (London: Longman, 1983).
15. For a description of instructional conversations and how they can be used to teach language and literacy, see chapter 12 in our book *Show, Tell, Build: Twenty Key Instructional Tools and Techniques for Educating English Learners*.
16. Ellis, *The Study of Second Language Acquisition*, 28–31, 764–65.
17. Ellis, *The Study of Second Language Acquisition*, 6.
18. Manfred Pienemann, "An Introduction to Processability Theory," in *Cross-Linguistic Aspects of Processability Theory*, ed. Manfred Pienemann (Amsterdam: John Benjamins, 2005), 1–60.
19. The Defense Language Institute categorizes languages by their similarity to English for purposes of establishing the number of weeks required of full-time, intensive study to develop basic skills in social language comprehension and use. Association of the United States Army, "DLI's Language Guidelines," http://www.ausa.org/publications/ausanews/specialreports/2010/8/Pages/DLI'slanguageguidelines.aspx.
20. Ofelia Garcia, *The Translanguaging Classroom: Leveraging Student Bilingualism for Learning* (Baltimore: Brookes Publishing, 2016).
21. Although the fields of second language acquisition and translanguaging may look at language learning phenomena differently, we believe that both perspectives can operate in productive complementarity, filling in voids around each approach's areas of focus. We also believe that some of the assumptions and practicalities popularly attributed to each approach do not reflect their philosophical grounding, such as the criticism that second language acquisition approaches intend to replace an L1 with an L2 or that they view the teaching and learning of an L2 as attempting to remedy some sort of linguistic deficit. Similarly, we believe that claiming translanguaging is messy and disorganized in practice does not take into account the clear and structured guidance that is part of its framework and the empirically driven movement that stretches its implementation in new directions.
22. Larry Selinker, *Rediscovering Interlanguage* (New York: Longman, 1992); Susan M. Gass and Alison Mackey, "Input, Interaction, and Output: An Overview," *AILA Review* 19 (2006): 3–17.
23. Selinker, *Rediscovering Interlanguage*; Mackey, "Input, Interaction, and Output."
24. Ellis, *The Study of Second Language Acquisition,* 846–47.

25. *Literacy* remains a dynamic concept, evolving and changing over time, reflecting different societies' forms of and needs for expression. Literacy activist Paulo Freire defined literacy as "discursive forms and cultural competencies that construct and make available the various relations and experiences that exist between learners and the world." Paulo Freire and Donaldo Macedo, *Literacy: Reading the Word and the World* (New York: Routledge–Taylor & Francis, 2013), 7. Even more technically, María Torres-Guzmán defines literacy as an "asset of cultural practices that includes the encoding and decoding of print and that is used to convey a message that has specific shared meaning for a group of individuals in a particular context." Bertha Pérez and María E. Torres-Guzmán. *Learning in Two Worlds: An Integrated Spanish/English Biliteracy Approach,* 3rd ed. (New York: Allyn and Bacon, 2002), 4. Similar to the culture-bound definitions we presented in previous chapters for communication and language, these definitions of literacy situate culture at its core. Similarly, our perspective on literacy is meaning and culture centered, encompassing the ability to perceive meaning from and express meaning in the *social semiotic system* of text.
26. An excellent synthesis of this research is summarized in Diane L. August and Timothy Shanahan, eds., *Developing Literacy in a Second Language: Report of the National Literacy Panel* (Mahwah, NJ: Lawrence Erlbaum Associates, 2006).
27. Nonie K. Lesaux et al., "Development of Literacy of Language Minority Learners," in *Developing Literacy in a Second Language: Report of the National Literacy Panel*, ed. Diane L. August and Timothy Shanahan (Mahwah, NJ: Lawrence Erlbaum Associates, 2006), 75–122.
28. Nonie K. Lesaux et al., "Uneven Profiles: Language Minority Learners' Word Reading, Vocabulary, and Reading Comprehension Skills," *Journal of Applied Developmental Psychology* 31, no. 6 (2010): 475–83.
29. Catherine E. Snow, "Cross-Cutting Themes and Future Research Directions," in *Developing Literacy in a Second Language: Report of the National Literacy Panel*, ed. Diane L. August and Timothy Shanahan (Mahwah, NJ: Lawrence Erlbaum Associates, 2006), 631–51.
30. Proctor and colleagues tested a second language reading comprehension model incorporating decoding and oral language measures on a sample of 135 Spanish- and English-speaking fourth graders and reported a high correlation of 0.73 between students' vocabulary knowledge and reading comprehension outcomes. C. Patrick Proctor et al., "The Intriguing Role of Spanish Language Vocabulary Knowledge in Predicting English Reading Comprehension," *Journal of Educational Psychology* 98, no. 1 (2006): 159–69. In another study, van Gelderen and colleagues administered tests of English vocabulary knowledge and reading comprehension to 397 Dutch students in grades 8 through 10 and found a strong correlation of 0.63. Amos van Gelderen et al., "Linguistic Knowledge, Processing Speed, and Metacognitive Knowledge in First- and Second-Language Reading Comprehension: A Componential Analysis," *Journal of Educational Psychology* 96, no. 1 (2004): 19–30.
31. Catherine E. Snow, M. Susan Burns, and Peg Griffin, *Preventing Reading Difficulties in Young Children* (Washington, DC: National Academy Press, 1998), 74.
32. See Kate Cain, *Reading Development and Difficulties* (West Sussex, UK: British Psychological Society and Blackwell, 2010) for an extensive discussion of this research and its application for practice.
33. One study that relates directly to the impact of text structure is Jill Fitzgerald and Alan Teasley, "Effects of Instruction in Narrative Structure on Children's Writing," *Journal of Educational Psychology* 78, no. 6 (1986): 424–32. For an extensive discussion of how awareness of text structure relates to children's and adult readers' reading and writing performance, see Walter Kintsch, *Comprehension: A Paradigm for Cognition* (Cambridge: Cambridge University Press, 1998).
34. See http://www.wida.us/assessment/access/ for information on the WIDA ACCESS for ELLs English proficiency assessment and http://www.elpa21.org/ for ELPA 21. You may wonder why it is necessary to use a test designed to measure MLEs' listening, speaking, reading, and writing when all children are given standardized reading tests. Tests for MLEs are sensitive to the stages they go through in developing proficiency in all four skill areas. In addition to language complexity, cultural content can also affect assessment of MLEs' knowledge of academic subjects. Culture-free testing does not exist. This is a result of the strong connection between culture and cultural content, on the one hand, and language, on the other, as our earlier discussion of communication, culture, and language described. In well-written tests, MLEs can understand the cultural content of test questions through context. Depending on an MLE's cultural heritage, what may be a common cultural occurrence in many places in the United States may be completely unfamiliar to the MLE. Consider this sentence:

    Tommy had cereal after he got up.

If MLEs are not familiar with cereal, they might not understand the meaning of the sentence, and the word *had* would not provide the specificity necessary to infer the general meaning. However, if the wording provides more background through specificity of terms, it becomes clear that *cereal* refers to food:

Tommy ate cereal for breakfast.

More specific word choices, such as *ate* rather than *had*, and specifying *breakfast* to provide additional context (*after he got up* may not be understood as rising in the morning), provide information that makes the content more comprehensible to the MLE.

35. The most recent update of the TESOL standards is from 2006: http://www.tesol.org/advance-the-field/standards/prek-12-english-language-proficiency-standards. WIDA stands for World-Class Instructional Design and Assessment. The latest set of WIDA standards was released in 2020. See http://www.wida.us/assessment/access/background.aspx. Information about the ELPA21 standards can be found at https://elpa21.org/elp-standards/.
36. We chose to present the WIDA English Language Development Standards for several reasons. First of all, the consortium includes 80 percent of US states, meaning that a majority of teachers will use them for their yearly testing of MLEs to satisfy the requirements of the Elementary and Secondary Education Act. Furthermore, the latest set of standards was released in 2020, whereas the latest TESOL language proficiency standards date back to 2006, and the TESOL standards were based on the language proficiency levels developed by WIDA.
37. Available at https://wida.wisc.edu/sites/default/files/resource/Performance-Definitions-Receptive-Domains.pdf and https://wida.wisc.edu/sites/default/files/resource/Performance-Definitions-Expressive-Domains.pdf.
38. Pienemann, "An Introduction to Processability Theory."
39. William M. Saunders, Barbara R. Foorman, and Coleen D. Carlson, "Is a Separate Block of Time for Oral English Language Development in Programs for English Learners Needed?," *Elementary School Journal* 107 (November 2006): 181–98.
40. Jim Cummins, *Bilingual Education and Special Education: Issues in Assessment and Pedagogy* (San Diego: College Hill, 1984).
41. William Saunders, Claude Goldenberg, and David Marcelletti, "English Language Development: Guidelines for Instruction," *American Educator* (Summer 2013): 13–25.
42. A reading development class may or may not be the best place for an ML whose reading is below grade level. It might be more advantageous to invest more time in the instructed second language acquisition that occurs in an L2 development (e.g., ELD) class, which integrates the four skills of listening, speaking, reading, and writing at the student's level of proficiency and which has been shown to expedite second language development. Wherever language arts and literacy instruction takes place, it should be targeted as closely as possible to the ML's L2 proficiency levels.
43. Because Gero is in Florida, a state that does not require the WIDA literacy components of the Kindergarten Screener, Ms. Levin only had listening and speaking scores to consider. She also used information from classroom observations and language samples, as well as knowledge about his home language literacy practices, to gauge his proficiency levels at this point in the school year.
44. WIDA's Interpretive Guide for Score Reports Spring 2024 document recommends referring to the WIDA performance definitions to understand proficiency levels. In addition to Individual Student Reports, WIDA provides Student Roster Reports for groups of students in a school and grade.
45. We wanted to help classroom teachers we worked with to understand how ELD teachers provide this quality of targeted language instruction for their MLEs. To determine what might help, we designed an empirical exploration of what qualified ELD teachers actually do differently when they use language arts and literacy teaching techniques that are common to both the L1 and L2 instructional environments. To isolate what is different about targeted language instruction, we recorded videos of ELD teachers using a dozen different language arts techniques that are commonly applied in regular elementary and secondary classrooms. The ELD classes that participated in these videos were composed exclusively of MLEs in grades K–2, 3–5, 6–8, and 9–12, and their teachers were certified and experienced in teaching ELD.

    After the videos were produced, we showed them over a year's time to more than a hundred regular language and literacy teachers and asked them to take notes regarding what was different about the execution of those teaching techniques with the MLEs. In other words, we asked them to note what the teacher and students did that was different from if a language arts or literacy teacher had been using the same strategy or technique with a class composed solely of native speakers of English, or non-MLEs. From teachers' observations and subsequent reflections, we identified qualities of scaffolding that made sense to regular language and literacy teachers. We held subsequent professional development sessions with the teachers, sharing these qualities of scaffolding for MLEs, which we termed pitch, pace, portion, and perspective/point (the 4 Ps of language arts scaffolding for MLs).

46. We would like to point out that although adjusting pitch as suggested in the TLI protocol may seem the same as moderating language demands in the SCC protocol, they are essentially different in purpose and practice. Although they have some similarities, they are different because the purpose of moderating language demands is to make the content of the language used or expected accessible to MLs, and the purpose of adjusting pitch is to adjust the language form and structure to slightly above an ML student's current level of proficiency to be able to engage in comprehending and using this language with the help of an expert instructor. For example, using a modified text in the SCC protocol might involve the teacher highlighting key terms and phrases in a long text to direct the ML to essential parts for understanding the concept being taught (e.g., photosynthesis), whereas a text adjusted in pitch would use grammatical structures and vocabulary that are slightly above the ML student's current proficiency level so the language and literacy instructor can use them as a springboard to learning and using new language.
47. Another example is using a grammatical focus rather than a semantic one for a cloze procedure, which means omitting specific parts of speech, rather than every *n*th word, to check an ML's grammatical competence.
48. Roland Tharp and Ronald Gallimore, *Rousing Minds to Life: Teaching, Learning, and Schooling in Social Context* (New York: Cambridge University Press, 1988).
49. This can also be accomplished through technology, using grammar mini-lessons available at free resources such as the app Show Me.
50. Emily C. Bouck et al., "Technology in Action: Rethinking Everyday Technology as Assistive Technology to Meet Students' IEP Goals," *Journal of Special Education Technology* 27, no. 4 (2012): 47–57.
51. Artificial intelligence (AI) tools such as Diffit (app.diffit.me) and MagicSchool (app.magicschool.ai) offer a plethora of customized teaching tools. Diffit has the option of providing readings in multiple languages. Magic School's Best Practices for AI Usage provide sensible guidelines for working with any AI resources: "Check for Bias—AI might occasionally produce biased or incorrect content. Always double-check before sharing with students. The 80-20 Approach—Use AI for initial work, but make sure to add your final touch, review for bias and accuracy, and contextualize appropriately for the last 20%. Your Judgment Matters—See AI-generated content as a starting point, not the final version. Always Adhere to Your School's Guidelines. Protect Privacy—Don't include personal student details like names or addresses." See also appendix C for a list of AI tools and guidelines for their responsible use.

Chapter 8

1. Gero is a bilingual French/Haitian Kreyòl speaker, but because of his dominance in Haitian Kreyòl, we will use Haitian Kreyòl as the primary language of discussion when referring to Gero's native language.
2. Lois A. Bader, *Bader Reading and Language Inventory,* 4th ed. (Upper Saddle River, NJ: Merrill, 2002). Available at https://ptgmedia.pearsoncmg.com/images/9780132943680/samplechapter/9780132943680.pdf.
3. Diane August and Timothy Shanahan, eds., *Developing Literacy in Second-Language Learners: Report of the National Literacy Panel on Language-Minority Children and Youth* (Mahwah, NJ: Lawrence Erlbaum Associates, 2006); Claude Goldenberg, "Reading Wars, Reading Science, and English Learners," *Reading Research Quarterly* 55, no. 1 (2020): 131–44, doi:10.1002/rrq.340.
4. National Institute of Child Health and Human Development, *Report of the National Reading Panel, Teaching Children to Read: An Evidence-Based Assessment of the Scientific Research Literature on Reading and Its Implications for Reading Instruction, NIH 00-4769* (Washington, DC: US Department of Health and Human Services, 2000).
5. Catherine Snow, "Cross-Cutting Themes and Future Research Directions," in *Developing Literacy in Second-Language Learners*, 641–42.
6. Nonie K. Lesaux and Esther Geva, "Development of Literacy in Language-Minority Students," in *Developing Literacy in Second-Language Learners,* 27–60.

7. National Institute of Child Health and Human Development, *Report of the National Reading Panel, Teaching Children to Read: An Evidence-Based Assessment of the Scientific Research Literature on Reading and Its Implications for Reading Instruction, NIH 00-4769* (Washington, DC: US Department of Health and Human Services, 2000); Claude Goldenberg et al., "A Response to 'Toward Comprehensive Effective Literacy Policy and Instruction for English Learner/Emergent Bilingual Students' by the National Committee on Effective Literacy (NCEL)," March 7, 2022, response to the NCEL White Paper, https://www.thereadingleague.org/wp-content/uploads/2023/09/TRLC-ELEB-A-Response-to-the-NCEL-Whitepaper.pdf.
8. National Institute of Child Health and Human Development, *Report of the National Reading Panel*, 639.
9. David L. Share, "Phonological Recoding and Self-Teaching: Sine Qua Non of Reading Acquisition," *Cognition* 55 (1995): 151–218, cited in Snow, "Cross-Cutting Themes and Future Research Directions," 646–47. Based on an extensive review of the literature on effective literacy instruction with a view to English learners, Claude Goldenberg calls for comprehensive oral English language development through listening and speaking instruction and read-aloud activities that expose students to text that is inaccessible to them because of their language proficiency. If students have not developed sufficient oral language by the time they pass beginning and early reading, more ELD instruction is necessary. Claude Goldenberg, "Reading Wars, Reading Science, and English Learners," *Reading Research Quarterly* 55, no. 1 (2020): 131–44, doi:10.1002/rrq.340. Claude Goldenberg et al., "A Response to 'Toward Comprehensive Effective Literacy Policy and Instruction for English Learner/Emergent Bilingual Students.' "
10. Snow, "Cross-Cutting Themes and Future Research Directions," 646.
11. Diane August, Margarita Calderón, and María Carlo, *Transfer of Skills from Spanish to English: A Study of Young Learners: Report for Practitioners, Parents, and Policy Makers* (Washington, DC: Center for Applied Linguistics, 2002), 647.
12. Nonie K. Lesaux et al., "Uneven Profiles: Language Minority Learners' Word Reading, Vocabulary, and Reading Comprehension Skills," *Journal of Applied Developmental Psychology* 31, no. 6 (2010): 475–83.
13. August and Shanahan, *Developing Literacy in Second-Language Learners.*
14. Chapter 7 provides a brief explanation of interlanguage. Although every teacher who teaches literacy should have basic knowledge about the ML student's current interlanguage in relation to their first language, Claude Goldenberg and his colleagues warn against overgeneralizing cross-language transfer, pointing to the danger of putting children into too-ridged categories just because they are part of a group or community rather than considering individual differences withing groups. Goldenberg et al., "A Response to 'Toward Comprehensive Effective Literacy Policy and Instruction for English Learner/Emergent Bilingual Students.' " See also note 18 below.
15. "D-Lab: Haiti," 2003, available at http://web.mit.edu/D-Lab/Website%20Redo/haiti/creole_grammar.pdf.
16. Jeffra Flaitz et al., *Understanding Your International Students* (Ann Arbor: University of Michigan Press, 2003), 178.
17. Michael DeGraff, "Haitian Creole," in *Comparative Creole Syntax: Parallel Outlines of 18 Creole Grammars,* Westminster Creolistics Series 7, ed. John A. Holm and Peter L. Patrick (London: Battlebridge Publications, 2007). For common American English pronunciation issues for native French or Haitian Kreyòl speakers, see http://www.confidentvoice.com/blog/american-english-pronunciation-problems-for-speakers-of-haitian-creole/.
18. Robert Kaplan's work on contrastive rhetoric has been criticized as overly general and his research methods as lacking adequate controls. Some have suggested that a person's first language (L1) and culture impact on their writing in the second language (L2) is less a result of interference from the L1 than an effect of the writer's current interlanguage. Today's general view is that the writer's experience linguistic repertoire also needs to be considered when reading discourse produced by MLs. Robert Kaplan, "Cultural Thought Patterns in Inter-Cultural Education," *Language Learning* 16, no. 1 (1966): 1–20.
19. William Grabe, "Notes Toward a Theory of Second Language Writing," in *On Second Language Writing,* ed. Tony J. Silva and Paul K. Matsuda (Mahwah, NJ: Lawrence Erlbaum Associates, 2006).
20. The best way to start with the protocol is to underline the verbs that indicate what the teacher and students are doing during the activity. The verbs and verb phrases are already underlined in the lesson description for illustration purposes
21. See table 8.1 for Gero's assumed WIDA performance definitions based on his ACCESS Screener results.

22. Florida B.E.S.T. Standards: English Language Arts, ELA.K.C.1.3, https://www.fldoe.org/core/fileparse .php/7539/urlt/elabeststandardsfinal.pdf.

Chapter 9

1. Bader Reading and Language Assessment Inventory, http://staging.indyreads.org/wp-content/uploads/2012/09/BaderAssessment.pdf.
2. Florida Department of Education, *Grade 4 2022 B.E.S.T Writing Scoring Sampler* (Tallahassee: Florida Department of Education, 2022). Available at https://fsassessments.org/resources/general/best-writing-scoring-samplers.
3. There are many free resources available for teachers who want to build background knowledge on morphology and incorporate morphology instruction. To start, we recommend the following: (1) Linguistics for Teachers of ELLs, https://linguisticsforteachersofells.weebly.com/; (2) a compilation of helpful instruction resources by the Training and Technical Assistance Center Literacy Team at George Mason University, https://gmuedu-my.sharepoint.com/:w:/g/personal/msekinge_gmu_edu/Edk5wkdPWrdKlLJ wK7g6ICwBACvUVBTw18joH5UIMwxQbQ?rtime=kjIG_RU33Ug; and (3) a list of commonly taught prefixes, suffixes, and root words in grades 4 and 5, https://torreytlc.wordpress.com/wp-content /uploads/2016/02/grade-4-morphology-instructional-sequence.pdf.
4. J. F. Carlisle, "Morphological Awareness and Early Reading Achievement," in *Morphological Aspects of Language Processing*, ed. L. Feldman (Hillsdale, NJ: Erlbaum, 1995), 189–209.
5. L. Green et al., "Morphological Development in Children's Writing," *Journal of Educational Psychology* 95, no. 4 (2003): 752–61.
6. M. Singson, D. Mahony, and V. Mann, "The Relation Between Reading Ability and Morphological Skills: Evidence from Derivational Suffixes," *Reading and Writing: An Interdisciplinary Journal* 12 (2000): 238–52.
7. E. Demont and J. E. Gombert, "Phonological Awareness as a Predictor of Decoding Skills and Syntactic Awareness as a Predictor of Comprehension Skills," *British Journal of Educational Psychology* 66 (1996): 315–32.
8. K. Mokhtari and B. Thompson, "How Problems of Reading Fluency and Comprehension Are Related to Difficulties in Syntactic Awareness Skills among Fifth Graders," *Reading Research and Instruction* 46, no. 1 (2006): 73–96; C. Scott, "Syntactic Contributions to Literacy Learning," in *Handbook of Language and Literacy: Development and Disorders*, ed. C. A. Stone et al. (New York: Gilford Press, 2004), 340–362.
9. S. Bentin, A. Deutsch, and Y. Liberman, "Syntactic Competence and Reading Ability in Children," *Journal of Experimental Child Psychology* 48 (1990): 147–72; E. Demont and J. E. Gombert, "Phonological Awareness as a Predictor of Decoding Skills and Syntactic Awareness as a Predictor of Comprehension Skills," *British Journal of Educational Psychology* 66 (1996): 315–32.
10. M. Leikin, "Processing Syntactic Functions of Words in Normal and Dyslexic Readers," *Journal of Psycholinguistic Research* 31, no. 2 (2002): 145–63, https://doi.org/10.1023/A:1014926900931.
11. Many teachers are not fluent in their MLE strudent' native languages, but we encourage them to learn a few words and phrases and features similar to English to enable basic communication and encourage the students to take risks.
12. Ms. Oliver chose to keep the morpheme *-s* for third-person singular present tense separate from the *-s* used to indicate plurality in nouns to reduce the potential for confusion in her fourth-grade students. This morpheme, along with *-'s* (possessive), *-en* (past participle), and *-est* (superlative), would be covered during the next round.
13. The best way to start with the protocol is to underline the verbs that indicate what the teacher and students are doing during the activity. The verbs and verb phrases are already underlined in the lesson description for illustration purposes.
14. Edith's full WIDA proficiency level descriptors are found in table 4.3.

Chapter 10

1. The State Board of Education approved the new standards in January 2023 with implementation during 2023–2024. Available at https://ed.sc.gov/instruction/standards/english-language-arts/standards/ 2023-sc-ccr-ela-standards-approved/.

2. Lois A. Bader, *Bader Reading and Language Inventory*, 4th ed. (Upper Saddle River, NJ: Merrill, 2002). Available at https://ptgmedia.pearsoncmg.com/images/9780132943680/samplechapter/9780132943680.pdf.
3. Florida Department of Education, *Grade 7 2022 B.E.S.T Writing Scoring Sampler* (Tallahassee, FL: Florida Department of Education, 2022). Available at https://fsassessments.org/resources/general/best-writing-scoring-samplers. The scores correspond to purpose/structure, development, and language.
4. Jacquelyn Schachter, "An Error in Error Analysis," *Language Learning* 24, no. 2 (1974): 205–14; Joy M. Reid, *Writing Myths: Applying Second Language Research to Classroom Teaching* (Ann Arbor: University of Michigan, 2008).
5. Robert B. Kaplan, "Cultural Thought Patterns in Inter-Cultural Education," *Journal of Research in Language Studies* 16, no. 1–2 (1966): 1–20: doi: 0.1111/j.1467-1770.1966.tb00804.x. Robert B. Kaplan, "Cultural Thought Patterns Revisited," in *Writing Across Languages Analysis of L2 Text*, ed. Ulla Connor and Robert B. Kaplan (Reading, MA: Addison-Wesley, 1987), 9–21.
6. See endnote 18 in chapter 8 for information about pushback against Kaplan's work and how practitioners currently view the question.
7. Min Wang, Keiko Koda, and Charles A. Perfetti, "Alphabetic and Nonalphabetic L1 Effects in English Word Identification: A Comparison of Korean and Chinese English L2 Learners," *Cognition* 87, no. 2 (2003): 129–49.
8. Megumi Hamada and Keiko Koda, "Similarity and Difference in Learning L2 Word-Form," *System* 39, no. 4 (2011): 500–9.
9. Minh Nguyen-Hoan and Marcus Taft, "The Impact of a Subordinate L1 on L2 Auditory Processing in Adult Bilinguals," *Bilingualism: Language and Cognition* 13, no. 2 (2010): 217–30; Wang et al., "Alphabetic and Nonalphabetic L1 Effects."
10. Alison Holm and Barbara Dodd, "The Effect of First Written Language on the Acquisition of English Literacy," *Cognition* 59, no. 2 (1996): 119–47.
11. Dana R. Ferris, *Treatment of Error in Second Language Student Writing* (Ann Arbor: University of Michigan, 2011); Keith S. Folse, *Vocabulary Myths: Applying Second Language Research to Classroom Teaching* (Ann Arbor: University of Michigan, 2004).
12. Hamada and Koda, "Similarity and Difference in Learning L2 Word-Form."
13. Hamada and Koda, "Similarity and Difference in Learning L2 Word-Form."
14. The work of Dana Ferris (2011) provides guidance on when and how to correct ML students' writing errors.
15. This could be a result of how native Arabic readers search for, recognize, and process vowels and consonants due to differences in the Arabic script, which may also impact reading the strategies they employ. See, for example, Katherine I. Martin, "Reading in English: A Comparison of Native Arabic and Native English Speakers" (MA thesis, University of Michigan, 2011).
16. See chapters 2 and 7 for a discussion of WIDA's levels and how we use them in the SCC protocol and the TLI protocol, but bear in mind that you can apply the two TASLL Framework protocols to any other scheme of proficiency levels, such as ELPA 21's English Language Proficiency at http://elpa21.org/wp-content/uploads/2023/02/1.2.2-ELP-Standards-2014.pdf, TESOL's International preK–12 English Language Proficiency Standards at https://www.tesol.org/media/fuwijiu4/bk_prek-12elpstandards_framework_318.pdf, or the Common European Framework of References used for all foreign/second languages at https://www.coe.int/en/web/common-european-framework-reference-languages/table-1-cefr-3.3-common-reference-levels-global-scale.
17. Robert Kaplan's articles on intercultural thought patterns might be helpful in this regard. Kaplan, "Cultural Thought Patterns in Inter-Cultural Education"; Kaplan, "Cultural Thought Patterns Revisited."
18. For strategies using graphic organizers to teach MLs text structures for reading comprehension and in planning writing, see chapters 17 (pp. 159–165) and 20 (pp. 183–189), respectively, in Joyce W. Nutta et al., *Show, Tell, Build. Twenty Key Instructional Tools and Techniques for Educating English Learners* (Cambridge, MA: Harvard Education Press, 2018).
19. Plateau of learning is a terminology of educational psychology. Students experience a period of little or no further progress (as seen by a flat part on a learning curve) in study after making rapid progress initially. L2 learners can face this plateau passing from the intermediate to advanced levels of language

proficiency. J. C. Richards, *Moving Beyond the plateau: From Intermediate to Advanced Levels in Language Learning* (New York: Cambridge University Press, 2008); Mehdi Mirzaei, Masoud Zoghi and Haniyeh Davatgari Asl, "Understanding the Language Learning Plateau: A Grounded-Theory Study," *Teaching English Language* 11, no. 2 (Summer and Fall 2017): 195–22, doi: 10.22132/tel.2017.53188.

20. The best way to start with the protocol is to underline the verbs and verb phrases that indicate what the teacher and student(s) are doing during the activity. We have already underlined them for illustration purposes.
21. For example, choose a few minutes of both "Persuasive Speech (Stop Eating Fast Food)," available at http://www.youtube.com/watch?v=bVJ8GlqbxkU, and "Speech 110-Summer 2011 (Persuasive Speech-Say No to Fast Food)," available at http://www.youtube.com/watch?v=XvkH-SXyH_E.
22. In addition to getting Tasir to contribute to the academic conversation, leveled questioning will also allow Mr. Grant to gauge how much she knows about the features of persuasive argument and plan for assisting her during writing and revising.
23. See, for example, Khan Academy or the online community of the app ShowMe.
24. Nutta et al. "Responding to Sentence-Level Errors," in *Show, Tell, Build*, 175–81.
25. Reading her own text during rehearsal and the mock city hall argument is easy for Tasir, but listening to her peers' arguments presents some challenges.

Chapter 11

1. English language proficiency assessments have different ways of reporting scores in language domains, categorizing proficiency levels, and calculating overall proficiency scores. WIDA, whose assessment reporting we are using in this book because it is widely used in the United States, calculates composite scores for oral proficiency (50% listening + 50% speaking), literacy (50% reading + 50% writing), comprehension (30% listening + 70% reading), as well as an overall score (15% each for listening and speaking + 35% each for reading and writing). Edgar's individual scores are shown in table 11.2. It is important to note that, although all students in Ms. Myers's ELD class are at the same overall proficiency level, not every student will have the same composition of scores
2. Lois A. Bader, *Bader Reading and Language Inventory*, 4th ed. (Upper Saddle River, NJ: Merrill, 2002). Available at https://ptgmedia.pearsoncmg.com/images/9780132943680/samplechapter/9780132943680.pdf.
3. Florida Department of Education, *Grade 10 2022 B.E.S.T Writing Scoring Sampler* (Tallahassee: Florida Department of Education, 2022). Available at https://fsassessments.org/resources/general/best-writing-scoring-.
4. Elizabeth Bernhardt, *Reading Development in a Second Language: Theoretical, Empirical, and Classroom Perspectives* (Norwood, NJ: Ablex, 1991).
5. Research has shown that it takes from four to seven years. Wayne Thomas and Virginia Collier, *School Effectiveness for Language Minority Students* (Washington, DC: National Clearinghouse for Bilingual Education, 1997).
6. Thomas and Collier, *School Effectiveness for Language Minority Students*.
7. William Nagy and Dianna Townsend, "Words as Tools: Learning Academic Vocabulary as Language Acquisition," *Reading Research Quarterly* 47, no. 1 (2012): 91–108.
8. Claude Goldenberg, "Teaching English Language Learners: What the Research Does-and Does Not-Say," *American Educator* 32, no. 2 (Summer 2008): 11-23, 42-43.
9. See chapter 9 for additional information about morphology.
10. For instance, although all human languages have subjects, verbs, and objects, some languages, such as English, German, and French, have a subject-verb-object (SVO) structure, whereas other languages, such as Pashto and Turkish, require a subject-object-verb (SOV) construction. German is one of the languages that use the SVO structure in main clauses, but subordinate clauses follow the SOV structure. Yet other languages, such as Arabic and Hebrew, use a verb-subject-object (VSO) structure. In addition, some of these languages differ in terms of script and direction. For instance, Arabic and Hebrew have twenty-eight letters and are read from right to left; English and French have twenty-six letters and are read from left to right. It is also important to note that there are significant differences in spelling systems. English spelling, for instance, is said to be more irregular than spelling in languages such as Spanish, which has a more regular orthography. It is estimated that about four hundred words in English have irregular

spellings, and these are among the most frequently used words in the language. David Crystal, *The English Language: A Guided Tour of the Language* (London: Cambridge University Press, 2002).

11. The lesson is gleaned from the tenth-grade Pearson's textbook series *Language Central*: Jim Cummins et al., *Language Central: English Language Development (ELD), Grade 10* (New York: Pearson Education, 2013). A commercial product was used because it highlights best how integrated English language instruction teaches all four language skills one by one, while allowing a focus on form.
12. Manfred Pienemann, ed., *Crosslinguistic Aspects of Processability Theory* (Amsterdam, the Netherlands: John Benjamins, 2005).

Conclusion

1. The breadth of the term *multilingual learner* allows the TASLL Framework to encompass all learners who are in the process of becoming bilingual (or trilingual, etc.), whatever their situations, contexts, and locations. However, much of this book focused on MLs who spend at least part of their school day in regular classrooms with native speakers (and other non-ML students) who are proficient in the majority language of instruction. Within this global group of ML students, we more pointedly focused most of this book on MLs in the United States who are learning English as a new language, whom we refer to either as multilingual learners (MLs) or multilingual learners of English (MLEs), when it's necessary to specify their second language for clarity.
2. This chapter specifies English language development (ELD) teachers and classes in its schoolwide collaboration approach, but this also would apply to a second language (L2) development specialist of any majority language of instruction. When reading ELD, please feel free to substitute second language development (L2D) or whatever specific L2 applies, such as Dutch language development, Japanese language development, or Spanish language development.
3. For research on the positive correlation between student academic achievement and levels of collaboration in schools, at both the elementary and secondary levels, consult Steve Gruenert, "Correlations of Collaborative School Cultures with Student Achievement," *National Association of Secondary School Principals Bulletin* 89, no. 43 (2005): 43–55; or Yvonne L. Goddard, Roger D. Goddard, and Megan Tschannen-Moran, "A Theoretical and Empirical Investigation of Teacher Collaboration for School Improvement and Student Achievement in Public Elementary Schools," *Teachers College Record* 109, no. 4 (2007): 877–96.
4. Some schools may not have an in-house L2D teacher and depend on bilingual aides who work alongside MLs for most of the day. For descriptions of the most frequently used ELD and bilingual program models that use ELD specialists, see Cheryl A. Roberts, "Bilingual Education Program Models: A Framework for Understanding," *Bilingual Research Journal* 19, no. 3–4 (1995): 369–78, or Jeanne Rennie, "ESL and Bilingual Program Models," Center for Applied Linguistics, September 1993, http://www.cal.org/resources/digest/rennie01.html.
5. Please see the discussion of language learning in academic settings in chapter 1 for more detail.
6. More teachers and school counselors need to become aware that MLs can be gifted and can thrive in a gifted class, even though they still must acquire academic language in their L2, and teachers need to learn how to better identify such students. As it stands, MLs are vastly underrepresented in gifted classes but traditionally have composed a disproportionate number of the students diagnosed with a disability, following a similar pattern to their culturally diverse native English-speaking peers.
7. Multilingual Department and Minneapolis Public Schools, "2011–2012 ELL Programming Framework," http://ell.mpls.k12.mn.us/uploads/programming_framework.pdf.
8. Sophie Arkoudis, "Negotiating the Rough Ground Between ESL and Mainstream Teachers," *International Journal of Bilingual Education and Bilingualism* 9, no. 4 (2006): 415–33; Chris M. Davison, "Key Assumptions about Effective Collaboration Between ESL and Content-Area Teachers," *International Journal of Bilingual Education and Bilingualism* 9, no. 4 (2006): 454–75.
9. For a description of ELD specialists and classroom teachers coteaching, see Maria Dove and Andrea Honigsfeld, "ESL Coteaching and Collaboration: Opportunities to Develop Teacher Leadership and Enhance Student Learning," *TESOL Journal* 1, no. 1 (2010): 3–22.
10. A. Richardson Love, "Collaborating for Student Success: Perspectives from the MetLife Survey of the American Teacher," *National Civic Review* 99, no. 2 (2010): 10–14.

11. Love, "Collaborating for Student Success"; Linda Darling-Hammond et al., *Professional Learning in the Learning Profession* (Dallas, TX: National Staff Development Council, 2009).
12. National Commission on Teaching and America's Future, *Team Up for 21st Century Teaching and Learning: What Research and Practice Reveal About Professional Learning* (Washington, DC: NCTAF, 2010).
13. Etienne Wenger, Richard McDermott, and William Snyder, *Cultivating Communities of Practice: A Guide to Managing Knowledge* (Cambridge, MA: Harvard Business School Press, 2002).
14. Clea Fernandez and Makoto Yoshida, *Lesson Study: A Japanese Approach to Improving Mathematics Teaching and Learning.* (New York: Routledge, 2004).
15. You can find information about these online learning management platforms at Istation Lectura (Powered by AMIRA Learning), https://amiralearning.com/istation-lectura; i-Ready, https://www.curriculumassociates.com/programs/i-ready-learning/personalized-instruction; ELLevation, https://ellevationeducation.com.
16. Artificial intelligence educational tools such as MagicSchool can generate questionnaires and notes to parents in multiple languages.
17. US Department of Education, "Newcomer Tool Kit, Chapter 5, Establishing Partnerships with Families," https://www.ed.gov/sites/ed/files/about/offices/list/oela/newcomers-toolkit/chap5.pdf; also for an international perspective, see *Learning Unlimited, Parents' Integration Through Partnership (PIP): PIP Project Toolkit* (London: Learning Unlimited, 2015). A useful resource on general parent engagement is Hanover Research, *Strategies for Fostering Parent Engagement* (Salt Lake City, UT: ULEAD Education, 2019).
18. French for "Thank you for your son. He is a gift to our class."
19. Linda Darling-Hammond, *Teacher Quality and Student Achievement: A Review of State Policy Evidence* (Seattle, WA: Center for the Study of Teaching Policy, University of Washington, 1999); Daniel Weisberg et al., *The Widget Effect: Our National Failure to Acknowledge and Act on Differences in Teacher Effectiveness* (Brooklyn, NY: The New Teacher Project, 2009), http://www.tntp.org.
20. Haitian Kreyòl, meaning "One cannot eat okra with one finger," which in turn implies that people must work together to accomplish tasks.

Appendix A

1. U.S. Code: Title 20 § 7801 (20) English Learner - Definitions
2. WIDA. (2020). *WIDA Guiding Principles of Language Development.* WIDA. https://wida.wisc.edu/

Acknowledgments

We thank Karen Adler, our insightful, brilliant editor, for being our steadfast partner throughout this journey and for raising our game with her spot-on guidance. We are grateful for Karen and many other professionals at Harvard Education Press for their expert suggestions in editing, attention to detail in design, and creative marketing plans.

We thank our colleagues and district partners who provided support, talked things over, and put the protocols through their paces in their classrooms. We are especially grateful for our colleagues Michele Regalla, Irina McLaughlin, Marjorie Ceballos, Vicky Zygouris-Coe, Su Gao, Laura Monroe, Sophie Cuocci, Nadia Garzon, Leslie Mendez, Kerry Purmensky, and Yvonne Cadiz, whose contributions shaped our thinking and writing, and for Padideh Fattahi Marnani and Laila Noor, who helped us identify recent research. Nirmal Ghimire shared his expert insights on the use of artificial intelligence with multilingual learners, for which we are very grateful. We thank our many district colleagues who have embraced the Teaching All Subjects, Language, and Literacy (TASLL) Framework and *Show, Tell, Build* and incorporated them into how they adapt lessons for multilingual learners of English and Spanish, including Anca Irimie, Lorena Kogan, Nivia Brito, Veronica Schmidt-Gomez, Julie Snyder, Betsy Sotomayor, Michelle Bonilla, Geri Chaffee, Timothy Delgado, and Jen Tapia. We have strived to ensure that everything in this book reflects the best practices and expert insights generously shared with us by the outstanding district leaders Natasa Karac and Melissa Morgado. We thank Matthew Lavery for helping us locate the latest data about multilingual learners in the United States.

We also greatly benefited from Wendy Williams's artistic vision, who interpreted our drawings and turned them into clear and concise graphics. Wendy is our invaluable artistic partner.

Most important, we thank the real students who were the basis for the stories of our four multilingual learners. Witnessing their struggles and accomplishments inspired us to tell the story of learning and teaching second languages from their perspectives. We hope they inspire our readers as much as they inspired us.

About the Authors

CARINE STREBEL tributes her parents for sparking her love for different cultures and language learning. While fulfilling field experience hours in an elementary classroom in Zurich, she noticed a tiny girl sitting alone, largely ignored by the teacher and classmates, and instinctively selected her to be the focus of the assigned case study. Although communication proved to be difficult, the experience was powerful and rewarding. The two grew close as they worked together, and their goodbyes at the end of the semester were difficult. While teaching French, German, and English as a second language (ESL) in the United States, Strebel's thoughts repeatedly returned to Rosa, and she decided to become a teacher educator to help immigrant children reach their highest potential. Dr. Strebel is the coauthor of three books published by Harvard Education Press and the cofounder of the *Journal of English Language Education* and has extensive experience in curriculum design and program evaluation. Since leaving Stetson University where she was English for speakers of other languages (ESOL) coordinator, taught pre- and in-service teachers, and provided professional development for departmental faculty, Dr. Strebel has been an independent contractor and occasionally teaches courses in teaching English to speakers of other languages (TESOL) and French. She plans to teach content and language integrated learning (CLIL)–focused courses in teacher education and offer French and English conversation courses in a nursing home as a volunteer when she remigrates to her native Switzerland.

JOYCE W. NUTTA and her parents moved to a small town in the Dolomites of Italy when she was in the ninth grade, where she was enrolled in an Italian-speaking high school even though she knew nothing of the language or culture. She spent two years in ninth grade, and although her social language developed by the end of her second year, she was unable to pass the rigorous essay exams of academic subjects and language arts in Italian and returned to Florida to continue high school. After volunteering to help immigrant students learn English, she became an ESOL teacher and eventually a teacher educator. Dr. Nutta is now a Professor Emerita of multilingual education at the University of Central Florida. She most recently published *English Learners at Home and at School: Stories and Strategies* with Harvard Education Press, for which she codeveloped and cofacilitates participatory multimedia storytelling events that create an aesthetic space for transformation. She is the founder and executive director of a nonprofit organization, the Bilingual Village (https://www.bilingualvillage.org), a physical and virtual network of schools and community partners that enables language learners to practice speaking their new language. She continues to research and write about multilingual learners (MLs) and to advocate for effective policies and practices for educating MLs and for the opportunity of bilingualism for all.

EDWIDGE CREVECOEUR BRYANT thinks fondly of the time spent in Haiti with her grandmother and siblings before the family joined her parents in the United States. Her father was her first teacher, and her mother ensured the family held on to many aspects of Haitian culture. As such, she became the first student in the United States to earn a BS in bilingual education with an emphasis on Haitian Kreyòl and English. She then proceeded to earn an EdD in applied linguistics with an emphasis in bilingual/bicultural education from Teachers College, Columbia University, New York. Currently, she is the professor and chair of the Education Department at Flagler College, St. Augustine, Florida. She also serves as the director of accreditation and assessment and ESOL coordinator. Dr. Crevecoeur Bryant is the general director of an education and community organization in Haiti called OAKA (Oganizasyon Agrikilti Kominote AlfaTeknik [Organization, Agriculture, Community and Literacy]). She regularly presents on Haitian history and language. Throughout her career in education, Dr. Crevecoeur Bryant has advocated for maintaining and respecting the native language of multilingual learners as they add English to their linguistic repertoire.

FLORIN M. MIHAI grew up in Iasi, Romania. In second grade, he started learning English in school and became fascinated by it. After he earned a BA in English and Romanian from Alexandru Ioan Cuza University in Iasi, he taught English as a foreign language (EFL) at a private language school in his hometown for several years. Because he wanted to further his education, he enrolled in the Multilingual and Multicultural Education Program at Florida State University, where he earned a master's degree and PhD. His research interests include language and content-area assessment for multilingual learners of English, grammar instruction, pre- and in-service teacher education, and curriculum development in global contexts. He is the author of *Assessing English Learners in the Content Areas: A Research-into-Practice Guide for Educators* (University of Michigan Press, 2017) and a coauthor of *Show, Tell, Build: 20 Key Instructional Tools and Techniques for English Learners* (Harvard Education Press, 2018) and *Language and Literacy Development: English Learners with Communication Disorders, from Theory to Application* (Plural Publishing, 2020). Currently, he is a professor in the TESOL program at the University of Central Florida.

KOUIDER MOKHTARI was born and raised in Morocco, a multilingual country where he learned to read in both Arabic and French. Outside of school, he communicated primarily in Moroccan Arabic, a colloquial variant of Modern Standard Arabic that is rarely written or used in formal contexts. His early fascination with the nature of language and its critical role in literacy development was further deepened in his first year of high school, when he began studying English.

After earning his teacher certification, Mokhtari taught English as a foreign language in high schools in Rabat and Casablanca, Morocco. His academic journey continued with a master's degree in applied linguistics and an interdisciplinary doctorate in psycholinguistics and reading from Ohio University.

Mokhtari is a distinguished scholar, researcher, and expert in education and literacy. Renowned for his work on reading comprehension, literacy development, and the integration of educational technology, Mokhtari has made significant contributions to understanding how individuals acquire languages and develop literacy skills. His research explores the intersection of cognitive processes, literacy acquisition, and the role of technology in enhancing learning outcomes.

Beyond his academic achievements, Mokhtari is deeply committed to bridging the gap between research and practice in education. He has collaborated as a consultant with educational institutions and governmental organizations worldwide, advocating for evidence-based literacy instruction. His workshops and lectures are in high demand among educators seeking to refine their teaching practices and improve student outcomes.

Currently, Mokhtari serves as the Anderson-Vukelja-Wright Endowed Professor and Director of the K-16 Literacy Center at the University of Texas at Tyler, where he dedicates his work to research, teaching, and service in the areas of literacy instruction and student achievement.

DONITA GRISSOM is an experienced educator, curriculum designer, and teacher trainer specializing in multilingual education. With a strong background in developing innovative curriculum, she has designed programs that support the success of multilingual learners in diverse educational settings. As a dedicated teacher trainer, she has worked with educators nationally and internationally, equipping them with effective strategies to enhance language acquisition and student engagement. A prolific writer, Dr. Grissom has authored books and professional development resources that empower teachers and elevate student achievement. With extensive experience in online and in-person teaching, she remains committed to fostering inclusive learning environments and advancing the field of multilingual education.

Index

K

L

M

R

S

T

U

V